WELL-KEPT SECRETS

WELL–KEPT SECRETS

The story of
William Wordsworth

Andrew Wordsworth

PALLAS ATHENE

Contents

Foreword

By the time Wordsworth died in 1850, at the age of eighty, his lit-
erary reputation was well defined and comfortably assured. New
editions of his poems were published regularly, and sold decently;
and a year after his death an official biography enabled readers to
relate the man and his life to the poetry that they had learned to
love. Appropriate tributes were paid, and a statue was commis-
sioned, to be erected in Westminster Abbey in memory of the for-
mer Poet Laureate. Even as his features were being chiselled out
of the block of marble, Wordsworth's poetry was being effortlessly
integrated into the national heritage, to be set in stone for all time.

At this point, however, readers became aware that their un-
derstanding of Wordsworth's work was in fact far from complete.
For in July 1850 *The Prelude* was published for the first time.[1] By
any account this event should have led to a radical rethinking of
Wordsworth's oeuvre – revealing his achievement to have been
greater, and his vision more complex, than previously imagined;
and shifting the emphasis in his writing firmly towards the auto-
biographical dimension. But as it turned out the poem, which
had been completed almost half a century earlier, and recounted
events – such as the French Revolution – from the previous cen-
tury, arrived too late to make the impact it deserved. Nonetheless
the fact that it was only published posthumously endowed *The
Prelude* with a significance of a different kind: it was the first clear
indication of Wordsworth's tendency to hold back, and to hide

important elements of his life and work from the public gaze, so as to preserve a private space that was inscrutable – at whatever cost to the overall coherence of his oeuvre.

This reticence became even clearer when, in 1922, Emile Legouis published *William Wordsworth and Annette Vallon*, which told the story of Wordsworth's time in France in 1791-2: of his love-affair with Annette; and of Caroline, the girl she gave birth to.[2] That whole episode had been systematically covered up during the poet's lifetime, and was subsequently kept secret by his family for over seventy years after his death. (Three years after Legouis' book came out the original (1805) version of *The Prelude* was published: this version of the poem did include a coded account of the love-affair with Annette, but without Legouis' book the reader would have been unable to read the code and make the necessary connections).

Three decades further on and another aspect of Wordsworth's private life came under the spotlight, when in 1954 the scholar F. W. Bateson put forward the theory – in *Wordsworth – A Reinterpretation* – that William had been in love with his sister Dorothy. The possibility of an incestuous relationship had indeed been voiced during the poet's lifetime – only to be dismissed or swept under the carpet. But when the theory resurfaced in the 1950s it would not go away. Too much had changed in the meantime, too much evidence and too many texts had come to light, for it to be possible to continue to believe in and uphold the image of the poet that had been so carefully defined a hundred years earlier.[3] And to complete the picture, the full text of Dorothy's *Grasmere Journals* was published for the first time in 1958, finally allowing readers to hear her side of the story.

★ ★ ★

Since the 1960s several different versions of Wordsworth have coexisted uneasily. The pillar of the literary establishment is still there, with his patriotic sonnets, his village schoolmasters and lonely travellers, his sunsets and wild flowers and flocks of sheep. This image has endured not only because his poetry appeals to people who may be nostalgic for a certain idea of pre-industrial England. It also suited the twentieth-century poets who had ostentatiously turned their backs on his work. Successive generations of poets and intellectuals chose to consider Wordsworth as being out of date and largely irrelevant. They saw him as a pompous moralising bore, part of the unwanted baggage which had found its way into the nation's cultural heritage, and which they were happy to be rid of. Besides, as so much of twentieth-century culture related to a world that was urbanised and industrialised, it was all too easy to emphasise the distance that separated Wordsworth's concerns from their own.

At the same time however another poet was emerging from the shadows. This was a person whose complex inner life defied any kind of definition: a man whose entire adult existence was structured by his relationships with different women, and who could not create or be happy without their help and presence; a writer whose career had turned him into a public figure, even though he depended on privacy and secrecy in order to explore those areas of human experience that meant the most to him. And, recognised at last as the great poet of memory, and of the play between the conscious and unconscious, he became the man who had rethought the terms by which literature defined itself. In the context of this re-evaluation of Wordsworth, *The Prelude* now came into focus as being central to his oeuvre. But like its author it remained ambiguous and hard to categorise. One could see it as the last of a line – arguably the last great long poem in

English literature – or one could see it as the first of its kind –
a groundbreaking enterprise that explored the workings of the
human mind in a way that had never been attempted before.

So in the late sixties, when I was growing up, Wordsworth
was becoming a much more interesting person and poet than
he had been. For my part I had my own reasons for wanting to
get to know him better. When I was six years old, my great-aunt
gave me a small chest that had belonged to the poet. It is made of
wood, and covered in sheepskin embossed with a pattern of brass
studs. On the lid smaller studs form the letter 'W'; inside, a label
indicates that it was made by T. Shaw, jun. of Kendal, Westmorland.
When open the chest gives off a musty smell that no amount of
cleaning will dislodge, and which evokes the tenacious cold and
damp of English country houses. The chest became my talisman.
I placed it next to my bed; and have had it in my bedroom, wher-
ever I have lived, ever since.

Wordsworth became my constant companion: by day we
shared the same surname (William's younger brother Christopher
was my great-great-great grandfather), and by night his spirit
slept close by me in the little wooden chest (or so I imagined).
But the man himself remained profoundly enigmatic. I had stud-
ied his poetry both at school and university, and knew it quite
well; but whenever I tried to explore a part of his work in depth
or in detail, I lost my way in a maze of half-meanings and coded
suggestions – a sort of labyrinth in which Wordsworth hid him-
self so successfully that I could never be quite sure of who he
really was. This began to irritate me – until one day I decided to
try and resolve the matter by studying both his work and his life
in a thorough and systematic way. Not with the aim of providing
a 'definitive version' of Wordsworth that necessarily had a general
validity, but rather of reaching an understanding of the poet and

of his poetry that I at least could be satisfied with. This book is the record of that quest.

★ ★ ★

As anyone who has studied literature (or art, or music) knows, a clear distinction is made in the academic world between an artist's work and his or her life. What really matters are the works themselves (and the scholarly criticism of them). Biography is of secondary interest: it is thought of as a valuable accessory — as photographs also can be — in documenting aspects of an artist's life, but there its usefulness ends. The work of art is considered as being autonomous, standing apart from — and slightly above — the mass of often messy and mundane material that constitutes a human existence. This principle is particularly hard to challenge where English literature is concerned, because of the example of Shakespeare. The great Elizabethan stands at the heart of English culture, and continues to speak to us with urgency and power four hundred years after his death; yet we know precious little about his life. One can invent endless possible scenarios (like the one in the film *Shakespeare in Love*), but the true drama rests in the plays themselves. The tacit assumption for students of literature is, therefore, that what holds true for Shakespeare must hold true generally.

But does it? Almost unintentionally Wordsworth demonstrated how fragile the assumptions were on which such judgements were based. By placing himself at the centre of his poetry (most obviously in *The Prelude*, but in reality in all his work), he showed that an individual's life has a direct bearing on the meanings generated by his or her art. Not just an influence, but a clear impact. With Wordsworth, the distinction between art and biography fails spectacularly. We cannot begin to understand his art if we do not also scrutinise his life, with the same rigour that an academic would apply to the texts.

This book therefore moves between two genres or categories. It is not a biography, nor is it a work of scholarship: it is a bit of both, and something different from either. I prefer to think of it as a portrait – of both the man and his work.

Curiously for someone who was so indifferent to outward appearances, Wordsworth seemed quite happy to sit for his portrait when asked to do so. In all, more than eighty portraits, sketches and busts were done of him while he was alive; and during one visit to London, in 1831, he agreed to pose for four different painters. In part this compliance can be explained as simple public relations: in middle age and beyond Wordsworth took great care about the way he presented himself and his work to the general public, even as he had ignored such niceties and conventions as a young man. But I like to think there was also another reason for his willingness to have his portrait done, and that was to see how unconvincing the result was. The tension between the visible and the real was central to his poetry – and what better way was there of confirming this than by contemplating portraits of himself which failed to reach inward to the poet's soul, paintings and drawings which really had nothing poetic about them at all?

Dorothy, who as always put herself on the same wavelength as her brother, summed up the Wordsworth sentiments nicely in a letter of 1831. Commenting on a request from the Master of St John's College, Cambridge (where Wordsworth had studied), for a portrait of the Poet to be hung in the College, she noted that,

> Of course my brother consents; but the difficulty is to fix
> on an artist. There never yet has been a good portrait of my

brother. The sketch by Haydon, as you may remember, is a fine drawing – but what a likeness! All that there is of likeness makes it to me the more disagreeable. (June 13, 1831)

Maybe though a portrait in words has a better chance of succeeding, by virtue of using the same medium as the poet used to express himself. A written portrait can weave together biographical material with lines or passages from the poetry, thereby recreating the ebb and flow between life and art that is the artist's natural condition; and – hopefully – dramatising honestly and accurately the interaction of inner and outer worlds that is at the heart of Wordsworth's poetry. Like all portraits this one is subjective – it offers a personal interpretation of the poet, rather than an impartial assessment of the man and his oeuvre. That said, 'I have at all times endeavoured to look steadily at my subject' (to use Wordsworth's own words from the Preface to *Lyrical Ballads*). I think that is what Wordsworth would have wanted, and I hope that in this way the book remains true to the spirit of his poetry.

Chapter I

On the Road

Movement delighted him. The early pages of *The Prelude* show us a boy who seems to be in a state of almost perpetual motion: running around like 'a naked savage'; 'leaping through groves / Of yellow groundsel'; scrambling up rock faces to rob birds' nests of their eggs; swimming; rowing; riding; roaming over the hills at night; ice-skating on the lake in the winter. And the pleasure in physical exercise stayed with him all his life: even when he was sixty his sister Dorothy declared him to be,

> still the crack skater on Rydal Lake – and as to climbing of mountains – the hardiest and youngest are yet hardly a match for him. (Letter to Mary Lamb, January 9, 1830)

Later that year his daughter Dora went to spend the winter with friends at Cambridge; and William, having decided that she needed a pony, bought one for her in the Lake District and rode it himself, on his own, all the way to East Anglia. He trotted across England at a leisurely pace, quite contentedly, and composed several poems during the time he was in the saddle.

But above all he walked – day in, day out, whatever the weather, for the whole of his long life. His appetite for devouring distances was matched only by his lack of interest in the food that was supposed to fuel these exertions: he could walk all day on the strength of a bowl of porridge (with maybe a mug of milk and some bread for lunch), and found it hard to understand why anyone should need to eat more than that, or why they should need to rest at any point in the journey. At the age of sixty he was essentially the same person as the undergraduate, still lean and fit, and with a toughness that was ingrained. His day was organised so that he could work well and take plenty of exercise, and when possible he took little or no account of the needs of other people. He ate little and drank no alcohol. He strode up a mountain before lunch as happily as another man strolling towards the drinks cabinet.

And then there were the walking tours – in Wales, Scotland, or wherever – which offered him (as he saw it) the best way of exploring a region, and which tended to be extremely demanding physically: during the last of them – to Ireland, in 1829 – he would be outdoors by half past five in the morning and walk or ride in the mountains all day, returning as late as ten o'clock in the evening. However the most remarkable of these tours must be the first one he made – the Continental tour that he and his friend Robert Jones embarked on in the summer of 1790, and which took in France, Switzerland and parts of Italy, Germany and Belgium. This was a truly epic performance. Averaging about 25 miles a day on foot, and only occasionally travelling by boat, the two students covered around 3,000 miles in three months. At the time he saw it simply as a better way of spending the summer than studying for exams (as he was supposed to be doing) – and so he slipped away from England without informing anyone in his family where he was going or what he was doing. The itinerary he and Jones had set themselves left no room for distractions or detours – they steered well clear of Paris for example, despite the fact that the capital was celebrating the first anniversary of the Revolution at the time. Their goal was the Italian Lakes, and in order to reach it they needed remarkable discipline and stamina. Characteristically, Wordsworth made light of the physical demands and difficulties: 'A march it was of military speed' (*The Prelude*, Book VI, line 428) was all he had to say on the subject when he came to write the story up more than a decade after the event.[4] Indeed, Napoleon would have been proud of him. And this throwaway assessment was not a case of time blurring the rough hard details of experience: when he wrote to Dorothy from Lake Constance, towards the end of the journey, he was equally light-hearted about the effort and exertion that the whole enterprise had involved:

> We have both enjoyed most excellent health, and we have been this some time so inured to walking, that we are become almost insensible of fatigue. We have several times performed a journey of thirteen leagues [about forty miles] over the most mountainous parts of Swisserland, without any more weariness, than if we had been walking an hour in the groves of Cambridge. (September 6, 1790)

And so they marched, day after day, with their few belongings in bundles on their heads. They danced with French peasants, got lost on a few occasions, crossed over the Alps without realising it, were disappointed by Mont Blanc and enthusiastic about the Swiss landscape in general. The patchwork of emotions and experiences that Wordsworth later described in *The Prelude* is one that any hiker will immediately recognise. And while the journey as it was narrated in *The Prelude* took on a new significance, with the Swiss Alps endowed with a spiritual grandeur both as a physical destination and as a metaphor for the human soul or mind, what is striking about the way Wordsworth actually lived that summer is how uncomplicated it all was. In deciding their itinerary he and Jones made no attempt to see any of the great Italian cities of the north – not even Venice; and they showed no interest in engaging meaningfully with the turmoil of the French Revolution. Instead, to use an image that would later inspire one of the finest passages of *The Prelude*, the two young men skated over the most important political event of the eighteenth century, barely grazing the surface. The beauty and meaning of the long march was located not in external events or places, but inside their own bodies, in the steady systematic rhythm that took them from one village to another, and in the silent relationship that grew up between their bodies and the land they moved through.[5]

London, where Wordsworth lived for about five months after graduating from Cambridge, was approached in the same way as the Lake District or the Swiss Alps – that's to say from a pedestrian's point of view. In Book VII of *The Prelude* he offered what is effectively a guided tour of the city, with the reader as his companion – the only time he ever used such a device. Normally he played down the presence of other people with him when he was out walking, but here he makes a point of taking the reader by the arm and leading him (or her) through the metropolitan labyrinth:

> Meanwhile the roar continues, till at length,
> Escaped as from an enemy, we turn
> Abruptly into some sequestered nook
> Still as a sheltered place when winds blow loud.
> At leisure, thence, through tracts of thin resort
> And sights and sounds that come at intervals,
> We take our way. A raree-show is here
> With children gathered round; another street
> Presents a company of dancing dogs,
>
> (Book VII, lines 184-90)

Thence back into the throng, until we reach,
Following the tide that slackens by degrees,
Some half-frequented scene where wider streets
Bring straggling breezes of suburban air.

> (Book VII, lines 205-8)

And so on. At times the poetry has a cinematic quality – fluid and restless but visually very precise – that is way ahead of its time:

midway in the street
The scavenger, who begs with hat in hand;
The labouring hackney-coaches, the rash speed
Of coaches travelling far whirled on with horn
Loud blowing, and the sturdy drayman's team
Ascending from some alley of the Thames
And striking right across the crowded Strand
Till the fore-horse veer round with punctual skill;

> (Book VII, lines 163-70)

Wordsworth's instinctive sense of space and distance was that of a pedestrian. He had no difficulty imagining the world from the point of view of people who almost always travelled on foot, whether to make a living or because they had no alternative. As he felt his way towards a poetic career, his affinity with all those who, quite literally, walked through life, would prove to be an important element in giving form and structure to his writing.

★ ★ ★

During the 1790s he was constantly on the move. Dissatisfied with himself, with society and with the world at large, he felt ill at ease wherever he was. Turning his back on the career options that his university education opened up (the most obvious one being the Church), and finding himself therefore without any form of steady income, he drifted into an aimless nomadic existence which obliged him to rely on the goodwill and generosity of others.[6] He went more or less where someone would have him; and so he invited himself to one friend's house after another, or stayed with relations somewhere else, or, when necessary, rented simple accomodation for a time... and then moved on.

For ten years he lived as a wanderer, and the poems written during that decade offer a challenging and totally unsentimental vision of the nomadic lifestyle. They present a series of brief encounters with people who found themselves on the road for reasons which were usually beyond their control: people whose lives had lost all semblance of stability and security, and who for the most part were travelling either because they had nowhere to live, or because they were trying to get home – or to find the loved ones they had lost. There were peasant farmers dispossessed of their properties by greedy and powerful landowners, and others – like the shepherd in *The Last of the Flock* – whose lives had buckled and snapped as a result of bad luck or unforgiving social and economic pressures. Then there were those who were caught up in the migration towards the cities that signalled the beginning of England's Industrial Revolution. And there were the casualties of the long war with France, or of the various overseas wars and adventures that went along with Britain's emergence as the world's dominant colonial power.

The people he portrayed were almost invariably presented as the passive victims of unthinking and ultimately cruel social mechanisms. They were as trees uprooted by powerful storms, or human driftwood washed ashore on the Northumbrian

coast: discarded or redundant or unwanted, they became travel-
lers, vagrants, beggars – a restless and disturbing population that
the middle classes did their best to keep at a safe distance. For
Wordsworth on the other hand the encounters with what he
called 'the wanderers of the earth' were precious and privileged
moments. He would try to draw the people he met into conver-
sation, teasing a little of their life story out of them like a thread
of silk from a cocoon. His curiosity was heightened by the sense
that he could learn from them: as he put it neatly in *The Prelude*,

> When I began to enquire,
> To watch and question those I met, and held
> Familiar talk with them, the lonely roads
> Were schools to me in which I daily read
> With most delight the passions of mankind,
> There saw into the depths of human souls –
> Souls that appear to have no depth at all
> To vulgar eyes.
>
> (Book XII, lines 161–8)

One of the things that clearly pleased Wordsworth in these
situations was their unpredictability: the encounters that the pub-
lic highway offered were valuable precisely because they were
random and unplanned. They allowed him to 'see into' the lives
of a wide variety of people, just as in *Tintern Abbey* he evoked
the state of being that allows us to 'see into the life of things'. He
could listen to a traveller's tale just as he could listen to the many
voices of the wind – in the trees, through the grasses, among
rocks and boulders – and he could learn from both of them.

Wordsworth was sympathetic to the plight of the 'road-peo-
ple' he met, but his response to the situations they evoked or de-
scribed varied considerably. He came to see that no two cases were

the same, and that the poems could only have general validity if they focused on what was particular to each story. To start with, there were those who depended on the roads for their living, however modest or precarious that might be: the peddlars, postmen, knife-grinders and the like. They formed a class apart: life for them was hard, but without the road it would be even harder. By contrast, the people he met who had been displaced – the casualties of war, or the discharged soldiers and sailors, who were usually trying to get home – moved Wordsworth to reflect on the destructive foreign policies that had led to these situations. This theme was first explored in *Salisbury Plain* and *The Ruined Cottage*, then developed in the study of *The Discharged Soldier* in early 1798 – a poem that was intended to stand on its own, but was later modified and incorporated into *The Prelude* (Book IV, lines 364-504). The soldier in question, tall, lean and exhausted, was encountered on a lonely road at night, and in the moonlight appeared like a ghost:

> His face was turned
> Towards the road, yet not as if he sought
> For any living thing. He appeared
> Forlorn and desolate, a man cut off
> From all his kind, and more than half detached
> From his own nature.
>
> (1798 version, lines 55-60)

Wordsworth was able to find a lodging for the soldier at the home of a labourer, and left him there. Four years later he offered a variant on the theme with *The Sailor's Mother*: the woman, having learnt that her son had died at sea, had travelled from Westmorland to Hull to collect any possessions he might have had. When Wordsworth met her she was returning home, carrying a bird in a cage – the sum total of his belongings.

A similar note of pathos was provided by *The Last of the Flock* (1798), in which Wordsworth meets a shepherd who is carrying the last of his lambs to market, having been obliged to sell off his entire flock one by one, in order to feed his growing family. The poem opens with the expression of shock felt by Wordsworth at this encounter:

> In distant countries have I been,
> And yet I have not often seen
> A healthy man, a man full grown,
> Weep in the public roads, alone.   (lines 1-4)

But the real question raised by the poem remains – typically for Wordsworth – unstated. For what will become of this man and his family once he has sold his last lamb? Deprived of his livelihood, how will he be able to avoid leaving his home and joining the general migration towards the cities – and towards desperate poverty? While not yet displaced, the shepherd is another expression of the social turmoil that uprooted the discharged soldier and the sailor with his bird cage, and which Wordsworth would consistently denounce throughout his career.

The poems about the soldier, the sailor and the shepherd could be considered as studies of certain social types and situations – each of them written about in a very personal way, certainly, but with their precedents in eighteenth-century literature (not to mention a long tradition of drawings and etchings of such people that goes back, via Rembrandt, to artists like Bosch and Brueghel). But there were other encounters on the open road that inspired poems which were completely original, and which provided early indicators of what would constitute the uniquely 'Wordsworthian' vision. These involved meetings with old men, whose ability to survive the worst that life had to offer moved the young man deeply.

Two poems of 1797-8 in particular engage with this theme – two poems that grew out of one. Wordsworth's original intention had been to write a poem about 'the old Cumberland beggar': an old man whose precarious situation offered Wordsworth the chance to make an emphatic piece of social criticism. As a head-piece to the poem, he described how these beggars were home-less, yet also part of rural communities, as they

> ...confined themselves to a stated round in their neighbour-hood, and had certain fixed days, on which, at different hous-es, they regularly received alms.

The criticism he then developed was not about the circum-stances that obliged people to survive in this way, but of the workhouses which were being set up to house the old and poor (and to get them out of the way and out of sight); and he ar-gued passionately against the loss of freedom and dignity that the workhouse inmates were condemned to:

> Then let him pass, a blessing on his head!
> And, long as he can wander, let him breathe
> The freshness of the valleys, let his blood
> Struggle with frosty air and winter snows;
> And let the chartered air that sweeps the heath
> Beat his grey locks against his withered face. ...
>
> May never HOUSE, misnamed of INDUSTRY,
> Make him a captive!   (lines 171-6; 178-9)

Given the choice between the workhouse and the open road, Wordsworth had no hesitation in leaving the old beggar out on the highway. Better to die like King Lear on some blasted heath, than to suffocate and wither away in 'prison'. Clearly anything was better than ending up in the workhouse. (Charles Dickens expressed exactly the same opinion in *Our Mutual Friend* (1865), with the story of Betty Higden. It seems that little or no progress had been made in the intervening seventy years).

Even as he argued in defence of the old beggar, however, another line of thought formed in the poet's head which suggested that perhaps the man was less to be pitied than envied. So at a certain point Wordsworth started a second poem – or, as he put it when chatting to his friend Isabella Fenwick in 1843:

> If I recollect correctly these verses were an overflowing from the old Cumberland Beggar.[7]

The verses in question were entitled *Old Man Travelling*, but after 1800 were renamed *Animal Tranquillity and Decay* (the original subtitle) – and that change reflected Wordsworth's realisation that this poem addressed quite different issues from those of the other 'road poems'. In a handful of lines Wordsworth evoked the long spiritual journey that the old man had made to reach a state of

> peace so perfect, that the young behold
> With envy, what the Old Man hardly feels.
>
> (lines 13-14)

The 'tranquillity' that he enjoys has been hard-won; and in such a context the adjective 'animal' in the title is surprising, as at first sight it sounds reductive, almost demeaning. But on reflection it is clear that it acts as an embrace: the old man has rejoined the great order of the natural world, from which civilised man has excluded himself, and he has done this before crossing the threshold of death. Some of the 'Lucy' poems, in particular '*A slumber did my spirit seal*', would evoke a similar state of peace and harmony, but at the highest price – Lucy reaches that state by virtue of dying before reaching adulthood.[8] The old man offers a counterpoint to the thinking that will lie behind the 'Lucy' poems: placed at the other extreme of life from the young girl, he attains a similar quietude through opposite means. Instead of being subtracted from adult life, he goes through it, accepting all that life throws at him, and through endurance emerges as if unscathed.

After the 1805 edition of *Lyrical Ballads* Wordsworth removed the last six lines of the poem, which had set the encounter in a specific context:

> – I asked him whither he was bound, and what
> The object of his journey; he replied
> 'Sir! I am going many miles to take
> A last leave of my son, a mariner,
> Who from a sea-fight has been brought to Falmouth,
> And there is dying in an hospital.
>
> (lines 15-20)

In cutting these lines Wordsworth extracted the poem from the ballad genre, and placed it instead close to works such as the *Ode: Intimations of Immortality* (which in 1805 he had recently completed) – poems which offer a message which can be read as timeless and universal. And the editing had two other consequences that were significant: it removed all dialogue between the poet and the old man, and it removed all trace of any relationship between the man and other human beings. From being a grieving father who is content to chat with another traveller while resting on his long journey, the old man is transformed into a profoundly solitary figure, who is uninterested in whatever or whoever he encounters, and who travels without seeking to reach any particular destination, as if compelled to do so by Newton's law of inertia.[9]

A variation of the *Old Cumberland Beggar* and the *Old Man Travelling* was developed in the study of the discharged soldier, written at about the same time; and it reappeared in 1802 in the figure of the leech gatherer, in *Resolution and Independence*. This time though Wordsworth, instead of merely recording what he sees, also expresses his response to the encounter:

> While he was talking thus, the lonely place,
> The old Man's shape, and speech, all troubled me:
> In my mind's eye I seemed to see him pace
> About the weary moors continually,
> Wandering about alone and silently.   (lines 134–8)

The verb 'to trouble' was not often used by Wordsworth, and its use here alerts us to the resemblance between these lines and those of Book I of *The Prelude*, in which, having 'borrowed' a boat for a night-time excursion, the boy is scared by the strange landscape in which he finds himself, and feels the consequence of the adventure for weeks afterwards:

> No familiar shapes...
> But huge and mighty forms that do not live
> Like living men moved slowly through my mind
> By day, and were the trouble of my dreams.
>
> (lines 422; 425–7)

What troubles the adult Wordsworth in his encounter with the leech gatherer is that he feels the old man to be like one of those 'huge and mighty forms' that troubled his boyhood dreams: that's to say the man has moved beyond the human dimension and become part of a wider natural world whose meaning is hard to decipher. Similarly, in Book VII of *The Prelude*, the blind beggar that he encounters seems to be,

> a type
> Or emblem of the utmost that we know
> Both of ourselves and of the universe;
> And, on the shape of this unmoving man,
> His fixèd face and sightless eyes, I looked
> As if admonished from another world.
>
> (lines 617–22)

As always the open road remained a school for Wordsworth; and the lessons he learned there were often harsh, and hard to digest.

For the people he encountered – the 'wanderers of the earth' – time was measured in footsteps, and distances were calculated in terms of a day's march. Their horizons were modest, but the landscape they crossed was known intimately, and nature was in a certain way humanised by the way they travelled through it. In the long run, that was perhaps the most important lesson Wordsworth learned on the road – one that transcended individual destinies, and which would call into question established notions about how time and space could be understood and measured in literature.

★ ★ ★

In the autumn of 1799 Wordsworth decided to settle in the Lake District. He took Dove Cottage in Grasmere (about thirty miles from his birthplace at Cockermouth) on a low rent, and set up home there with Dorothy. The move led to a significant shift of focus in his poetry, as he felt, for the first time in his adult life, a sense of belonging to the place he lived in. Surreptitiously the vagabond started to take root, and in so doing he began to identify with country people whose lives were settled and relatively stable.

The lives of the road-people continued to interest him, but from this time on they were relegated to the background of his imagination – they were there when it suited him to turn to them, but were no longer a prime source of inspiration for his poetry.

Michael, written in the autumn of 1800 and one of the most significant additions to the second edition of *Lyrical Ballads* that was published that winter, makes this new attitude clear from the outset:

> If from the public way you turn your steps
> Up the tumultuous brook of Green-head Ghyll...
>
> (lines 1-2)

Wordsworth here leaves the open road, with all the unpredictable encounters and endlessly varied perspectives that it provided, and leads the reader into a landscape that has a specific identity, and place-names that have a pleasantly local flavour, like 'Green-head Ghyll'. The change of direction could not be more explicit. At the same time though Wordsworth skilfully managed to graft these new poems onto the existing body of work that made up the first edition of *Lyrical Ballads*. For the drama of Michael, whose sheep-farm and family life are ruined when his son is obliged to leave for the city and never returns, develops one of the main themes explored in the first edition, namely the erosion of the rural lifestyle. Wordsworth felt strongly enough about this issue to write about it in detail to Charles James Fox, leader of the Whig opposition in Parliament. He enclosed a copy of *Lyrical Ballads* with his letter, in which he explained how poems such as *Michael* were intended as criticisms of recent government policies:

> ...by the spreading of manufactures through every part of
> the country, by the heavy taxes on postage, by workhouses,

Houses of Industry, and the invention of Soup-shops &c &c superadded to the encreasing disproportion between the price of labour and that of the necessaries of life, the bonds of domestic feeling among the poor, as far as the influence of these things has been extended, have been weakened, & in innumerable instances entirely destroyed... parents are separated from their children, & children from their parents; the wife no longer prepares with her own hands a meal for her husband, the produce of his labour; there is little doing in his house in which his affections can be interested, and but little left in it which he can love. (January 14, 1801)

Wordsworth's concern with family values and domestic affection was not new: they were evoked as early as *An Evening Walk*, written in his late teens. But it was only once he had returned to live near his birthplace, and had felt deep down the rightness of that choice, that he was able to articulate these feelings in a way that went beyond the purely personal. Living at Grasmere allowed him both to explore the most intimate sensations and memories that the contact with nature inspired, and also to give a wider social coherence to his poetic vision. Michael's sheepfold, laboriously constructed with local stones and then abandoned, remains fixed in the landscape as an indictment of the same politics and economic pressures as provoked the fleeting glimpse of another shepherd carrying his last lamb to market to be sold. Likewise, the old Cumberland beggar who went the rounds of the villages according to a well-established pattern, found his match in the leech-gatherer who, high up on the moors, roamed from pond to pond in a desperate attempt to scrape a living. They were two facets of the same unforgiving social reality.

★ ★ ★

In moving to Grasmere, Wordsworth may have turned his back on an itinerant lifestyle – but there were almost as many encounters with travellers and beggars as before, for Dove Cottage was situated next to the road, and a constant stream of people came knocking at the door, most of them asking for money or food. Suddenly, by virtue of having somewhere to live, William found himself in a completely different relationship to the road-people. Instead of being the one who accosted the strangers he met in the hope of learning something about their lives, he found himself being approached by travellers who hoped he would give them something. As he had very little money to live on he was seldom inclined to respond to these requests; and it is revealing that one of the few poems about this kind of encounter, written after settling in Grasmere, tells of how some child-beggars tried to cheat him by pretending that their mother was dead when she clearly wasn't. The incident must have rankled – enough at least for the *Beggars* of 1802 to inspire a sequel fifteen years later, entitled specifically *Sequel to the Foregoing – Composed many years after*.

Dorothy, stimulated perhaps by the way her brother had tried to understand the lives of the poor and the homeless in *Lyrical Ballads*, took up where he left off and recorded her meetings with travellers and beggars carefully – and often in considerable detail. The opening pages of her *Grasmere Journal* contain an impressive number of these encounters – two on the first day alone – and although they are much less frequent in the later part of the journal, Dorothy's keen interest in people as individuals endows each brief exchange with a particular flavour. She comments on the clothes, or the accent, or the small details of the traveller's life-story; and in this way her style offers a nice counterpoint to William's. In his poems the people all speak in Standard English (while Dorothy's accounts make it clear that they invariably used dialect), and the particular details of their situations are always subservient to the wider picture – that of the destiny they unknowingly follow, and of the artist's all-embracing vision.

It's a question of taste as to whether one prefers the style of Dorothy's diary or of William's poems. However, very soon the attitudes of brother and sister converged. The incident that provoked William to compose *Beggars* also stuck in Dorothy's throat like a fishbone – enough for her to recall it in her entry of June 10, 1800, a fortnight after the event. Thinking back, she adopted a tone which had none of the sympathy she normally showed towards those who came knocking on her door. Speaking of the child-beggars she wrote that 'they addressed me with the Begging cant & the whining voice of sorrow', and that a bit later she watched them 'creeping with a Beggars complaining foot'. Clearly the endless requests for food and money were starting to irritate her – or at least to make her take a certain distance from the plight of the homeless poor. As the journal proceeded less and less space was devoted to such encounters, so that by the beginning of 1802 they were treated as blandly as a comment on the weather:

> It is now 7 o'clock – I have a nice coal fire – Wm is still on his bed – 2 beggars today. (February 11, 1802)

However the desire to sympathise remained dominant: the next day's entry included a detailed account of a meeting with a homeless woman and child, and ended with the reflection that,

> When the woman was gone, I could not help thinking that we are not half thankful enough that we are placed in that condition of life in which we are. We do not so often bless god for this as we wish for this 50£ that 100£ &c &c.

It was the kind of sentiment that her brother, who seemed to feel that a relatively stable and comfortable way of life was his by right, never felt moved to express – or if he did he never set it down on paper.

Once Wordsworth had a home of his own walking became a daily pleasure rather than a metaphor for a way of life. The fundamental difference between himself and the travellers he met on the road became apparent: they were on the road out of necessity, while he was out walking because he enjoyed it. They had no home to go back to, and usually no destination that could offer any sort of comfort or relief. For them the open road offered neither pleasure nor freedom, and in many cases they would have given a lot to be able to say goodbye to it for ever. If they were stoical about their condition, it was with the resignation of Edgar's 'Poor Tom' in *King Lear*, or of 'The Seafarer' and 'The Wanderer' in the Anglo-Saxon poems of the same name. Wordsworth's situation in the 1790s had nothing in common with the misfortunes of the people who wandered more or less aimlessly along the English roads: he was a Cambridge graduate who could easily have found steady and respectable employment if he had chosen to. But he had preferred to opt out of the system, and to live on just the right side of poverty, so as to preserve the intellectual and personal freedom that was as vital to him as the oxygen he breathed.

Once the conditions were right this need for freedom found expression. At some point in the first three years at Grasmere Wordsworth composed his wonderful celebration of walking on the open road – a sort of pedestrian's *Ode to Joy* – which became the exhilaratingly fresh and optimistic beginning of *The Prelude*:

> The earth is all before me. With a heart
> Joyous, nor scared at its own liberty,

I look about; and should the guide I choose
Be nothing better than a wandering cloud,
I cannot miss my way. I breathe again!

(lines 15-19)

The passage fuses the promise of spiritual grace ('O there is blessing in this gentle breeze' – line 1) and of political emancipation ('Now I am free, enfranchised and at large'– line 9) with the near ecstasy of physical well-being, the lines coming in a rush of energy that seems to be directly inspired by the lungfuls of country air that the poet inhales as he leaves the city further and further behind him. He even finds the courage to stand up to Milton, whose sobering comment at the end of *Paradise Lost*, as Adam and Eve are banished from the Garden of Eden –

The world was all before them
(Book XII, line 646) –

is answered by the insouciant

The earth is all before me

which suggests that for Wordsworth Eden may still be attainable – even in a country that was already marked by the Industrial Revolution. At any rate nothing occurs to trouble the mind, or to detract from the sense of instinctive pleasure that suffuses the whole passage. After ten years of wandering in the wilderness he had rediscovered the unalloyed happiness in movement that he had known as a boy – and which, now that he had a home of his own, he was determined never to lose again.

A major component of this rediscovered pleasure was Dorothy's company. Occasionally he set out for a walk on his own, but usually they went together; and this would be the pattern for the next thirty years. William's pace was relentless, and he was incredibly lucky that his sister was so tough and resilient: despite being as small as he was tall (she measured less than five feet, while he was almost six feet tall), she was always a match for him. With three steps for every two of his, she could keep up with her brother even on the steepest climbs, or on the longest circuits, or in the worst weather conditions. He didn't have to wait for her – and she never complained, never asked to stop, or said she was hungry. It was almost as if they were one person and not two.

Over and beyond the pleasure of Dorothy's company and conversation, her presence at his side during these long walks in the hills accentuated the intimate nature of the experience. The public roads offered the chance of unexpected meetings with other people; but while the hills and moors also yielded occasional encounters (such as with the leech gatherer), their true importance for the poet lay in the fact that nature there reigned supreme, unchallenged by man. The hill walks gave Wordsworth the time, the space, and the silence in which to take the true measure of the natural world; to feel its pulse beat; and, gradually, to measure himself against nature. Dorothy's presence made this endeavour more complete and satisfying. They shared precious childhood memories, and she was an integral part of the physical and emotional landscape which nourished his work. With her beside him, he could reassure himself that time had not distanced him irremediably from the past. With her beside him, the long hill walks could help him feel that he was indeed a part of nature, and that he had not been irrevocably banished from the natural world by the alienating experiences of adult life.[10]

★ ★ ★

When he was sixty Wordsworth told a friend that 'he never wrote down as he composed, [but he] composed walking, riding, or in bed, and wrote down after'.[11] His favourite way of composing poetry when at home was to walk up and down the gravel path in the garden, muttering to himself. And he would do much the same when out in the fields or woods. The locals took him for a harmless eccentric, as he 'went bumming and booing about',[12] while Dorothy, referring in a letter of 1804 to Catherine Clarkson to the way *The Prelude* was being composed, said that

> He walks out every morning, generally alone, and brings us in a large treat almost every time he goes. The weather with all its pleasant mildness, has been very wet in general, he takes out the umbrella & I daresay, stands stock-still under it during many a rainy half-hour, in the middle of road or field.
>
> (February 13, 1804)

Writers tend to enjoy regular walks: they are part of the pattern of their daily lives, a necessary counterpoint to what T. S. Eliot called their 'sedentary trade'. But while for most writers the daily walk offers a break from work, as well as a chance to mull over what they are writing, Wordsworth's attitude was completely different. Sitting down at a desk and composing poetry made him physically unwell (indeed he disliked most aspects of the writing profession – revising texts and publishing them were also necessary evils, to be delegated or postponed or ignored whenever possible). He found that his brain functioned well when his body was in motion, but tended to seize up when he sat still in front of a blank piece of paper. In itself this is no amazing discovery – there are people everywhere who feel the same way – but what is significant is the way Wordsworth, having decided on writing as a career, baulked at the basic premises for that profession; and in creating conditions for himself in which he could work satisfactorily, produced a completely new kind of verse, one which depended on a different relationship between mind and body.

He worked as he walked. As he crunched and squelched his way over the gravel, clay, scree and bogs of northern England, words and phrases formed in his mind. At first the lines jostled each other, stopped and started and looked around for help; but gradually a sort of sense imposed itself, the breathing became steadier, and thought began to flow with its own rhythm and logic; overlapping at the end of lines, pausing, shifting direction, moving forward again. Under the pressure of this gentle but relentless natural energy the formal constraints of eighteenth-century verse soon gave way. The couplets became uncoupled; and the rhymes, which up till then had gone in two by two like the animals in Noah's ark, disbanded and dispersed like those same animals on reaching dry ground after the waters had receded. Feeling was able to flow freely, and phrasing became a matter of intuition.

The Prelude, with its supple rhythms and its complex and unpredictable shifts of thought and feeling, shows how this method of composition could be sustained over long periods, moving the narrative effortlessly forward. Indeed, *The Prelude* is a poem that reads well when read aloud, and gives very much the impression of someone reminiscing as they walk. But Wordsworth's practice of composing '*en plein air*' is perhaps seen at its purest in *Lines Written a Few Miles above Tintern Abbey*. If we take – almost at random – a dozen lines, and mark a brief pause with a /, and a more significant pause or change of direction with a //, we can see how closely the written words replicate the pattern of natural breathing and thinking, and how far they disregard the formal rules and measures of late eighteenth-century verse:

// I cannot paint
What then I was.// The sounding cataract
Haunted me like a passion:// the tall rock,/
The mountain,/ and the deep and gloomy wood,/
Their colours and their forms,/ were then to me
An appetite;// a feeling and a love,/
That had no need of a remoter charm,/
By thought supplied,/ nor any interest
Unborrowed from the eye.//– That time is past,/
And all its aching joys are now no more,/
And all its dizzy raptures.// Not for this
Faint I,/ nor mourn nor murmur;// other gifts
Have followed;/ for such loss,/ I would believe,/
Abundant recompence.//   (lines 75-88)

The impression we have here is not so much of listening to the poet as he talks, as of following the actual movement of his thoughts. And this is not fortuitous: for it seems that *Tintern Abbey* was unique among Wordsworth's compositions in having been the product of a single journey on foot – and then of not having been reworked at a later date. In the notes he dictated to Isabella Fenwick in 1843, he was quite specific:

Tintern Abbey. July 1798. No poem of mine was composed under circumstances more pleasant for me to remember than this: I began it upon leaving Tintern, after crossing the Wye, and concluded it just as I was entering Bristol in the evening, after a ramble of 4 or 5 days, with my sister. Not a line of it was altered, and not any part of it written down till I reached Bristol.

Wordsworth immediately recognised the special qualities of *Tintern Abbey*, placing it at the end of *Lyrical Ballads*, to provide a climax to the collection. It remains one of the best loved of his poems, and is invariably included in any selection of Wordsworth's poetry; and one cannot help feeling that the poem's success is directly related both to the way it was composed, and to the fact that it wasn't reworked. It was one of those happy events that occur in the careers of artists, when everything comes together at the right moment, taking the artist by surprise and resulting in a work whose fluidity and elegance may, perhaps, never again be repeated.

★ ★ ★

It is tempting to see physical movement and exertion as having a purely liberating effect on the mind, with the supple rhythms and subtle thought processes of a poem like *Tintern Abbey* as a perfect example of what can be achieved when mind and body work in harmony. According to such a formula words flow, and feeling is released, in time and in tune with the body as it moves. But in Wordsworth's case the mechanism was complex, and no single or simple equation held true. Depending on the circumstances his daily walk might help him in the composition of a poem anywhere between fourteen and nine thousand lines in length. A sonnet, an ode, a ballad, or an epic. And the difference between the genres is not simply one of length. A sonnet works in a way that is the exact opposite of a poem like *The Prelude* or *The Excursion*, being not just concise but formally extremely demanding. Rhymes and metres have to be respected to the letter. Thought needs constantly to be disciplined and concentrated, and feeling must be properly contained within the corset-like structure of the poem.

It is here, one imagines, that the gravel path outside Dove

Cottage came into its own. The path, about the length of a cricket pitch, provided a sort of physical equivalent to a line of poetry: pacing up and down it could help the poet first articulate his ideas and then fit them to the metrical requirements of the sonnet. One of the locals at Grasmere remembered him at work as he strode up and down the garden path:

> He would set his head a bit forrad and put his hands behind his back. And then he would start a bumming, and it was bum, bum, stop, then bum, bum, bum, reet down till t'other end, and then he's set down and git a bit o'paper and write a bit.[13]

No doubt the fixed limits of the garden path did provide a useful discipline for the composition of his poetry, but there was no straightforward correlation between the kind of exercise he took and the poetry he produced: for example, during his journey on horseback from Lancaster to Cambridge in 1830, he composed a sonnet, a medium-length poem in rhyming couplets, and 'a few Stanzas of an Ode to May'. Clearly the important thing was simply to be in movement – for the rest the form he employed would depend on his feeling about the subject he was working on, rather than be determined by the circumstances of the moment.

The flip side to this habit, which consisted of working on poems while lying in bed, brought him close to his hero Milton, who composed *Paradise Lost* in that way (though of course in Milton's case working habits were to a large part determined by his blindness).[14] But whether by choice or necessity, and whether – in Wordsworth's case – outdoors or in bed, the practice of composing poetry without the help of pen and paper obliged the poet to use his powers of memory to the full. He had to be able to hold long passages of freshly invented poetry in his head for hours, before committing them to paper. And this in turn made him write in a particular way, leaving out any elements that might prove a distraction from the central thrust and purpose of the poem. Anything that might be forgotten was discarded, only lines that were bound by an internal logic and sense that made them memorable would be retained. The result was poetry that was designed to be recited as much as read: poetry that, although written to be printed, published and read, could also be said to be part of an archaic oral tradition stretching back to Homer. Such poetry has a double status similar to that of plays, whose texts can be read silently but were intended first to be memorised by the actors, and then to be spoken out loud. The result as far as the reader is concerned is poetry which, however complex or difficult the thought, is relatively easy to learn by heart: a passage from Milton or Wordsworth can be memorised just as a passage from Shakespeare can be memorised.

★ ★ ★

A road runs through the whole of Wordsworth's oeuvre, impinging on his writing in so many different ways that it could fairly claim to be an emblem of his vision. Yet it is significant that he showed no interest in creating any such metaphor. However much he loved walking and enjoyed travelling, he never thought of representing his life as a journey, any more than he thought of using his beloved River Derwent to stand for 'the river of life'. Certainly there is a journey of sorts in *The Prelude*, but the sub-title *Growth of a Poet's Mind* indicates that the journey is significant more for what takes place inside the poet's head than for where he travels from and to. One only has to compare *The Prelude* with an allegory like *Pilgrim's Progress*, or an eighteenth-century picaresque novel such as *Tom Jones* or *Joseph Andrews*, to see how little Wordsworth relies on the open road, and all the encounters and experiences it offers, to move the narrative forward and to endow the work with meaning.

After witnessing the misery of the homeless poor he encountered on the public highway, Wordsworth found it hard to subscribe to the myth of the open road, except in moments of purely personal pleasure, such as when he set out on holiday. And however much he loved movement, he believed passionately that rural society could flourish only if people were encouraged to live and work in one place – preferably the place where they were born and had grown up. Movement inevitably implied disruption, and almost invariably placed families under stress. If one could believe in the progress promised by the burgeoning Industrial Revolution, then all well and good – the movement of people towards the cities would be seen as something positive, a painful change leading to a greater good in the long term. But Wordsworth was always profoundly sceptical about the benefits of industrialisation and capitalism. He dug in his heels like a discontented donkey and refused to countenance the idea of social progress. For this he was branded in his later years as a reactionary; but while his political views did indeed change in middle age, it is worth noting that his views on rural society were clearly articulated by the time he was twenty-eight (when *Lyrical Ballads* was published), and never altered from that time on.

'Journeys end in lovers' meetings', wrote Shakespeare, and the idea of a destination is crucial to one version of the 'journey through life' motif: we travel, through good times and bad, with the hope of arriving finally at a situation that gives meaning to our life. The other version, best articulated in north American literature and cinema from the 1950s onward, saw travelling as an end in itself: here the starting-point is fairly irrelevant, and there is no particular destination. This was the aesthetic of a society that did not have its origins on the American continent, and which had evolved thanks to a principle of mobility (which turned the rootlessness of the immigrant population to advantage). In mid-twentieth-century America one could imagine travelling long distances as enjoyable – thanks to cars and cheap petrol – and something that could be done in relative comfort.[15]

Wordsworth would have been horrified at the idea that travelling should be effortless – for him the exertion and discomfort involved in 'seeing the world' was an integral part of the experience. Nonetheless his vision of 'the road' is closer to that proposed by twentieth-century American culture than to that articulated in European literature from Dante to Cervantes and beyond. For Wordsworth, as for Kerouac, the road was simply a fact of life; apparently endless, it was an end in itself – both undefined and self-defining. It could be heaven or hell: it could open onto new perspectives, but it could also confine the traveller in a straitjacket of monotonous complaints and deprivations. Cold, hunger, dirt, exhaustion, boredom, loneliness. For the female vagrant of his early poems the open road was a form of purgatory, while for the young man released from the city at the beginning of *The Prelude* it was a promise of freedom: both of them were right, both reactions were honest and true, reflecting the condition and situation in which these individuals found themselves. The road was a conductor of meanings rather than meaning itself. A road is a road is a road.

Chapter II

Spontaneous and Overflowing

Before he was out of childhood and into puberty both of Wordsworth's parents had died, and the family had fallen apart. Ann Wordsworth (William's mother) succumbed to tuberculosis and died in 1778, when she was only thirty. Following his wife's death John Wordsworth decided he could not look after his five children properly as well as earn a living: so Dorothy, then aged six, was sent to live with relatives in Halifax, while her four brothers were sent to boarding-school at Hawkshead. The boys returned home to Cockermouth during the school holidays, but 'home' as a concept was at this point more fiction than fact – and disappeared altogether when John Wordsworth caught pneumonia in the autumn of 1783, and died. He was forty-two. From then on holidays were spent at Whitehaven, where their uncle Richard lived.

William, after being abruptly deprived of both his mother's and his sister's company at the age of eight (he would only be reunited with Dorothy nine years later) therefore spent most of his adolescence in an environment that was exclusively masculine. The only feminine presence was offered by Anne Tyson, a lady in her sixties who, together with her husband Hugh, took in boys from Hawkshead School as boarders. To all intents and purposes the Tysons' house became home for the Wordsworth boys.

Anne provided William with a maternal presence and affection that seem to have gone a long way to compensating for the loss of his real mother. She was warm, reassuring and utterly dependable, without being strict. Though no teacher, the values she lived by – such as frugality, straightforwardness and domestic harmony – were easily absorbed by him, and her values became a reference point for him throughout his life.[16]

If we are to believe *The Prelude* he was not unhappy. Book II celebrates the freedom he was allowed outside of school, the friendships he formed, and the intense pleasure of feeling himself close to nature. The poems that survive from his schooldays though are less serene, and suggest that the loss of his parents remained an open wound for a long time. So, for example, in *Written in very early youth* (probably composed when he was sixteen),

> Now, in this blank of things, a harmony,
> Home-felt, and home-created, comes to heal
> That grief for which the senses still supply
> Fresh food; for only then, when memory
> Is hushed, am I at rest.

The feelings he expressed at the age of sixteen may be slightly at variance with his understanding of them fourteen years later, but he remained consistent in his belief that domestic stability and emotional security were prerequisites for happiness and well-being. Like charity, love begins at home. Even in the turbulence of adolescence he sought to reconcile the sexual impulses that surged in his body with conventional notions of domestic bliss. We see this in the English version of a classical Greek poem that he produced while at school. In the original by Anacreon (from the sixth century BCE) the poet gives instructions to a painter as to how best to represent the body of the woman he loves – a device that allows Anacreon to evoke the charm and seductive qualities of his mistress. Wordsworth's version overlays natural landscape onto the forms and contours of the body to create an effect that is quite different from the original. Exploiting the potential of the analogy between the woman's robe (or 'veil') that both hides and exposes her body, and the mist which, as it moves, conceals and reveals different parts of the landscape, Wordsworth invents his own highly personal striptease:

> While Fancy paints beneath the veil
> The pathway winding through the dale,
> The cot, the seat of Peace and Love,
> Peeping through the tufted grove.

('Cot' is used here as a contraction of 'cottage' rather than in the modern sense of the word, meaning 'a small bed'). Wordsworth's playful metaphor leads us towards the woman's sex, 'peeping through the tufted grove', guided by the underlying sense that it is precisely in the domestic haven of the cottage bedroom that Love can be celebrated and the woman's body enjoyed.[17] It is one of his most erotically subversive images – and all the more intriguing for offering a synthesis between orthodox puritan thinking, which eulogised domestic values, and pagan classical thought. The verse also alerts us to an important characteristic of Wordsworth's writing, which was its obliqueness – that's to say, his preference for whatever was unstated or implicit. Like the mist that floated over the autumn landscape his writing tended to veil its true intention: it suggested rather than defined its meaning, which was left to 'peep through' the metaphor – and which could therefore easily be missed or overlooked by a casual reader.

The sexual fantasies he occasionally indulged in moved

between the domestic environment and the natural world out-
side, as he looked for a way of reconciling potentially conflicting
needs and desires. So for example, in another poem (known as
Beauty and Moonlight), also written when he was sixteen, a young
man wanders around the hills and vales while trying to forget the
girl he is in love with. In the course of his rambling he dreams up
a curious erotic metaphor:

> Then might her bosom soft and white
> Heave upon my swimming sight
> As these two swans together ride
> Upon the gently swelling tide. [18]

However when he came to write *An Evening Walk* a year or
two later, Wordsworth took the cluster of words and associations
from these earlier poems – tuft, cottage, bosom, swans, lake – and,
having shuffled the cards, dealt a hand which generated a quite
different meaning. In *An Evening Walk* the swans are considered
not as metaphors but as real birds, and Wordsworth develops an
elaborate comparison between the 'tender Cares and mild do-
mestic Loves' shown by a family of swans and their cygnets, and
the desperate situation of an abandoned and homeless woman
with her young children. The poet follows the swans to their
nest, which is described as if it were a human habitation:

> Yon tuft conceals your home, your cottage bow'r,
> Fresh water rushes strew the verdant floor;
> Long grass and willows form the woven wall.

> (lines 227-229)

Wordsworth is not trying to anthropomorphise the birds.
The point he is making is that nature is ordered, and to that
extent more 'humane' than human society often is. Animals live

and behave in a civilised way, while human beings can easily find themselves reduced to a condition which is completely barbaric. Addressing the swans, Wordsworth says:

> Ye ne'er, like hapless human wanderers, throw
> Your young on winter's winding sheet of snow
>
> (lines 239-240)

while the following passage (lines 241-300) recounts the sad story of a female beggar who, despite her best efforts, did just that. In this context, where security and family values are seen as all-important, the female breast is less an object of desire than a source of comfort and nourishment. So, when the female beggar's children die of cold and hunger, Wordsworth's comment is that,

> No tears can chill them, and no bosom warms,
> Thy breast their death-bed, coffined in thine arms.
>
> (lines 299-300)

★ ★ ★

While the vision of soft white breasts that 'heaved upon the young man's swimming sight' in *Beauty and Moonlight* is clearly no more than adolescent fantasy, it is a sight that Wordsworth could have glimpsed for real a few years later in London. Between 1793 and 1796, with libertine behaviour in the capital at its most visible and emphatic, the neckline of women's dresses dropped to a historic low. In Elizabethan times unmarried women might wear dresses that were cut so low as to reveal their nipples, but Regency London went one better, and for a while could offer the sight of 'society women' exposing the whole of their breasts in public (for example, a print by Isaac Cruikshank from 1794 depicts

Lady Buckinghamshire and Mrs Fitzherbert dressed (or rather undressed) in this way, in an opera box in a London theatre.)[19]

The date of the print is significant. This fashion (short-lived and exclusively metropolitan) took its inspiration from the French Revolution, where the figure of Marianne, *la fille du peuple*, had been chosen to symbolise the aspirations of the newborn Republic, and in particular the principle of Liberty that the Revolution upheld. As such she had been thought up in a demure classical pose in September 1792 (just at the time of the September Massacres!); but a year later, with the Terror well under way and a more aggressive ideology being disseminated by the French authorities, Marianne bared her breasts and could also be represented leading the people into battle.

The London fashion followed this second version of Marianne. As England was by this time at war with France, the 'Amazon' references of the bare-breasted *fille du peuple* were deftly ignored. What was preserved was the uncorseted and liberated image of a woman. Sexual and political freedom were proposed as being identical, or at least complementary. Liberty shading into libertinism. The idea was never likely to last long in a puritanical culture like that of England, nonetheless it did have its moment – and that moment coincided precisely with Wordsworth's formative years. (Delacroix's famous painting of *Liberty leading the people*, with Marianne bare-breasted on the Parisian barricades – the work which became the most popular image of the Age of Revolution – was painted much later, in 1830 – by which time the good ladies of London were once again firmly trussed up in their corsets of whale-bone.)

Given Wordsworth's exposure to the full force of the French Revolution, it is significant that his thinking at this time went in the opposite direction, emphasising the maternal role of women and underplaying their sexual energy. In his poetry the sensual qualities associated with the female breast were gradually subtracted from the human body, and offered, along with a matronly bosom, to the natural world. Lake Windermere (or Winander), which in the earlier poem (*Beauty and Moonlight*) was simply the flat expanse on which the shapely bosom / swans glided, became the maternal breast:

> bosomed deep, the shy Winander peeps
> 'Mid clustering isles
>
> (*An Evening Walk*, lines 13-14)

The image stood the test of time. In Book V of *The Prelude*, written more than fifteen years later, Wordsworth thought of Lake Windermere in the same way: the famous passage which begins,

> There was a Boy, ye knew him well, ye Cliffs
> And Islands of Winander!   (lines 389-390)

and which describes how the owls would answer the boy's 'mimic hootings', ends with silence:

> the visible scene
> Would enter unawares into his mind
> With all its solemn imagery, its rocks,
> Its woods, and that uncertain Heaven, received
> Into the steady bosom of the lake.
>
> (lines 409-13)

By now the bosomed lake has become a symbol of placid maternity, capable of accepting anything and everything without losing its natural calm and serenity.

★ ★ ★

An Evening Walk, completed when Wordsworth was nineteen, was published in 1793 with a subtitle, '*Addressed to a Young Lady*'. One naturally supposes this young lady was a girl or woman he was courting, and to whom he wanted to dedicate his first substantial composition; but a note dictated to Isabella Fenwick fifty years later specifies that, 'The young Lady to whom this was addressed was my Sister'. The subtitle neatly illustrates the ambivalent nature of William's feelings towards Dorothy: for at what point does brotherly affection risk shading into another kind of emotion? The way the idea of the swans was used in these years is indicative of that tension: from being in his earlier poem (*Beauty and Moonlight*) a seductive image of a woman's breasts the swans are purged in *An Evening Walk* of all erotic content, and presented instead as an example of tender feelings and domestic harmony – precisely the kind of sentiments that were compatible with a poem addressed to his sister Dorothy.[20] But it would be a mistake to imagine that Wordsworth's thinking or vision had changed in any significant way: in his mind the second image (of the happy family of swans and cygnets) is overlaid onto the first, rather than replacing it. For him nothing was ever discarded or forgotten: experiences accumulated and were superimposed in the brain like geological strata in the earth; and the function of memory (or rather one of its many functions) was to hold these strata together and to give a meaning to the relation that existed between them.

The impulses were not easily reconciled. Wordsworth's next long poem, *Salisbury Plain*, written between 1793 and 1795, ushers in another pair of swans:

> Like swans, twin swans, that when on
> the sweet brink
> Of Derwent's stream the south winds hardly blow,

'Mid Derwent's water-lillies swell and sink
In union, rose her sister breasts of snow,
(Fair emblem of two lovers' hearts that know
No separate impulse)   (lines 208-13)

The synthesis he seeks to achieve here is complicated, in that he carries forward meanings or associations generated both by *Beauty and Moonlight* and *An Evening Walk*. From the early poem comes the swans / breasts metaphor, and the linking of this to the love between a man and a woman. But the tone here is placid and not sexually charged; and the placing of these lines in the middle of a passage in which the homeless woman recounts the loss of her husband and three children creates a clear link to the comparison of a family of swans with a human family that he developed in *An Evening Walk*. One feels Wordsworth hesitating between an instinctive eroticism and a self-imposed correctness of feeling. And it may be the epithet of 'sister breasts' that holds the key to this tension. The coupling here of 'sister breasts' and 'two lovers' hearts that know/ No separate impulse' may be too much of a coincidence. *An Evening Walk*, which this passage evokes, was addressed to Dorothy, and includes a similar epithet – apparently innocuous but potentially troubling. There he describes the farmyard cock surrounded by hens as 'Gazed by his sister-wives' (line 130). The image uncannily prefigures the Wordsworth household of around 1805 in which William's female company consisted of his wife Mary; his sister Dorothy; and his sister-in-law Sara Hutchinson – the ensemble being enviously referred to by Coleridge as 'Wordsworth's harem'. The idea that Dorothy could somehow be both sister and wife to him was one that William had great difficulty in rejecting; and when they set up house together in Grasmere in 1799 he meditated at length on this difficulty in *Home at Grasmere*. The tension was only resolved (in so far as such things are ever resolved) by his marriage to Mary Hutchinson in 1802.

★ ★ ★

The man who eulogised kindness and gentleness in his poetry showed a rather different disposition while growing up. Outside of school his energy was largely uncontrolled and, in response to the magnificently untamed natural landscape he lived in, it curdled into a kind of wild and restless intensity that always ran the risk of expressing itself in acts of disobedience or violence. The evidence for this comes in a patchwork form: there are the episodes remembered in Book I of *The Prelude*, such as setting traps for woodcocks; stealing from traps set by others; climbing steep rock-faces to steal eggs from birds' nests; or 'borrowing' someone's boat for a night-time outing on the lake. Then there is Wordsworth's confession to his nephew Christopher (who was gathering material for a biography of his uncle) that 'I was of a stiff, moody and violent temper': as an example he described how once as a boy he had used a whip he was carrying to slash through a oil painting of an old lady (part of a collection of family portraits) that was hanging in his grandfather's house.[21] Or there is the opinion of his sister Dorothy, who, writing about him in 1792 in a letter to her friend Jane Pollard, spoke of 'a sort of violence of Affection if I may so Term it which demonstrates itself every moment of the Day when the Objects of his affection are present with him...'.[22] Or else the poem *Nutting*, written in 1798, in which the assault on the hazel-nut tree is tinged with sexual undertones. Remembering a walk he took in the woods as a boy or teenager, Wordsworth describes how the purity of the natural setting provoked powerful emotions in his spirit –

the hazels rose
Tall and erect, with milk-white clusters hung,
A virgin scene! – A little while I stood,
Breathing with such suppression of the heart
As joy delights in; and with wise restraint
Voluptuous, fearless of a rival, eyed
The banquet

which, unresolved, led him to violate the peace and order of the place:

Then up I rose,
And dragged to earth both branch and bough,
    with crash
And merciless ravage; and the shady nook
Of hazels, and the green and mossy bower,
Deformed and sullied, patiently gave up
Their quiet being.

(lines 17-23; 41-46)

The exploration of the 'dark / Invisible workmanship' thanks to which this unruly and impulsive ugly duckling was turned into a mature and socially responsible swan, is the story of *The Prelude*. At the level of narrative it is a very selective account, and the process of understanding exactly what Wordsworth experienced as a young man is complicated for the reader by the self-censorship which is one of the hallmarks of his poetry. But however economical he chose to be with the raw facts of his life story, and however much he sought to gloss over the inner conflicts and tensions that he had to deal with, it is impossible to imagine his youth as anything other than turbulent. And it was not merely a question of having to come to terms with an unruly or difficult character – or with the trauma of being orphaned. The trajectory he followed between the ages of seventeen and twenty -two – from Hawkshead to Cambridge, then on to London, and from there to France – obliged him to absorb massive social and political contradictions, and to somehow reconcile apparently incompatible realities.

First, the scholarship he won to St John's College, Cambridge, plucked him from the landscape of sheep, heather and rainwashed boulders that he had known since birth and set him down among the sacred honeystoned cloisters and musty libraries of the great university. There he rubbed shoulders with young men who would smile at his northern accent, and consider the good folk of Westmorland as country bumpkins. While they were no cleverer than Wordsworth they felt themselves superior because they had more money to spend, and could indulge themselves in a whole range of hedonistic pleasures that were out of his reach. For example, they had the means to transform their sexual fantasies into experiences that they could brag about, while the lad from the Lakes had to make do with reading about such adventures in Chaucer's *Canterbury Tales*. Casual prostitution was an intrisic part of university life at that time, but it had to be paid for, and Wordsworth's meagre budget had no room for such expenses. No doubt there were plenty of ways in which an undergraduate could enjoy some form of sexual gratification at little or no expense, but Book III of *The Prelude* makes no mention of any such encounters, and suggests that Wordsworth followed a monastic lifestyle in keeping with the principles of College life at the time. Oxford and Cambridge Colleges, like English public schools for most of the twentieth century, were unusual microcosms: all-male territories which resembled monasteries in that study and learning were revered as much as any religious doctrine could be, yet which felt and smelt more like military barracks, and which could engender among friends the sense of comradeship and complicity that professional soldiers experience. Still, given that the Fellows of the various Colleges were expected to remain celibate, one would have to consider a Cambridge College as more monastery than barracks. While we have no evidence about Wordsworth's emotional and sexual development at this time (other than the account he later presented in *The Prelude*), it is likely that he toed the monastic line, and that that he left Cambridge at the age of twenty every bit as inexperienced sexually as when he had arrived there three years earlier.

To London then he came, where (to paraphrase St Augustine's account of his own arrival in Carthage) a cauldron of unholy loves sang all about his ears. The 'great tide of human life' that ebbed and flowed through the streets of the capital fascinated and bewildered him. While he loved the spectacle that the crowds produced – represented in Book VII of *The Prelude* as part travelling circus, part fair, and part zoo[23] – he insisted on the distance that separated him from the people he observed, tacitly claiming to occupy the moral high ground by virtue of the 'natural values' instilled into him through his rural upbringing. Where, in the middle of the 'blank confusion' that he saw around him, he found a focus, it tended to draw his attention to women who for one reason or another had fallen from a state of grace. The most obvious of these were the prostitutes, of whom there was no shortage – it is reckoned that one woman in ten in the streets of London at that time was employed in the world's oldest profession. William Blake predicted that

> The Harlot's cry from Street to Street
> Shall weave Old England's winding sheet[24]

and Wordsworth's attitude towards 'shameless women' was equally disapproving, if a little less apocalyptic. In Book VII of *The Prelude* he remembered how in London he

> for the first time in my life did hear
> The voice of woman utter blasphemy –
> Saw woman as she is to open shame
> Abandoned, and the pride of public vice.
> Full surely from the bottom of my heart
> I shuddered, but the pain was almost lost,
> Absorbed and buried in the immensity
> Of the effect: a barrier seemed at once
> Thrown in, that from humanity divorced
> The human form, splitting the race of man
> In twain, yet leaving the same outward shape.
>
> (lines 416–26)

The shock Wordsworth felt at the slack morals of the Londoners was compounded by the oppressive omnipresence of peoples' bodies – what he called in his 1850 version of *The Prelude* 'that huge fermenting mass of human-kind' (Book VII, line 621). 'Fermentation' was a bit of a euphemism for the smells that the streets and houses of the city gave off, and which provided a constant reminder of the body's various needs and functions. Indoors there were the odours of unwashed bodies, chamber pots, cooking, and excrement; outdoors the human waste was mashed together with household waste, along with horse dung, urine, and liberal quantities of mud. Writing in the 1850s Charles Dickens called the Thames 'an open sewer',[25] and much the same could be said of many of the streets and alleys that the young Wordsworth walked along sixty years earlier. Having grown up in a poor and remote rural community, Wordsworth knew all about the tough facts and truths of human existence; but his was a knowledge

based above all on the natural cycles of life and death, an under-
standing of the world which had a logic – and therefore a dignity
– which helped to make sense of the mess of everyday life. In
London he was obliged to exist in a continual present tense, to
see and hear and inhale the 'fermenting' appetites and desires of
tens of thousands of adult human beings, day after day, night after
night, as they made a living or reproduced or enjoyed themselves,
without feeling that there was any underlying order or meaning
to all the frenetic activity. Instinctively he recoiled from such a
debauchery of the senses, his disgust reaching a climax in his de-
scription of Bartholomew Fair, which he likened to a 'parliament
of monsters'. However it would be wrong to see Wordsworth
as prudish or self-righteous in using phrases such as this: they
were the common language of popular printmakers such as
Rowlandson and Gillray, whose work repeatedly emphasised the
most basic needs and functions of the human body with a sort of
provocative insouciance typical of the eighteenth century. When
Wordsworth concludes his passage on Bartholomew Fair with
the image of tents and booths

> vomiting, receiving on all sides,
> Men, women, three-years' children, babes in arms
> (Book VII, lines 693-4)

he creates the kind of synthesis between the body and the urban
environment that the fashionable printmakers of the time would
have approved of. And it is perhaps worth adding that these prints,
which could be extremely crude and explicit, were displayed in
the windows of the printmakers' shops – like pornographic im-
ages in newspaper kiosks or newsagents' shops today. Someone
like Wordsworth who loved walking in the streets could not fail
to notice them – and they would surely have had a powerful

effect on him, given the sober and restrained manners, with their emphasis on reserve and discretion, that he had been taught.

London was a tough school for Wordsworth, and the opening passage in Book I of *The Prelude* shows how relieved he was to be released from it, and to find again the space and silence of the countryside. Nonetheless the congested metropolis would have taught him (among other things) to recognise the adult needs and impulses of his body, to articulate and debate the sexual desires that he might feel, and to see himself as one among many – a young man not so different from the thousands of other healthy young men in the capital that wanted to make a way for themselves.

In November 1791 Wordsworth left London for France. Thirteen months later he was back again in London, having fathered an illegitimate child from a French woman, and having abandoned mother and child before the girl was even born. The wheel had come full circle, revealing the inadequacy of Wordsworth's high-sounding moral code, and throwing his emotional world into apparently hopeless turmoil.

★ ★ ★

In 1643 Milton published the first of four tracts on the subject of divorce, *The Doctrine and Discipline of Divorce*. It is generally agreed that this work was prompted in part by the experience of his own marriage. The previous year he had married a girl half his age (he was thirty-four, she was seventeen). His biographer, his nephew Edward Phillips, described the event neatly and eloquently:

> About *Whitsuntide* it was, or a little after, that he took a Journey
> into the Country; nobody about him certainly knowing the

Reason, or that it was more than a Journey of Recreation: after a Month's stay, home he returns a Married-man, that went out a Batchelor; his Wife being *Mary*, the Eldest Daughter of Mr. *Richard Powell*...[26]

Mary Powell was clearly very unhappy in her role as Milton's bride, and after little more than a month she returned to the family home. The couple were not reconciled until the summer of 1645, and in the meantime Milton had plenty of opportunities to reflect on the consequences of his hasty and imprudent actions. In one of the most revealing passages of the *Doctrine* he wrote,

...it is not strange though many who have spent their youth chastly, are in some things not so quicksighted, while they hast too eagerly to light the nuptiall torch...[27]

It is the nearest that Milton came to confessing the personal motivation that lay behind the tract, though other passages (in the extended second edition published the following year) also showed themselves, by the urgency or violence of the language, to be branded by personal experience. He was clearly disgusted by sexual intercourse when there was no love felt or expressed, describing such an act as grinding 'in the mill of an undelighted and servil copulation', and portraying it as a crime against nature:

...the most injurious and unnaturall tribute that can be extorted from a person endew'd with reason, (is) to be made to pay out the best substance of his body, and of his soul too, as some think, when either for just and powerfull causes he cannot like, or from unequall causes finds not recompence.[28]

Wordsworth's sexual history was quite unlike Milton's: when he found himself the father of an illegitimate child before reaching the age of twenty-three he obviously had very different worries to those of the man who was (it would seem) still a virgin at the age of thirty-four. Nonetheless they were both quintessential puritans, with that unrelenting insistence on individual rights and moral responsibility that is the hallmark of true protestant thought; and Wordsworth's admiration for Milton was such that his thinking tended to offer echoes of, or musical variations on, that of his guide and mentor – even when he did not intend it to. So Wordsworth's *Letter to the Bishop of Llandaff* of 1793, in which the young poet pinned his republican colours to the mast, was modelled both in style and content on Milton's tracts. As usual when Wordsworth measured himself against Milton, he failed – in this case because he backed away from publishing the controversial essay (whereas Milton stood by every polemical word he ever wrote, and accepted the consequences).[29] Nonetheless there is an uncanny resemblance between Wordsworth's *Letter* and Milton's *Doctrine* in that they both used a social or political issue of general interest to reflect on matters that were intensely personal and intimate. Just as in his earliest poetry Wordsworth had overlaid imagery of the human body onto the natural landscape, so in his *Letter to the Bishop of Llandaff* he imagined a sexual dimension implicit in the contemporary political landscape. After setting the tone by declaring that the decade was pregnant with historical significance – 'At a period big with the fate of the human race' – he went on to examine the relationship between prostitution and poverty (among other matters), expressing the hope that social change in the wake of the French Revolution might lead to a condition in which,

> the miseries entailed upon the marriage of those who are not rich will no longer tempt the bulk of mankind to fly to that promiscuous intercourse to which they are impelled by the instincts of nature, and the dreadful satisfaction of escaping

the prospect of infants, sad fruit of such intercourse, whom they are unable to support.[30]

The phrase 'the dreadful satisfaction of escaping the prospect of infants' is ambiguous: does it refer to avoiding conception (and hence the prospect of being a father in the future), or to escaping from the sight of a child already conceived and born? – (which is pretty much what Wordsworth himself had done, except that he left France just when his illegitimate daughter Caroline was born, and without having set eyes on her). Either way, it is hard to believe that Wordsworth would have written the sentence if he had not himself had to confront the dilemma of an unexpected (and unwanted) pregnancy outside of marriage.

Further on, referring to the French Revolution, Wordsworth wrote,

> The coercive power is of necessity so strong in all the old governments that a people could not but at first make an abuse of that liberty which a legitimate republic supposes.
>
> The animal just released from its stall will exhaust the overflow of its spirits in a round of wanton vagaries, but it will soon return to itself and enjoy its freedom in moderate and regular delight.[31]

The idea of representing the violence of revolution in terms of pent-up animal energy is a bit forced; and bearing in mind Wordsworth's earlier comments on 'that promiscuous intercourse to which (men) are impelled by the instincts of nature' it suggests that Wordsworth is brooding here on more than social upheaval. He is reflecting on the power that nature and instinct exert over man, and on how these forces can best be channelled so as to have a beneficial influence. He understands that sexual energy is a major component in the vitality of all animals and yet, when he looks back on the disastrous consequences of his own unbridled sexual adventure in France, he feels that energy must be harnessed, and instinct controlled, if they are not to be destructive.

Wordsworth is usually represented as a diehard republican who in middle age made a complete U-turn and ended up as a diehard Tory. But such radical changes of heart and mind are rare; and in Wordsworth's case there are plenty of signs that there was much more continuity of thought and feeling in the course of his long life than he has been given credit for. The underlying message of the *Letter to the Bishop of Llandaff* is of the need for moderation; and the cautionary tone of the *Letter* finds an echo in the famous *Preface to Lyrical Ballads* written seven years later, even though the theme and register are quite different there.

Students of Wordsworth remember from the *Preface* that 'all good poetry is the spontaneous overflow of powerful feelings'. It sounds like the definitive Romantic creed, in opposition to the formal artificiality of eighteenth-century verse. But Wordsworth goes on to qualify this statement drastically: 'I have said that Poetry is the spontaneous overflow of powerful feelings: it takes its origin from emotion recollected in tranquillity...'. It is hard to see how feeling that is filtered and distilled by memory can hope to be spontaneous: indeed, Wordsworth seems rather to be looking for a way to avoid the emotional quicksands that spontaneity would drag him into. His problem – and it lasted well into middle age – was that he felt too much and too strongly: he had great difficulty in controlling his natural impulsiveness and in articulating his emotions honestly without upsetting the mental and moral order he had constructed in his mind and which he depended on. He needed the distance that time offered in order to write in a way that he could trust to be both truthful and coherent. When he criticised the excesses of the French Revolution he was also criticising his own tendency towards excess, and stressing the need for self-control. The 'overflow' of spirits of the French revolutionaries was echoed by the 'overflow of powerful feelings' in his own poetry: both needed to be moderated in order to be acceptable.

Wordsworth's mistrust of real spontaneity had its roots in his experiences in France: there the uncontained passions of the Revolution that he witnessed at first hand had been echoed, in his personal life, by the uncontained passion that led to him fathering an illegitimate child. Political and sexual energies dovetailed neatly. The 'overflow' of spirits among the new *citoyens de la République* was matched by the ejaculation of sperm − (for what better definition of ejaculation could be offered than 'a spontaneous overflow'?) − which marked Caroline's conception. The personal and the political confuse (with the political discourse serving as a camouflage for a personal discourse that the writer cannot confront openly). Similarly, when writing about his time in France in Book X of *The Prelude*, he speaks regretfully of

> the errors into which I was betrayed
> By present objects   (lines 881-2)

but makes no attempt to specify whether he is referring to mistaken political convictions or to personal misdemeanours of a very intimate kind. What is clear though is that the consequences of having followed the instincts of nature preyed on his mind for decades, and were a major factor in his development of an aesthetic which, through the constant exercise of memory, enabled him to keep a certain distance from the confused and contradictory impulses that made up the present tense.

★ ★ ★

Whether because he was embarrassed by his youthful excesses and adventures, or because he felt that the subject was not suitable for poetry, Wordsworth left no record of his sexual development. But he did something else that was perhaps more interesting: he allowed his feelings about sex and gender to dilate and diffuse themselves in the natural world, so that the all-important relationship between man and nature acquired at times a sexual undertone. As we have seen in the passages quoted above, this way of thinking had been present in his verse since adolescence; but when he came to work on *The Prelude* he had the chance of developing his ideas in a more coherent way.

One important strand in his thinking was the attribution of genders to natural phenomena which the English language normally denied them. As a consequence nature would be 'read' in more human terms than had ever been the case before; and at the same time the world that had always been considered specifically human would be shown to be part of a much larger universe.

Although English has no clear genders for anything which is not part of the animal world, a certain poetical consensus had formed over the centuries which attributed masculine or feminine qualities to the major protagonists of the natural world. The most obvious of these was that the sun – life-giving and dominant over all things – was masculine, while the moon – ever-changing, elusive, beautiful yet unattainable – was feminine. Almost all European languages which have genders (that is to say almost all Indo-European languages except for English) had agreed on this basic distinction between sun and moon (German being an exception to the rule), and even English poets (such as Shakespeare and Spenser, for example) had been moved to give them genders. Wordsworth was happy to stick to the general rule: and so the sun is masculine in Book II, line 185 of *The Prelude*, and in Book VIII, line 118; while the moon is feminine in Book II, lines 198 & 199; IV, 81; and VI, 654.

Water proved more problematic. Perhaps because it made itself felt in the Lake District in so many ways – lakes, streams, rain, waterfalls, rain again, ponds, yet more rain, rivers, lakes that turned into ice rinks… and in the distance the sea – that it was impossible for him to categorise it neatly. And there was no real consensus to help him among the main European languages: for example, the sea was feminine in French, masculine in Spanish, and neuter in German; a river was masculine in German (though individual rivers could be feminine), while French had both a masculine noun for a river (*un fleuve*) and a feminine noun (*une rivière*), and individual rivers could be masculine (*le Rhin, le Rhone*) or feminine (*la Seine, la Loire*). All very confusing. When he came to write *Finnegans Wake* Joyce reverted to global archetypes, and had the River Liffey speak with a woman's voice as it flowed silently between the earthy banks of the rural landscape and through the man-made city of Dublin. Wordsworth however decided that his beloved River Derwent was masculine (*The Prelude*, Book I, lines 273-5; 288; 290); and, in linking the river to his father –

> Behind my Father's House he passed, close by
>
> (I, 290)

suggests that he considered it to have been a benevolent, trusted and watchful presence during his childhood.

Although the sea lay less than twenty miles from Grasmere as the crow flies, and was visible from the tops of the mountains he loved to climb, Wordsworth felt no particular affinity for it (and no doubt appreciated it even less once his brother John had drowned at sea in 1805). Unlike his contemporary Turner, Wordsworth never felt any desire to explore the sea as a subject;

and in *The Prelude* he left the sea neuter (XIII, 50) as if to show
his indifference to it – or else returned it to the vocabulary of
classical mythology,where it would have been masculine ('...
and dry up / Old Ocean in his bed...' (V, 31-2)). Lakes how-
ever were quite a different proposition: they were daily compan-
ions for most of his life, and touched him intimately, prompting
some of the most subtle thoughts and sensations in his poetry. For
Wordsworth lakes were implicitly feminine: still and serene, they
were not only beautiful themselves, but also reflected the splen-
dour of the mountains and the sky, or of the full moon. Calm
and contained, and generous with the life they in turn contained,
their presence was maternal – and it is not hard to see where epi-
thets like 'the bosom of the steady lake' (V, 413) come from. And
of course they did not move – unlike rivers and streams – and
they were not subject to tides, as the sea was. They were constant,
and could be relied on as points of reference – just as Anne Tyson,
'my old Dame' (IV, 17), who took care of the young Wordsworths
after their mother died – was always there when he returned from
an outing or an expedition or a journey. Dependable and wel-
coming, the Lakes became symbols of far more than the District
that was named after them.

★ ★ ★

In *The Prelude* the poetry wove its way between 'male' and 'fe-
male' in nature – and at the same time conspired to suggest an
interpenetration of the human and the natural world. A clear ex-
ample of this occurs in the famous episode of the boy who knew
how to 'talk with owls' (Book V, lines 389-413). The boy became
as one with the owls not just because they answered his calls, but
because his body and his heart shared the same language as the

landscape of lake and hills in which this game took place. In other words, Wordsworth has Nature create its own metaphors in us, even as we create metaphors in the natural world. The dynamic in this case is provided by the word 'into', with its suggestion of depth and distance:

> ...a gentle shock of mild surprise
> Has carried far into his heart the voice
> Of mountain torrents; or the visible scene
> Would enter unawares into his mind,
> With all its solemn imagery, its rocks,
> Its woods, and that uncertain heaven, received
> Into the bosom of the steady lake. (V, 407-413)

'Into his heart', 'into his mind', and 'Into the bosom of the steady lake' together reveal the intent of Wordsworth's thought, which was to develop a poetic language capable of cross-pollenating different elements of the natural world – of which human beings are one element, but only one.

Wordsworth's poetry neither denies the body, nor attempts to transcend it. Rather it is the writing of a man who was so at ease in his body, so active, and living in such constant and intimate contact with the natural world, that he took physical well-being for granted. Like an athlete or a dancer, he appreciated his body above all for what it allowed him to do and feel, and was grateful for the freedom it offered him. By the same token though the body was felt and thought of above all as a means to an end, and became in a way depersonalised. It was perhaps this, together with the puritanical constraints that he had grown up with, that led him to write about women in a rather abstract way, that seemed to deny their sexuality. Nonetheless, Wordsworth's personal history reveals a man who could not live without women, and who needed female company every day of his life. Managing those needs, and managing the women who were supposed to satisfy those needs, would take up a large part of his adult life.

Chapter III

France

There is a Candide-like quality to Wordsworth's early experience of France, starting from the moment the Cambridge undergraduate first set foot on French soil. When Voltaire's ingenuous hero sailed to Lisbon, his arrival there coincided with the terrible earthquake of 1755 which destroyed much of the city; and when a year later the young man's ship reached Portsmouth, he witnessed the execution of Admiral Byng – immortalised by Voltaire in the maxim that '*il est bon de tuer de temps en temps un amiral pour encourager les autres*'.[32] Wordsworth's arrival in France likewise occurred in the middle of historical events of which he was blithely unaware. He and his friend Robert Jones disembarked at Calais on July 13, 1790, the day before the first anniversary of the fall of the Bastille, a holiday that was all the more popular and significant for celebrating at the same time Louis XVI's oath of loyalty to the new constitution, which took place on the Champs de Mars in Paris the next day. The same ceremony of oath-taking took place all over France; Wordsworth and Jones watched it, and the celebrations that followed, in Calais. It must have been an exciting and moving event to witness – yet Wordsworth made no mention of it either in the letter he wrote to Dorothy later in the journey, nor in that part of *The Prelude* that refers to their arrival in France. *The Prelude* is lyrical on the mood of the French people at that time, and offers glimpses of open-air 'Dances of Liberty' and other celebrations; yet nothing that was happening in France could bring the two Englishmen to alter or modify their pre-established route. They avoided Paris, where history was being made, and instead, following small country roads and paths and occasionally taking lifts on boats or barges, made for the Alps.

The letter written to Dorothy almost two months later offered a perspective on the French Revolution that would have delighted Voltaire:

> ...During the time which was near a month which we were in France, we had not once cause to complain of the smallest deficiency in civility in any person, much less of any positive rudeness. We had also perpetual occasion to observe that chearfulness and sprightliness for which the French have always been remarkable. But I must remind you that we crossed it at a time when the whole nation was mad with joy, in consequence of the revolution. It was a most interesting period to be in France... (September 6, 1790)

The letter was sent from one of the Swiss lakes which, along with the Italian lakes, had been the true destination of this special version of the Grand Tour. The place where Wordsworth was staying was called Kesswil, but in the letter heading he miswrote it as 'Keswill (a small village on the lake of Constance)'. The lapsus was revealing: Wordsworth was apparently doing his best to elide his destination into his starting-point. 'Keswill' looks and sounds remarkably like 'Keswick', a small town in the Lake District which overlooked Derwent Water, and which was one of the landmarks of Wordsworth's childhood and youth. To confuse departure and arrival in this way made perfect sense in the context of a journey whose main aim had been to reach the Italian

equivalent of the Lake District. Indeed the whole thrust and pur-
pose of this adventure was to reconcile the unknown with the
familiar, to reach a landscape that felt like home while exploring
strange and exotic territory in foreign lands.

Much has been made of the impact of the French Revolution
on Wordsworth's political thinking, and of the radical attitudes
that he evolved during the 1790s as a consequence of his experi-
ences in France. At the same time it is worth noting that his first
trip to France, made exactly a year after the Revolution began,
was a walking tour which avoided any of the major places of
conflict (in particular Paris). The second visit to France, organised
two years later when the revolution was still in full swing, was
planned with a view to improving his French, so that he could
qualify as a travelling companion to a gentleman. Wordsworth's
uncle Richard, who was expected to finance the project, insisted
that his nephew spend the time in 'some retired Place' in France.[33]
Whether or not William would have preferred to live somewhere
lively and challenging, we do not know; the fact remains that
politics were clearly not high on the agenda when planning the
trip, and that the quiet provincial town of Orléans, about eighty
miles south of Paris, was chosen as a suitable place of residence.

Here, in the town that Jeanne d'Arc made famous, he met and
fell in love with his own 'Maid of Orléans'. Annette Vallon was
twenty-five when she met William, four years older than him and,
being on home territory as well, quite sure of herself and of what
she had to offer. While biographers, basing their judgement on
one miniature portrait which is presumed to be of her, prefer to
speak of her as pretty rather than beautiful, that judgement seems
harsh. Assuming the portrait to be of her, and to be reasonably
accurate, it suggests a sensual, lively and curious woman, whose
combination of long curly brown hair, dark eyes and mischievous

smile should have been enough to seduce any young man she fancied – indeed the wonder is that she was attracted to the awkward, hook-nosed and extremely serious Englishman, with his poor grasp of the French language and of French culture. But there is a long-standing tradition in France of a woman initiating a younger and inexperienced man into a relationship that is both sexual and romantic, and it may be that Annette was, at least in part, acting that kind of role in her relationship with William. It may be that the fact that he was poor and vulnerable and young and a foreigner acted in his favour – we will never know. But what is clear is that the chemistry between them functioned, and the two fell in love. '*La langue s'apprend sur l'oreiller*', as the French say, ('the best method for learning a foreign language is pillow talk') – and whether or not Wordsworth was doing his best to improve his French (as Voltaire would no doubt have intimated), he also fell into the arms of, and the bed of, Annette Vallon; where he no doubt perfected his understanding of many nuances and subtleties of the French language, even as he explored the new-found land and infinite pleasures of her body.

One morning he woke up to the news that Annette was pregnant. We do not know when she told him (she became pregnant within weeks of their meeting); nor – more to the point – do we know how he reacted. For right from the start Wordsworth did his best to hide the affair in secrecy and silence. He kept no diary, and never once in later life referred directly to this part of his French experiences in letters or in his poetry. Letters written at this time to Dorothy or other members of the family may have been lost; all we can say is that no traces remain of how his mind was working as he came to terms with the fact that he was going to be a father, and as he faced up to the implications of the complex and difficult situation in which he found himself.

Still, we can form a picture of the inner debate that preoccupied him during the following months from what he didn't do. Most significantly, he didn't wash his hands of the whole business and head back to England, to carry on with his life as if nothing had happened. That was clearly the easiest option, and would have been quite acceptable for the kind of people he had studied with at Cambridge or had known in London. But such behaviour went completely against the stern moral code he had been brought up on in the Lake District. Of all social types the libertine was one of those that he loathed the most, as the libertine was both depraved and privileged: usually a member of the upper classes – or at least with the financial means and social status to obtain whatever pleasure he desired – and, in France, a perfect embodiment of all that was bad with the Ancien Régime, and that the Revolution was trying to eradicate. Whatever else he might be or do, he had no intention of being branded as a libertine (later on Byron would be the one Romantic poet he could not stomach, and, unsurprisingly, Byron had nothing kind to say about Wordsworth's poetry).

Nor, however, did he marry Annette – as the unwritten laws of Westmorland would have required. Unwanted pregnancies and single mothers were common currency in rural England, but while people were used to seeing the evidence of extra-marital sex, they felt it should not be sanctioned. A man who got a girl into trouble should marry her, and that was that. Wordsworth was well aware of this, but could not find a single rational argument to support this course of action. For his relationship with Annette was a meeting of opposites. Over and beyond the obvious difference of nationality, language and culture, Annette was a royalist and a Catholic while William was a republican and a Protestant. The religious difference was more important than the political, as ordination had been mooted time and again as a career option for William, and that of course meant that he would be made a priest in the Church of England. Were he to marry a Catholic he would automatically disqualify himself from such a career, as the Roman Catholic Church insists that for a marriage between a Catholic and a non-Catholic to be authorised, the non-Catholic must first convert to Catholicism.

A career in the priesthood had never interested William, and for him had never been more than a possible option that he could talk about now and again, and which served as a kind of alibi, allowing him to trundle along peacefully from day to day without seeking gainful employment elsewhere. But the problem was that his options were extremely limited, as he had made no visible effort to find any kind of work anywhere (and in fact had no intention of looking for any). Therefore, as he was dependent on his uncle Richard for the small amounts of money he survived on, he had few legitimate means for resisting family pressure on him to accept a career in the Church and become financially self-sufficient.

For the crux of the matter was that he had no money with which to support a wife and child (or children). At the end of *Sense and Sensibility* Jane Austen comments on Elinor and Edward that

> they were neither of them quite enough in love to think that three hundred and fifty pounds a-year would supply them with the comforts of life[34]

while William's income was a fraction of that amount – and would continue to be so for years to come. He could live on next to nothing, but he knew that he couldn't hope to raise a family in the same spartan manner as he was used to… And to cap it all there was, hanging over all these existential, financial, and philosophical preoccupations and dilemmas, a massive black cloud caused by the increasing political uncertainty in France.

William followed Annette from Orléans to Blois, where her family lived, and they spent the summer of 1792 there. He spent his time worrying, and walking by the river, and writing. Significantly, given the dramatic situation in which he found himself, he made no attempt to draw on what he was living, and chose instead to finish his *Descriptive Sketches*, a poem based on the walking tour of France and the Alps that he and Robert Jones had made two years earlier. In part he was motivated by the idea that he might be able to make some money by finishing and publishing this poem; but what was really manifesting itself here was a trait that would define much of his writing, namely a desire both to keep an emotional distance from the subject of his poems, and also to rediscover his subject as if for the first time, by waiting until circumstances placed him in a situation similar to that of the initial experience (in this case, quite simply, the fact that he was back in France). The convergence of these two impulses would allow him to measure his immediate response to whatever the experience had been against his understanding of it at a later date: the poem that emerged from this confrontation of past and present would be the closest he could hope to get to a truthful interpretation in art of the process of living.

These attitudes would only be articulated eight years later, in the 1800 Preface to *Lyrical Ballads*; but they were clearly present right from the beginning of Wordsworth's career. He found it perfectly natural to write about his first experience of France while living another and completely different experience in the same country a couple of years later. And while the subject matter (of the walking tour in the Alps) did not correspond to his present situation, there was a serious point to revisiting the summer of 1790 two years later: for in the summer of 1792 he had to make up his mind urgently as to what he should do in his relationship with Annette, and *Descriptive Sketches* allowed him to reflect on his feelings for France, to put a possible commitment to continental Europe in the balance and set it against his natural allegiance to England. Where did his loyalties lie and where should he make his life? The debate was sufficiently intense for the present to irrupt towards the end of the poem, unannounced and unexpected, into the narrative of the past:

> And oh, fair France! Though now the traveller sees
> Thy three-striped banner fluctuate on the breeze
>
> . . . .
>
> Yes, as I roamed where Loiret's waters glide
> Through rustling aspens heard from side to side
>
> . . . .
>
> – But foes are gathering – Liberty must raise
> Red on the hills her beacon's far-seen blaze:

Descriptive Sketches is not a very good poem but, regardless of the quality of individual lines or passages, is important in that it reveals Wordsworth's feelings towards France to have been extremely positive during those crucial months of 1792: there is nothing in the poem to suggest that at that point he was thinking of beating a retreat from France, from his relationship with Annette, and from the responsibilities implicit in the imminent paternity that he contemplated as he walked along the banks of the Loire.

For the previous six months Wordsworth had been surfing a euphoric wave of excitement and enthusiasm. To fall in love with an exotic French woman in the middle of a revolution was a dream come true, and it is reassuring to see that when he came to write *The Prelude* more than ten years later, and looked back on that period, he made no attempt to qualify with hindsight and the wisdom of experience the validity of those feelings:

> Bliss was it in that dawn to be alive,
> But to be young was very heaven!
>
> (Book X, lines 692-3)

Wordsworth's deep desire in 1792 was that his relationship with Annette would match and mirror the destiny of the whole country: their love would echo the new-found happiness of the French people, and the birth of their child would be a perfect expression of the rebirth of the nation. Yet as Annette moved into the fifth month of her pregnancy the political atmosphere in France became increasingly tense and volatile, and the aspiring poet's vision of youth, love and social equality working together in unison appeared to him to be more and more of a mirage. In August fighting broke out in Paris, the king was imprisoned and the monarchy suspended. The following month mobs invaded the prisons of Paris, killing over a thousand prisoners – most of whom were non-political. The September Massacres, as they became known, marked the end of the first phase of the French Revolution, and heralded the beginning of the Terror.

During this time Annette's belly continued to swell, in perfect harmony with the sunwarmed grapes and pears and peaches that grew in the orchards through which she and her lover strolled each evening, by the banks of the slowflowing Loire. They walked and talked, but resolved precious little. William managed to get his uncle Richard to send him some more money, but was also told that no more would be forthcoming. The French adventure would no longer be subsidised. And as he had no reason to believe that Annette's family would provide much financial support, even were they to marry, he found himself unable to plan a future for himself in France, even though it became increasingly urgent to reach some sort of decision.

Wordsworth left Annette in Orléans in October 1792, and set off for England. It's not clear exactly what his intention was, or what pushed him to make that decision. In the 1805 version of *The Prelude* he wrote that,

> Reluctantly to England I returned,
> Compelled by nothing less than absolute want
> Of funds for my support.
>
> (Book X, lines 190-92)

while the 1850 version of the poem plays down the financial embarrassment and makes his return out to have been in a way inevitable:

> Dragged by a chain of harsh necessity,
> So seemed it, – now I thankfully acknowledge,
> Forced by the gracious providence of Heaven, –
> To England I returned.
>
> (Book X, lines 222-25)

Leaving aside the possible intervention of divine providence, the truth probably rests somewhere between these two versions. Clearly the lack of money was (as any stranded holidaymaker or traveller knows) a sufficient reason for returning home as quickly as possible. But against that we have to set the fact that he knew his uncle wouldn't give him any more money for the purpose of returning to France. So the idea that he went back to England in order to find the money that would allow him to go back to France, to Annette, and to their child, is hard to believe. At the back of his mind he knew that if he took the boat at Calais he would be unlikely to return; and that, after staying with his lover for the first seven months of her pregnancy, he would be abandoning her just when his presence mattered the most. Before leaving he arranged for someone to represent him legally at the child's baptism. In thus acknowledging paternity of the child he was offering a measure of support to Annette; but in failing to marry her before leaving for England, and by the simple of fact of delegating someone to replace him at the baptism, he was tacitly acknowledging that he had no clear idea as to when – if ever – he might return to France, nor under what conditions or for how long.

As it turned out his indecision was made redundant by the onrush of historical events. He arrived in England a few days before his daughter Caroline was born – on December 15, 1792. She was baptised the same day in Orléans cathedral – her surname variously spelt as 'Wordwodsth', 'Wordsodsth' and 'Wordsworsth' at different places on the baptismal certificate. From the safety of England Wordsworth could watch his great romance disappear without trace. The following month Louis XVI was imprisoned, then executed; and on February 1, 1793, France declared war on England. Apart from a ten-month truce in 1802-3, the two countries would be at war continuously for the next twenty-two years, and all communication between them would be broken.

None of this – the Terror, the rise of Napoleon and the unending Napoleonic Wars – would have been easy to predict when he reached Paris in October 1792. At that point Wordsworth might still have believed that he could sort out his money matters in England, and be back in France by the time the baby was born – or soon after. In which case one would expect him to keep going, and to spend as little time in Paris as was necessary.

But he stalled when he saw the confusion and turmoil caused by the September Massacres, and instinctively paused to take stock of the situation. By now he was competely out of his depth, and all around him events were spiralling out of control. His dream – of personal happiness intertwined with national renewal – was fast curdling and turning into a nightmare. In an unforgettable sequence in *The Prelude* (Book X, lines 54-77), he evoked the state of mind – of anxiety bordering on panic – that he experienced. The passage contains lines of apocalyptic force unique in Wordsworth's oeuvre –

> 'The horse is taught his manage, and the wind
> Of heaven wheels round and treads in his own steps;
> Year follows year, the tide returns again,
> Day follows day, all things have second birth;
> The earthquake is not satisfied at once'
>
> (lines 70-74)

– and culminates in an echo of Macbeth's despairing cry after murdering Duncan –

> Methought I heard a voice cry 'Sleep no more,
> Macbeth does murder sleep' –
>
> (*Macbeth*, II, II, 35-6)

but with a neat twist that makes the sense of guilt collective rather than personal:

> And in such way I wrought upon myself
> Until I seemed to hear a voice that cried
> To the whole city 'Sleep no more!'

In Wordsworth's mind the parallel between individual and social destinies was maintained, even as the whole adventure

veered towards disaster: his own mistakes and unhappiness ech-
oed the failure of the French Revolution to fulfil the promises
it had offered to the French people. And just as he had sought in
nature, and then in politics, a dimension which both embraced
and transcended human dreams and aspirations, so he discovered
in the nightmare of the Terror an echo to the chaos that he had
created for himself in his own life, with no sign of any possible
solution.[35]

And so after two troubled months in Paris Wordsworth left
for England. He would not return to France until the summer
of 1802, ten years later, while his next visit to Paris would be in
1820, by which time his daughter Caroline was married and her-
self the mother of two girls.

★ ★ ★

One of the minor consequences of the twenty-year war between
France and England was that personal correspondence between
citizens of the two countries was officially censored. As a result
we know next to nothing about the course that Wordsworth's
feelings for Annette took during the 1790s. Not a single letter
of his to her remains, and just three letters written by her to
William and Dorothy have come down to us – preserved, thanks
to a bureaucratic oversight, in the archives of the Mairie de Blois
(one of the letters is to William, and two are to Dorothy).[36] As
Wordsworth never kept a diary we have very little idea of what
their correspondence amounted to, or whether he imagined that
there could be any future for the relationship. For almost a decade
the affair – the first great crisis of his adult life – was consigned
to silence and secrecy. Not a single poem addressed to her, or in
memory of their relationship, exists; not a single love letter has

Letter from Annette Vallon to William Wordsworth, March 20, 1793

come down to us. Superficially it was as if she had never played a part in his life.

Wordsworth however mistrusted all that was superficial, and liked nothing better than to explore the hidden and deeper strata of meaning in all that he lived. It is clear from traces left in his poetry that Annette and his little girl remained on his mind, and were a trouble to his dreams. But it is also very likely that the Iron Curtain of censorship that existed between England and France actually suited him. Not only at a practical level, given that for the whole of that decade he remained to all intents and purposes penniless and homeless, an unemployed vagrant who had no means of looking after a would-be wife and daughter properly. In emotional terms also censorship may have suited him – as Annette probably realised. 'Loin des yeux, loin du coeur' ('out of sight, out of mind'): the proverb's warning was clear. She knew that once her lover was back in England their affair was doomed to the archives unless real communication was possible. For his part Wordsworth, who liked to express himself in a straight-forward, even blunt, manner, would have had great difficulty in manufacturing sentiments when there was nothing of substance happening in the relationship. Fiction was never his strong point – and the censorship of letters freed him from the necessity of maintaining a fiction he could no longer believe in.

So he said and did little or nothing, and let time run its course. In any case he couldn't hope for any kind of dialogue on the subject with his brothers or uncles. Even before the outbreak of war his family would have been against him marrying Annette, so there was clearly no point in opening his heart to them once the French and English nations became entrenched in hostilities. At least not to the male members of the family – but of course there was also Dorothy. His sister, he soon realised, saw things very differently from the men – and she was not afraid to speak her mind, and was also keen to develop an intimate dialogue with the brother she loved so intensely. From the time that she and William were reunited in 1794 Dorothy took an active interest in every aspect of William's life and work, and knew exactly how to engage with him on any subject that mattered to him. She became his confidante for questions concerning his relationship with Annette, which as time went on centred on finding a way out of the impasse that would not be dishonourable. That was no easy matter, as William had no money to spare to contribute to-wards Caroline's upbringing, and was unable to set up a dialogue with Annette which might have led to an understanding which released him from any moral obligation towards her, and left him free to marry another woman. For her part Annette considered that she and William were as good as married – she referred to herself by his Christian name, calling herself '*la femme Williams*' or '*la veuve Williams*' (his surname being impossible for her to pronounce). She continued to hope that their relationship would be formalised, and even when it became clear that this would not happen, she chose not to marry another man. So William remained emotionally entangled long after their affair had died a natural death.

Of the three letters from Annette that have survived two were addressed to Dorothy – (one dates from the spring of 1793, the other from 1834): in the first of these she referred to Dorothy as her 'dear sister', and entreated her to help persuade William to take matters in hand and find a way of reuniting himself with his 'wife' and daughter. The warm and spontaneous tone of the writing corresponds to what we know of Annette's character, and is repeated in the letter to William (also from the spring of 1793) that has come down to us. There she pleaded with her lover with the same desperate urgency that she expressed in the letter to Dorothy:

> '…Viens , mon ami, mon mari, recevoir les embrassements tendres de ta femme, de ta fille. Elle est si jolie, cette pauvre petite, si jolie que la tendresse que j'ai pour elle m'en fera perdre la tete si je ne t'ai pas continuellement dans les bras. Elle te ressemble de plus en plus tous les jours. Je crois te tenir dans mes bras, son petit coeur bat contre le mien, je crois sentir celui de son père;…' (modernised spelling)

('Come to me, my friend, my husband, come and enjoy the tender embrace of your wife and your daughter. She is so pretty, poor little thing, I feel such tenderness for her that I'm sure I'll go out of my mind if I don't have you with me all the time. She looks more and more like you with each day that passes. I feel that I'm holding you in my arms; I feel her little heart beat against mine, and have the impression of listening to her father's heart;…')

She signed off by saying that she kissed him

> sur la bouche, sur les yeux et mon petit que j'aime toujours, que je recommande bien à tes soins.

'Mon petit' refers to his penis, and Annette's phrase gives us a good idea of how she would have expressed herself in her intimate moments with William, both in the words that she used and in the language of her own body. French culture has traditionally been far more open and straightforward than English in the way it speaks of the human body, of its needs and functions and desires; and Annette's way of talking and behaving would have been perfectly normal for a young French woman. For her English lover on the other hand it must have been a huge shock, both exciting and rather frightening, like an emotional tidal wave which swept away the barriers and landmarks that a provincial and puritanical upbringing had imprinted on his mind – the taboos, the secrecy, the things felt but not said, and the things dreamed of but never realised. Here was a situation in which desire did not need to be sublimated in poetic metaphors, and in which immediate and tangible pleasure created its own language and vocabulary. A language within a language: and for Wordsworth the strain must have been enormous, as he not only needed to communicate with his lover in a foreign language (French), but also had to learn how he should express himself within that language in a way that made sense to the woman who was to be the mother of their child. He was being asked, explicitly or implicitly, to feel and speak and act as another person than the one he had been till then – and he had absolutely no idea how to go about such a task.

It is true that in London he had heard and seen and read examples of an extremely explicit way of talking about the human body – it was the language of the prints and cartoons and satires that he couldn't fail to register and absorb. But it expressed an attitude that was typically English in that it tended to debase whatever it spoke of: it took pleasure in deflating pretensions, and in reminding the reader / listener / spectator that noone is really superior to anyone else. It delighted in bringing things down to earth, whereas the French equivalent of this kind of attitude delighted in the earthiness of human life – which is not the same thing.

Wordsworth was in no way prepared for the French experience; but given his physically active, energetic and impulsive character one feels he must have been happy to enter into the adventure. With Annette he not only enjoyed sexual gratification, but also came into possession of his natural birthright – his own body. Thanks to the contact with her, and to the intimacy they shared, he became aware of the physical reality of his existence. Until then one imagines that his body had existed for him as a kind of ever-present soulmate, on whom he could always rely, and through which he experienced and made sense of the natural world. In France he would have come to understand it as something which could be observed and itemised and whose different parts, and their functions, could be casually and innocently referred to in conversation. But it was not clear whether he was ready to embrace this alien way of being and feeling about himself. And given that not a single letter from William to Annette has survived we have no way of knowing how he expressed himself when communicating with her. All that we have are poems which refer more or less directly to the relationship and its consequences, together with the language of the poetry, in particular *The Prelude*, which evolved in the years that followed his time in France.

The thrust of that evidence is unequivocal: as he matured as a poet he developed a subtle and supple language of his own which enabled him to express the body without referring to it, and which used consciousness as a filter in which sensual desires, fears and aspirations could be both purged and distilled. As a result we have poetry that is often described as 'disembodied', and whose author has a reputation for being cold and detached and otherworldly. It is puritan poetry *par excellence*, just as *Paradise Lost* is: in both cases sensuality is sublimated to the point where it threatens to negate the sensations it sublimates. The body wishes continually to dissolve, to disappear, to become redundant. And at the same time it remains obstinately centre stage, and shows no signs of agreeing to vanish discreetly into the wings until such time as nature has run its course and the human life has ended.

Wordsworth was a man who could neither forget nor invent.

All that he lived was branded on his skin; and the more significant an experience was, the greater the need to make sense of it in poetry. The significance of his relationship with Annette lay in part in the intensity of the emotions and feelings it had generated, but most of all in that it had given birth to a healthy child. Even if his memory had been less powerful than it was, he could never have hoped to relegate the affair with Annette to the archives of experience, as Caroline was the living and breathing reminder of what he had known and loved and believed in. But the very fact that the relationship continued to float between past and present made it more complicated to deal with in writing, as what Wordsworth liked best was to meditate on an experience that was well and truly finished. And matters were further complicated by the fact that when he came to write about his French experiences in *The Prelude* he was married to another woman – Mary Hutchinson – and she read everything that her husband wrote. Mary was by all accounts extremely tolerant and understanding, and not at all the kind of wife who would resent a poetic reference to some 'other woman' from her husband's past. But there are limits to anyone's good-natured comprehension, and Wordsworth had no wish to test where Mary's lay. So any account he might offer of his time with Annette was going to be seriously flawed – if not doomed – from the outset.

Wordsworth's solution was – inevitably – unsatisfactory. During the 1790s he maintained this strategy of obliquely exploring his feelings of guilt and loss with tragic stories of crazy or abandoned mothers and their children (such as in *Salisbury Plain*, 1793-4; *The Thorn*, 1798; *Her Eyes are Wild*, 1798). More generally a sense of loss permeated much of his best poetry in that decade, and can in part be traced back to the unhappy ending of his affair with Annette. When he came to write *The Prelude* he maintained this strategy of oblique reference to the past, and this time included the story as a sort of fable inside the main narrative, with the story of Vaudracour and Julia.

By the early 1800s (when he was working on *The Prelude*) Wordsworth had convinced himself that he had taken the right course in leaving Annette and returning to England, and that no other outcome to the affair with her would have been possible. Having decided that things could not have turned out otherwise, Wordsworth elevated the tone of his fable to the level of tragedy, casting the two lovers in a modern-day version of the Romeo and Juliet story, who were kept apart, and whose love was doomed, because of circumstances beyond their control. Aesthetically it was a neat synthesis, and the Shakespearian echoes gave added flavour to the narrative; but above all it allowed Wordsworth to come to terms with his own conscience, and to acquit himself of any lingering sense of responsibility for what had happened, for what he had – and had not – done.

The story of Vaudracour and Julia takes up 380 lines of Book IX of the 1805 version of *The Prelude*. One need look no further than the names of the two lovers to have a good idea of Wordsworth's intentions in creating the fable. That 'Vaudracour' is a coded substitute for 'Wordsworth' becomes clear when one remembers that in French *vaudra* is the third person singular of the future tense of *valoir* ('to be worth'), and means 'he/she/it will be worth'. *Cour* – in French a 'court' or 'courtyard' – is pronounced exactly the same as *court*, which in English means 'short'. Therefore *Vaudra-cour(t)* would translate into English as 'Short-worth'. As a coded surname for Wordsworth it is hardly flattering, all the more so when set against a 'literal' reading of 'Words-worth', which would be 'he who is worth his word'. For in abandoning Annette after promising to return to her once he

had obtained more money in England, Wordsworth demonstrat-
ed that he was not worth his word; on the contrary he came well
short of it. And he refers to his own sense of worthlessness in
Book X of *The Prelude* when, speaking of whatever potential role
he felt he might play in the French revolution, he says

> That I both was and must be of small worth
>
> (line 192)

'Small-worth' or 'Short-worth', the sense is clear (in the 1850
version of the poem, which radically shortens the Vaudracour-
Julia episode, 'small worth' is replaced by 'small weight', making
it impossible to make a connection between Words-worth and
Vaudra-cour).[37]

So much for the hero; and given the way the story of
Vaudracour and Julia unfolds it is easy to see Shakespeare's Juliet
behind the name of Julia. However, to be sure the reader did
not miss the point Wordsworth included an explicit reference to
Shakespeare's play at a critical moment of the narrative:

> I pass the raptures of the pair; such theme
> Hath by a hundred poets been set forth
> In more delightful verse than skill of mine
> Could fashion, chiefly by that darling bard
> Who told of Juliet and her Romeo,
> And of the lark's note heard before its time,
> And of the streaks that laced the severing clouds
> In the unrelenting east.   (Book IX, 634-41)

Julia's fate differs from that of Shakespeare's Juliet, but is not
much less tragic: she ends up in a convent, her illegitimate child
dies in childhood, and her lover loses his mind and becomes a
complete recluse. Superficially the story sits awkwardly within

the narrative of *The Prelude* – unless and until the reader realises that it is actually a form of autobiographical fiction. That opportunity was long in coming for readers of Wordsworth's poetry, as Wordsworth, who spent the second half of his life revising and modifying the image of himself that he had created in the first half, decided to remove the Vaudracour – Julia episode from *The Prelude*. The 1850 version of the poem, which was the only version available to the public until 1926, reduces the story from 380 lines to a mere 33-line parenthesis; while the whole story was included, as a poem in its own right, in the 1820 collection of his poems. Wordsworth's strategy is clear: as the years passed he wanted to put as much distance as possible between himself and his experience in France. At the same time he could not deny what he had lived and known – so the best he could hope for was to bring a scalpel to the whole affair, cut it out of the body of his autobiographical poem, and present it as something completely different, something that had happened to someone else, just like the stories that made up *Lyrical Ballads*.

And so it appeared in the anthology published in 1820 and entitled *The River Duddon, A Series of Sonnets: Vaudracour and Julia: and Other Poems. To Which Is Annexed, a Topographical Description of the Country of the Lakes, in the North of England*. Buried in the middle of a mass of poems and prose eulogising the landscape of the north of England, the story could no longer do much harm.

Along with this, Wordsworth charged his nephew Christopher with the task of writing the poet's official biography. The *Memoirs of William Wordsworth* duly appeared in 1851, a year after his uncle's death and less than a year after the publication of *The Prelude*. In it Christopher Wordsworth provides the account of Wordsworth's time in France that was to be the exclusive and definitive version of events for the next seventy-five years:

Wordsworth's condition in France was a very critical one; he was an orphan, young, inexperienced, impetuous, enthusiastic, with no friendly voice to guide him in a foreign country, and that country in a state of revolution....The most licentious theories were propounded; all restraints were broken, libertinism was the law. He was encompassed with strong temptations; and although it is not the design of the present work to chronicle the events of his life except so far as they illustrate his writings, yet I could not pass over this period of it without noticing the dangers which surround those who in an ardent emotion of enthusiasm put themselves in a position of peril without due consideration of the circumstances which ought to regulate their practice.[38]

The story was dead and buried: all that remained to suggest the presence of a corpse was a slight mound of disturbed earth. But soon the grass grew and covered it, and everything was as it should be. (It was only with the publication in 1922 of Emile Legouis' book, *William Wordsworth and Annette Vallon*, that the general public had any knowledge of that episode in his life).

★ ★ ★

When, in the 1850 version of Book X of *The Prelude*, Wordsworth gratefully acknowledged 'the gracious providence of Heaven' in obliging him to leave France and return to England it was, according to the lines that follow, because he believed that he had escaped from a dangerous situation just in time, and that he might well have been killed had he remained in France. But it was not only that which he thanked Heaven for: the return to England marked a turning-point, and effectively determined the course the rest of his life took. It led him to explore and then portray his sense of identity as being related to a particular place – the Lake District – and as having a profound connection with his childhood. This was not something he stumbled on by chance; rather it came out of years of aimless wandering and soul-searching during the 1790s. And it was a discovery he made – and perhaps could only have made – in the company of Dorothy. Nonetheless, when he sailed from France in December 1792 he was not only leaving behind his mistress and their newly-born baby girl; he was also turning his back on the possibilty of a European dimension for his life and work. In this he was remarkably in harmony with the national mood. The war with France, the Continental Blockade, and the Napoleonic wars isolated Britain from continental Europe to an almost unprecedented extent. The English were urged to respond to a new kind of patriotism, which blurred more and more frequently with xenophobic nationalism (and Wordsworth participated actively in articulating this rallying-cry). Once the English emerged victorious from the Napoleonic Wars, and with their colonies intact and their imperial ambitions ever more likely to be realised thanks to their command of the seas, and thanks to the power and technical support offered by the Industrial Revolution – at that point the English felt no particular need to go towards their 'friends and neighbours' in Continental Europe. 'Britannia rules the waves' was the order of the day, and 'Rule Britannia' installed itself comfortably as the mentality that would dictate British attitudes towards the rest of the world for a very long time to come.

Wordsworth's assertion of his Englishness, which became more and more pronounced as the years passed, was therefore a political gesture as well as a personal expression. In his case the price he had to pay was exceptionally high, for it entailed repudiating his first love and his first-born child, as well as curtailing the curiosity and spirit of adventure that had prompted him to travel in Europe.

But if Wordsworth in 1850 thanked Heaven for bringing him back safely to England, it was also a tacit tribute to Mary, after more than forty-five years of married life together. For Annette led William slowly but surely to Mary. As it turned out, Wordsworth's love-life would prove a perfect example of the law in physics which states that every action provokes a counter-reaction of equal force. The two women stood at opposite poles of Wordsworth's psyche: Annette represented otherness, and dramatised the seductive force that came with strangeness... while Mary was a childhood friend. He had known her since the age of five or six, when they went to the same school in Penrith (and having been born in the same year, were no doubt in the same class). They had seen each other occasionally when they were in their teens, and when they began to spend more time together it was in a family context. Everything about Mary was familiar to him: they spoke with the same accent, shared the same cultural references, were used to the same weather, the same food...

Annette and Mary were worlds apart. In choosing Mary William set such a distance between himself and Annette's world that it is easy to discount the importance of that first love, to make it seem almost an accident and peripheral to the poet's growth and development. The way that the story was sidelined in *The Prelude* only adds to that impression. But to imagine that Annette was in any way a 'minor character' in the Wordsworth saga, and that Mary was the true love of his life, would be quite wrong. It is not for nothing that Wordsworth used Shakespeare's *Romeo and Juliet* as a paradigm for recounting a version of his relationship with Annette. Whatever he may have said fifty years

after the event, the separation from Annette seemed to him trag-
ic at the time. And if war between England and France had not
been declared, it is likely that he would have felt morally obliged
to honour the commitment he had made to Annette in acknow-
ledging Caroline as his daughter – in which case the whole
course of his life would have been different.[39] A puritanical sense
of duty and moral responsibilty ran very deep in Wordsworth (his
loathing for Byron stemmed from the latter's casual and libertine
attitude towards women), and it is hard to imagine that the man
who wrote *We are Seven* or *The Last of the Flock* would have been
able to dismiss Annette and Caroline from his memory as simply
belonging to another life.

Wordsworth's *vie sentimentale* may have had the trajectory of
a boomerang, but there was nothing inevitable about the course
it took. Between Annette and Mary stood Dorothy; and without
her William may never have reached as far as Mary. For it was the
years spent living with his sister that showed him the beauty of a
relationship based on complicity and familiarity, and made him
believe that it was possible as an adult to reestablish continuity
with the experiences of childhood. In sexual terms Dorothy was
forbidden to him, and he was obliged to sublimate his feelings to-
wards her in one way or another. Mary though was available; and
if he could claim her as a woman he could also keep intact the
memories he had of her as a girl. The girl would be the mother
of the woman, just as the boy was father of the man.[40] Mary, over
and beyond the personal qualities that attracted William to her,
was the key to solving the intricate puzzle about identity that had
taken shape in Wordsworth's mind. But Dorothy was the catalyst:
both because of the intensity of William's feeling for her, and be-
cause of her sexual inaccessibilty, she provided the necessary stim-
ulus that pushed her impulsive and sexually frustrated brother

towards Mary. The price was Annette, and that was a price that Wordsworth by this point was more than willing to pay.

★ ★ ★

Something of the French connection remained – echoes and memories that lodged in the poet's inner ear, where no one was likely to disturb them, and which perfumed the English he wrote with the scent of another language. So, for example, the phrase '*ça ne te regarde pas*' ('it's none of your business') – most often heard in quarrels between lovers or married couples – seems to surface in the poem of the *Old Man Travelling* of 1797, where,

> The little hedge-row birds,
> That peck along the road, regard him not.

Both the word order and the choice of verb here are out of place in a poem which uses familiar vocabulary and a simple narrative to make its point: Wordsworth uses the French '*regarder*' to make the English phrase memorable. And thanks to the two-way functioning of the French verb, the English becomes more subtle and interesting: 'him' becomes subject as well as object of the action – for just as the birds don't take any notice of the old man, so he ignores them. The birds don't concern him, their lives are none of his business – *ça ne le regarde pas*. The mutual indifference, made possible by the fact that the man poses no threat to the little birds, indicates how completely the man is integrated into the natural world.

The most significant of Wordsworth's Gallicisms though must be the one in the opening passage of *The Prelude*. Line 9 of Book I, which in the 1805 version reads,

Now I am free, enfranchised and at large,

introduces a complex set of associations into writing that was already dense with references and suggested meanings. The word 'enfranchised' is pivotal in the line, referring both back to 'free' and forward to 'at large', and needs to be understood well – the more so as it doesn't really seem to fit into the context. In English the word has a precise and specific meaning, 'to be entitled to vote' – and what do elections have to do with the rest of the passage, which celebrates physical well-being and the pleasure of being in the countryside? Nothing – unless one thinks of the context of the French Revolution, and the idea of the political emancipation of an entire nation. Wordsworth here pins his republican colours firmly to the mast, and identifies himself with the French people as a whole. But to understand the full significance of 'enfranchised' here we have to delve into its etymology. The word comes to English from the French (*affranchir*), and was used in French (from the thirteenth century) to describe the setting free of a slave by his or her owner at the time of the Romans. In this context *franc* means 'free'. Exactly the same word – *un franc* – is also used to describe a member of the Germanic tribe of Franks from whom the French took their name. Thus there are two parallel senses for *franc* which the French may well choose to confuse, so as to claim for themselves the status, by definition, of a free people. Be that as it may, it is clear that Wordsworth not only identifies himself with the French people and their aspirations, but also suggests that he has become one of them: 'I am... enfranchised' has a curious sound to it in the middle of a passage of English poetry, and sounds a bit like 'I have become French' or 'Frenchified'. (The reader's ear has already been alerted to this connotation by 'immured' in the previous line – 'A prison where he has been long immured': 'immured', a word never normally used in English, comes from the French *'emmurer'*, meaning to imprison within walls. If one dates the French Revolution from the fall of the Bastille on July 14, 1789, then Wordsworth's identification with those who were freed from the Bastille makes his pro-revolutionary feelings even clearer).

The Gallic etymology of 'enfranchised' is reinforced by 'at large', which also comes from the French – (*au large*) – where it is generally used to refer to a boat sailing off the coast – thus reiterating in a marine context the sense of liberation felt when walking or riding out of a city into the country. But in the English the phrase has a quite different meaning, which is that of a prisoner or wild animal that has escaped from captivity. Wordsworth skilfully picks up and reiterates associations he has already suggested – (the city as a prison, the people set free from slavedom) – but at the same time he introduces a note of danger, and a warning: for the escaped prisoner or animal are both dangerous, and must be caught and returned to captivity if people are to feel safe.

In just one line Wordsworth manages to compress apparently incompatible themes and attitudes, and expresses perfectly the conflicts of thought and feeling that plagued him at that time; and he does this thanks to the way he plays the French element in English against the Anglo-Saxon. But the fine ambivalence of the 1805 version of *The Prelude* was doomed to pass away, as Wordsworth's personal loyalties and political sympathies altered. The man who opposed the Reform Act of 1832 no longer wished to be considered as part of a nation that was free and enfranchised. For the 1850 version of *The Prelude* Wordsworth removed all political and Gallic references or undertones from the passage: instead of,

FRANCE

...from yon city's walls set free,
A prison where he has been long immured,
Now I am free, enfranchised and at large.

(1805 version)

lines 7–9 read as,

From the vast city, where I long had pined
A discontented sojourner: now free,
Free as a bird to settle where I will.

(1850 version)

There is no longer any debate, nor anything to debate.

Chapter IV

Our Lords and Masters

Poetry and poverty are so close to being anagrams that they are seen as natural bedfellows. No decent poet should expect to make a living from his craft. Painters and novelists can earn good money and even become rich without necessarily compromising their talent, but a poet is like a monk, and is expected to live apart from and above the mundane, mercenary or mercantile activities that make up so much of human existence. His work is to distil human experience into language by removing all that is superficial, casual or anecdotal, while preserving and then purifying the essence that emerges from that process. Wordsworth offered a wonderfully succinct and precise description of that creative process in his Preface to *Lyrical Ballads*:

> ...the emotion is contemplated till, by a species of reaction, the tranquillity gradually disappears, and an emotion, kindred to that which was before the subject of contemplation, is gradually produced, and does itself actually exist in the mind. In this mood successful composition generally begins, and in a mood similar to this it is carried on.

The best metaphor for this time-consuming process is probably that of distilling fruit to make strong alcohol (something that monks became very skilled at): the slim volume of poems that are the end product offering the concentrated nectar of personal experience, much as the slim and costly bottle of eau-de-vie or brandy is alcoholic nectar to be sipped and enjoyed in small doses.

Very few poets have made a living – even less support a family if they had one – by writing poetry. However strong the sense of vocation, however much the muse occupied their thoughts by day and by night, nonetheless the business of composition was almost always carried on in their spare time. To make ends meet they needed a job that guaranteed a steady income, and which left them enough time and energy afterwards to be able to work at their own creations. Over the centuries poets – even the greatest of them – have had a wide range of parallel professions (the roles inevitably changing along with social conditions). They have been diplomats, teachers, private tutors, clergymen, clerks, civil servants, librarians; or they have relied on prose writing – novels, magazine articles, or essays – to subsidise the unprofitable poetic work. A handful of men managed to muddle along as court poets, relying on allowances or handouts from kings and princes; in more recent times others have enjoyed private incomes, or have been maintained by wives or lovers.

The crucial point for poets has always been to avoid compromising their artistic integrity. But however unworldly they may have appeared or aspired to be, in separating their work from the material and economic demands of everyday life, such a distinction was artificial and seldom stood up to scrutiny. Worries about money, patronage, developing a career, or satisfying the reading public not only weighed on the poet's mind but also influenced the tone, style and content of the poetry itself. And Wordsworth was no exception to this general rule – on the contrary, his oeuvre stands as a perfect example of poetry created under stress (despite all his efforts to hide or gloss over the social and economic constraints which defined him even as he tried to defy them.)

Wordsworth is famous for having achieved one of the biggest U-turns in literary history, going from being an ardent republican who had found inspiration in the French Revolution to a morose Conservative who wrote poems advocating acceptance of the death penalty; opposed the Reform Bill of 1832; and resisted change of all kind in his beloved Westmorland. *The Prelude* traced the first part of this long curve, recounting his disillusion with the course taken by the French Revolution, and with its aftermath; while later poems gave increasing expression to the patriotism and religiosity that went hand in hand with his political conservatism. A couple of letters written in middle age show that he was well aware of the extent to which his opinions had changed, and felt the need to demonstrate that there was a sense and coherence to his thinking even though this might not be obvious to others. So in a letter to Lord Lonsdale written in 1818, he explained his support for the landowning class, saying that,

> It appears to a superficial Observer, warm from contemplating the theory of the Constitution, that the political power of the great Land holders ought by every true lover of his Country to be strenuously resisted; but I would ask a well intentioned native of Westmorland or Cumberland who had fallen into this mistake, if he could point out any arrangement by which Jacobinism can be frustrated, except by the existence of large Estates continued from generation to generation in particular families, with parliamentary power in proportion.
>
> (January 21, 1818)

Three years later he wrote to his friend James Losh:

> I should think that I had lived to little purpose if my notions on the Subject of Government had undergone no

modification – my youth must in that case have been without enthusiasm & my manhood endued with small capacity of profiting by reflexion.

He went on to cite various examples of how and when his opinions had changed, such as:

I disapproved of the war against France at its commencement, thinking, which was perhaps an error, that it might have been avoided – but after Buonaparte had violated the Independence of Switzerland my heart turned against him…

When I was young … I thought it derogatory to human Nature to set up Property in preference to Person, as a title for Legislative power: that notion has vanished.

(December 4, 1821)

Whether or not one agrees with Wordsworth's arguments, it is clear from the tone that they were the fruit of steady reflexion rather than irrational impulse; and that he established his social and political values in just the same way as he defined his feelings or thoughts in poetry, namely by measuring his present opinions against some benchmark from the past. Wordsworth's coherence – or at least his desire for coherence – is clear; and by aligning this insistence on coherence with an appeal for continuity in all things social and political (at the same time qualifying the whole by insisting that it is natural for people to change their opinions as they grow older), he did his best to erase or at least minimise whatever contradictions there might have been in his attitudes and arguments. But the story as he told it was – as usual – meagre and partial, and the image he presented of his thinking and behaviour was fairly disingenuous and misleading.

★ ★ ★

Westmorland, where Wordsworth grew up, was in many ways still a feudal society at the end of the eighteenth century, with disproportionate amounts of power and money concentrated in the hands of the landowning class, and with a rigid system of social hierarchies which it was virtually impossible to challenge or alter. Not far away, the manufacturing cities of the north were being transformed out of all recognition by the Industrial Revolution – (Manchester and Liverpool were just seventy miles from Grasmere as the crow flies) – and were putting to good capitalistic use the wealth generated by worldwide trade and colonialism; while London, as the centre of a burgeoning Empire, experienced a period of unprecedented growth, acting as a steady magnet for people from all over the British Isles (one in ten of all English people lived there in the mid-eighteenth century, and its population in 1801 was just less than a million, twice the size of Paris). At the same time the class structure of English society underwent a profound and irreversible change, with the emergence of a substantial middle class which owed no allegiance to the aristocracy and which, as generators of much of the wealth that was flowing into England from trade, commerce, business and industry, demanded greater political representation and influence. In 1789, when the Ancien Régime was swept away in France, the time of the English middle classes had not quite arrived; but during the nineteenth century the Bourgeois Revolution would change England for ever – eventually bequeathing to the nation, under the umbrella epithet of 'Victorian', a weird and wonderful assortment of values and attitudes.

Wordsworth was aware of these widespread and radical changes in English society; nonetheless he found it hard to be moved by them. His vision had been formed in a world which recognised clearly defined hierarchies, and which preferred to conceive of personal misfortune as being the workings of fate rather than the product of social injustice – (or else, as in the story of 'Goody Blake and Harry Gill', trouble begins when individuals fail to respect the obligations and responsibilities that come with their position in society).

From his early years Wordsworth's fortunes were bound up with his relations to the landed gentry. John Wordsworth (his father) worked as agent to Sir James Lowther (Lord Lonsdale), an extremely powerful, hard and unscrupulous man whose aim was to gain complete political control – by whatever means were necessary – of Cumberland and Westmorland. As Lowther's agent John Wordsworth was expected to keep strict accounts of a wide range of activities, including rent-collecting and electioneering (i.e. buying votes) – work which brought him into direct and frequently painful contact with the good people of Westmorland. Large sums of money were involved in managing the annual accounts, and since his employer was as harsh and strict as a Dickensian villain, John Wordsworth's position was difficult and stressful, as mediating between the demands of his employer and the needs or requests of Lowther's tenants or constituents was a thankless and often impossible task. William therefore grew up in a sort of social no-man's land, in which the family's loyalties were divided between serving the interests of the aristocracy (to which they could never belong) and maintaining normal social relationships with their fellow-citizens (from whom they were necessarily alienated by the nature of John Wordsworth's work). In his Preface to *Lyrical Ballads* Wordsworth tried to gloss over the fault lines running through the social landscape that he had grown up in, by declaring that a poet is, quite simply, 'a man speaking to men'. But his childhood, youth and early manhood all led him to think and feel quite differently, and to be all too aware of the conflicts inherent to the English class structure that made that kind of universalising phrase sound empty and almost meaningless.

★ ★ ★

In eighteenth-century England power was synonymous with patronage; and patronage was a double-edged weapon that could do good as well as harm. In Wordsworth's case it proved to be enormously important. His first experience of benevolent patronage came long before he was aware of what it signified, when, a year after the death of their mother in 1778, William and his brother Richard were enrolled in Hawkshead Grammar School. The school was a charitable foundation which, besides offering boys a good education, had also been endowed with the means (thanks to the bequest of £250 from a seventeenth-century patron) to provide scholarships for local boys to study at St John's College, Cambridge. And it was with one of these scholarships that Wordsworth was able to take wing and, at the age of seventeen, leave rural Westmorland for the exotic intellectual stratosphere of Cambridge University.

In the meantime though Wordsworth had felt the full force of all that was cruel and unjust in eighteenth-century social re-lations. William's father died when the boy was just thirteen, and it was discovered that Sir James Lowther owed John Wordsworth £4,660 – a huge sum in those days (roughly £250,000 today).[41] Sir James refused to honour this debt to John Wordsworth's heirs, and as a result the five orphaned children found themselves pen-niless. Uncles and cousins stepped in to offer what support and help they could (though never gratuitously, as all expenses were charged to the Wordsworth estate, to be repaid as and when possible). Having lost all emotional security with the death of both his mother and father (and furthermore separated now from the sister he was so fond of), William found himself without any material security either as he reached the threshold of adolescence. Whether he knew then that this situation was the direct consequence of Sir James Lowther's behaviour, or whether he found that out during the course of the next few years, is not important. Certainly by the time he went to Cambridge he would have known the facts; and the resentment and sense of grievance would colour his perception of society for the next fifteen years.

The experience of Cambridge would have done little to change his mood, as he would have rubbed shoulders there with the sons of the rich and powerful – young men who more often than not were spoilt, arrogant and self-satisfied, and whose main concern at university was to spend money and have a good time. But the excesses of undergraduate life were nothing compared to the mindless extravagance and sustained debauchery that he could have observed in London, where he lived for about a year after graduating.

By the time he left for France, in November 1791, he had an ingrained antipathy towards the aristocracy and a well-rooted dislike of the Establishment they represented. The battle-cry of the French Revolution was music to his ears at this time, and there is no doubt he believed in its message of social renewal. But it also became clear to him that there was no obvious way his personal situation was likely to be transformed even by a major social upheaval, and this for two simple reasons: one being that he had no money, and the other that he didn't want to work. His laziness in this respect was all the more striking given his extraordinary physical energy, but that is how it was: for over twenty years after graduating he had no steady employment and earned next to nothing. It was only after he had fathered six children and had a whole household to maintain that, in 1811, aged forty-one, he grudgingly decided he had to look for a job – and only on the condition that it didn't prevent him from writing poetry, of course.

Back in 1790, when he was at Cambridge, his uncles wanted him either to follow an academic career or to go into the Church (his maternal uncle William Cookson was a Fellow at St John's and could have helped Wordsworth in either of these directions.) Wordsworth used the idea of ordination as a ploy for several years, as a way of keeping his uncles quiet – but he had no wish to go down that path. He also produced his own breadwinning alternatives: he would give private lessons; he would translate from European languages; he could write articles for reviews or newspapers; he would be a travelling companion to a gentleman....In the end he never even attempted to do any of these – and almost certainly never intended to try. Nor did he seem to worry much about his future – unlike Dorothy, who shared her concern about William with her friend Jane Pollard:

> I am very anxious about him just now as he will shortly have to provide for himself: next year he takes his degree; when he will go into orders I do not know, nor how he will employ himself. He must, when he is three and twenty either go into orders or take pupils. (letter of April 30, 1790)

But her brother did neither of these, preferring to live on next to nothing and wait for his uncle to send him some money through the post. Even when Caroline was born and he recognised her as his daughter, he did nothing to find a job that would allow him, hopefully, to provide for her. Like a horse that balks at an obstacle, he stubbornly refused to engage with the world of adult employment. The idea of poetry as his vocation matured slowly inside his mind during the 1790s, but he wrote irregularly and without a sustained voice, and the verses earned him little or no money. The only real work he had during this period was that of looking after a young boy, which he did between 1795 and 1798, and for which he was paid a very modest amount of money.

Wordsworth's motives for accepting this employment probably went beyond the basic facts of the narrative. The story goes like this: the wife of a friend of his had died very soon after childbirth, leaving her widowed husband, Basil Montagu, with a boy to raise. Montagu was unable to reconcile this task with trying to make a living (as well as drinking heavily, getting into debt, etc.); but instead of farming the child out to some nanny, he came up with an original proposition. His friend Wordsworth was, as he would say, a poet in the making, and poets need time and space and freedom in which to create. Wordsworth also had a sister of whom he was exorbitantly fond, and who appeared to be at a bit of a loose end – no suitor or fiancé in sight as far as one could tell. Maybe Wordsworth and his sister could look after Basil junior (the boy having inherited the father's name, for want of a better). He (Basil senior) would find them somewhere to live out in the country, where the boy would get plenty of fresh air and be kept well away from the insalubrious fleshpots of London from which he (Basil senior) had difficulty in extricating himself; Wordsworth would have somewhere to live – rent-free, quiet, and close to nature – and would be able to wander around composing poetry to his heart's content; and Dorothy would provide the essential maternal presence for young Basil (aged just under three at the time), as well as having the pleasure of living with her brother (which was what it seemed she wanted to do).

The plan suited all concerned (except perhaps Basil junior), and was put into operation in the summer of 1795. William and Dorothy moved to the south-west of England, where they lived in the country, looked after young Basil and gave him the beginnings of an education, and got on with their own lives. Wordsworth discovered that he was happy living with Dorothy; he also met Coleridge, and opened a crucial dialogue with him, and so gradually moved towards the poems that would make up *Lyrical Ballads.* In short the experience was formative, and would bear fruit in different ways well after they returned to London in the spring of 1798.

As so often with Wordsworth though there was also a kind of sub-plot which would never be acknowledged, but which at the very least contributed towards giving significance to whatever he was involved in, and sometimes offered the true explanation for a particular initiative, in contradiction to the official version of events. In this case what was striking was that little Basil had been born just twelve days after Wordsworth's daughter Caroline – (Caroline on December 15, 1792, Basil on December 27); moreover the boy had been saddled not only with his father's name, but also that of his recently deceased mother – and had duly been christened Basil Caroline Montagu.

For Wordsworth such a combination of coincidences must have been very unsettling. Young Basil offered Wordsworth the chance to come close to the fatherhood that he had failed to live in France, to experience vicariously something of what he would have known with Caroline if he had stayed in France. Not that this would prevent him from brooding in his poems on the fate of half-crazed single mothers – but it was better than nothing. Small wonder then that he accepted the proposition.

There are contradictory accounts of the treatment Basil received while in the care of William and Dorothy. Dorothy's version, as relayed in letters to friends, gives the impression that they did all they could to offer the boy a carefree and healthy childhood close to nature – something similar to Wordsworth's own boyhood, as recounted in Books I and II of *The Prelude*. For his part Basil as an adult remembered those years quite differently, saying he had been treated cruelly and came close to starvation while with the Wordsworths. William, typically, did not go into details about the fostering / education of Basil in the letters he wrote to friends; nonetheless the deprivations evoked by Basil are not at odds with Wordsworth's idea of what a normal childhood was like. He himself had been brought up strictly, and had quickly grown used to a very meagre diet. Given his very limited financial resources, he no doubt spent far less on food than he should have, but without realising there was anything wrong in this. As for the punishments handed out to the boy, both William and Dorothy would, at a later date, treat William's own children with a strange kind of severity – so Basil's complaints are both perfectly credible and not particularly surprising.[42]

In any case, the real significance of this whole experience for anyone interested in Wordsworth's poetry, is that he spent two and a half years looking after a little boy while in his mid-twenties – an age when most men are staking out careers for themselves. In accepting the commitment to look after Basil, Wordsworth tacitly turned his back on the career choices – teaching, or the Church, or whatever – that would have satisfied his uncles, opting instead for an occupation that left him free to live exactly as he pleased. In a sense he managed to reclaim the kind of liberty that children take for granted, and at the same time subtracted himself from the demands of the adult world.

It was not however as if Wordsworth was imagining he could sustain a childlike mentality while developing as an adult. On the contrary, what counted for him was to engage with a child's vision of the world while never losing sight of the distance that separated it from an adult vision. And what began to take shape during those years would prove to be one of Wordsworth's most important contributions to literature – namely the exploration of childhood as a realm in its own right, quite independent of the adult world into which it was supposed to merge seamlessly through the process of education.

The first edition of *Lyrical Ballads* contained two poems on this theme – *Anecdote for Fathers* and *We are Seven* – both of which were composed towards the end of the time Wordsworth spent looking after Basil. Wordsworth noted at a later date that *Anecdote for Fathers* related directly to his relationship with Basil, while *We are Seven* was inspired by an encounter with a young girl five years earlier. But the premise of both poems – that there is no straightforward dialogue between adults and children – is the same, and constituted the first stage on that journey towards a new understanding of the child's world – the other major stages being the 'Lucy' poems and the first two books of *The Prelude* – that would in turn influence his thinking on the nature of time, the cycles of life and death, of growth and decay – in short, the whole structure of human existence.

Given the complication for Wordsworth that was implicit in young Montagu's name being 'Basil Caroline' it is perhaps not surprising that one of these two poems should refer to Basil, while the other refered to a meeting with a young girl in 1793 – the year after Wordsworth's return from France, when the fate of his baby daughter Caroline was very much on his mind. *We are Seven* suggests that Wordsworth saw his 'virtual' relationship with Caroline as running parallel with his real relationship with Basil. The fact that *We are Seven* turns around the deaths of two of the

OUR LORDS AND MASTERS

seven children who, for their sister, are not in fact dead, reinforces the sense that Wordsworth was exploring the angst created by his own situation as an absent father who had effectively abandoned his daughter to her fate – even though in reality she remained alive and well. Caroline was dead to him even though she was actually alive, just as the girl's brother and sister were alive for her, even though they were actually dead.

A third poem, written like the other two in 1798 and also forming part of the first edition of *Lyrical Ballads*, reflected on the lifestyle that, for better and for worse, Wordsworth had committed himself to at this time. In *Expostulation and Reply* the schoolmaster reproaches the poet for his passivity and apparent inactivity: the poet answers that there is no simple way of measuring and evaluating true creativity:

> 'Think you, 'mid all this mighty sum
> Of things for ever speaking,
> That nothing of itself will come,
> But we must still be seeking?' (lines 25-28)

At one level Wordsworth's reply suggests an oriental aesthetic for poetry – in which creativity is equated with a state of awareness, itself the result of a process of mental preparation and discipline. But at the same time the verse offers a defence for Wordsworth's refusal to earn money, asking quite simply if from the mighty sum of capital floating around, none of it will come his way without him having to seek it out. Wordsworth's argument (had he been forced to justify his way of life at this time) would have been that these two forms of passivity were complementary, and that both were necessary for the creation of good poetry.

★ ★ ★

In May 1802 Sir James Lowther died, and his heir declared that he would respect all debts incurred by Sir James. As a result the Wordsworths obtained £8,500 (the original debt plus interest). This made a huge difference to William's finances (his joint share with Dorothy eventually amounted to £3,825), and inevitably prompted him to reconsider his opinion of the aristocracy. Until then he had only known or seen their bad side; now, as luck or fate would have it, he was to witness the opposite...

Enter Sir George Beaumont. Sir George, having previously developed a malicious fever during a recent Grand Tour of Italy, had been advised by his doctors of the need to reside for a sizeable part of each year in the country, with the aim thereby of avoiding a deleterious aggravation of his pulmonary condition consequent on excessive exposure to the noxious fumes that tainted the air of the great capital. To this end and in this manner Sir George, together with his wife, Lady Margaret, found themselves in the summer of 1803 in the Lake District, where Sir George, a keen and gifted amateur painter, enjoyed sketching the picturesque and suggestive landscape. And there, while lodging at Greta Hall, they met Coleridge, who was also staying at the Hall.

Coleridge, master impresario that he was, and scenting both the generosity and good taste of the worthy baronet, realised the opportunity that had presented itself and seized it with both hands. He spoke warmly of Wordsworth's poetry and lent Sir George a copy of *Lyrical Ballads*. Beaumont responded by buying for Wordsworth a small property near Greta Hall, with the idea not only of helping the poet financially but also of drawing him closer to where both Coleridge and he were guests. It was a remarkably generous gesture to make, the more so as he had neither met Wordsworth nor written to him first to find out

whether or not the proposition interested him; and the language
he used in the letter he wrote to Wordsworth once the property
had been bought, is a perfect example of the enlightened and
well-intentioned attitude that coloured all his actions:

> I thought with pleasure on the encrease of enjoyment that
> you would receive from the beauties of nature by being able
> to communicate more frequently your sensations to each
> other, & that this would be a means of contributing to the
> pleasure and improvement of the world by stimulating you
> both to poetic exertions.[43]

'Each other' and 'both' are references to Wordsworth's rela-
tionship with Coleridge, which Beaumont took for granted. In
fact, by 1803 Wordsworth's friendship with Coleridge was on the
wane, and he had no wish to have him as a close neighbour. But
he must have been startled and touched by the sensitivity and en-
couragement that Beaumont expressed in his letter. Wordsworth
was not used either to praise or to offers of help. The reviews
of *Lyrical Ballads* had been mixed, and had criticised the 'lowly'
subject matter of the poems; yet here was a cultured man – and a
member of the aristocracy – who believed that such poems were
not only enjoyable to read, but also socially beneficial. Coming
just a year after the new Lord Lowther's pledge to honour his de-
ceased cousin's debts, Beaumont's spontaneous gesture must have
made a powerful impression on Wordsworth, and certainly con-
tributed to altering his view of aristocratic landowners in general.
While he was reluctant to have anything to do with the proper-
ty that Beaumont had bought for him, Wordsworth was glad to
accept Beaumont's friendship – which was offered on terms of
absolute equality, ignoring differences in wealth and social stand-
ing. Wordsworth's assertion in the 1800 Preface to *Lyrical Ballads*

that he was 'a man speaking to men' was beginning to prove itself. Maybe poets were not, as Shelley was later to claim, 'the unacknowledged legislators of the world', but their writing surely had the potential of transcending class barriers, and of speaking to and for humanity as a whole.

So during 1804 Wordsworth found himself in the curious position of becoming friendly with two members of the English landowning class, while at the same time working on Books IX and X of *The Prelude*, in which he recounted his enthusiasm for the French Revolution and for ridding the country of all vestiges of the Ancien Régime. There was no direct contradiction in this (his sonnets of 1802 had already made clear his disillusionment with the course French politics had taken after the Revolution). Nonetheless it points to the conflictual nature of Wordsworth's mindset at this time in his life. The 'great U-turn' he accomplished was not a single and coordinated change of heart and mind that took place in middle age, between the ages of forty and fifty-five; but rather a complex series of shifts in thinking that began when he was in his early thirties, even when the poetry that he was producing spoke out loud and clear against the abuse of wealth and power and inherited privilege, and in favour of republican values.

Beaumont would prove as good a friend as the new Lord Lowther would be a source of help and support. During the decades that followed both men would do whatever they could to encourage Wordsworth and help him financially, while doing their best to avoid being patronising. They were discreet, they respected him as an individual in his own right, they addressed him as an equal, and they honestly admired his writing and took an active interest in everything he did. Wordsworth kept Beaumont in touch with progress (or lack of it) in his work, and sent him a copy of any edition of his poems that appeared. Sir George clearly enjoyed this dialogue with a true artist, and responded by showing Wordsworth the landscapes he painted. On one occasion Wordsworth then returned the compliment by writing a poem in appreciation of Beaumont's work, which he later published under the title of *Elegaic Stanzas, suggested by a Picture of Peele Castle in a Storm, painted by Sir George Beaumont*. And so it went on, polite courtesies impinging on creative impulses in a way which Wordsworth would never have imagined possible before meeting Beaumont – and which, it must be said, went completely against his natural instincts.[44]

Beaumont was particularly active as a patron of the visual arts. His own collection included a very fine landscape by Claude le Lorrain, which he treasured so much that he had a special case made for it, which allowed him to take the painting with him when he was travelling. In 1805 he helped set up the British Institution, which, thanks in large part to Beaumont, proved to be the precursor to the National Gallery in London (in 1824 Beaumont offered to give sixteen paintings from his collection to the nation, on condition that another private collection was bought up when it became available: on the basis of these acquisitions, plus the works already in the British Institution, the National Gallery was set up in 1825). Beaumont also bought Michelangelo's bas-relief, the *Taddei Tondo*, during a trip to Italy in 1821, and then gave it to the Royal Academy. While his great love was for the work of the Old Masters, he also took an active interest in contemporary painting, and – (though he disliked Turner) – was a patron of Constable; however it was only with Wordsworth, among contemporary artists and writers, that he became friends.

One of the very best landscapes by Claude in English

collections was owned by the Earl of Egremont, who was as keen a patron of the arts as Beaumont, though with different tastes. The Earl is best known today as having been the patron of Turner, and for enjoying the same sort of easy-going relationship with Turner as Beaumont did with Wordsworth. Egremont's main residence was at Petworth House, and Turner was always welcome there as a guest; rooms on the upper floor were set aside for him to use as a studio. Given that Turner came from the working-classes of London (his father was a barber), this kind of familiarity was quite significant. Still, it seems that Turner felt at ease in these odd surroundings, which savoured more of the eighteenth century than of the nineteenth: Egremont was known to maintain about fifteen mistresses, who between them gave birth to more than forty children – and (of course) to countless conflicts and tensions. The atmosphere at Petworth House must have been lively and colourful.

Beaumont and Egremont showed the English aristocracy at its best (at least as far as artists were concerned); and Wordsworth and Turner were lucky to be on friendly terms with these men – Wordsworth in particular, given that he had decided to live so far from London, and in a place where dialogues of the sort that mattered to him were few and far between. The attitudes of these aristocrats – enlightened open-mindedness, and a generous use of their wealth to the greater good of the community – seemed to call into question some of the consequences of the French Revolution. In France the aristocracy had been decimated, after which the Revolution had led first to the Terror and then to the 'ogre' that was Napoleon. In England, despite all the upheavals of that period, a certain continuity was maintained; and it is striking that both the great poet and the great painter of the Romantic period enjoyed the patronage of aristocrats whose values and lifestyles carried an eighteenth-century perfume deep into the body of the nineteenth century.

★ ★ ★

Wordsworth did not enjoy the same sort of easy-going friendship with Lord Lowther; but Lord Lonsdale (as he became) was better placed than Beaumont to provide practical and financial help if it was needed.[45] He was there in the background, wealthy and influential, and well disposed towards Wordsworth. So when at the end of 1811 Wordsworth's financial situation – with a wife and five children to support, together with his sister and sister-in-law – became desperate, he knew who to turn to. He wrote to Lonsdale, asking if his Lordship could offer him any kind of job that would allow him to earn some money without preventing him from writing poetry. Lonsdale replied that he was unable to help at the present time. However, he did not forget Wordsworth's request, and in September 1812 offered him an annuity of £100, until such time as a suitable position could be found. After some hesitation Wordsworth accepted. As it turned out the right sort of job did become available a few months later, and in March 1813 Lord Lonsdale was able to have Wordsworth appointed Distributor of Stamps for Westmorland. At last the poet had a steady income.[46] He kept the job for the next twenty-nine years. It wasn't a sinecure, but neither did it take up too much time or energy – nor did it have the slightest impact on what he wrote. Bread-winning and creativity were separated as daily activities (though of course if he could earn money from his poetry as well, then so much the better). It wasn't perfect as a solution, but it lifted a huge number of worries and preoccupations from his shoulders. And it came through the good offices of Lord Lonsdale

(assisted by Sir George Beaumont – together they provided
£8,000 of sureties necessary for Wordsworth to assume the
position). Without them it seems inconceivable that Wordsworth
would have managed to get the job (or a similar one), and to put
his finances onto a steady footing.

★ ★ ★

In January 1801 Wordsworth sent a copy of the second edition of
Lyrical Ballads to Charles James Fox, leader of the Whig opposi-
tion in Parliament, together with a letter in which he expressed
some of the beliefs and convictions that motivated him in his
writing. Referring to the characters portrayed in *The Brothers* and
Michael he noted that,

> They are small independent <u>proprietors</u> of land here called
> Statesmen, men of respectable education who daily labour on
> their own little properties. The domestic affections will always
> be strong amongst men who live in a country not crowded
> with population, if these men are placed above poverty. But if
> they are proprietors of small estates which have descended to
> them from their ancestors, the power which these affections
> will acquire amongst such men is inconceivable by those who
> have only had an opportunity of observing hired labourers,
> farmers, and the manufacturing Poor. Their little tract of land
> serves as a kind of permanent rallying point for their domes-
> tic feelings, as a tablet upon which they are written...
>
> (January 14, 1801)[47]

Wordsworth was effectively using his poetry to try and lobby
support from Fox for the cause of small landowners. In this he
was disappointed. But as is so often the case with Wordsworth,

there was a kind of sub-plot in the letter that he wrote to the politician. At this stage in his life his sense of his own profession was still vague and unformed; but as the years passed, and the need to provide for a wife and family became urgent, he came to identify at a certain level with the small landowners he had written about in *Lyrical Ballads*. For even as he imagined the holdings of shepherds to be 'tablets' on which their personal values were inscribed, so he came to see his own writing as a 'little tract of land' from which he could earn a modest income – and which he desperately wanted to be able to pass on to his children, as a heritage. The first tacit use of this analogy came a year later, in the sonnet known as 'Nuns fret not at their Convent's narrow room', when he wrote that,

> 'twas pastime to be bound
> Within the Sonnet's scanty plot of ground
> (lines 10-11)

– the small dimensions of a sonnet neatly matching the size of the garden in which he and his sister could grow some vegetables to feed themselves. But the argument only took real form in his mind when he became aware of the limits of the copyright laws in England: when he realised for example that his collection *Poems, in Two Volumes*, published in 1807, would cease to earn him any money in 1835, and would bring no money to his children were he to die in the meantime. At that point he began to campaign for a radical extension of the copyright laws, seeking to extend the time they remained in vigour, and to enable a writer's children to inherit the rights to published works. He lobbied and argued for thirty years, and was finally rewarded in 1842 by a watered-down version of the Bill that he wanted – Parliament voting to extend copyright from twenty-eight to forty-two years from the date of first publication, or seven years after the writer's death (whichever was the longer). It was a good deal less than he had hoped for, but at least he had established the principle of literature as intellectual property, that could be passed from one generation to the next (even if only briefly), just as a house or piece of land could be. He had carried his sense of affinity with small landowners through to its logical conclusion, and had asserted once again the importance of continuity in social and financial relations.

Wordsworth's models during this marathon campaign may have come from the stable pre-industrial world of rural England, but the issues it raised belonged very much to the future. The next great campaigner for copyright was Charles Dickens, who took on the United States (where at the time there was no copyright law), and helped to establish the principle that writers and composers had an 'inalienable right' over their creative production. During the twentieth century this principle became more or less taken for granted (except in countries under Communist rule); however in recent years technological innovations have made piracy – above all of music and films – increasingly easy. And so in some ways the world could be said to have returned to a situation not unlike that which made Wordsworth despair in the early 1800s. The difference is that nowadays intellectual property is recognised as involving a whole body of law (most of which has to do with patents and business and industry, rather than with works of art); so that while debates continue to rage, the premises for those debates are no longer called into question.[48] From being a near anagram of poverty, poetry has shifted its position considerably, and can now claim to be a near anagram of property (or at least a poor relation of the same). And that change is due in part to Wordsworth.

Chapter V

Lucy in the Sky

In September 1798 William and Dorothy, together with Coleridge and a friend of his, John Chester, set off for what was intended to be a two-year residence in Germany. The aim was to stay near a university town such as Hamburg, learn German, and improve their understanding of German (and European) culture in general. The project bore all the hallmarks of Coleridge's many and various adventures, being intellectually ambitious, financially unrealistic, and more or less doomed to failure from the outset. But at this time Coleridge still had considerable influence over Wordsworth – who would never have thought up a scheme like this himself, but seemed to have been happy to go along with his friend's initiative, in order to be close to Coleridge and enjoy his company and conversation.

However after just twelve days together in Germany the Wordsworths separated from Coleridge and Chester. The problem was money. The Wordsworths' budget was too meagre to allow them to follow the programme that Coleridge and Chester wanted for themselves, and so they decided to look for some

Overleaf: Letter written by William and Dorothy to Coleridge, and sent from Goslar, December 1798. It is addressed, 'an der Herrn Coleridge, Ratzeburg', and includes boyhood scenes from The Prelude *as well as two of the 'Lucy' poems*

and troubled pleasure; not without the voice
of mountain echoes did my boat move on;
Leaving behind her still on either side
small circles glittering idly in the moon,
Until they melted all into one track
of sparkling light. A rocky steep uprose
above the cavern of the willow tree
And now, as fitted one who proudly rowed
with his best skill, I fixed a steady view
Upon the top of that same shaggy ridge,
The bound of the horizon, for behind
was nothing, but the stars & the grey sky.
She was an elfin pinnace; twenty times
I dipped my oars into the silent lake,
And as I rose upon the stroke my boat
Went heaving through the water, like a swan
When from behind that rocky steep, till then

The bound of the horizon, a huge cliff,
As if with voluntary power instinct,
Upreared its head: I struck & struck again,
And growing still in stature the huge cliff
Rose up between me & the stars, & still
with measured motion, like a living thing,
Strode after me. with trembling hands I turned,
And through the silent water stole my way,
Back to the cavern of the willow tree;
There, in her mooring-place I left my bark,
And through the meadows homeward went with grave
And serious thoughts; & after I had seen
That spectacle for many days my brain
Worked with a dim and undetermined sense
Of unknown modes of being. In my thoughts
There was a darkness, call it solitude

B

Have you been able to get any information ~~either~~ concerning the earliest poets of Germany? I find in Monsieur Raimond's translation of Coxe's Travels in Switzerland, that Mr Bodmer a German poet of Zurich had presented him with a volume of amorous verses of the poets of the thirteenth century. This work is extracted from a manuscript which the King of France entrusted to the city of Zurich in the year 1752. I will transcribe the sentence which follows "Il m'a encore donné (that is Mr Bodmer) le recueil de ses tragedies historiques & politiques, ouvrage aussi savant qu'interessant & &" It had been son recueil the meaning of this sentence would have been evident but the word savant seems to imply that it is a collection of which Mr Bodmer is only the editor: unless, being original tragedies they are accompanied with notes. As to your hexameters, I need not say how much the sentiment affected me. I have not been sufficiently accustomed to the metre to give any opinion which can be depended upon. One thing strikes me in common with the German ladies, that the two last feet are what principally give the character of verse to the Hexameters—the sum of my feeling is that the two last are more than verse, & all the rest not so much. I mean to say that there should be none of the sensation of metre in the whole of the verse to break the monotony of the two last feet. The lines also are not sufficiently run into each other, but that might be easily remedied. You do not ~~know~~ how you liked the poem of Wieland which you had read. Let me know what you think of Wieland—You make no mention of Klopstock; and what is the merit of Goethe's new poem? — Dorothy has written the other side of this sheet while I have been out. She has transcribed a few descriptions—you will read them at your leisure. She will copy out two or three little Rhyme poems which I hope will amuse you. As I have had no books I have been obliged to write in self-defence. I should have written five times as much as I have done but that I am prevented by an uneasiness at my stomach and side, with a ~~tendency to~~ dull pain about my heart. I have used the word pain, but uneasiness & heat are words which more accurately ~~express~~ my feeling. At all events, it renders writing unpleasant. Reading is now become a kind of luxury to me. When I do not read I am absolutely consumed by thinking & feeling & bodily exertions of voice or of limbs, the consequences of those feelings. ~~For~~ the last stanza of this little poem you will consider the words "long time" as put in merely to fill up the measure but as syntonious to the sense.

My hope was one, from cities far,
Nursed on a lonesome heath;
Her lips were red as roses are,
Her hair a woodbine wreath.

She lived among the untrodden ways
Beside the springs of Dove,
A maid whom there were none to praise
And very few to love;

A violet by a mossy stone
Half-hidden from the eye!
Fair as a star when only one
Is shining in the sky!

And she was graceful as the broom
That flowers by Carron's side;
But slow distemper checked her bloom,
And on the heath she died.

Long time before her head lay low,
Dead to the world was she:
But now she's in her grave, and oh!
The difference to me!

The next poem is a favourite of mine & is of me Dorothy —

quiet provincial town in Lower Saxony where they could find cheap lodgings and study German at their own pace, without ruining themselves financially. On October 6 they arrived in the town of Goslar, took lodgings there, and settled in for the winter. The months that followed would prove to be a truly Dantesque experience.

The town turned out to be unfriendly and dreadfully dull. Communication with the locals was limited: they met only one German with whom they felt inclined to chat – and he was deaf and had no teeth! Even before the winter set in they had turned in on themselves, and when the winter arrived it turned out to be the worst in living memory. William and Dorothy were stranded in Goslar for four months; and their lodgings were so cold that even indoors they were miserable. They had to wear overcoats to go from one room to another. William's bedroom lay over a corridor that had no ceiling, and was so cold that the other inhabitants of the house always expected him to die during the night. The stove was inevitably the focus of their attention, and Wordsworth was moved to write a poem about it, in which he compared his present situation to that of a fly he observed stumbling around on top of the lukewarm stove:

> Alas! How he fumbles about the domains
> Which this comfortless oven environ!
> He cannot find out in which track to crawl,
> Now back to the tiles, then in search of the wall,
> And now on the brink of the iron.

> Stock-still there he stands like a traveller bemazed:
> The best of his skill he has tried;
> His feelers, methinks, I can see him put forth
> To the east and the west, to the south and the north;

But he finds neither guide-post nor guide.[49]

They would have left if they could, and headed in any direction of the compass in order to escape, but the weather was too bad and the roads were impossible. For the first time in his life Wordsworth, whose childhood had passed in continual movement and who had spent the previous five years as a restless nomad, found himself trapped, unable to go any further than the edge of the town. This sense of paralysis could easily have provoked a state of depression and mental inertia in someone whose intellectual activity had always relied on physical exercise and well-being. But curiously it didn't. Instead the desperate conditions actually concentrated his attention, and forced him to write in a new way. As Coleridge elegantly put it in his poem *Frost at Midnight*,

> The Frost performs its secret ministry,
> Unhelped by any wind.

Even as Wordsworth presented himself as being as hopelessly lost and clueless as a fly in midwinter, the freezing cold and isolation which he thought were numbing his brain and making him lose his sense of direction were in fact having the opposite effect. A secret and miraculous ministry was at work. Far from losing direction the poet was, without realising it at the time, opening up new paths of thought and feeling that were to prove vitally important for his development. The winter at Goslar laid the bases for the work for which Wordsworth later became famous, and pushed him to a degree of self-knowledge that might have eluded him had he not been held there as an unwilling captive for more than four months.

There were three kinds of poems produced in this short period: the 'Matthew' and 'Lucy' poems (most of which would be included in the second edition of *Lyrical Ballads*); a large part of Book I of *The Prelude*, together with the 'There was a boy...' episode from Book V (lines 389-413); and *Nutting*, which was originally intended to be part of *The Prelude*, but was then taken out of the scheme for the long poem and published separately. While the work was very varied it had a certain unity which would make itself felt in Wordsworth's oeuvre at different intervals. For example the 'Matthew' and 'Lucy' poems, while they belong to the *Lyrical Ballads*, also prefigure one of the fundamental dynamics of *The Prelude*. Matthew and Lucy are diametrically opposed. They are represented as an elderly schoolmaster and a young girl – but the difference in age and gender is only the starting-point for a more significant dialectic: between the influence of education and that of nature, between articulacy and intuition, between thought and feeling, between discipline and freedom, between rational thought and irrational impulse. And so on.

Another kind of dialectic animates the Goslar work as a whole, and that is the tension between poems about imagined or real characters (as in *Lyrical Ballads*), and poems that were specifically autobiographical. One way of looking at the Goslar experience is to see it as a moment of crucial transition from the kind of writing Wordsworth had been engaged on in the 1790s, in which he explored and dramatised the lives of other people, to the more introspective work that would characterise the next five years, and which would result above all in *The Prelude*. When Wordsworth and Coleridge set off for Germany they had just delivered *Lyrical Ballads* to the printers, and it was published two days before Wordsworth reached Goslar. One of the functions of the German trip was clearly to allow him to take stock of what that collection of poems represented, and to work out how best to proceed. The 'Matthew' and 'Lucy' poems show him feeling his way forward to a new, more private idiom (especially in the 'Lucy' poems), while still maintaining the style and voice of *Lyrical Ballads* (especially in the 'Matthew' poems). At the same time the months spent away from England deprived him of all his usual routines, company and habits, and gave him the time and mental space he needed to move towards a radically different kind of poetry.

The 'Matthew' poems are affectionate testimonials to all that the modest village schoolmasters represented and achieved. But in the end Wordsworth maintained a certain emotional distance from his character, and specified in the notes he dictated to Isabella Fenwick towards the end of his life, that, 'this schoolmaster was made up of several both of his class and men of other occupations'. In the 'Lucy' poems however the register is different: more intense, more involved, and more complex – even though the poems themselves are shorter, at times almost lapidary. None of the 'Matthew' poems contains lines of such anguish as, 'But she is in her Grave, and Oh! / The difference to me.' From the moment they were composed everyone has felt the particular quality of these poems, and almost everyone has found themselves asking the question, who is Lucy? Who is the girl or woman who could have inspired such strong feelings in this stern and stoical man's heart? In a letter of April 6, 1799, in which he referred to the poem *'A slumber did my spirit seal'* Coleridge wrote that: 'Most probably in some gloomier moment he had imagined the moment in which his Sister might die.' Given Coleridge's privileged position as an intimate friend of Wordsworth, and given all that we know about Wordsworth's relationship with his sister, this thesis has become the favourite one for all those who believe that there was 'a Lucy' – that's to say that the poems refer to one specific person. In the opposite camp stand those who find such detective work irrelevant, and who prefer to see Lucy only as a figment of the poet's imagination, a girl who existed as an example of certain social realities – much as Matthew did. For them there is no one Lucy, and the cause of literature would be better served if more attention was paid to the text itself, and less to the private story that may or may not lie behind it.

Wordsworth himself gave no clues as to who he might be referring to in the 'Lucy' poems – but that, given his ingrained reticence about all aspects of his private life, is not so significant. And while he made it clear that Matthew was a composite figure drawn from a number of men he had known, Wordsworth made no such comment about Lucy – yet she also was in a different way a composite figure. In her case it was not so much that he drew on different girls or women to create a single identifiable person, rather that he drew on different feelings of his own to create a mood and vision that would be the synthesis of a complex whirlpool of emotions. While the poems are united by the sense of loss that permeates them all, the scenarios evoked are quite different from each other, and make it hard to imagine a single Lucy inspiring all the poems. The two ballads, *Lucy Gray* and *'Strange fits of passion I have known'*, are already incompatible, as the first tells the story of a small girl who disappears in a snowstorm, never to be seen again, while the other expresses the anxieties of a lover about the well-being of the young woman he is in love with. The three elegaic pieces, *'Three years she grew in sun and shower'*, Song (*'She dwelt among th'untrodden ways'*), and *'A slumber did my spirit seal'*, are similar in tone, but the first clearly evokes the death of a child, while the 'maid' of *Song* seems to reach adulthood before dying, and the Lucy of the third poem is ageless and completely anonymous.

By writing a cluster of poems in a short space of time on the theme of premature death, and by giving the same name to the girl who is the subject of each of the poems, Wordsworth created a generic feel to the name of Lucy. A 'Lucy' poem was a poem about loss, about nostalgia and memory and the passing of time. The themes were universal, and the anonymity that he established for the girl fitted the themes, in that it emphasised the impersonal nature of death – and the way premature death was an everyday occurrence at the time.

No family was safe from that threat. Obviously the poor were more at risk, but even the rich and powerful lived in the knowledge that children were extremely vulnerable during the first ten years of their lives. And every woman knew that giving birth was dangerous and unpredictable: either she or her baby – or both of them – could die in the hours and days following birth. The standard response was to produce large families; for the rest infant deaths were stoically accepted, and seldom referred to in art, literature or music. Likewise the premature deaths of women were seldom remembered in poetry or music – although the seventeenth century did offer two masterpieces of this kind: Milton's sonnet *Methought I saw my late espousèd saint* (1658), which almost certainly refers to his second wife Katherine (but could also refer to his first wife Mary, as both died prematurely), and Purcell's *Music for the funeral of Queen Mary* (1695). (The near coincidence of dates for these compositions suggests a general shift in attitudes: instead of being taken for granted and passed over, premature death could now be considered a subject worthy of attention, as it not only allowed the artist to express feelings of loss or grief, but also offered a chance to reflect on the inevitability – or the injustice – of such events in a world where human destinies were decided by God.)

But it was Wordsworth who, in the 'Lucy' poems, was the first writer to give voice to the grief felt when a child dies (it is worth noting that while he had no direct experience of this kind of loss when he wrote the poems, two of his children died in 1812, aged five and three, while his favourite daughter Dora also died before he did). In all there are six poems, written between 1798 and 1802, that refer specifically to Lucy: *Song* (*'She dwelt among th' untrodden ways'*); *'Strange fits of passion I have known'*; *Lucy Gray*; *'Three years she grew in sun and shower'*; *'I travelled among unknown men'*; and *'Among all lovely things my Love hath been'*. The last of these (and the least successful), written in 1802, is quite different in tone from the others, and cannot really be considered as forming part of the group; while *'A slumber did my spirit seal'*, written during the winter in Goslar, clearly does form part of the group even though Lucy is not named. The theme Wordsworth elaborated in these poems belongs to the years before his marriage in 1802 – from then on the tone changes, becoming more affirmative and less melancholic. The series was anticipated by the 1798 poem *We are Seven*, which offered a child's reflection on infant death, and grafted neatly onto the 'Matthew' poems in *The Two April Mornings*, in which Matthew stands over the grave of his dead daughter, and broods on his love for her.

Song and *Lucy Gray* are the most straightforward of the series. *Lucy Gray* is a simple narrative, typical of most of the poems in *Lyrical Ballads*; while *Song* is an intensely felt lament which nonetheless relies in part on precedent. The lines,

> A Maid whom there were none to praise
> And very few to love:
>
> A Violet by a mossy stone
> Half-hidden from the Eye!   (lines 3-6)

reply to and develop Gray's comment on rural life in his *Elegy written in a Country Churchyard* of 1751:

Full many a flower is born to blush unseen,
And waste its sweetness on the desert air.

(lines 55-6)

But then in *'Three years she grew in sun and shower'* Wordsworth used the image of the flower in a decidedly new way, moving beyond eighteenth-century thinking:

Three years she grew in sun and shower,
Then Nature said, 'A lovelier flower
On earth was never sown;
This Child I to myself will take;
She shall be mine, and I will make
A Lady of my own.   (lines 1-6)

Here Nature usurps the place usually ascribed to God ('The Lord giveth and the Lord taketh away'). Wordsworth tacitly refutes the logic that had sustained Christian belief for centuries, according to which a divine purpose underlies even such a cruel event as the death of a child, and instead evolves a different argument. For him a baby is born into a state of grace which has less to do with Christian concepts of innocence than with its unconscious yet umbilical connection with nature. That connection is broken by the necessary processes of education and social development; but should a child die before that process is begun it preserves intact the bond with nature. What appears tragic to us can also be seen to be the child's salvation. In Book I of *The Prelude* Wordsworth put this thinking about childhood to the test, by delving into memories of his own boyhood – or maybe it was the other way round, and the thinking behind the 'Lucy' poems developed as a result of the autobiographical meditations that the 'winter's crucible' at Goslar helped him to produce. No matter.

We know that Wordsworth worked on Book I of *The Prelude* while he was at Goslar (and that he also composed there the episode in Book V in which the boy communicates effortlessly with the owls); and it was during that winter that all but one of the 'Lucy' poems were composed. The thinking behind the 'Lucy' poems runs parallel to that which motivated *The Prelude*; to this extent they offer a vital link between the first two phases of Wordsworth's major output, that is to say between the publication of *Lyrical Ballads* and the composition of *The Prelude*.

'*A slumber did my spirit seal*' stands alongside '*Three years she grew in sun and shower*' in that it also interrogates a point of Christian doctrine – this time concerning the transience of human life. 'Earth to earth, ashes to ashes, dust to dust', is the message of the Burial Service. To the principle of return to a point of origin Wordsworth proposes instead a dynamic based on a scientific rather than religious concept of the universe:

> No motion has she now, no force;
> She neither hears nor sees;
> Rolled round in earth's diurnal course,
> With rocks, and stones, and trees.

Here the body of the dead girl is subject to the laws of motion as set out by Galileo, Copernicus and Newton: she moves thanks only to the force of inertia, because she is once again part of the Earth that turns around the sun. And along with this the linear notion of time which is used to measure a human life, or historical change or progress, is replaced by a cyclical conception ('earth's diurnal course') which subverts notions of progress and achievement, and reminds the reader of the greater patterns that control the workings of the universe.

Wordsworth produced a strange variation on this theme in the famous 'skating' episode in Book I of *The Prelude*, which he also wrote while in Goslar. To start with he created a mood which was the complete antithesis of the 'Lucy' poems – a scene full of noise and movement and childish excitement. Then the tempo changes abruptly:

> Not seldom from the uproar I retired
> Into a silent bay, or sportively
> Glanced sideway, leaving the tumultuous throng,
> To cut across the image of a star
> That gleamed upon the ice; and oftentimes,
> When we had given our bodies to the wind,
> And all the shadowy banks on either side
> Came sweeping through the darkness, spinning still
> The rapid line of motion, then at once
> Have I, reclining back upon my heels,
> Stopped short; yet still the solitary cliffs
> Wheeled by me – even as if the earth had rolled
> With visible motion her diurnal round! (I, 474-86)

As in a Vermeer painting, in which the casual and apparently superficial subject matter gradually reveals a vision of great complexity and subtlety, so here the banal incident being described – a boy comes to a sudden stop while skating on the ice – can be seen to contain a whole cluster of meanings that endow the moment with significance. First there is the casual transgression of deliberately skating over the reflection of a star, which creates a connection between the boy and the vast universe in which he is no more than an insignificant atom – rather as Lucy, in dying, is absorbed back into the infinite order of nature.... Likewise the boy, on stopping short, sees himself swept along in 'earth's diurnal round', just as Lucy is 'rolled round in earth's diurnal course'. But

there is a fundamental difference in the connections and relation-
ships that are suggested: little Lucy exists in a state of harmony
with all things – 'The stars of midnight shall be dear / To her'
(*'Three years she grew…'*, lines 25-6), while the boy's glimpse of
the universe in motion is the accidental result of a sort of instinc-
tive aggression. In the 1850 version of *The Prelude* this dynamic
was emphasised by adding an extra line that suggested a hunter
chasing his prey:

> To cut across the reflex of a star
> That fled, and, flying still before me, gleamed
> Upon the glassy plain;   (450-52)

But the extra line also works in another way, underlining the
exactness of the visual and physical perceptions in this passage.
The reflection of a star or of the moon would indeed seem to
stay constantly ahead of him as he moved towards it; similar-
ly, on stopping short on his skates after travelling at speed he
would indeed have the impression that the landscape continued
to move past him – just as happens when you turn round and
round fast on one spot, and then stop: everything continues to
whirl round you. The sensations evoked are grounded in a real
perception of the physical world. In this respect it is worth noting
that Wordsworth took a real interest in some aspects of science.
He was in particular fascinated by the discoveries of Newton.
The son of Wordsworth's headmaster at Hawkshead School re-
lated how his father, who used to lend Wordsworth (then aged
fifteen or sixteen) books from his library, one day found him
completely engrossed in Newton's *Opticks*. Later, when at
Cambridge, Wordsworth found that if he stood on the bed in
his room at St John's and looked at just the right angle through
the window, he could see Trinity College Chapel, which housed

the marble statue of Newton (as related in Book III, lines 56-9, of *The Prelude*). However much Wordsworth may have sensed a divine purpose in the workings of nature and of the universe, and however close to a state of mystical awareness he may have come at times in his poetry, his understanding of the natural world was essentially empirical, and as such owed just as much to the laws of Newton as to the poetry of the Book of Genesis.

The 'Lucy' poems have their origin in the folktales of *Lyrical Ballads*, but carry in their simple verses the seeds of a debate about science and religion, and the laws governing life, death and the workings of the universe. It was a debate which engaged Wordsworth profoundly, and which he never resolved. Still, the drift of his thinking across the decades is clear: the 1805 version of *The Prelude* maintains a wonderful balance between doubt and faith; while in the second half of his life that balance was lost, as he recoiled from what he saw as an anarchistic cocktail of atheism and arguments about evolution, and retreated towards the shelter of established religion.

★ ★ ★

Even for those who wish to see Lucy as no more than an anonymous figure plucked out of folk culture it must be clear that the writing in the 'Lucy' poems goes way beyond the impersonal dimension of the ballad form. And it is easy to imagine – independently of Coleridge's supposition – that Wordsworth could have been brooding on his feelings for his sister during that long cold winter, when the two of them were cooped up together in a house in Germany, isolated from the rest of the world and left to their own devices. Nonetheless, Dorothy made no reference to the 'Lucy' poems in her *Grasmere Journal*, so it is hard to know how she reacted to them. The closest thing to a response came in her entry for April 29, 1802, when she described how she and her brother lay near to each other in a field:

> William heard me breathing & rustling now & then but we both lay still, & unseen by one another – he thought that it would be sweet thus to lie so in the grave, to hear the *peaceful* sounds of the earth & just to know that ones dear friends were near.

Significantly it is William, not Dorothy, who conjures up this otherworldly scenario reminiscent of the 'Lucy' poems (in particular that of '*A slumber did my spirit seal*'). If Dorothy made any reply to this daydream she did not record it; nonetheless she seems to have let herself go, wanting to share in and sustain the fantasy. Later in the day, as they lay close to each other in another field, she observed how the sheep had,

> something of strangeness, like animals of another kind – as if belonging to another world.

And when they returned home she noted that,

> We went to bed immediately – I slept upstairs.

That is to say, she did not sleep in her normal bedroom, which at that time was on the ground floor, but in the spare bedroom on the first floor, next to William's bedroom. It was a way of prolonging until the next morning the sweet sensation of lying next to her brother for all eternity, that he had teasingly imagined earlier that day.

One can imagine that the 'Lucy' poems were a sort of code, which neither brother nor sister felt they should be asked to break. Dorothy could guess at their hidden meaning even as she copied them out or re-read them for the umpteenth time; but she knew that her brother would always remain evasive as to Lucy's real name. And she knew that it had to be like that if the peace and harmony of their household was to be maintained. And as long as she did not know for sure she could believe whatever she liked; and as her fantasy world was every bit as rich as his, and was becoming ever more vital to her as her real prospects of marriage and fulfilment shrank by the day, it was in her interest to keep that fantasy alive and well, and to do nothing that might call it into question or put it at risk.

If Dorothy made no claim, even in her private journal, to be the Lucy of those poems, then she acted wisely: for her brother had a young girl on his mind who could just as well have been a candidate for the role – and that was his illegitimate daughter Caroline. No doubt she had been on his mind more or less all the time since she had been born six years earlier; but when Wordsworth found himself in Germany in the winter of 1798, and with so much time on his hands in which to reflect and take stock, he could not but think of all that he had lived in neighbouring France in 1792.

All his adult life Wordsworth lived with two secrets which he elevated to the level of taboo: one was his true feelings towards his sister, and the other was the existence of his illegitimate daughter. His refusal to explore either of these subjects openly in his poetry, or even to admit that there was anything in particular that was worth exploring, must have created enormous tensions in the heart and mind of a man whose sense of artistic integrity was based on plain speaking and honesty. He carried in himself the awareness that he had a daughter who, although she was alive and well in France, was effectively unknown to him and thus to a certain extent dead. Wordsworth's relationship to Caroline was more imaginary than real: that's to say that like Lucy she was as much a product of his imagination as a real person. Indeed in the course of his long life he only met her three times (once in 1802 at Calais, a second time in Paris in 1820; and again in Paris in 1837). What had died when he abandoned Caroline and her mother was the relationship itself; that could have been the loss he wrote about in the 'Lucy' poems – a loss made all the sharper by the fact that when he wrote the poems he was still unmarried and had not yet started a family of his own. Whether or not he felt responsible for the way things had turned out between Annette and himself, he had to live with that sense of loss for the rest of his life.

Lucy is not an anonymous person plucked out of folk culture; neither is she Dorothy, nor Caroline. She is all of them. With the 'Lucy' poems Wordsworth introduced a new dimension into his writing, in which different meanings coexist in the same verses. The writer's mind and attention shift continually between one focus and another, creating a texture which is both personal and universal, as the Romantic aesthetic would want it to be.

★ ★ ★

The coupling of youth and death, or of erotic love and death, had provided music, art and literature with one of its most powerful impulses ever since the days of Classical Greece and Rome. The nineteenth century offered a particular contribution to this time-honoured theme thanks to its intense interest in the deaths of girls and young women – the women usually dying either of consumption or as a result of tragic love affairs, and the girls generally dying on their own of unspecified illnesses. The roll-call in this respect is illustrious. Schubert's string quartet of 1824,

Death and the Maiden, carried the idea in its title (the name for the quartet came from the theme of its second movement, which was taken from a setting by Schubert (in 1817) of a poem with the same title by Matthias Claudius). Sixteen years later Little Nell's death proved to be the most famous and most memorable moment in *The Old Curiosity Shop* (Dickens, who wrote the novel in serial form, kept readers on both sides of the Atlantic in a state of suspense for weeks as the girl's health slowly deteriorated). And then it was the turn of the Italians — Verdi, Bellini and Puccini among others — to kill off their leading ladies, with works such as *La Traviata, Norma,* and *La Bohème* offering up sacrificial victims whose decline and distress provided the most beautiful arias in the operas. In France, Emma Bovary committed suicide while still young and healthy, and in Russia Anna Karenina followed suit. Back in England Catherine Earnshaw, the heroine of Emily Bronte's *Wuthering Heights,* died young, while Jane Eyre, the heroine of Charlotte Bronte's novel of the same name, just managed to avoid death by starvation, exhaustion and hypothermia; and Thomas Hardy's magnificent portrait of Tess Durbeyfield led inexorably to her death. Not to be outdone, Scandinavian theatre presented the world with the tragic heroines of Strindberg and Ibsen, while the paintings of Edvard Munch depicted a similarly feverish and angst-ridden culture (Munch's painting of his sister dying of tuberculosis (entitled *The Sick Child*) was used by Penguin in the 1970s as a book cover for their edition of an anthology of Ibsen's plays that included *Hedda Gabler* and *The Wild Duck* — both of which end with the deaths of their heroines.)

These are only a few well-known examples of a theme that was the nucleus for a wide range of preoccupations and anxieties. The fate of pre-pubescent girls naturally provoked quite different emotions and responses from that of nubile young women, or that of single women saddled with illegitimate children, or of married women with irresponsible lovers. And if consumption or tuberculosis hung like a sword of Damocles over the heads of everyone in the nineteenth century (just as cancer does nowadays), such diseases would not always be responsible for the deaths of girls and women in the prime of life. A mass of other factors intervened, which articulated sexual and social tensions and conflicts that were endemic to nineteenth-century Europe, and which went way beyond the individual stories that they encompassed. Nonetheless it is fair to say that the killing off of girls and young women – for whatever reason – is one of the leitmotifs of nineteenth-century European culture (along with its counterpoint, the desire to preserve the principle of feminine purity and innocence); and in chronological terms Wordsworth was a front-runner here, his poetry set the trend. The 'Lucy' poems, written on the cusp of the eighteenth and nineteenth centuries, belong in spirit only to the nineteenth.

Chapter VI

Adam and Eve

In November 1799 Wordsworth announced to his sister that he had taken the lease on a cottage just outside Grasmere, for £8 a year. The next month they set up home together – and they would remain living under the same roof until Wordsworth's death over fifty years later. After William's marriage Dorothy necessarily gave way to his wife Mary, and learnt the new role of maiden aunt – but she never lost her position as William's confidante and close companion; and the intense complicity which characterised their relationship has made it one of the most famous man–woman partnerships in the history of literature.

That a brother and sister should decide to live together was not odd, particularly in a rural community in which family structures were all-important. For William and Dorothy though it was not merely a practical solution, but also the realisation of a dream that they had nurtured more or less consciously for six years, from the time that they had been reunited in the summer following his return from France. And that reunion had in itself been the consummation of a dream, as Dorothy had been separated from her four brothers after their mother's death in 1778. Brought up by relatives over seventy miles away from her brothers, she had seen little of William during the next fifteen years, and when in June 1793 she heard that he was coming to visit her, she was ecstatic at the idea of being with him again. And so apparently was he, judging from the passages she copied out from recent letters of his to her, and which she forwarded to her close friend Jane Pollard:

> Oh my dear, dear sister with what transport shall I again meet you, with what rapture shall I again wear out the day in your sight. I assure you so eager is my desire to see you that all obstacles vanish. I see you in a moment running or rather flying to my arms.[50]

The following April they set off on the first of many journeys and tours they would make together. For the twenty-two year old Dorothy it would be an introduction to the Lake District, which she had been obliged to leave when she was six, and had not visited since. It would also be an initiation into the travelling style of her brother. If intended as a sort of test she passed it brilliantly, keeping pace with him quite happily as they walked eighteen miles to Grasmere on one day, and fifteen miles from Grasmere to Kendal the next day. From then on she would be his favourite walking companion – and given the amount of time he liked to dedicate to walking, and the fact that he composed while walking, this meant a lot. And of course these long walks in the wild open spaces of the hills and valleys created a special kind of intimacy between them, for the emptiness and vastness of the landscape emphasised the fact that there was no one else with or near them. Together they created a quiet dialogue of kindred spirits, forming a microcosm whose warmth and cosiness was set off by the limitless horizons and unbridled elements of the landscape they moved through.

The journey through the Lake District in 1794 opened up for William and Dorothy the prospect of a New World: the beauty of the landscape, and the childhood memories it evoked, suggested to them the possibility of a completely new way of life. When they returned in 1799 it was to claim possession of this natural birthright. This time they walked into their Promised Land; and when they set up home together there was an almost sacred quality to the enterprise.

Needless to say, the reality of the adventure was at variance with the dream. Mid-December in the Lake District was unlikely to correspond to any normal person's idea of either the New World or the Promised Land: it was cold and damp and misty, it rained and snowed. Dorothy had terrible toothache, both she and her brother developed bad colds. The cottage was cramped and the ceilings impossibly low – William had to walk around with a permanent stoop. And so on. It was not an easy start to their new life together.

And yet. During the following year Wordsworth worked on *Home at Grasmere* – a long poem (1049 lines) celebrating their return to the region in whch they had been born, which completely ignored the difficulties they had to overcome and instead endowed the adventure with an almost mythical status. The bold premise of this poem was that the Vale of Grasmere represented a second Eden. Wordsworth proposed the metaphor at the very beginning of the poem, saying that he was writing and living, 'With paradise before me' (line 9), and then developed it further:

> The unappropriated bliss hath found
> An owner, and that owner I am he.
> The Lord of this enjoyment is on Earth
> And in my breast.   (lines 85–88)

> The boon is absolute; surpassing grace
> To me hath been vouchsafed; among the bowers
> Of blissful Eden this was neither given,
> Nor could be given,   (lines 122–5)

Coming from the man who had spent the previous decade recording the harshness of life in the country such lyricism seems surprising – and is a measure of just how happy Wordsworth was at this time. Clearly he felt an enormous rush of energy and enthusiasm at the idea of constructing his life in his beloved Lake District; and when William's younger brother John arrived unexpectedly in late January 1800, his happiness was even greater. John was a sailor, and finding himself in between voyages, was able to stay with his brother and sister for eight months. For the first time in their adult lives they could feel themselves almost a family, and it was this as much as the beauty of nature that Wordsworth was revelling in when he likened the Vale of Grasmere to paradise.

But more than celebration was involved in writing *Home at Grasmere*. The reference to the Garden of Eden inevitably invited comparison with *Paradise Lost*. For Wordsworth references to the authors he admired – and in particular to Milton – were never made just for the sake of it. With this poem Wordsworth measured himself for the first time against his great master – but why now? The idea may have come to him right at the beginning of his great adventure; for when in December 1799 he and Dorothy made the journey to Grasmere to move into their new home they covered most of the distance – forty-four miles – on foot (with the remaining twenty-four miles on horseback). At some point Wordsworth realised that he could tease a certain significance from the way they chose to travel. For *Paradise Lost* concludes with Adam and Eve leaving Paradise on foot:

> They hand in hand with wandering steps and slow,
> Through Eden took their solitary way.
>
> (Book XII, lines 648-9)

while William and Dorothy's adventure had begun with them

returning to the Lake District on foot. Could this symmetry not offer the starting-point for recounting their enterprise as a response to *Paradise Lost*? If he and his sister had returned on foot to live together in one of the wildest and most beautiful parts of England, which was also their birthplace, could they not justly portray themselves as a modern Adam and Eve moving against the current of history, travelling upstream to a point of origin where human and natural values could be maintained intact? It would be an example not of life imitating art, but of life inverting or reversing art... After *Paradise Lost* Milton had written *Paradise Regained*. Could Wordsworth not offer, through an honest exploration of his own story, a sort of '*Paradise Rediscovered*', a modern version of Milton's poem which would be both a tribute to the master and an affirmation of the values that Milton had asserted in his great poems? Could he, Wordsworth, show that it was possible to recreate the state of Eden in some part of England in 1800? And if the poem seemed to be valid and coherent, what would that say about the values on which contemporary English society based itself?

The vast range of subjects discussed in *Paradise Lost* was clearly beyond the reach of the twenty-nine year old Wordsworth, who sensibly decided to leave most of them aside and focus on the essential paradigm of the couple, and the moral values that they were supposed to uphold in a puritan vision of society. But here of course the young poet stubbed his toe on a crucial problem. Adam and Eve were sexual partners, and, according to both the Authorised Version of the Bible and Milton, specifically husband and wife. Whatever William's feelings might have been towards his sister it was out of the question that he should suggest even remotely that there was a sexual connotation to their relationship, much less make out that they were living like husband and wife.

Although, sex apart, that is just what they were doing. Briefly, he needed to prise the potentially sexual component of the relationship away from the other elements that mattered – such as trust, affection, companionship and fidelity – and hope that his improvised formula for model relationships between man and woman stood the test of scrutiny.

To this end Wordsworth widened and deconsecrated as far as was possible the idea of the couple – choosing instead the term 'pair' to refer equally to human beings and animals; as if he and his sister formed a pair as naturally as two butterflies or two anteaters, all of them ready to embark on Noah's ark when the moment was come. So for example he longed to see two eagles in the sky above the valley:

> And if the banished Eagle Pair return,
> Helvellyn's Eagles, to their antient Hold,
> Then shall I see, shall claim with those two Birds
> Acquaintance, as they soar amid the Heav'ns.
>
> (lines 738-40)

Similarly he called to mind a couple who had planted a grove of fir-trees , and praised

> this Pair,
> Who in the prime of wedlock, with joint hands
> Did plant this grove, now flourishing, while they
> No longer flourish.   (lines 638-4)

He and Dorothy formed another human pair –

> we twain,
> A pair seceding from the common world,
>
> (lines 248-9)

which he identified emphatically with another pair of birds – this
time swans:

> But two are missing – two, a lonely pair
> Of milk-white swans – ah, why are they not here
> To share in this day's pleasure? From afar
> They came, like Emma and myself, to live
> Together here in peace and solitude....
>   to us
> They were more dear than may be well believed,
> Not only for their beauty and their still
> And placid way of life and faithful love
> Inseparable, not for these alone,
> But that their state so much resembled ours,
> They having chosen this abode;
> They strangers, and we strangers; they a pair,
> And we a solitary pair like them.
>
> (lines 322-6; 333-41)[51]

The choice of swans as metaphors for their lifestyle was in no
way casual, as Dorothy well knew. It looked back to the poem
An Evening Walk which Wordsworth had written in 1788-9, and
had dedicated to his sister when he published it in 1793. In the
poem Wordsworth devoted forty lines (lines 200-40) to a study of
a family of swans, seeing in them a model of harmony, grace and
order; he then contrasted this image of natural well-being with
the situation of a female beggar, a single mother unable to feed
and protect her children properly (lines 241-300). The pair of
swans were described in an eighteenth-century manner, blandly
lyrical and based on generalisations:

> On as he floats, the silvered waters glow,
> Proud of the varying arch and moveless form of snow.

> While tender Cares and mild domestic Loves,
> With furtive watch pursue her as she moves;
> The female with a meeker charm succeeds,
> And her brown little ones around her leads,
>
> (lines 205-10)

What Dorothy may not have been familiar with is the ode (*Beauty and Moonlight*) that William wrote during his teens (referred to in chapter II), which treats the theme of swans in a much more erotic way:

> Then might her bosom soft and white
> Heave upon my swimming sight
> As these two Swans together ride
> Upon the gently swelling tide.[52]

Had she known this poem she might have found the epithet of 'milk-white swans' in *Home at Grasmere* disturbing. For Wordsworth creates here a kind of poetic synthesis that establishes meanings across time through associations. We find a similar kind of synthesis in Dickens' *Great Expectations*, where Magwitch is first presented to us in chapter 1 as 'a fearful man, all in coarse grey, with a great iron on his leg'; then, when he re-appears much later in the book the 'grey' and the 'iron' are brought together, as a powerful hint of who the stranger is, before he discloses his identity:

> I made out....That he had long iron-grey hair.
>
> (Chapter 39)

The difference is that in *Great Expectations* Dickens uses a narrative strategy quite deliberately, to tease the reader before revealing Magwitch's identity; while Wordsworth's meditation on associations – two swans on the lake – 'bosom soft and white' – breasts contain milk and milk is white – swans are white – 'milk-white swans' – operates at the level of the unconscious. About fourteen years separate *Beauty and Moonlight* and *Home at Grasmere*, and no attempt is made to establish a connection between the two texts. The play of meanings is therefore extremely elusive, and Wordsworth's true intent remains submerged , but no less real for that – the more so when one adds in the precedent of the 'sister breasts of snow' in the description of the swans in *Salisbury Plain* (quoted on page 51).[53]

★ ★ ★

Wordsworth could indulge in all kinds of playful fantasies about his sister, as long as they never went beyond daydreams (and were coded as well); but there were clearly defined limits to what he allowed himself to think or feel. His natural paradise could only prosper if the rules were respected; there could be no Garden of Eden without some form of prohibition. In the Bible it was the Tree of Knowledge that was forbidden; in *Home at Grasmere* it was unlawful sexual knowledge. Wordsworth used two vignettes to make his point: first the tale (lines 469-532) of a local resident whose rural idyll was destroyed when he, a married man who found himself attracted to the 'blooming Girl' who was the couple's servant,

> became
> A lawless suitor of the Maid, and she
> Yielded unworthily.   (505-7)

Bit by bit his world disintegrated: he lost touch with his wife and children, abandoned his sheep and his fields, and died of grief. This cautionary tale is immediately followed by an 'improving story' about a widower who was left with six girls to bring up,

six fair Daughters budding yet, not one,
Not one of all the band a full-blown flower!

(545-6)

The 'budding' and 'flower' epithets, echoing the 'blooming' of the girl in the first tale, emphasise that a direct comparison is being made between the two families – and the contrast could not be clearer. The widower understands exactly what his duty is, respects the character and inclinations of each of his daughters, and never behaves incorrectly towards any of them. As a result,

they are gay,
And the whole House is filled with gaiety.

(605-6)

These studies functioned in two ways: they provided examples of bad and good behaviour against which Wordsworth could measure himself and define his own moral code for life with Dorothy; and they widened the scope of the poem beyond the purely personal, as Wordsworth sought to articulate a vision that could have meaning for a whole society. For *Home at Grasmere* was the ambassador for a very ambitious project, that had been dreamed up in conversation with Coleridge in 1798. The project came to be known as *The Recluse*, and was destined to be the Holy Grail of Wordsworth's poetic endeavours for the next thirty years.[54] For much of that time it served him as an alibi for failing to produce new compositions: when asked what he was working on, he would say it was *The Recluse*. But at the outset he believed passionately in the enterprise, and was convinced that having settled in Grasmere he was at last in a position to realise the great project – hence the subtitle to the manuscript of *Home at Grasmere* was *Book First, Part First of The Recluse*.

The project failed for a multitude of reasons. The title in itself was problematic: why should a long poem designed to address the state of contemporary society be called *The Recluse*? How could the lives of William and Dorothy, 'a pair seceding from the common world', serve as a model for the vast majority of the population who did not enjoy such freedom? There was no easy answer to this question. The writing he had done at Goslar had convinced Wordsworth of the importance of rooting artistic creation in personal experience – but how to give a general significance to personal meaning, that was the question. Luckily he was well organised (as all functioning artists need to be). He kept different compartments in his brain, and allowed the Goslar material to exist quite separately from the Grasmere debate that was going on at the same time. In the fullness of time the authentic autobiographical material evolved gradually into *The Prelude*, without being shackled to, or modified by, the grandiose ideas of *The Recluse* (*The Prelude* was conceived of as constituting part of *The Recluse*, but as an autonomous entity). So while Wordsworth never resolved the tension between the autobiographical and social dimensions of writing to his satisfaction, it didn't matter unduly. We have *The Prelude*, intact and free-standing – while the last part of *Home at Grasmere* (lines 959-1049) was published in 1814 as a *Prospectus* to *The Recluse*.

★ ★ ★

At the same time as he mulled over *Home at Grasmere*, Wordsworth wrote a short series of poems on the theme of names and places. They are not remarkable poems, and have been largely ignored by modern editors; yet they clearly had a particular significance for him, as they were grouped together under their own heading – *Poems on the Naming of Places* – in the 1815 collection of his poems. As with the 'Lucy' poems, reference to an element of folk culture is used to cover a meditation that is personal and intimate. In this case Wordsworth's starting-point was the rural tradition of giving names to places 'where little incidents must have occurred, or feelings been experienced, which will have given to such places a private and particular interest'. Five poems were written between December 1799 and October 1800, attributing a small valley to Dorothy; a sheltered resting-place to Mary Hutchinson (William's future wife); a rock to Mary's sister Joanna; and a lonely peak to William; while another remote spot next to Grasmere Lake was named as 'Point Rash-Judgement'. To these were added in later editions a poem written between 1800 and 1804, attributing a grove to William's brother John, and a poem from 1845 naming two peaks after Mary (his wife) and her sister Sarah.

Leaving aside the ostensible reason for writing these poems – which is certainly valid, but only up to a point – there are two possible ways of interpreting them. The one that springs immediately to mind is that the act of naming is synonymous with asserting control over, or possession of, the thing, place, animal or person named. The period in which Wordsworth lived was one of constant naming and re-naming: at one end of the spectrum scientists like Linnaeus were busy classifying the plant and animal kingdoms in terms of species, and giving names to even the least impressive insects and plants; at the other end explorers and colonialists were re-naming vast tracts of the globe that had been known to indigenous people by other names for hundreds or thousands of years. In this way Wordsworth's playful naming of places could be seen as an attempt to impose a recognisable form on the landscape – to make the untamed territory in which he had chosen to live more familiar.

However, as one reads the poems it becomes clear that the name of a place was chosen on the basis of association: that is to say that the qualities of a particular place corresponded (in Wordsworth's opinion) to the character of one or other of the group of young people who were exploring the area. This involves a quite different thought-process, one that is based on complementarity rather than possession, and which works in two directions: 'this place makes me think of you' being balanced by, 'when I think of you this place comes to mind'. People become a part of the landscape – just as William and Dorothy were at this time trying to create a sense of belonging to the Lake District – and natural elements are chosen by virtue of what they can express about human beings. In this respect it is significant that while William locates his future wife in a resting-place, he sees his sister as essentially undomesticated, untamed. A waterfall courses through the 'dell' or little valley with which she is associated, a 'wild nook' abundant with 'wild growth'. The poem ends with the hope that even after he and his sister are dead, local people,

> When they have cause to speak of this wild place,
> May call it by the name of EMMA'S DELL.

Wildness was a quality that Wordsworth feared in women more than he admired it. He associated it with the half-crazed and more or less hysterical women – abandoned mothers and jilted mistresses – that he had written about during the 1790s in poems such as *Her Eyes are Wild*:

> Her eyes are wild, her head is bare,
> The sun has burnt her coal-black hair;
> Her eyebrows have a rusty stain,
> And she came far from over the main.

She has a baby on her arm,

Or else she were alone: (lines 1-6)

No doubt the bold and lively character of Annette had been one of the things that had attracted him to her, but in general he liked women to be quiet and home-loving, self-contained and self-controlled – so to celebrate Dorothy's 'wildness' in verse was quite exceptional. It could only have been possible because it was self-evident that he was referring to her intellectual spirit and independence, rather than to any aspirations she might have towards sexual freedom; and because there could be no insinuation on her brother's part that she might ever be classed among the unhappy 'wild women' he had previously portrayed, the sad victims of a breakdown in moral codes or social stability.

The other thing that is striking about the poem on the naming of 'Emma's Dell' is that it is not 'Dorothy's Dell.' William's sister is renamed even as the little valley is named – unlike Mary and Joanna, whose true names are respected in the places named after them. John's name is not given to the grove with which he is associated, but reference is repeatedly made to 'my brother', so it is quite clear who is the subject of the poem. Not so with Dorothy: there are no references in the poem to 'Emma' being William's sister, and editors are obliged to add a note to make the fact clear. The poem operates in a strangely contradictory way, dispossessing Dorothy of her identity even as it endows her with a dell of her own.

Why change Dorothy's name? And why 'Emma'? There are no obvious answers to these questions. 'Emma' appears for the first time in Wordsworth's verse in one of the 'Matthew' poems: in *The Two April Mornings* (composed in 1798-9) it is the name given to the schoolmaster's daughter, who died at the age of nine:

Six feet in earth my Emma lay,
And yet I loved her more,
For so it seemed, than till that day
I e'er had loved before.   (lines 37-40)

The poem was published in 1800, the year in which the poem
on 'Emma's Dell' was written. If it was a coincidence that he used
the name of a dead girl for his sister, so be it; but one imagines
that Dorothy would have wondered about the possible impli-
cations of the name he chose for her – the more so in that the
young Emma, six feet under, closely resembled poor Lucy, about
whom her brother had written so movingly. Apart from this prec-
edent, one can play with various hypotheses. The name 'Emma'
comes from the German '*ermen*', meaning 'whole' or 'universal':
it's possible that Wordsworth learnt this while he and Dorothy
were living together in Germany, and that he used it as a nick-
name for her – in which case it would be both a very private
form of address, and a great compliment to the qualities of his
sister. Alternatively one could say that 'emma' read backwards is
close to 'ame', which in French means 'soul' – and that William
considered Dorothy as his natural soul-mate. Or one could say
that 'my Emma' – the formula that Wordsworth preferred –
almost elides into 'Mamma' or 'Mama', and that with this nam-
ing of his sister William sublimated his desire to find again the
mother he had lost at the age of eight....

What's in a name? Often, as in this case, it's impossible to say.
But the fact of naming has in itself a certain significance. Hegel
described Adam's naming of the rest of God's creation as '*der erste
Akte*' ('the first act'); and among those he named was Eve. In giv-
ing a new name to his sister William was reenacting the part of
Adam in the garden of Eden; and to this extent the small poem

on the naming of 'Emma's Dell' fits perfectly with the long and ambitious meditation on Grasmere as Eden, that was laboriously worked out in *Home at Grasmere*.

★ ★ ★

Home at Grasmere is an intensely personal debate that turns round and round the idea of possession. The starting-point is the fact of setting up home, of having a home of one's own. But Wordsworth elides this into another form of possession: Dorothy, the woman who had chosen to live with him, became in a certain way his:

> behold
> Yon Cottage, where with me my Emma dwells.
>
> (lines 97–8);

> My Emma (line 647)

Of course Dorothy could never truly be his, and he knew it. But the emotional congestion is such that it ushers in thoughts of marriage. As the poem opens he suggests that his commitment to living in the Lake Distrcict can be compared to a marriage vow, and that the landscape in all its beauty is offered to him as a dowry:

> If e'er the acceptance of such dower was deemed
> A condescension or a weak indulgence
> To a sick fancy, it is now an act
> Of reason that exultingly aspires.   (lines 79–82)

By the end of the poem he has argued himself into believing that the true marriage is between the inner and external worlds, between the individual mind and the natural world we live in:

Paradise, and groves
Elysian, fortunate islands, fields like those of old
In the deep ocean, wherefore should they be
A History, or but a dream, when minds
Once wedded to this outward frame of things
In love, find these the growth of common day?

(lines 996–1001)

Home at Grasmere is not able to celebrate that longed-for wedding day, but it does articulate very well not only the emotional turbulence of a man who longs to take a bride (if only he could find her!), but also the awareness that he needs to prepare himself for such a step. Entering into and taking possession of a house, a place, an artistic vocation and, hopefully, the state of marriage are all possible only if a man first enters into possession of himself and becomes master of his own destiny. This is something Wordsworth understands perfectly as he moves towards the conclusion of the poem:

Possessions have I wholly, solely, mine,
Something within, which is yet shared by none,
Not even the nearest to me and most dear,
Something which power and effort may impart.

(lines 987–90)

I wish,
I burn, I struggle, and in soul am there.
But me hath Nature tamed and bade me seek
For other agitations or be calm,
Hath dealt with me as with a turbulent stream –

(lines 932–6)

Self-possession is the ultimate goal of the long meditation that makes up *Home at Grasmere*, as it is the key to other forms of knowledge and achievement. The price to pay is the firm control of all emotions and thoughts that are unruly or illegitimate, and the means to that end are close to those employed by a monk – a systematic purification and sublimation of feelings and desires, combined with a rigorous programme of discipline and self-denial. The emphasis on the need for purity increases as the poem progresses:

> whatever else of outward form
> Can give us inward help, can purify,
> And elevate, and harmonize, and soothe
>
> (lines 390-2)

> Many are pure, the best of them are pure; ...
> Joy of the highest and the purest minds
>
> (lines 678 & 681)

> How goodly, how exceeding fair, how pure
> From all reproach is this aetherial frame
> And this deep vale, its earthly counterpart
>
> (lines 851-3)

And the poem ends with an emphatic affirmation of the most important of his various good resolutions:

> all pure thoughts
> Be with me and uphold me to the end!
>
> (lines 1048-9)

The logic is fairly straightforward: self-possession leads to a lessening of desire to possess others; and it creates a space in which inner spiritual liberty can exist, just as it guarantees the physical and spiritual liberty of others, through a principle of respect. In short, the application of strict puritanical morality offers individuals the chance to recreate conditions similar to those that Adam and Eve enjoyed before the Fall. That in essence was the meditation that Wordsworth elaborated as he explored the uncontaminated landscape of the Lake District, and as he reflected on Milton's achievement and wondered if there was any way that he could offer a sequel or reply to *Paradise Lost*.

The trouble was that Wordsworth was never very happy with theories — and as theories go this one was pretty tenuous. It was not only the evidence of the reality of his neighbours' lives — unfaithful husbands, abandoned wives, and (no doubt) incest and forms of sexual abuse — that caused his thinking to unravel. There were the unresolved tensions inside himself, generated by cohabitation with his sister; and the memories of his relationship with Annette — of natural impulses unchecked by moral constraints which had unleashed new feelings and had given him true sexual pleasure, and which had only been wrong in that the child they had conceived was illegitimate. He simply could not square the theory with the practice. Life was not like that. At the same time he had to find a way of making sense of the situation in which he found himself — living alone in the wilds of Westmoreland with an unmarried sister who loved him passionately and seemed prepared to give her life for him, placing herself entirely at the service of her brother and his art.

The immediate result of this crisis — *Home at Grasmere* — was a literary mess, a mish-mash of feelings and voices and aspirations, with its Miltonic diction and phrasing —

> Come, thou prophetic Spirit, Soul of Man,
> Thou human Soul of the wide earth that hath
> Thy metropolitan Temple in the hearts
> Of mighty Poets   (lines 1026-9) —

designed to help elevate the tone and guarantee the worthiness of the endeavour. But it was not only because the poem tried too hard, and then failed to achieve a satisfactory form or message, that Wordsworth never published it.

★ ★ ★

William invariably showed his poems to Dorothy – and then asked her to copy them out, as his handwriting was appalling. One wonders what she made of this long and tortuous 'cry from the heart', which was both a declaration of love to her and a refusal of that same love. Where was her place in this enterprise, what was her role, and what identity did her brother allow her? To start with he insisted on giving her a name that wasn't hers, and never once used her real name in his poetry when referring to her. Why? What was she really to him? Did anyone really exist for him apart from himself? Or was he so locked into his imaginary world that nothing counted but the integrity of that fine construction?

Dorothy loved her brother ardently, but she had a powerful character and an independent mind, and was not an undiscriminating admirer of everything and anything her brother wrote. Writing to her friend Jane Pollard in February 1793 about the poems *Evening Walk* and *Descriptive Sketches* that Wordsworth had just published, she showed herself to be an acute and impartial critic:

> the Poems contain many Passages exquisitely beautiful, but they also contain many Faults, the chief of which are Obscurity, & a too frequent use of some particular expressions & uncommon words for instance <u>moveless</u>, which he applies in a sense if not new, at least different from its ordinary one; by moveless when applied to the Swan he means that

sort of motion which is smooth without agitation; it is a very beautiful epithet but ought to have been cautiously used, he ought at any rate only to have hazarded it once, instead of which it occurs three or four times.

(February 16, 1793)[55]

The weighty symbolism of the swans, and the fact that the poem was dedicated to her, failed to move her. Her comments were limited to technique and poetic diction; nonetheless she clearly felt that she could dialogue with her brother on equal terms; and the next part of the letter suggests that she wished to be his confidante and adviser as much where his writing was concerned as in other aspects of his life:

> I regret exceedingly that he did not submit the works to the Inspection of some Friend before their Publication, & he also joins with me in this Regret.

As the years passed she tended to keep negative comments about his poetry to herself – or at any rate she seldom wrote them down. However the journal entry for February 7, 1802, when William was working on a poem provisionally called 'The Pedlar', shows that she had not lost her ability to judge for herself:

> ...We sate by the fire & did not walk, but read the pedlar thinking it done but lo, though Wm could find fault with no one part of it – it was uninteresting & must be altered. Poor William!

For Dorothy it was vital to the Grasmere adventure that she should exploit the trust that William had in her to the full, and accompany him in his literary career in any way she could. This led to her needing to move between different roles in quick succession. The most mysterious of these was as her brother's constant companion on their long walks together. While we know that poems such as *'I wandered lonely as a cloud'* or *Resolution and Independence* were based on walks William and Dorothy had made together, and that she had already written up in her journal, it is impossible to know how much Dorothy's company and conversation impinged on her brother's thoughts and feelings, as she accompanied his 'lonely' cloud o'er hills and across dales and vales. As we have seen, walking for Wordsworth was synonymous with composing, and it is hard to believe that Dorothy's presence did not affect the way Wordsworth saw things when they were out together. Such things are impossible to quantify – but that does not mean we should overlook or discount them.

Once William had put pen to paper, two other roles opened up for Dorothy. The exciting one was to be – almost invariably – the first person to read (or rather hear) a new poem. Once again, we don't know how far she was invited to make comments, or allowed to criticise; but we do know that she was as plain-speaking as she was unaffected in dress and appearance. Given that her brother appreciated her intellectually, and given their enormous emotional complicity, it is likely that she would have spoken her mind quite freely – even though her overriding desire was always to help and encourage him.

That, however, was not the end of the matter. It was not even the beginning of the end. For Wordsworth's mania for revision and correction – (of which more later) – condemned Dorothy to a Sisyphean fate, endlessly writing out and recopying draft, 'finished' and 'final' versions of her brother's poems. Along with his distaste for writing poetry (sitting down and composing for any period of time made him physically unwell), William had a talent for delegating; and as a consequence Dorothy found herself volunteered as a permanent scribe. Once he married, his wife Mary would help with this task, and later on his daughter Dora would join the 'typists' pool' of Rydal Mount; but during the first two years at Grasmere Dorothy alone helped see the poems through to their definitve versions. It was both drudgery and a privilege. Probably Dorothy took it for granted as a simple household task – a pleasant change from washing and baking and making jam. (And although she and Mary were obliged to write out the 9,000 lines of *The Prelude* again and again, they were at least spared the fate of Tolstoy's wife, who had to write out *War and Peace* seven times....)

And then there was the role for which Dorothy is best known today – that of a writer in her own right. Although she never had publication in mind, her *Grasmere Journals* have never been out of print since they were published in full (in 1958), and her account of 'life with William' is considered the perfect complement to his poetry. Her prose is compared to his verse, her feminine sensibility set against his all-embracing vision of the world: here indeed they made a perfect pair! And her writing was modest in scale and remained tucked away in a corner, while editions of her brother's verses rolled one after another off the printer's press: that too corresponded to public expectations. All in all it seemed a literary match made in heaven.

Needless to say, it wasn't quite as simple as that. While it is clear that Dorothy wanted to respond in kind to William's writing, the motivation behind the *Grasmere Journals* was intensely personal, and the notebooks were never intended to be read as decorative complements to her brother's more important work. The first entry of all is revealing in this respect:

> *May 14, 1800.* Wm & John set off into Yorkshire after dinner at ½ past 2 o'clock – cold pork in their pockets. I left them at

the turning of the Low-wood bay under the trees. My heart
was so full that I could hardly speak to W when I gave him
a farewell kiss. I sate a long time upon a stone at the mar-
gin of the lake, & after a flood of tears my heart was easier.
The lake looked to me I know not why dull and melancholy,
the weltering on the shores seemed a heavy sound. [...] I
resolved to write a journal of the time till W & J return, & I
set about keeping my resolve because I will not quarrel with
myself, & because I shall give Wm Pleasure by it when he
comes home again.

Dorothy's distress at seeing William leave stemmed from the
fact that he was going to visit Mary Hutchinson, and Dorothy
by this time knew that William had marriage in mind (in fact it
would seem that John was thinking along the same lines – and
he had better prospects than William to offer Mary). The men
were going courting, and that explains why Dorothy – normally
William's constant companion – was left behind. But what upset
Dorothy was not being left behind, rather the understanding that
her exclusive relationship with William was condemned to end.
Even as he worked on *Home at Grasmere,* with its Adam-and-Eve
metaphor which established his sister in such a privileged posi-
tion, he was taking steps to disentangle himself from the scenario
that he conjured up. Small wonder that she burst into tears as
soon as he was out of sight.

But the sadness was swiftly brought under control, as she gave
herself the task of writing a journal during her brother's absence
– which she would be able to show him when he returned. The
journal, in other words, was originally conceived of in much
the same way as the other tasks that filled her days. It was not
something that came naturally to her, but rather something that
needed to be done, and which she could tick off from the list

of things to do once the entry had been completed. This may help to explain the wonderful patchwork style of the journal, in which completely disparate information and observations sit side by side, with no authorial comment or guiding principle to make us understand what is more or less important. At the same time Dorothy's ability to engage emotionally with her subject matter – people, landscapes, birds, flowers – creates a sort of electric current which energises the writing. Keeping a diary was a bit of an effort for her, but once she got going she could write with great fluency and power.

The current though fluctuated wildly. There were times when she lost interest in the business of recording daily life, and wrote one-line entries, or simply skipped a day or two. And then there were moments when she blocked because of an emotional congestion inside herself: feelings that were too strong or too difficult to put into words, which made her physically unwell and reduced her to silence. These moments occurred frequently, and were invariably connected in one way or another with her relationship with William. For if she was intellectually self-confident, she was emotionally dependent on her brother. Her life was bound up with his in a way that – visibly at least – his was not bound up with hers. Not that he loved Dorothy less than she loved him; but he had no intention of sacrificing his happiness to a principle and a lifestyle that did not convince him. Even as he tried laboriously to resolve the mish-mash of hopes and aspirations that constituted *Home at Grasmere*, he was taking steps to construct his future on a quite different basis.

Dorothy began writing her *Grasmere Journal* because she realised what was happening, and could foresee what the outcome might well be. He would marry, and she would lose the exclusive relationship with her brother which her happiness depended on.

The journal was born out of crisis, and was suffused from start to finish with a sense of anxiety. The tension was always there, though it showed in Dorothy's headaches far more often than in her tears. Like her brother, she knew all about self-control – it was just that in her case it wasn't so effective.

William and Dorothy were both people of great emotional intensity, and they had chosen to live together in a wild and isolated part of England: it was a recipe for all kinds of difficulties. The most obvious problem was how to manage their relationship in such a way as not to hurt each other. But as they were both writers there was the added problem of weighing feelings against words, and of deciding what they could afford to translate into language. For William, as a poet who was beginning to place more and more emphasis on the autobiographical element in his work, this represented a major difficulty – and one that was compounded by the fact that he showed all his poems to Dorothy, and relied on her to make fair copies of them. And while Dorothy never intended her journal to be read by anyone but herself (and, presumably, William), her need to speak openly and honestly, whether in her journal, or in conversation, or in the letters she was always writing, made it hard for her to keep important feelings to herself. Though that is precisely what she was obliged to do on a daily basis.[56]

If William suffered far less than his sister in these circumstances, it was not only because he knew that for himself, at the age of thirty, marriage, a family and a career were all attainable – while for Dorothy, at twenty-nine, the die was cast, and any change to her situation in the future was extremely unlikely. William was helped also by the strategy that he had developed to deal with his own emotional turbulence – namely to wait until enough time had passed before writing about it. In France he had seen all too clearly where instinct and impulse led him if he allowed it, and he had learnt the importance of caution. He exercised great self-control in all that he said or did, and relied on time to do the rest. Time would reveal the essential order and meaning in things, and memory existed to reveal that order, and that meaning, in language.

★ ★ ★

British codes of behaviour have often been different from those practised on the Continent. During the winter that William and Dorothy spent in Germany, they discovered that many people in Goslar – including their landlady – assumed that the brother-sister relationship was a fiction, and that Dorothy was William's mistress (a similar assumption would almost certainly have been made in France). They probably found such whispered rumours upsetting, and would have been relieved once they returned to England, where people were willing to take their rather unusual lifestyle at face value, and to respect their choices without asking embarrassing questions.

Those questions were raised, inevitably, much later. The possibility of an incestuous relationship between William and Dorothy has been discussed at length over the last fifty years, with theories proposed and rejected as energetically as political aguments in a television debate. As if in reaction to the censorship which effectively hid the issue from the public gaze for about 150 years, the question of William's real relation to his sister has come to be seen as extremely important, something that needs to be clearly understood, defined and evaluated. For anyone interested in Wordsworth's poetry, or English literature in general, this has had some very positive consequences, as it has encouraged readers to study the poems more attentively: the bland and anodyne image of Wordsworth which had been purveyed for so long has been called into question, and new interpretations of different aspects of his writing have been aired and argued over.[57]

And who in all honesty could deny that the question of their relationship was critical to understanding his poetry, when brother and sister were inseparable throughout their adult lives? Certainly it matters. The problem is that any opinion that is given on the subject is no more than that. The documentary evidence we have to work with is meagre, and we can be sure now that no further evidence will come to light. We have to make do with suppositions and theories, and accept that the truth – if there ever is such a thing in cases like this – will remain a mystery.

My opinion is that there never was a physically incestuous relationship between William and Dorothy – and in a sense there never could be, for a variety of reasons. Incest, as anthropologists like Lévi-Strauss have shown, is *the* universal taboo, almost the only one that is common to all cultures in all ages. It is the taboo which allows societies to function, and without which they risk imploding and collapsing.[58] Even if in eighteenth-century rural England there was a certain amount of tolerance for incest and other forms of sexual misbehaviour, noone was in any doubt as to the weight of the taboo, least of all someone like Wordsworth, with his strict puritanical upbringing; university education; his brother who was ordained and married to a Quaker; and so on. The voices on the side of 'Thou shalt not' were overwhelming. And any aberration on his part would also have made a mockery of the principles and values that underscored his poetry – and that would have precipitated a crisis that could easily have prevented him from writing any more. And what was his life worth without his poetry?

Home at Grasmere acted like a safety valve for the extreme mental and sexual pressure that had built up in Wordsworth. But this does not mean, as some have suggested, that Dorothy drove William towards marrying Mary, as a way of resolving the impossible situation in which he found himself. Brother and sister had worked out a logic for their relationship long before they settled together in the Lake District; and if Dorothy found it harder to act out the terms of their understanding than he did, she was also lucid about the choices she had made.

For a long time no questions were asked about Dorothy's life; little or no mention was made of the mental breakdown that left her confined to her bedroom for the last twenty years of her life; and it was enough to see her in her role as her brother's faithful companion and confidante. And in the same way and for the same reasons her lifestyle and her destiny have been called into question in recent times. The faithful companion is recast as a sort of vestal virgin sacrificed on the altar of poetry. But it is hard to see the forthright and energetic Dorothy as a victim; the problem, if there is one, is that the choices available to her were few, and each one had its drawbacks. The most important decision she had to take was whether or not to marry. Presumably she could have found a suitable husband if she'd wanted to, yet we don't hear of her being seriously courted by anyone. Did she turn her back on the very idea of marriage, when she was in her mid-twenties, because it would have taken her away from William? We don't know.[59] What would have been clear to her though is that in committing herself to living with her brother in Grasmere, just before her twenty-eighth birthday, she was making it very hard for herself to find a husband: she was 'withdrawing from circulation', as it were, and fast approaching an age when she would no longer be necessarily considered marriageable.

Dorothy's commitment in the winter of 1799 had much wider repercussions than William's: he had nothing to lose, while she was more or less consigning herself to spinsterhood. Did she ever imagine that they would simply live together as brother and sister, for the rest of their lives? Again, we don't know – but I doubt it. William's French adventure had shown enough of his sexual needs and energy for Dorothy to understand that he would need to marry. And given that Annette became pregnant within weeks of meeting William, the chances were that once married William would soon have children (as in fact turned out to be the case, Mary's first child being born just eight months after the wedding).

Dorothy's love for her brother was unquestioning and unwavering, and when she decided to make her life with him it was for emotional reasons. But she was also lucid and extremely intelligent, and no doubt thought through what would be the consequences of deciding otherwise. She really did not have enough money to live on her own, and would have needed to find some sort of employment, presumably as a governess or lady's companion. She would have found herself, like Jane Fairfax in *Emma*, obliged to spend her days in the company of people with whom she had little in common; or, like Jane Eyre or the two sisters who help her, Diana and Mary Rivers, face the prospect of earning a meagre salary as a teacher, with little chance of personal happiness and fulfilment. Instead of which Dorothy was able to converse on equal terms with writers and intellectuals; and, as resident aunt participated fully in looking after and bringing up William's five children – and thus was able to enjoy most aspects of maternity even without having children of her own. Her life was difficult, certainly, and in many ways painful – but she chose it willingly, and never expressed on paper any regrets for that choice. Given the options open to a woman at that period, it is hard to argue that her life would necessarily have been richer or happier if she had decided to live it differently.

Chapter VII

Wordsworth & Co.

The poet who liked to represent himself as 'wandering lonely as a cloud' was in fact seldom alone. Finding himself an orphan at the age of thirteen he made sure, once he reached adult life, that there were always people close to him that he was fond of and could rely on. He clearly could not survive on his own. In the years following his return from France in December 1792 he went from one friend or relative's house to another, mixing and mingling with a wide variety of people. In 1795 the nightmare threat of solitude was finally dissipated, when Dorothy became his permanent companion. She would remain by his side for the next fifty-five years, while others came and went. And of course there was Mary, whom he married seven years later. Thanks to the presence of these two women, Wordsworth would never have to 'walk alone' again. If he chose to be on his own in order to compose his poems, well and good. But when he needed help or company there would always be someone there.

1795 was also the year in which Wordsworth was introduced to Coleridge – a meeting of minds that led to one of the most famous partnerships in English literature. For the next few years most of what Wordsworth thought, said and wrote was coloured by the dialogue with Coleridge. And as Coleridge could always be relied on to introduce new friends and acquaintances into 'the group', Wordsworth found himself drawn into dialogues with men like Southey, de Quincey, Lamb and Hazlitt.[60] Wordsworth enjoyed the company, and found the intellectual exchanges stimulating (and was no doubt also happy for Dorothy, who thrived in this environment). It was in these years that he found his poetic voice, and it is hard to imagine that he could have worked with such confidence, and achieved so much, if he had been left on his own and obliged to work in a vacuum.

One only has to compare the quality of Wordsworth's writing once Coleridge was no longer part of his landscape with what it had been when the two men's lives were intertwined, to come to the conclusion that without Coleridge Wordsworth had difficulty expressing himself completely. The chemistry between the two poets was complex and fluctuated continuously – but it worked. And when they drifted apart they both lost out. It was not unlike the relationship between John Lennon and Paul McCartney, neither of whom managed on their own to write songs as memorable as those they composed together while The Beatles existed. John Lennon (like Wordsworth) may have been the true creative force, and McCartney (like Coleridge) more of a lightweight; but Lennon's indolence, or cynicism, or complacency reduced his creative drive when he did not have McCartney's spontaneous and uncalculating enthusiasm to work against and feed off.

Within the Wordsworth-Coleridge partnership the gravitational pull at first worked in Coleridge's favour. During the second half of the 1790s William and Dorothy did their best to live near to Coleridge, so as to be able to enjoy his company as much as possible; and they followed him as far as they could in his many and various projects. The journey to Germany in the autumn of 1798 was thought up by Coleridge: on his own Wordsworth would never have dreamed of undertaking such an adventure.

And Wordsworth was seduced by the force of Coleridge's intellect to the point where his own projects were sketched out in accordance with ideas proposed by Coleridge. *Lyrical Ballads* was probably more his child than Coleridge's, but *The Recluse*, that mammoth undertaking of which *The Prelude* was supposed to be only the first part, was definitely Coleridge's conception.

After William and Dorothy settled definitively in the Lake District it was up to Coleridge to go towards them – which he duly did, sometimes with his wife Sarah and/or their children, sometimes on his own; and at times Sarah would come without her husband but with her children. The Coleridge household existed like a nomadic caravan, and for a time the Wordsworth household was one of their oases. In return for the stability and affection that the Wordsworth household provided, Coleridge offered enthusiasm in abundance, and constant encouragement. He believed in Wordsworth's talent long before it was recognised by others, and never failed to make his admiration clear. When he said of the 'There was a boy…' passage in Book IV of *The Prelude* that, 'Had I met these lines running wild in the deserts of Arabia, I should instantly have screamed out, "Wordsworth!"', he spoke with the instinctive generosity that made his own company so pleasant; but he also put his finger on an essential quality of Wordsworth's poetry, without weighing that quality down by definition. For it is true that when he was writing well Wordsworth's poetry was quite unique. There are cadences, rhythms, elisions and allusions that no other poet could hope to imitate. Or he might have been thinking of Wordsworth's ability to articulate complex thought and feeling in simple homespun words and phrases, so that one generally needs to read a passage twice: first one gathers the immediate sense of the writing, then there is a pause in which one realises there is a second meaning contained in the straightforward writing which is more obscure and complex, and then there is the process of exploring that second meaning and linking it to the more obvious sense of the writing. Or he could have been referring to Wordsworth's understanding of silence, and to the way Wordsworth played silence so well against language. In part this was a question of phrasing – just as in music the interval between notes is as important as the notes themselves – but in Wordsworth there was a special dimension to silence, which the French would call '*le non dit*' – 'that which remains unspoken' – and which constitutes an important part of the meaning of the whole (a bit like the mass of the iceberg which remains invisible beneath the surface of the water). '*Le non dit*' plays a very important part in Wordsworth's poetry, as it allowed his secretive and elusive character to express itself without fear of being trapped by clear-cut meanings.

Coleridge however was very difficult to live with. The particular conditions in which he existed – physical restlessness, intellectual ferment, emotional hyperactivity, financial precariousness and psychological fragility – meant that the atmosphere of the Wordsworth household changed radically whenever he made an appearance. It all became very complicated, as professional ambitions, personal attractions and antipathies, and sexual needs and desires created some heady and potentially explosive cocktails. Coleridge was responsible for most of the trouble, as his marriage fell apart, his health deteriorated, and his jealousy of Wordsworth increased. At one point, having fallen in love with Wordsworth's sister-in-law Sara Hutchinson (whom he referred to in his journal as Asra, to distinguish her from his own wife Sarah), he had hallucinations of Wordsworth making love to Asra-Sara in the local inn. These visions may well have been fuelled by the opium to which he was addicted; in any case they did nothing to help a friendship that was becoming increasingly strained and formal. By 1800 Wordsworth was already setting a distance between himself and his friend. The critical moment came with the preparation of the second edition of *Lyrical Ballads*. Wordsworth's name appeared on the title-page without that of Coleridge's – a decision that could be justified by the fact that he contributed fifty-nine poems to the volume while only five works by Coleridge were included. And then Coleridge's long poem *Christabel* was rejected at the last minute, in part because it was not fully resolved and completed, and in part because the tone and style were too much at variance with Wordsworth's poems. In its place Wordsworth decided to include his own poem, *Michael*; and to make it clear to everyone that the volume was essentially his creation, he also added the Preface which has since become famous as Wordsworth's literary creed.[61]

Overnight the team was radically rethought. 'Wordsworth & Coleridge' became, as it were, 'Wordsworth & Co.' For Coleridge the change was humiliating. From being the prime instigator and promoter of this new generation of poets, Wordsworth's intellectual superior, literary partner and unstinting admirer, he found himself relegated to the status of an expendable accessory – in some ways more of a burden than a blessing, and in any case less useful than the various women whose role it was to copy out Wordsworth's illegible manuscripts and multiple revisions.

It was the beginning of the end for their true friendship. As time passed and Coleridge came to terms with the new reality, his resentment and sense of injustice increased. He could not begin to see himself as others saw him: a penniless, overblown, self-destructive, and completely unreliable drug addict, incapable of managing either his love life or his professional career, and who seemed determined to ruin his family along with himself.

Wordsworth's distancing of Coleridge was in part a response to Coleridge's impossible character and behaviour – but only in part. The hard truth that Coleridge had such difficulty in facing up to was that Wordsworth was not interested in collaborating with anyone. His was a one-man show. If others were prepared to help him keep the show on the road, so much the better. Otherwise he would manage on his own.

The Wordsworth-Coleridge relationship is seen now as one of the great literary partnerships, similar to Ezra Pound's close association with James Joyce and T. S. Eliot at the beginning of the twentieth century. Given the tensions between Wordsworth and Coleridge that were palpable from 1800 onwards, and the acrimonious way their collaboration ended, commentators have tended to take sides, blaming one or other of the poets for damaging the relationship and ruining the common cause. Maybe it would make more sense to view the relationship as a meeting of two minds that were very different, and which thrived on the dialectic they created until the differences became incompatible (again, one could make the same analysis of the Lennon-McCartney dialogue – or of Pound and Joyce, or of Jung and Freud…). Such dialogues are in any case rare, and one should be grateful that they exist at all, and accept that they will inevitably have a limited life-span.

It is impossible for us to measure or quantify the extent and importance of the exchanges between Wordsworth and Coleridge. They were the result of countless unrecorded conversations, jokes, witticisms; the fruit of long walks together, and of idle evenings in front of the fire; of things said but also of other things left unsaid. Like one of Wordsworth's beloved streams that surfaced in the mountainside at some point, burbled its way downhill, disappeared, reemerged more turbulent than before yet also created little pools where the water was almost static, and turned slowly round and round and didn't seem to be going anywhere at all – so the dialogue with Coleridge took its own form, which altered constantly with the years that passed – always the same stream, but with a shape and voice that was always changing.

One can imagine how this kind of interaction might have worked. For example, Coleridge's poem *Frost at Midnight*, written in February 1798, could have helped Wordsworth in different ways and at different moments. The central theme, in which Coleridge reflects on childhood and nature as he sits next to his sleeping son, might have prompted Wordsworth towards composing *Anecdote for Fathers* a few months later. In that poem of course the little boy is wide awake and engages in dialogue with the man – quite the opposite of the situation in Coleridge's poem. Nonetheless both poems explore the relationship between two worlds – that of the child and that of the adult. And at the end of 1798 Wordsworth picked up the other strand of Coleridge's thought in *Frost at Midnight* – that of the sleeping child – and developed it in the 'Lucy' poems, in which infant death was imagined as a form of sleep which conserves intact the child's relationship with nature.[62] Again, the last verse of Coleridge's poem, which begins,

> Therefore all seasons shall be sweet to thee

is strongly reminiscent of the passage in Virgil's *Fourth Eclogue*, which begins,

> At tibi prima, puer, nullo munuscola cultu
> Errantis hederas passim cum baccare tellus
> Mixtaque ridenti colocasia fundet acantho.
>
> (lines 17-19)

('And for you, boy, the uncultivated earth
Will pour out her first gifts:
Straggling ivy and cyclamen everywhere')

– a poem with which both Coleridge and Wordsworth would
have been familiar, from their studies at Cambridge if for no
other reason. And when Wordsworth came to publish his *Ode:
Intimations of Immortality* in 1807 he chose the first line of Virgil's
Fourth Eclogue as epigraph – to a poem which, like *Frost at Midnight*,
explores the relationship between childhood and adulthood. Of
course Wordsworth's *Ode* goes far beyond *Frost at Midnight* in the
range and depth of its thought; but it may be that Coleridge's
poem sowed ideas in Wordsworth's mind that would bear fruit
almost a decade later.

All these conjectures are no more than that; but the point is
not to prove definitively a particular connection or influence, but
rather to get a sense of the possible interplay between Wordsworth
and Coleridge, and to appreciate that much of that dialogue took
place in ways that cannot easily be set down in print.

★ ★ ★

Between 1803 and 1810 Mary gave birth five times; and bit by
bit the cottage became impossibly congested. 'We are crammed
into our little nest edge-full', Dorothy wrote to a friend in 1806,
when only two of the five children had been born, and she was
not exaggerating. Dove Cottage had been cosy when only she
and her brother had been living there, but was far too small for a
growing family to be comfortable in. And of course there were
guests: Mary's unmarried sister Sara had been one, but with time
had become a more or less permanent resident. She shared a bed

with Dorothy (by this point every bed in the house was shared by two people).

Wordsworth's inner calm didn't seem to be affected by all the noise, disturbances and smells that reverberated through the cottage from dawn to dusk. Of course, without more money than he had there wasn't much he could do to improve or alter the situation, so maybe he just decided to take things as they were. At any rate he never suggested in letters or conversation that he found his living and working conditions difficult. And deep down he was probably very happy to feel and see and hear a large and extended family around him. He had grown up with four siblings, only to have the family group split after his mother's death, and then further fragmented after the death of his father. By 1810, with five children of his own in the house, he could feel that he had restored a sense of continuity from childhood to adulthood. Plus he had his own sister living with him, as Mary had hers. If there was a price to pay for all of this in terms of discomfort, so be it. What mattered was the bigger picture, and he was happy with that.

His work didn't seem to suffer. Between his marriage in 1802 and the family's move to a larger house in 1808, Wordsworth wrote some of his best poetry.[63] It helped enormously that he had developed the habit of composing outdoors, while walking. Nature offered him space and silence in abundance in which to dream up his verse; and with three women at home who were always willing to serve as secretaries, he had little to worry or complain about. He could enjoy human warmth and company when he wanted it, and isolate himself quite easily when he needed to be alone.

At another level however Wordsworth's domestic set-up did have an effect on the poetry he wrote. The poems became more introspective, less concerned with relating the stories of other people and more concerned with exploring the inner world of the individual. During the 1790s, when he had been rootless and homeless and often lonely, he peopled his solitude with the characters that we find in *Lyrical Ballads*, or in his play *The Borderers* (1796-7). But in the 'crammed nest' of Dove Cottage the last thing he wanted or needed was additional human presences in his work. On the contrary, what he desired most was to empty his head of domestic worries and disturbances, and to fill his lungs with fresh air. Walking was less the counterbalance to intellectual exertion that it had been prior to his marriage, and more an escape route from the suffocating atmosphere of the cottage. And he needed to spend time with himself, to concentrate on his private thoughts and feelings, in order to regain an inner balance and calm.

More often than not Dorothy accompanied him on his walks, but by then she was so much a part of himself that her presence didn't disturb him. In any case he could always write her out of his poems, and so reclaim in the verse (which he would then ask her to copy out for him) the absolute solitude which in reality was often diluted. The clearest example of him doing this is the untitled poem which is known by its first line, 'I wandered lonely as a cloud...', written between 1804 and 1807 but based on the memory of a walk made with Dorothy on April 15, 1802. Critics like to debate whether or not William stole from Dorothy's journal to compose the poem; what is clear is that even if he did consult his sister's account of that day (which given his extraordinary memory he probably wouldn't have needed to do) he changed

Overleaf: Dorothy's Grasmere Journal, *entry for April 15, 1802 – her account of seeing the daffodils by the shore of Ullswater*

black and green, the birches
here & there greenish but
there is yet more of purple
to be seen on the Twigs.
We got over into a field to
avoid some cows — people
working, a few primroses
by the road side, wood sorrel
flowers, the anemone, violets, strawberries, & that
starry yellow flower which Mrs
C calls pile wort. When we
were in the woods beyond
Gowbarrow park we saw a
few daffodils close to the water
side, we fancied that the
lake had floated the seeds
ashore & that the very
little colony had so sprung
up — But as we went along
there were more & yet more

& at last under the boughs
of the trees we saw that there
was a long belt of them the
~~[crossed out]~~ along the
shore, about the breadth
of a country turnpike road.
I never saw daffodils so
beautiful they grew among
the mossy stones about & above
them, some rested their heads
upon these stones as on a
pillow for weariness & the
rest tossed & reeled & danced
& seemed as if they ~~[crossed out]~~
laughed with the wind ~~[crossed out]~~
tossed so gay ever glancing
~~this wind the breath~~ ever
ever changing ↑ here was
here & there a little knot
and a few stragglers a few
yards higher up but they
were so few as not to disturb

the tone significantly by making the experience personal rather than shared. In recounting the episode Dorothy uses the pronoun 'we' seven times, and 'I' just once: the whole point for her is that this was a special moment that she was sharing with her brother, and that the sharing of it was part of what made it special. In William's eighteen-line poem any reference to Dorothy's presence is ruled out, while 'I' occurs four times, 'my' is used twice, and 'me' once – and the exclusive nature of the experience is underlined by his evoking 'the bliss of solitude' which fills his heart with pleasure.

From a purely literary point of view a comparison of Dorothy's account of seeing the daffodils, with William's memory of the experience, is revealing. Dorothy writes that,

When we were in the woods beyond Gowbarrow park we saw a few daffodils close to the water side, we fancied that the lake had floated the seeds ashore & that the little colony had sprung up – But as we went along there were more & yet more & at last under the boughs of the trees, we saw that there was a long belt of them along the shore, about the breadth of a country turnpike road. I never saw daffodils so beautiful they grew among the mossy stones about & about them, some rested their heads upon the stones as on a pillow for weariness & the rest tossed & reeled & danced & seemed as if they verily laughed with the wind that blew upon them over the Lake to them. There was here & there a little knot & a few stragglers a few yards higher up but they were so few as not to disturb the simplicity & unity & life of that one busy highway –.

William's representation of the moment is orchestrated quite differently:

I wandered lonely as a cloud
That floats on high o'er vales and hills,
When all at once I saw a crowd,
A host, of golden daffodils;
Beside the lake, beneath the trees,
Fluttering and dancing in the breeze.

Continuous as the stars that shine
And twinkle on the milky way,
They stretched in never-ending line
Along the margin of the bay:
Ten thousand saw I at a glance,
Tossing their heads in sprightly dance.

The waves beside them danced; but they
Out-did the sparkling waves in glee:

(lines 1-14)

Dorothy's narrative works like a tracking movement in cinema, that gradually reveals the full extent of the daffodils in a way that nicely dramatises the overall effect they create. She then suggests two different metaphors: the expanse of daffodils is compared to a country road (and that idea is reiterated by the 'highway' at the end of the passage), while the movement of the flowers is likened to a dance – that image being backed up by 'reeled', which clearly refers here to the folk dance of the same name. In turn that suggestion that the mass of daffodils is like a crowd of people is reinforced by 'laughed' and 'a few stragglers' and, with the sort of empathy that came so naturally to Dorothy, by the observation that 'some rested their heads upon the stones as if for weariness'. William's version is meagre by comparison: he sees the daffodils all at once; and uses the dancing metaphor three times without varying the verb. His one original image is of the flowers as stars – for the rest his text is less interesting, and less poetic, than Dorothy's account in prose. If he did indeed steal from Dorothy's journal, he did not profit much from the exercise; nonetheless, it is his poem that schoolchildren the world over are invited to read, while Dorothy's journal remains in the background, even as her presence beside the lake was ignored by her brother in his verses.

Dorothy never complained in her journal of being excluded from poems which referred to experiences that they had shared. On the contrary her thoughts were always for her brother and for his well-being. When she found herself written out of the poem '*The Leech Gatherer*' (better known as *Resolution and Independence*), which was based on a walk they made together on October 3, 1800, she made no comment about her exclusion, noting instead in her journal for May 9, 1802:

> William worked at the Leech gatherer almost incessantly from morning till tea-time. I copied the Leech-gatherer & other poems for Coleridge – I was oppressed and sick at heart for he wearied himself to death.

Wordsworth's difficulty in admitting that important experiences can spring from moments that are shared could be taken as an example of how self-centred he was (and there is plenty of biographical evidence to support that idea). Alternatively it can be seen as stemming from the Romantic aesthetic which gave great importance to the individual and intuitive basis of any profound and meaningful experience of, or relationship with, nature. As in a painting by Caspar David Friedrich, Wordsworth needed to be represented contemplating Nature on his own.[64] Of course there are paintings by Friedrich which include more than one person in a natural landscape; similarly the conclusion of *The*

Prelude (Book XIII) begins with the ascent of Snowdon in the company of two other men, who are not entirely excluded from the moment of revelation at the summit of the mountain. But the main impetus in Romanticism was always towards the marriage of the individual with the universal.[65]

★ ★ ★

During the intensely creative period that went from 1798 to about 1807, 'Wordsworth & Co.' achieved an extraordinary balancing act. The group somehow managed to maintain an aura of social respectability, which allowed them to dialogue with the aristocracy as well as to stay on good terms with their working-class neighbours, while at the same time enjoying a bohemian lifestyle worthy of Parisian artists a century later (colourful moments of this period included having to rescue Hazlitt after he tried to have his way with various local girls, none of whom would yield to him: the townsmen wanted to throw Hazlitt into the lake – if not into prison – and Wordsworth was obliged to help him escape). Indeed one could say that the Lake poets, together with their everchanging entourage of lovers, wives, relatives, children and friends, formed the first true bohemian community of modern times. This was all the more remarkable as it took root in a remote part of the English countryside, far from the metropolis (which such communities generally depended on for mental oxygen), and in a social situation which was extremely conservative.

The group preserved its freedom at a price. While they were accepted and tolerated by the local community (above all because William and Dorothy were born and bred there), and while liberal-minded patrons like the Beaumonts were happy to indulge their eccentricities, knowing that odd behaviour was only to be expected from artists, nonetheless they remained not only poor but also extremely isolated. Occasional expeditions to London to deal with publishers and catch up on social and political news could not alter that underlying reality. The relationships they developed among themselves were formed in what was essentially a vacuum; and they had to find a way of articulating those bonds, and the feelings that created them, which would make sense both to them and to other people.

Coleridge was no help in this. While he was not naturally transgressive as Byron was, nor a habitual womaniser like Hazlitt, he was morally childish and irresponsible, and created tensions and problems wherever he went. No doubt he relished the fact that the woman he had fallen in love with had virtually the same name as the wife he continually abandoned when he set out on one of his quixotic adventures. Coding Sara as Asra to distinguish her from Sarah must have seemed to him just a private witticism; though one might wonder whether the similarity in names was a complete coincidence, for given the way he treated the two women, they seem to have been more or less interchangeable for him. The Sara–Sarah drama was a tough knot in a tangled ball of wool which constituted the love lives and close relationships of the group. Isolated as they were, and accustomed to the idea that everything should be lived intensely, there was always the danger that any relationship that was formed would become unmanageable.

Wordsworth, who despite his turbulent youth was turning out to be a lover of stability and order, worked out a formula which both satisfied himself and also provided a gloss on the emotional lives of the members of the group that was socially acceptable. He decided that they were all friends. Virtually any adult relationship other than that of husband and wife could be considered as friendship. Of course there were degrees of friendship, but as to the degree, that didn't concern anyone other than the two people involved. As far as the printed word was concerned, Sir George Beaumont could be his friend, and so could his sister Dorothy. And that was that.

Dorothy had been alert to the possibilities for emotional camouflage offered by the concept of friendship long before William articulated them in his poetry. In June 1793, not long after her brother's return from France, she wrote to her close friend Jane Pollard:

> ...I have paced that walk in the garden which will always be dear to me from the Remembrance of those long, long conversations I have had upon it supported by my Brother's arm. Ah! Jane! I never thought of the cold when he was with me. I am as heretical as yourself in my Opinions concerning Love & Friendship; I am very sure that Love will never bind me closer to any human Being than Friendship binds me closer to you my earliest female Friend, and to William my earliest & dearest Male Friend. (letter of June 16, 1793)

Wordsworth took the hint and developed it forcefully in his *Lines Composed a Few Miles above Tintern Abbey* of 1798, when in the last part of the poem he turned to address his companion (Dorothy) directly:

> For thou art with me here upon the banks
> Of this fair river; thou my dearest Friend,
> My dear, dear Friend;
>
>   ...Oh! yet a little while
> May I behold in thee what I was once,
> My dear, dear Sister!...   (lines 115-7; 120-2)

But when he came to write *The Prelude*, Wordsworth was obliged to modify his wordplay slightly. The basic friend–sister ambiguity remained, but as he had decided to dedicate his long poem to Coleridge, Dorothy was deprived of the status of 'Friend' with a capital 'F' (that privilege passed to Coleridge), and had to be content with a small 'f' – though she kept the capital 'S' in 'sister'. So in Book VI Wordsworth addressed Coleridge directly, and reminded him of how during the summer he (Wordsworth) had been blessed with,

> the presence, Friend, I mean
> Of that sole Sister, she who hath been long
> Thy treasure also, thy true friend and mine,
>
> (213–5)

Wordsworth's juggling-act here is not elegant; nonetheless Coleridge also recognised the potential in the notion of friendship that Wordsworth promoted. It could be used to create the sense of a group, while being vague enough to allow people who had precious little in common to imagine they shared a common vision or identity. And so in 1815, when he decided to launch a weekly newspaper, he called it *The Friend*. It was as short-lived as all of Coleridge's projects, closing after twenty-eight issues – but no matter. The idea of the group had been sown, and it proved to be remarkably resilient and long-lasting. For the next hundred and fifty years artists and intellectuals with radically different characters and personal agendas would gather together under one banner or another – loose associations that in retrospect would be defined as movements and be classified as some sort of 'ism': Symbolism, Impressionism, Vorticism, Surrealism, or whatever. In Wordsworth's case he was in due course pigeonholed as one of the great poets of British Romanticism (having graduated to that title from being a leading representative of 'the Lake School of Poets').

The modern condition of the artist was coming to the light of day. Writers, painters and musicians gradually disengaged themselves from the shackles of aristocratic patronage, and formed themselves into groups that hovered like gypsy encampments on the fringes of society. And to give more credibility to the often improbable meeting of minds that these associations represented, the group portrait was thought up and wheeled out whenever appropriate. So, for example, an imaginative etching of 1815 by Charles Mottram brought together, among others, Sheridan, Wordsworth, Coleridge, Southey, Byron, Walter Scott, Francis Jeffrey, and Turner, for a fictitious breakfast party at the house of Samuel Rodgers.[66] The etching pushes artifice to the extreme: Sheridan was a playwright whose work had nothing in common with Romantic poetry; by 1815 Wordsworth and Coleridge had lost contact with each other, and Southey had become increasingly critical of Wordsworth's work; Byron and Wordsworth disliked each other intensely, while Francis Jeffrey poured unremitting scorn on Wordsworth's poetry in his articles for the Edinburgh Review. Turner meanwhile had no personal or professional relationship with any of the other members of this fictitious party. As far as Wordsworth was concerned only the presence of Walter Scott would have had any resonance, among the group of nineteen men represented in the etching. Nonetheless the group portrait persisted for well over a century as an affirmation of one '-ism' or another, from Impressionism to Surrealism and beyond, with artists and intellectuals bundled together to pose for the painter or the camera as if they were a team of footballers, or politicians at a conference.

Chapter VIII

Brother John and Brother William

Weep no more, woeful shepherds weep no more,
For Lycidas your sorrow is not dead,
Sunk though he be beneath the watery floor,

(John Milton, *Lycidas*, lines 165–167)

The pairing principle which Wordsworth brought into play in *Home at Grasmere*, and which helped him to structure and define his more intimate relationships at this time, could also be deployed to include his brother John; for as the four brothers grew up a certain symmetry had developed between them that suggested John as a natural companion for William. The eldest of the four (Richard) and the youngest (Christopher) already formed a pair of their own, in that they had chosen to remain inside the 'system' that their education had prepared them for, and had embarked on orthodox and respectable careers: Richard became a lawyer, while Christopher chose to go into the Church and to couple that with a university career – he became Master of Trinity College, Cambridge, and later on was Vice-Chancellor of the University. The two brothers in the middle, on the other hand, had made more adventurous choices. Unlike William, John accepted the idea of steady employment, but in joining the Navy he was able to preserve a good deal of freedom, and up to a point could make what he wanted of his career. In 1800 he used that freedom to spend eight months with William and Dorothy at Grasmere.

John was an easy person to live with, adaptable and self-contained, and he fitted in comfortably to life at Dove Cottage. For William it was a precious experience – the nearest he ever came to reconstituting the family that had been unceremoniously split up after the death of their father seventeen years earlier. But it also brought hidden tensions to the surface, testing William's character and pushing him to articulate the values that lay behind his writing. To start with there was the serious business of courting. As we saw earlier (in chapter VI), William and John set out in May 1800 on a journey to visit Mary Hutchinson – their departure then providing Dorothy with the impetus to begin her *Grasmere Journal*. No doubt John's role was simply to keep William company (normally Dorothy would also have been included in the expedition, but given that William was going to Mary as a potential suitor, he preferred to leave his sister at home). However it would seem that John (being as independent-minded as William and Dorothy) decided to play things a little differently, and put himself forward as an alternative husband for Mary. Certainly at that time his prospects were better than those of the penniless ballad-monger that was his brother; and once he had been appointed captain of the *Earl of Abergavenny* in September 1800, he pointed this out in a letter he wrote to Mary, saying that he expected to be 'a very rich man' within ten years, thanks to the trade with China. However John proved to be as discreet in courtship as he was in everything else, and deferred to William once the latter showed how serious his intentions were. He retreated, but did not forget; and when Mary wrote to John two years later to tell him of her engagement to William, his reply betrayed an intensity of emotion that went beyond simple friendship:

> I have been reading your Letter over & over again My dearest Mary till tears have come into my eyes & I known (*sic*) not how to express myself thou ar't a kind & dear creature But what ever fate Befal me I shall love to the last and bear thy memory with me to the grave

> Thine affly
> John Wordsworth[67]

The intensity of feeling here is palpable; what is striking also is (as has often been noted) that John chooses to end the brief letter by quoting from his brother's poem 'Michael':

> but whatever fate
> Befall thee, I shall love thee to the last,
> And bear thy memory with me to the grave.
> (lines 415-7)

It is hard to know just how to interpret the quotation: maybe the explanation is simply that, coming after the characteristically modest 'I known not how to express myself' he deals with the problem by leaving such matters to the professional – in this case the Poet. Who also happens to be his elder brother, and who has won the woman he also had his eye on, thereby proving himself to be 'the better man' on all counts. (One can't help wondering though if John might not be getting his own back on William, saying to Mary 'You want to marry a poet, alright then, let him make the pretty compliments on my behalf – I've got better things to do').

Whatever one chooses to read into the letter, it is revealing in a way that was not intended: for it shows the same difficulty in containing and articulating feelings that both William and Dorothy had to deal with. Here indeed was something that the siblings had in common, and that each of them learned to deal with in a different way. For all their self-control and studied courtesies, these three had a greater resemblance to such characters as Heathcliff and Catherine Earnshaw (in *Wuthering Heights*) than they have been given credit for.[68] Indeed the tone of John's letter to Mary is uncannily similar to that of William's letters to Mary, written during periods when he was travelling, and after years of married life together:

> Every day every hour every moment makes me feel more deeply how blessed we are in each other, how purely how faithfully how ardently, and how tenderly we love each other.... O Mary I love you with a passion of love which grows till I tremble to think of its strength...
>
> (August 11, 1810)

> My sweet Love how I long to see thee; think of me, wish for me, pray for me, pronounce my name when thou art alone, and upon thy pillow; and dream of me happily and sweetly. – I am the blessedest of Men, the happiest of husbands –
>
> (May 9, 1812)[69]

William's way of dealing with powerful emotions in his work was, as we have seen, to wait until time gave him distance from them.[70] John's strategy was to retreat into silence, and, if necessary, to disappear. For her part Dorothy had no clear strategy, and simply suffered in silence.

William paid John the compliment of calling him 'a *silent Poet*', and no doubt found his company a welcome counterpoint to that of the endlessly talkative poet that was Coleridge.

When the three of them set off for a walking tour together in the autumn of 1799, the contrast was sharp: Coleridge, with his constant chatter and witticisms and his puppy-like enthusiasm for any and every argument that the conversation might conjure up, set against the shy and self-contained character of John, a man who seemed to have little need to put his thoughts and feelings into words. William found himself in the middle of this strange trio, unsure who to turn towards, uncertain whether Coleridge or John was the more natural companion. It was as if he was listening in stereo to the two prime impulses which, when synthesised successfully, made his poetry so distinctive, but which when separated out, seemed to belong to two worlds which were barely compatible. From one side came an articulate, energetic and intelligent voice, from the other a quiet and intuitive murmur that sounded soft and discreet as a pulse-beat.

The dialectic was difficult to resolve. For years he and Coleridge had walked side by side: together they had produced, in *Lyrical Ballads*, a volume of poems that did its best to be easy to read and understand, using standard English, avoiding dialect and obscure references, and relying on forms that grafted a highly personal vision onto an essentially popular tradition; and they had launched the highly ambitious project to be known as *The Recluse*. But when *Lyrical Ballads* appeared on October 4, 1798, Wordsworth was in Germany where, after being left in the lurch by Coleridge, he began to delve into his childhood and into some of his most private thoughts and feelings, so as to produce a completely different kind of writing. When John unexpectedly re-entered William's life in 1799, he inevitably reminded his brother of the boy that he had been and that he had been writing about in Germany. Like a lodestone John's character, together with the simple fact of being his brother and of having shared so much of his early life, worked on William's imagination, giving him the impetus to develop the autobiographical writing begun in Germany, and as a consequence drawing him away from the abstract intellectual concerns that Coleridge preferred to focus on.

In the autumn of 1799 Wordsworth was coming home. Like a salmon laboriously working its way upstream to the place where it was spawned and where it will breed, he made his way along the valleys and over the hills to his birthplace, while his mind moved upstream against the current of time to reenact the events and experiences of his childhood. Like Dorothy, John could be a perfect companion on that journey back to where he once belonged – the more so in that he seemed to have preserved intact so much of the character of a boy. William could, perhaps, measure the distance he had travelled from his own childhood by comparing himself with John. And when he wrote how as a child,

> I held unconscious intercourse
> With the eternal beauty, drinking in
> A pure organic pleasure from the lines
> Of curling mist, or from the level plain
> Of waters coloured by the steady clouds.
>> (The two-part *Prelude* of 1799, first part,
>> lines 396-8)

he could well imagine John as being able to use the present tense to say the same thing. And he could imagine John and himself developing an intense and precious relationship, based on affinities that gave added life and meaning to simple family affection and loyalty: the two brothers could form a pair, just as he formed a different kind of pair with his sister, and another kind of pair with his great friend Coleridge.

But John was not someone who adapted easily to another

person's scheme, and after a week of walking with his brother and Coleridge, he informed them that he had to get back to organising his next voyage; they carried on without him. A week later, when passing through Ennerdale, they (Coleridge and Wordsworth) were told the story of a local man who had fallen to his death from a rocky crag, apparently while sleepwalking. It was the kind of story that Wordsworth had used in *Lyrical Ballads*, and a few months later it became the nucleus for a new poem, called *The Brothers*. He then introduced a second strand to the narrative which complicated the reading of the piece considerably: the dead man's brother, on returning to his birthplace after many years spent at sea,

> With a determined purpose to resume
> The life which he lived there; both for the sake
> Of many darling pleasures, and the love
> Which to an only brother he has borne
> In all his hardships   (lines 66–70)

is shocked to learn of his brother's death – and moreover is told that the habit of sleepwalking – which probably led to the shepherd's death – was caused by grief for his long lost brother: he used to walk about in his sleep looking for him.

There is no reunion, and no homecoming for the sailor, who returns to his ship and spends the rest of his life at sea. The theme – of two people who are thwarted in their desire to meet or to reveal themselves to each other – reminds one of certain episodes in Thomas Hardy's novels: Fanny missing out on her wedding to Troy because she goes to the wrong church, for example; or Tess failing to tell Angel about her past because the letter she writes him slips under the carpet as well as under the door. In Hardy as in Wordsworth there is the sense that people's destinies are shaped by forces that take no account of individual wills – though Wordsworth's ability to accept and absorb what-ever came his way disarms the event of its tragic thrust. For him the failed reunion of the two brothers is not the fault of a capri-cious and malicious 'President of the Immortals', but simply an example of how misfortune is (like death) an intrinsic part of life, which people must learn to live with from an early age.

Further on in the poem, in a passage (lines 135-64) in which the priest talks about the world in which the local community exists, he reflects on

> two Springs which bubbled side by side
> As if they had been made that they might be
> Companions to each other: (lines 138-40)

and tells how

> ten years back,
> Close to those brother fountains, the huge crag
> Was rent with lightning – one is dead and gone,
> The other, left behind, is flowing still.
>
> (lines 140-43)

Clearly the two streams stand in for the two brothers just as the pairs of eagles and swans speak for William and Dorothy in *Home at Grasmere*. What is significant is that the wordplay which elabo-rates the metaphor suggests that the absent and vagabond brother, the one who is 'gone', loses his vital energy, while the brother who is 'left behind' continues to thrive and be productive. We see that William, after a decade of often aimless wandering, wanted to repudiate that aspect of his character, and project himself instead as a deeply rooted and home-loving man; while his brother John, who drifted in and out of other peoples' lives like a ghost, and whose choice of profession meant that he would always be absent for long periods of time, was cast as the rootless vagabond.

It was a harsh judgement for William to make; but it was intended less as a criticism of John than as a lament for the the break-up of the family unit. Just as he felt that governments had a duty to try and preserve continuity in the rural communities, so Wordsworth believed that families should at all costs be maintained intact. In likening the bond between two siblings to a massive rock formation, Wordsworth in *The Brothers* made the point as forcefully as he could. But it was not the first time that this kind of image had occurred to him. A year earlier, in the two-part draft of the poem that would become *The Prelude*, he had singled out, as one of the significant moments in his youth, his distress at discovering that a large boulder which had been a feature of the village square had been split in two:

> A grey stone
> Of native rock, left midway in the square
> Of our small market-village, was the home
> And centre of these joys; and when, returned
> After long absence, thither I repaired,
> I found that it was split, and gone to build
> A smart assembly-room that perked and flared
> With wash and rough-cast, elbowing the ground
> Which had been ours. But let the fiddle scream,
> And be happy! Yet I know, my friends,
> That more than one of you will think with me
> Of those soft starry nights, and that old dame
> From whom the stone was named, who there had sat
> And watched her table with its huckster's wares,
> Assiduous for the length of sixty years.
>
> (1799 version, Second part, lines 33-40)

The passage is seldom commented on, but the fact that it is among the first of the so-called 'spots of time' to occur to Wordsworth, and that it was transcribed unchanged into the 1805 version of *The Prelude*, endows it with a particular significance. And the sharp irony of the phrase, 'But let the fiddle scream, / And be happy!' is also noteworthy, given that Wordsworth almost never expressed himself with irony (and that he loved the dances that would have been put on in the assembly-room). Whether it is man or the forces of nature that split the rock, the fact of splitting is seen as destructive. For a man whose family had disintegrated before he reached adolescence, unity was all.

★ ★ ★

After John's premature death at the age of thirty-two – he drowned when the *Earl of Abergavenny* sank off Weymouth in February 1805, at the beginning of a journey to India and China – William inevitably emphasised how close he had been to his brother, and how much they had had in common. But in many respects John was as much William's alter ego as he was his soulmate. The course John had taken professionally was both enterprising and risky, and it had implicitly called into question his elder brother's values, and William's carefully argued vision of society and social relations. Up to a point this could be read as a typical contrast between siblings, with John as the younger brother who refused the safety and security of life at home, along with its obligations and responsibilities, and preferred to make his own way on his own terms. But he had also proved himself as a sailor and an officer; and when he wrote to Mary in September 1802 (the letter quoted above), he was a man with real prospects. He was twenty-nine years old, and captain of the *Earl of Abergavenny*, the largest ship belonging to the East India Company. Thanks to the profits he could make through trade, he could become rich as well as successful in his Navy career. Potentially he was a much better match than his elder brother, and if he had tried to win Mary's hand instead of retreating into the shadows, he might have claimed her for himself.

This was a period of extraordinary expansion in English history, and one in which fortunes could be, and were being, made by men who had the right abilities and training and were prepared to take risks. A class of self-made men was forming that owed nothing to the landed aristocracy, and that during the first half of the nineteenth century would impose the principles of a meritocracy on English culture, leading inexorably to a major shift in both power and values throughout English society. In 1802 John looked set to be part of that tidal wave. His situation could have served as a model for the beginning of Jane Austen's novel *Persuasion* (1818), when Anne Elliot, following the advice of her friend Lady Russell, rejects the marriage proposal of Captain Wentworth:

> Captain Wentworth had no fortune. He had been lucky in his profession, but spending freely, what had come freely, had realized nothing. But, he was confident that he should soon be rich; – full of life and ardour, he knew that he should soon have a ship, and soon be on a station that would lead to every thing he wanted. He had always been lucky; he knew he should be so still....She was persuaded to believe the engagement a wrong thing – indiscreet, improper, hardly capable of success, and not deserving it.....He had left the country in consequence. (Vol. 1, chapter 4)

At the end of *Persuasion* Captain Wentworth finally secures the heart and hand of Anne Elliot. But there would be no happy ending for John after the years of risk and danger and overcoming obstacles. During his short-lived career he saw some of his investments fail, and other projects curtailed by restrictions imposed by the East India Company. Nonetheless he remained as optimistic and upbeat in his professional life as he was modest and unassuming in personal matters. And the bigger picture makes it clear that there were plenty of other young men like John Wordsworth in the England of the 1800s, and that together they created a new social dynamic which called into question the basic assumptions about order and hierarchy and progress on which English society had been based during the eighteenth century.

William had no easy answer to the challenge that John's profession, lifestyle and achievements represented, but he did his best. A few months after writing *The Brothers* he followed up its criticism of a rootless and vagabond lifestyle with another poem that addressed the same issues in a different key. In essence it is a love poem, and as he took the unusual step of sending a copy of it to Mary (Hutchinson) once it was completed, it is safe to say that the message of the poem was designed for her, and that it forms part of their long and unobtrusive courtship. Given the warmth of feeling apparent in the letter John wrote to Mary just before her marriage to William, it is possible that William thought in 1801 that he might lose Mary to his younger brother: that John, after being welcomed to Dove Cottage, might turn out to be a cuckoo in the nest, and rob of him of his treasure.

The poem in question was untitled – it comes to us with its first line, 'I travelled among unknown men', as the title – and it uses the 'Lucy' motif (with its by then familiar resonances) to argue that steady and stable lifestyles are the basis for happy relationships. It refutes the exotic element in foreign travel, advocating instead the kind of homely happiness that Gabriel

Oak would later aspire to in *Far from the Madding Crowd* (with
Sergeant Troy as his opposite number, the tragically seductive
wanderer). Referring to England he writes,

> 'Tis past, that melancholy dream!
>   Nor will I quit thy shore
> A second time; for still I seem
>   To love thee more and more.
>
> Among thy mountains did I feel
>   The joy of my desire;
> And she I cherished turned her wheel
>   Beside an English fire.   (lines 5-12)

The tension or conflict between William and John was not just
one of individual character or lifestyle: it reflected the profound
dichotomy that existed in the English psyche between an earth-
bound culture and a seafaring way of life. Today the sea around
Britain is for most British people little more than a border: what
matters is what happens on dry land. But during Wordsworth's
lifetime the elements were finely balanced: in many ways it was
the sea, and the navy, that held the key to Britain's destiny, both
in peace and in war. It was thanks to the navy that the British
were able to establish colonies across the globe, and develop the
trade on which their Empire was based; and it was thanks to the
navy that Britain gained the upper hand over Napoleon. Battles
such as Waterloo were pivotal or decisive, but long before then
Nelson had thwarted Napoleon's ambitions at sea, and established
effective control of the Mediterranean. Without that naval super-
iority it would have been much harder for the British to bring
Napoleon's seemingly endless campaigns on land to a halt.

At the level of individual destinies also the sea played a vital role. Apart from the sailors working in the merchant navy, and those who had either chosen or been pressganged into the fighting navy, there were the countless men who made their living as fishermen – and of course there were the wives and sweethearts and families of all these men, whose happiness and well-being depended on the fate of those who spent a large part of their lives at sea. Out of sight, but not out of mind.

It would have been easy for Wordsworth, living about twenty-five miles from the sea, to engage with this dimension of English life, but he chose not to. On the other hand his great contemporary, Turner, understood perfectly the potential of the subject-matter. For him the sea, with its shipwrecks and storms, its great fighting ships and humble fishing boats, its everchanging light effects and unpredictable weather and extraordinary beauty, became an inexhaustible metaphor both for the individual's experience of life and for national destiny. Although Turner was a Londoner by birth, and had no obvious connection with the sea, he was able, through his skilful handling of the many ways in which the sea can speak to us, to articulate preoccupations that were shared by a large part of the population at that time – and to become in a sense the 'national painter'.

But the sea did not call to Wordsworth. It did not feed his imagination; and while he was happy to explore the 'river of life' analogy in his poems, he never referred to the sea or the ocean in this way. He preferred to contemplate the sea from a distance, seeing it as a sort of vanishing point for human experience, an image of infinity like the sky; but he held back from any intimate contact with it. Nonetheless the sea's presence inspires several unforgettable passages in *The Prelude*, such as the moment in Book IV when he returns home from an all-night dance, and describes the landscape as echoing the exultation that he feels:

The sea was laughing at a distance... (line 333)

Or when, from the top of Snowdon, he traces the outlines of the
hills that gradually recede and fade

> Into the sea – the real sea, that seemed
> To dwindle and give up its majesty
> (Book XIII, lines 49-50)

And the sea shore itself is the scene for the wonderfully evoca-
tive moment in Book II when, at the end of a cross-country ride,
he gallops with other boys along the beach:

> or when,
> Lighted by gleams of moonlight from the sea,
> We beat with thundering hoofs the level sand.
> (lines 142-4)

The contact is almost there, but not quite; for while he comes
right to the sea's edge, Wordsworth does not once put his feet in
the water. At no point in his poetry does he show any interest
in the sea as an element in its own right. And what was sim-
ply a matter of taste became much more than that after John's
death by drowning. In the *Elegaic Stanzas* written for Sir George
Beaumont the following year (1806), he states explicitly that he is
no longer able to contemplate the sea with any pleasure, because
of the way his brother died:

> Not for a moment could I now behold
> A smiling sea and be what I have been:
> The feeling of my loss will ne'er be old;
> (lines 37-39)

No doubt his grief did affect him in this way. However it is
worth noting that Wordsworth's instinctive antipathy towards the

Plate 1: William Shuter, William Wordsworth, *1798*

Plate 2: Benjamin Haydon, Wordsworth, *1818. The loose white shirt, open at the neck, reminds us of portraits of Shelley and Byron, and clearly points to presenting a romantic image of the poet*

Plate 3: Francis Chantrey, Marble bust of Wordsworth, *1820
(commissioned by Sir George Beaumont). Wordsworth here assumes
the appearance of an Augustan poet (see page 390)*

Plate 4: Margaret Gillies, William and Mary Wordsworth, *watercolour, 1839*

Plate 5: Margaret Gillies, Dora Wordsworth, *1839*

Plate 6: Miniature portrait of Annette Vallon

Plate 7: Silhouette of Dorothy Wordsworth, 1806 — the only portrait we have of her as a young woman

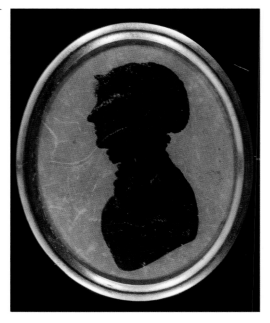

Plate 8: The four
notebooks that
hold Dorothy's
Grasmere Journals,
1800-1803

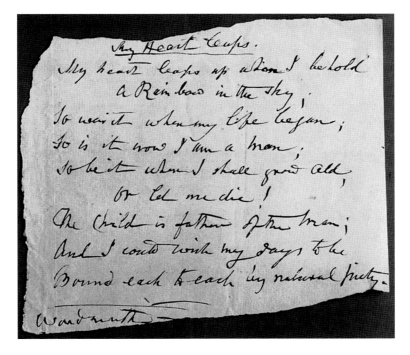

Plate 9: Copy by Constable of Wordsworth's poem 'My heart leaps up...',
some time after 1829

Plate 10: Peter Vandyke, Samuel Taylor Coleridge, *1795*

Plate 11: Wordsworth's Garden of Eden: Martindale

Plate 12: Postcard showing Dove Cottage

Plate 13: Wordsworth's chest; see page 10

Plate 14: Print by James Gillray, Un Petit Souper, à la Parisienne…*(1792), shows a family of 'Sans-Culottes' cooking and eating French aristocrats (see page 57)*

Plate 15: Isaac Cruikshank, Symptoms of Lewdness, or a Peep into the Boxes, *1794; see pages 47-8*

Plate 16: John Warwick Smith, Village of Stonethwaite and Eagle Cragg, Borrow-
dale, *1792. The Lake District was a popular destination for painters from the early 1790s*

Plate 17: Joseph Wright of Derby, Rydal Waterfall, *oil painting, 1795. The use of a
brownish tonal filter for depicting landscape, instead of true colour, was fashionable in the
second half of the eighteenth century. Rydal Mount (near this waterfall) was Wordsworth's
home for the last thirty-seven years of his life*

Plate 18: Turner, Mt Snowdon, *1799-1800, watercolour. See page 372*

Plate 19: Sir George Beaumont, Peele Castle in a Storm, *1805-1806. See pages 117 and 434 (note 44)*

And all the while my eyes I kept
On the descending moon.

My horse moved on; hoof after hoof
He raised, and never stopped:
When down behind the cottage-roof,
At once, the bright moon dropped.

What fond and wayward thoughts will slide
Into a Lover's head!
"O mercy!" to myself I cried,
"If Lucy should be dead!"
1799.

VIII.

SHE dwelt among the untrodden ways
Beside the springs of Dove,
A Maid whom there were none to praise
And very few to love:

A violet by a mossy stone
Half hidden from the eye!
—Fair as a star, when only one
Is shining in the sky.

She lived unknown, and few could know
When Lucy ceased to be;
But she is in her grave, and, oh,
The difference to me!
1790.

IX.

I TRAVELLED among unknown men,
In lands beyond the sea;
Nor, England! did I know till then
What love I bore to thee.

'Tis past, that melancholy dream!
Nor will I quit thy shore
A second time; for still I seem
To love thee more and more.

Among thy mountains did I feel
The joy of my desire;
And she I cherished turned her wheel
Beside an English fire.

Thy mornings showed, thy nights concealed
The bowers where Lucy played;
And thine too is the last green field
That Lucy's eyes surveyed.
-799.

X.

ERE with cold beads of midnight dew
Had mingled tears of thine,
I grieved, fond Youth! that thou shouldst sue
To haughty Geraldine.

Immoveable by generous sighs,
She glories in a train
Who drag, beneath our native skies,
An oriental chain.

Pine not like them with arms across,
Forgetting in thy care
How the fast-rooted trees can toss
Their branches in mid air.

The humblest rivulet will take
Its own wild liberties;
And, every day, the imprisoned lake
Is flowing in the breeze.

Then, crouch no more on suppliant knee,
But scorn with scorn outbrave;
A Briton, even in love, should be
A subject, not a slave!
1826.

XI.

TO ———

LOOK at the fate of summer flowers,
Which blow at daybreak, droop ere even-song;
And, grieved for their brief date, confess that
ours,
Measured by what we are and ought to be,
Measured by all that, trembling, we foresee,
Is not so long!

If human Life do pass away,
Perishing yet more swiftly than the flower,
If we are creatures of a *winter's* day;
What space hath Virgin's beauty to disclose
Her sweets, and triumph o'er the breathing rose
Not even an hour!

The deepest grove whose foliage hid
The happiest lovers Arcady might boast
Could not the entrance of this thought forbid
O be thou wise as they, soul-gifted Maid!
Nor rate too high what must so quickly fade,
So soon be lost.

Then shall love teach some virtuous Youth
"To draw, out of the object of his eyes,"
The while on thee they gaze in simple truth,
Hues more exalted, "a refinèd Form,"
That dreads not age, nor suffers from the worm
And never dies.
1824.

XII.

THE FORSAKEN.

THE peace which others seek they find;
The heaviest storms not longest last;
Heaven grants even to the guiltiest mind
An amnesty for what is past;
When will my sentence be reversed?
I only pray to know the worst;
And wish as if my heart would burst.

O weary struggle! silent years
Tell seemingly no doubtful tale;
And yet they leave it short, and fears
And hopes are strong and will prevail.
My calmest faith escapes not pain;
And, feeling that the hope is vain,
I think that he will come again.

XIII.

'TIS said, that some have died for love:
And here and there a church-yard grave is found
In the cold north's unhallowed ground,
Because the wretched man himself had slain
His love was such a grievous pain.
And there is one whom I five years have known
He dwells alone
Upon Helvellyn's side:
He loved—the pretty Barbara died;
And thus he makes his moan:
Three years had Barbara in her grave been laid
When thus his moan he made:

"Oh, move, thou Cottage, from behind that oak
Or let the aged tree uprooted lie.

"I only pray to know the worst;
And wish as if my heart would burst."

Plate 21: Benjamin Haydon, Wordsworth, *1842. Mt Helvellyn forms an artificial backdrop, in the manner of theatrical scenery, but the rendering of Wordsworth is convincing*

Previous page: Plate 20: A Complete Edition *of Wordsworth's poems, probably from 1896. The edition presents the poet's oeuvre thematically, disregarding a chronological order; and it offers a suitably Victorian image of Lucy*

sea had already led him to consider it as anything but friendly
several years earlier. The decisive event was his trip to France in
1802, to meet Annette – during the course of which he could
observe the English Channel from both coasts, and also observe
a large number of English ships, rigged out and equipped either
for trade or for war. The poems of that year make it clear that the
sea defined itself for him as a barrier – one that above all could
keep the 'ogre' of France (i.e. Napoleon) at bay, but more gener-
ally helped to preserve British values and identity from foreign
contamination. Wordsworth's vision – from which he would not
waver during the rest of his life – was almost identical to that
expressed centuries earlier by John of Gaunt on his deathbed (in
Shakespeare's *Richard II*), when he describes England as,

> This precious stone set in the silver sea,
> Which serves it in the office of a wall,
> Or as a moat defensive to a house
> Against the envy of less happier lands;
>
> (I, III, 46-49)

From this time the sea was for Wordsworth a necessary evil:
he didn't like it, but had to be grateful it was there, because
without it things would be even worse than they already were.
It led (or forced) men to leave their families, and it was the
theatre of costly and useless wars – but it kept the nation safe.
So much for his opinions in general. But between 1802 and 1805
the sea also dramatised the differences between William's and
John's characters and choices, and it was there that a number of
significant tensions came to the surface. As captain of a ship owned
by the East India Company, John had the opportunity to earn
large sums by trading in a private capacity. Over and beyond the
ship's recognised cargo, it could transport goods for the captain.

However, in order to set up this kind of business, John needed capital. Once the first instalment of the debt to the Wordsworths had been paid by Lord Lowther (in February 1803), John invested his share in his enterprise, and pressured his reluctant siblings into investing their shares also. From a commercial point of view the voyage was not very successful; nonetheless John persisted in trying to earn a fortune in this way. So when he was due to sail to China again in 1805, he once more asked Dorothy and William to invest their money in his venture – and once again they reluctantly complied. By the time the *Earl of Abergavenny* set sail in February 1805, he had about £20,000 personally invested in money and goods.[71]

On February 5 the ship sank off Weymouth, and John's investments went to the bottom of the sea along with his body. In William's mind any little belief he might have had in the virtues of an economy based on free trade and enterprise sank also. Unlike John's body, those ideas were never to be salvaged. John's death was above all a personal tragedy: but it also served to extinguish in William's mind what little belief he had in the policies that John had subscribed to. He mistrusted capitalism and had no time for colonialism, both of which were vital in those decades to the creation of the British Empire. He had no feeling for private enterprise; and the difficulties that John had had in making the fortune that could have been his if his career had proceeded smoothly, highlighted for William the pitfalls of the way the British economy was developing, and pushed him to react against those tendencies. Ironically therefore, the conservatism for which Wiliam became famous (or notorious) was also a reaction against the economic principles on which Conservative governments have operated ever since the early nineteenth century. It is a tension in Wordsworth's political thinking which tends to be overlooked, and is at least in part the result of his distress at the loss of his younger brother.

★ ★ ★

Given the tensions and contradictions of feeling that John inspired in William, as well as Wordsworth's preference for writing in retrospect, it is not surprising that his two poetic tributes to John – *To the Daisy* and '*I only looked for pain and grief*' – were posthumous, written in the months following John's death.[72] The only poem published during John's lifetime which referred (indirectly) to him was *The Brothers*, and that was highly critical of the choices John had made. And while John eventually had a place named after him, like Dorothy, Mary, Sara Hutchinson and Wordsworth himself, 'John's grove' did not find its place in the group until 1815 (under the title '*When first I journeyed hither*'). It was in that poem – effectively posthumous, though probably finished before John's death – that Wordsworth made John the compliment of being 'a silent Poet': no small tribute from a man who believed in the importance of the dialectic between language and silence. Nonetheless, the 'landlubber poet' refused to shift from the positions he had adopted years earlier: he contrasted 'Esthwaite's chearful Lake' (line 44) – where he lived – with the 'barren seas' (line 47) and 'joyless ocean' (line 92) that John had condemned himself to live on; and reiterated the judgement made in *The Brothers* when he concluded that,

'I think on thee
My Brother, and on all which thou hast lost.

(lines 103-4)

In settling his account with his brother William pulled no

punches. But in focusing on questions of lifestyle and profession Wordsworth may have overlooked the fact that he too was a loser – and not simply because he lost the brother he was fond of, and who died so young. The poetic vision that had underpinned *Home at Grasmere*, and had been put to the test in *The Prelude*, was based on a few alarmingly simple premises, such as family unity, continuity in time, and individual affinities. And that vision had not resisted the simple facts of reality. The pairing principle proved inadequate in terms of exploring his relationships both with Dorothy and with John: he found himself in the first case moving towards marriage with Mary Hutchinson, while in the second his brother John remained elusive and distant. And his desire for some sort of reassuring monolithic psychological structure (in essence the family unit), was shattered by nature's laws: the 'huge crag' of *The Brothers* or the 'grey stone / Of native rock' in Book II of *The Prelude* are both split in two. But the two halves do not form a pair, there is no way of making sense and order out of the division. Life goes on its way, in blind disregard of the patterns that the human mind conjures up to please or comfort itself.

Chapter IX

1802

Friar Barnardine: *Thou hast committed* –
Barabas: *Fornication? But that was in another country;
and besides, the wench is dead.*

(Marlowe, *The Jew of Malta*)

Even as he worked on *Home at Grasmere* during 1800, Wordsworth
found it impossible to sustain either the myth or the dynamic that
underpinned the poem. Setting up house with Dorothy had been
the realisation of a dream, but the dream soon started to go sour.
The sense of the sublime that he felt in the landscapes of the Lake
District found no echo in his own body. He could not sublimate
his instincts. He was not made for the monastic life, and refused
to pretend to himself that he was content to live that way. *Home
at Grasmere* remained in a drawer, unresolved and unpublished –
while he set about looking for a wife.

This, he knew, was going to be tricky. There were two ob-
stacles to overcome, and several problems to deal with. The first
obstacle was Annette. While she had no formal hold over him, he
had recognised the paternity of their daughter; and by the same
token, he did not feel morally free to commit himself in mar-
riage to another woman without her agreement. Obtaining that
consent was next to impossible while England and France were

at war, with communication between the two countries blocked by censorship. The second obstacle was provided by Dorothy's presence. Wordsworth's hypothetical future wife would not only have to accept the idea of 'another woman' in France, but also the daily reality of having yet another woman in the household – and one who enjoyed a privileged relationship with her brother from which she, his wife, might well be excluded. Only a woman with an unusual capacity for tolerance and understanding would be able to handle this cocktail – for even if the principle of un-married sisters living with their siblings was commonly accepted, the degree of intimacy that William and Dorothy knew was quite exceptional.

The problems to be dealt with were more or less significant, depending on how one looked at them. The most obvious was that he was permanently short of money. By this point in his life he had learnt to live on very little, and Dorothy seemed content to do likewise. But a wife might well expect more in material terms than his sister did. He earned next to nothing from his poetry, and had no alternative source of income, no job, no career prospects. He could hardly claim to be a good match. The other difficulty was harder to analyse, but just as troublesome: given the wild and remote place that he had chosen to live in, how likely was it that he would find a bride with whom he felt affinities, and who would be happy to share his life among the mountains?

The prospect was daunting: he needed to disengage himself from one relationship (Annette) and engineer another (i.e. find a wife), as well as realign his relationship with Dorothy without damaging it or hurting her unduly. All at the same time. Any normal man would have thrown up his hands in despair at such a challenge, but within a few months of arriving at Grasmere Wordsworth had embarked on this highly ambitious 'project', determined at whatever cost to see it through. Inevitably the process was riddled with contradictions – (evidence, one might say, of the mess he had got himself into). In May 1800, while he worked on *Home at Grasmere*, which celebrated the pact he and Dorothy had made to live together in pre-lapsarian platonic harmony, he set off with his brother John in a quite different direction – more precisely, into Yorkshire, where they were going to spend three weeks with Mary Hutchinson, and to get to know her better.

We don't know when it was that William had started to think about Mary as a possible wife. They had known each other since they were seven years old, when they had gone to school at Penrith together (Mary was the same age as William, so a year older than Dorothy). The Wordsworth and Hutchinson families were related by marriage, and on friendly terms. Dorothy had kept in touch with Mary during her teens, and this made it easier for William to renew contact with Mary – in 1787 – and to keep the friendship alive over the following decade, despite his nomadic lifestyle. At a certain point friendship drifted into courtship, but it is not clear when, as the good relations that existed between the Wordsworth and Hutchinson families, and the fact that William and Mary had known each other since childhood, meant that either he or she could go and stay at the other's home without eyebrows being raised – (though if Dorothy had not been present as a sort of buffer or mediator, things would have been much more complicated.)

He advanced towards Mary on tiptoe. William had learnt from his affair with Annette the need to control his natural impulsiveness, and no doubt decided to play things quite differently when he started to feel himself attracted sexually towards Mary. And given the difficulties he had to resolve, he needed time. Luckily

Mary was placid and easy-going by nature, and gave him that time. But even so it was awkward, and there were moments when his dealings with all three women – Annette, Dorothy and Mary – became entangled. For example, while he and John were staying with Mary in May 1800, Dorothy wrote to William to say that she had received a letter from Annette. In his reply to her, William made the following request,

> When you are writing to France say all that is affectionate to A. and all that is fatherly to C.[73]

The sentence is revealing in several ways. First, it shows that the censorship of letters between England and France was not total: and that begs the question as to how much correspondence there was between William and Annette during all those years – but unfortunately we have no answer to the question. Then there is the shock of realising that William was asking his sister to write affectionately to his former lover, despite the fact that the two women had never met: essentially William was asking Dorothy to put herself in his place, and speak on his behalf, even to the point of making 'fatherly' remarks to Caroline! One senses that Wordsworth was by now as much out of his depth as he had been in France in the autumn of 1792. Annette represented the past and Mary represented a possible future, while Dorothy was the present. Their conflicting voices, claims and needs must have made a confusion in his head similar to the noise of the waterfall in the Alpine valley that had robbed him of his sleep in Book VI of *The Prelude*, when he lay 'deafened and stunned / By noise of waters' (lines 578-9). He simply could not handle the different languages that were expected of him, and so delegated to Dorothy a responsibility which was his and his only. And this in turn reveals how important her presence was in the whole situation. Dorothy was both a major part of the problem that William had to resolve, and vital to the working out of a solution. She was both his confidante and his trusted secretary – as well as being the natural go-between in his relations with Mary prior to their marriage. Almost nothing survives of the correspondence between Annette and William, but the fragments that we have show that Annette trusted Dorothy, and tried to reach William through her. Dorothy's performance during this period was remarkable: caught up in a mechanism that she could not easily have anticipated and which risked ruining her life and her dreams, she could have sabotaged all that her brother was trying to engineer – or at least made his life a misery. Instead of which she did all she could to help him on his way, using the advantages of her gender to smooth or simplify his relations with the women he was or had been attracted to. And what thanks did she get for her generosity? Well, once married to William Mary responded by living in harmony with Dorothy under the same roof – it is said that there was never a bad word passed between them. Annette expressed her gratitude in her own way, by making it clear to Caroline that Dorothy had done whatever she could to help them. And when Caroline became a mother she called her first daughter Louise Marie Caroline Dorothée. Dorothée is not a common name in French, and in choosing it Caroline was no doubt showing her appreciation for Dorothy's efforts at mediation and for all she had done to keep the fragile link between William and Annette alive.[74]

As for William's response to Dorothy's efforts that was, as we shall see in due course, more complicated.

★ ★ ★

During the summer and autumn of 1800 Wordsworth prepared a second edition of *Lyrical Ballads*, and this kept a sense of momentum going in his work, despite the impossibility of resolving *Home at Grasmere*. However it also soured his relationship with Coleridge, as a result of what one might call the '*Christabel* crisis' of October 1800.[75] From the time they had met in 1795 Coleridge had offered Wordsworth constant moral support and intellectual stimulation. But his own poetic production remained imperfect, often unfinished and lacking overall coherence of vision. That, combined with his increasingly difficult and unpredictable behaviour, wore away at Wordsworth's patience. By the autumn of 1800 Wordsworth had had enough of the partnership. The second edition of *Lyrical Ballads* was almost ready, but Coleridge seemed unable to finish *Christabel*, which was supposed to be his major contribution to the volume. On October 6, Dorothy noted briefly in her journal,

Determined not to print Christabel with the LB.

(the pronoun is missing, but the decision was obviously William's and not hers). William had decided to cut free, at whatever cost. The next day Coleridge left, obviously unhappy – his departure recorded by Dorothy in an almost dismissive manner:

Tuesday. Coleridge went off at 11 o'clock –

He re-appeared just over a fortnight later, on October 22:

Wm composed without much success at the Sheepfold. Coleridge came in to dinner. He had done nothing. We were very merry.

Here Dorothy's comments betray her, especially when linked to her entry for the previous Friday (17th):

> I found Wm at home where he had been almost ever since
> my departure – Coleridge had done nothing for the LB –
> working hard for Stuart.

Dorothy pitches Coleridge's lack of involvement with *Lyrical Ballads* against her brother's commitment to the project (Daniel Stuart was editor of the *Morning Post*, and Coleridge was clearly more occupied writing newspaper articles than composing poems); she also emphasises that this didn't spoil their fun when together. The remarks suggest a small family conspiracy to agree, masking – perhaps – a sense of guilt. As far as the Wordsworths were concerned the right decision had been taken, and everything could go on as before.

But it wasn't like that really. The cost for cutting Coleridge out of the second edition of *Lyrical Ballads* was considerable. The friendship inevitably suffered, and never regained the easy intimacy and complicity that the two men had enjoyed until then. And he lost the chaotic yet fertile input of ideas that Coleridge produced at the drop of a hat. Without Coleridge's constant stimulus and encouragement Wordsworth's self-confidence faltered, and he doubted his ability to be the kind of poet he aspired to being.

In the end he decided to go underground. While maintaining in public that he was working on *The Recluse* – a fiction that he would keep up for the next thirty-five years – he allowed the seeds of *The Prelude* that he had sown in his mind to germinate in secret: three years later he would resume work on the project and bring it to a conclusion in the space of a year and a half. But at the end of 1800, when so many elements of his life were unhappy and unresolved, that great work was no more than a daydream. What was real at the end of 1800 was the crisis, the tensions, the impasse.

Once he had sent the second edition of *Lyrical Ballads* to the printers his writing stalled. Today we see that whole period from 1798 to 1805 as a sort of golden age, in which Wordsworth went from strength to strength, and when, between publishing *Lyrical Ballads* and finishing *The Prelude*, he revolutionised English poetry and established himself as the greatest of the Romantic poets. But Wordsworth's perception of those years – of how he lived them and of the choices and decisions he had to make – would have been radically different. As far as he could see at the end of 1800, his personal life was a mess and he had no clear sense of direction for his work. *Lyrical Ballads* had been reasonably successful, but the ballad form had its limits: it tended to present human lives as motifs woven into a pattern that transcended individual destinies, and this reduced the potential for emotional involvement available to the poet. During the 1790s he had experimented with other genres and techniques as well: short, medium-length and long poems, some of them very personal in tone; he had inserted dramatic monologues inside a poem (*The Brothers*) and had even written a proper play for the theatre (*The Borderers*) – though it was never staged. There was nothing strange about working in such a wide variety of styles – almost all artists do so in their twenties as they seek to establish their voice; but by 1800 he had reached the point where he needed to assess which kind of work offered the most potential for the future. And then there were the autobiographical fragments that he had jotted down during the winter of 1798-9 in Goslar: what was he to do with them? The two-part version of *The Prelude* (reworked and elaborated in Books I and II of the 1805 version of the poem) was completed in the autumn of 1799, but Wordsworth was clearly unsure as to how to develop it further; and while he did work on Book III during 1801, it was only in the spring of 1804 that he returned to the project in a serious and focused way, reorganising it and greatly extending its range and scope. For most of the first three years spent at Grasmere the poem by which he would be best known, and thanks to which he would be forever identified with the Lake District, hibernated. Whether or not it was taking shape in his mind, it was totally invisible to anyone else – even to Dorothy.

To say that 1801 was a fallow year would be an understatement. He produced just one poem in the whole year, *'I travelled among unknown men'*; and this, as we saw in the previous chapter, had more to do with promoting his qualities as a potential husband – and sidelining his brother John – than with literary concerns. By a curious coincidence Dorothy's writing disappeared from sight at the same time. The first of the four notebooks that make up the *Grasmere Journal* tailed off in mid-sentence on December 22, 1800:

> Monday. S & Wm went to Lloyds. Wm dined, it rained very hard when he came home at...

after which there was a gap of ten months, the second note-book resuming on October 10, 1801. Scholars assume that the notebook(s) for the intervening months have disappeared – and maybe they are right. But it could be that Dorothy, in line with her brother, simply stopped writing. The most casual glance at the journals shows that she was not a natural diarist, in the way that someone like Samuel Pepys was: there were times when she felt she had nothing of interest to say, or simply lost interest in the idea of keeping a journal, while at other times she revelled in re-cording even minor events at length and in great detail. Dorothy's journals were as much a projection of her inner world as they were a commentary on the world around her; and it is possible that she, like William, found the situation in the winter of 1800-1 so uninspiring – with *Lyrical Ballads* wrapped up; Coleridge offended; John no longer with them – that they both lost the motivation to write. Similarly, in October 1801 she had good reason to start writing again, for William's life was once more on the move. At the beginning of that month the newspapers announced that a preliminary agreement for a truce with France had been reached at Amiens, making it possible for the English to communicate with and travel to France once again. Wordsworth jumped at the opportunity to settle his unfinished business with Annette: during the following months Dorothy's journal records a regular exchange of letters with Annette (as many written by herself as by William); and it seems that it was at this time (perhaps in November) that William and Mary became engaged.

Dorothy knew that everything would change for her also. Just as William's visit to Mary in May 1800 had stimulated her to begin her Grasmere Journals, so it may be that the treaty of Amiens jolted her into resuming the writing. Her second notebook begins a few days after the announcement of the peace treaty; and from that time on she wrote regularly until January 1803, three months after William's marriage to Mary – at which point her life with William had been relegated to the archives, and she once again lost interest in the idea of recording her life. Apart from occasional journals, in particular during Continental tours or other travels, she never returned to the practice.

At first (in October 1801) the entries were hopelessly meagre – maybe because her writing was rusty. So, for example,

Tuesday 13th. A thorough wet day.
Sunday 18th. I have forgotten.
Monday 26th October. Omitted. They went to Buttermere.
Friday (6th November). (Coleridge) came.

And then suddenly the writing begins to flow. The protagonists of her drama – William, Mary, Coleridge and herself – are all assembled at Dove Cottage. Her future happiness and well-being is out of her control, and she becomes a prey to a thousand anxious thoughts, fears and wishes. She has a reason to write, and finds the words to match her emotions. The entry for November 10 reads,

> Poor C left us & we came home together....C had a sweet day for his ride – every sight & every sound reminded me of him dear dear fellow – of his many walks to us by day & by night – of all dear things. I was melancholy & could not talk, but at last I eased my heart by weeping – nervous blubbering says William. It is not so – O how many, many reasons have I to be anxious for him.

As usual her thoughts are for others: her affection for Coleridge is unchanged, and she worries for William – while he is scornful of her tears. But the passage is also interesting in another way: it resembles the first entry in her *Grasmere Journal*, written on May 14, 1800:

> ...My heart was so full that I could hardly speak to W when I gave him a farewell kiss. I sate a long time upon a stone at the margin of the lake, & after a flood of tears my heart was easier. The lake looked to me I knew not why dull and melancholy...

With her heart once again full, and her soul melancholic, and her mind besieged by worries for those she loves, and her own identity fragile and easily lacerated, Dorothy in the autumn of 1801 is ready to write. But, like her brother, she is never self-indulgent, and the entry for the next day (November 11) has a no-nonsense edge to it that Pepys would have admired:

Wednesday 11th. Baked bread & giblet pie put books in order – mended stockings, put aside dearest C's letters & now at about 7 o'clock we are all sitting by a nice fire – W with his book & a candle & Mary writing to Sara.

The following twelve months would prove critical for William, in more ways than one. The winter was spent in laying the foundations for a new life – gaining Mary's hand and heart, and coming to some sort of understanding with Annette. At the same time he had to reassure Dorothy that she would not lose her 'special relationship' with him once he married. That was easier said than done. It was not that Dorothy did not trust him, but her love for her brother was so absolute that she found it hard to believe that a *ménage à trois* could function, and that she would not be excluded from William's company in a way that made her suffer. With a sort of animal instinct Dorothy's journal registers her fear of being abandoned: the tone and language change, insisting on the exclusive nature of their relationship. So, for example, the entry for February 16, 1802, brings the reader as close as is possible to William's body:

> ...I had persuaded myself not to expect William, I believe because I was afraid of being disappointed – I ironed all day – he came in just at Tea time, had only seen Mary H....his mouth & breath were very cold when he kissed me. We spent a sweet evening – he was better...

From this point on the journal acquires, at moments, the sublimely erotic quality of the *Song of Songs* in the Bible. The next time that he leaves (presumably to visit Mary) on March 4, Dorothy gives herself tasks to do to fill his absence, but is nonetheless unable to contain the intensity of her feelings:

Now for my walk. I *will* be busy. I *will* look well and be well when he comes back to me. O the Darling! here is one of his bitten apples! I can hardly find it in my heart to throw it into the fire — I walked round the two Lakes crossed the stepping stones at Rydale Foot. Sate down where we always sit I was full of thoughts about my darling. Blessings on him.

When they are together the language is no less intense:

After dinner we made a pillow of my shoulder, I read to him & my Beloved slept...

Thus I was going on when I saw the shape of my Beloved in the Road at a little distance (March 17)

...he is now reading Ben Jonson I am going to read German it is about 10 o clock, a quiet night. The fire flutters and the watch ticks I hear nothing else save the Breathings of my Beloved... (March 23)

The tension remains constant during the following weeks, culminating on April 29 in the moment (quoted earlier in the chapter on the 'Lucy' poems) when William and Dorothy lie close to each other in a field. Again, the pulse-beat of the relationship is affirmed by the slightest of sounds:

William heard me breathing and rustling now and then but we both lay still, and unseen by one another — he thought that it would be sweet thus to lie so in the grave, to hear the *peaceful* sounds of the earth and just to know that ones dear friends were near.

By now Dorothy is obliged to console herself with the idea that she and William may be permanently united after death, precisely because it is increasingly obvious that they are soon going to lose their unique relationship. Indeed, when they go for a walk the next day Dorothy stares aimlessly at the view,

> looking at the prospect as in a vision almost I was so resigned to it. (April 30)

What she is resigned to is not the visual 'prospect' of the landscape in front of her, but the prospect of the future – of a life that she must learn to share with Mary, and of a new role that she must accept. After these entries the tone of the journal becomes more subdued, and phrases like 'my Beloved' disappear: Dorothy resigns herself to the inevitable, and until the crisis of William's wedding day she avoids explicit statements of her feelings for her brother. Instead she projects her modest desires and extreme sensibility onto other creatures, with whom she can easily identify. She is particularly responsive to birds, and follows them attentively through the spring and early summer of 1802, as they court, sing, build nests and rear families. Her observations of birds more or less coincide with her acceptance that everything is about to change for ever, and they begin in a simple matter-of-fact way:

> the Owls had not begun to hoot, & the little Birds had given over singing (March 17)

> The Rocks glittered in the sunshine, the crows & the Ravens were busy, & the thrushes & little Birds sang (March 18)

During the next two months she continues to watch – and listen to – the birds around her. Then the focus shifts to nesting and breeding. On May 7 she notes that,

> The sparrows are now fully fledged. The nest is so full that they lie upon one another, they sit quietly in their nest with closed mouths.

This must be the same nest that stimulated Wordsworth to write his poem *The Sparrow's Nest* in these months. For him it triggered off childhood memories of,

> The Sparrow's dwelling, which, hard by
> My Father's House, in wet or dry,
> My Sister Emmeline and I
> > Together visited.   (lines 7–10)

From being 'Emma' in *Home at Grasmere* poor Dorothy is re-christened a second time; but to compensate she is offered a special tribute:

> She gave me eyes, she gave me ears;
> And humble cares, and delicate fears;
> A heart the fountain of sweet tears;
> > And love and thought, and joy.   (lines 17–20)

The same strategy – a reference to their childhood, and the use of 'Emmeline' for 'Dorothy', is used in another poem written that spring, entitled *To a Butterfly*:

> Oh! Pleasant, pleasant were the days,
> The time, when, in our childish plays
> My sister Emmeline and I
> Together chased the Butterfly!   (lines 10–13)

This poem was started on March 14, and 'altered' – so maybe finished – on March 24. The dates correspond to entries in Dorothy's journal, which also notes that the idea for the poem came from the sharing of childhood memories:

> The thought first came upon him as we were talking about
> the pleasure we both always feel at the sight of a Butterfly. I
> told him that I used to chase them a little but that I was afraid

of brushing the dust off their wings, & did not catch them –
He told me how they used to kill all the white ones when he
went to school because they were frenchmen.

(entry for March 14, 1802)[76]

The anecdote provides a good example of the violence that
Wordsworth at times had difficulty in controlling when he was
a boy, and which gave an unforgettable edge to some of the epi-
sodes in Book I of *The Prelude*. In *To a Butterfly* though the kill-
ing of white butterflies is omitted and the violence toned down,
leaving a lightweight reflection on childhood that is not very
exciting. What is of more interest is the unwritten subplot that
accompanies the composition of the poem. For this was exactly
the time when Wordsworth set in motion the plan to settle his
account with Annette and propose marriage to Mary. Dorothy's
journal makes this quite clear with the entry for March 22:

> Mr. Luff came in after dinner and brought us 2 letters from
> Sara H. & one from poor Annette....we resolved to see
> Annette, & that Wm should go to Mary.

There is a theatrical quality to the situation here, with
Dorothy acting as vital intermediary in a sequence of commu-
nications that must inevitably involve an unhappy redefinition
of her relationship with William, and which will lead to a dis-
tance being established between them, where previously there
had been unalloyed complicity and intimacy. For Wordsworth the
challenge was to make it clear to Dorothy that she would not lose
him once he married, and to reassure her that their dialogue was
unique and irreplaceable. *The Sparrow's Nest* and *To a Butterfly* are
part of that strategy: by focusing on shared childhood memories
they emphasise that there is an important part of William's world

that includes Dorothy, and from which Mary will always be excluded.

As part of that strategy he once again renames Dorothy, this time turning 'Emma' into 'Emmeline' – presumably because 'Emmeline' sounds like a childish variation of 'Emma'. 'Emmeline' does also sound curiously close to 'Caroline' (especially with the French pronunciation of Caroline); and Caroline, Wordsworth's daughter in France, was by now nine years old, close to the age of 'Emmeline' in the poems. And Caroline was very much on Wordsworth's mind in March 1802, as he had to prepare for the prospect of meeting her for the first time and, in closing with Annette, of saying goodbye to her at the same time. As always with Wordsworth, past and present were overlaid in his mind, creating strata of meaning that poetry – and perhaps only poetry – could hope to dramatise and articulate, thanks to its potential for almost infinite ambiguity and ambivalence.

And what of the white butterflies, innocent victims of childish cruelty? They may have been written out of the poem, but they provided its starting-point. Wordsworth in 1802 remembered that as a boy he killed all the white butterflies 'because they were frenchmen' – a reminder that the French had been the traditional enemy of the British for centuries. In Wordsworth's case though the antipathy was neutralised by his intellectual curiosity, and then completely overturned by his experiences in France: first his discovery of the beauty of the French landscape (in 1790), and then his love-affair with Annette. Wordsworth in 1792 may well not have remembered that as a boy he wanted to kill anything that made him think of Frenchmen; but in 1802, when the Treaty of Amiens gave him the chance of closing with Annette and starting a new *vie sentimentale* with Mary, the childhood memory was much more present in his mind. For in March 1802 he knew that he had to kill off the French connection in order to move forward. It was a case not of killing 'frenchmen' but of repudiating a French woman and of denying a French girl the right to have a true father. And that weighed heavily on his conscience. The mother would understand that at this point their relationship was fit only for the archives, she could move on and look after herself; but for the little girl, the Caroline who was so like Emmeline, it was different. The author of *We are Seven* and *Anecdote for Fathers* had a fair idea of the complexity of child psychology, and knew that in closing with Annette he would also be aborting all possibility of a dialogue with his daughter – a dialogue that could have enriched his life and which she surely needed.

For William the violence that could not be avoided concerned his severing of the 'French connection'. For Dorothy this was secondary to the irrevocable damage that his marriage to Mary would do to their relationship. She knew that it was unfair to reproach him for wanting to marry, but at the same time it seems she couldn't avoid giving him hints of the distress he caused her. Picking up on his admission of cruelty towards butterflies (made on March 14), the entry in her journal for April 28 offers a similar reflection:

> Wm was in the orchard – I went to him – he worked away at his poem, though he was ill & tired – I happened to say that when I was a Child I would not have pulled a strawberry blossom.

This last comment makes best sense if one imagines that Dorothy came across William absent-mindedly pulling blossom from a strawberry bush as he tried to find the words for his poem, and that Dorothy, in rebuking him for this, tried to make her brother understand that she could never have acted as he had done, in sidelining their relationship. She did not have the capacity for violence that he had; and she had chosen not to marry, and to keep their relationship intact, rather than jeopardise a dialogue and partnership which were vital to her well-being, and provided the structure around which she organised her daily life.

William could not afford to listen to her at these moments; but he must have appreciated her ability to sublimate her feelings, by finding a simple and modest image in the natural world that served to conduct emotions that she could not express openly. Clearly she had read his poetry well, and had learned how to crack the codes it depended on.

★ ★ ★

Everywhere the birds were nesting and laying eggs. Dorothy's attention meanwhile shifted from the sparrow's nest which her brother had chosen to write about to a swallow's nest close to her bedroom window. On June 16 she noted that,

> The swallows come to the sitting-room window as if wishing
> to build but I am afraid they will not have courage for it, but
> I believe they will build at my room window.

This was confirmed three days later, and all seemed to be well – but on June 25 things went badly wrong:

> I looked up at my Swallow's nest & it was gone. It had fallen
> down. Poor little creatures they could not be more distressed
> than I was I went upstairs to look at the Ruins. They lay in a
> large heap upon the window ledge; these Swallows had been
> ten days employed in building this nest, & it seemed to be
> almost finished – I had watched them early in the morning,

in the day many & many a time & in the evenings when it was almost dark I had seen them sitting together side by side in their unfinished nest both morning & night.

Dorothy's capacity for empathy was always generous, but she had a special reason to identify with the poor swallows: she had spent more than two years patiently building her nest in Dove Cottage, only to find that construction now in tatters, blown away in the wind. She had wanted nothing more than to be allowed to sit with her brother 'side by side in their unfinished nest both morning and night', yet she now had to accept that that time of quiet and exclusive intimacy was about to end. As she surveyed the wreckage of the nest, she asked herself if she had the strength and the means to fashion a role and an existence for herself in the changed circumstances – one that would have meaning, and not cause her undue suffering. In this regard she found encouragement a few days later:

> It is now 8 o'clock I will go & see if my swallows are on their nest. Yes! There they are side by side both looking down into the garden. I have been out on purpose to see their faces.
>
> (June 29)

And on July 6 she was able to state that,

> A letter came from Mary in the morning & in the evening one from Coleridge by Fletcher. The swallows have completed their beautiful nest. I baked bread and pies.

Two days later, and it was time for William and Dorothy to set off for France. Dorothy said goodbye to her swallows – and to the life she had enjoyed until that moment – with a pathos worthy of a soprano in an Italian opera:

O beautiful place! – Dear Mary William – The horse is come Friday morning, so I must give over. William is eating his Broth – I must prepare to go – The Swallows I must leave them the well the garden the Roses all – Dear creatures!! they sang last night after I was in bed – seemed to be singing to one another, just before they settled to rest for the night. Well I must go – Farewell. – – (July 8)

As a postscript to this sequence, it is worth recalling the comment made by Dorothy to her friend Catherine Clarkson in March 1806, and quoted in the previous chapter: 'We are crammed into our little nest edge-full.' Dorothy here was referring once again to Dove Cottage, but this time the nest is a human one, containing four adults and two children. What is significant is that the cottage / nest image remained valid for Dorothy despite all the upheavals. She was able to overcome the distress at seeing her cosy 'brother-sister' nest destroyed and, with time, could imagine herself as part of a larger nest – in which she could only be one among many, but, crucially, from which she was not excluded. Her ability to adapt and to embrace was remarkable, and it was thanks to this generosity of spirit that she was able to make the most difficult of transitions, and carry on living in the house after William and Mary's marriage.

★ ★ ★

The gods help those who help themselves. Wordsworth's determination to give a new direction to his life, without having any kind of financial security to underwrite his desires, was rewarded just when it mattered most. For it was in May 1802, with his trip to France planned and marriage on the horizon, that Lord Lonsdale died. A month later his heir Sir William Lowther announced his readiness to honour all debts incurred by Lord Lonsdale. William's share (once repaid) meant that he would feel moderately comfortable for the first time in his life, and made it much easier for him to look forward to married life and hopefully start a family. And so in July he and Dorothy set out on the decisive journey. They went first to see Mary in Yorkshire, then travelled south to London and Dover. They crossed the Channel to Calais, spent a month there with Annette and Caroline, then made the long journey back to Yorkshire, where William and Mary were married on October 4. They then returned, together with Dorothy, to Grasmere.

All in all the journey lasted three months, and must have been as demanding emotionally as it was physically. William, who during it not only had to manage the intimate relationships he had with three different women – (Dorothy, Mary, and Annette) – but was also confronted by his daughter for the first time in his life, helped himself through the experience by composing sonnets on political themes, while maintaining a silence worthy of his brother John on the subjects closest to his heart. For her part Dorothy tried to deal with her emotions by turning the trip to France and its sequel into a travel narrative. Putting aside the breathless whispered thoughts that she had noted down just before leaving Grasmere, she established a deliberate distance from herself by launching into a matter-of-fact account of the journey:

> On Friday morning, July 9th William & I set forward to Keswick on our road to Gallow Hill – we had a pleasant ride though the day was showery.

For the next three months she did her best to maintain this attitude and this style – only twice relapsing into the diary mode, and otherwise offering a seamless narrative that could have been written at any suitable moment. Clearly she did not trust herself to articulate her emotions on a day-to-day basis. Even so, when she reached the wedding-day, her self-discipline cracked, and the narrative with it. She started out in the no-nonsense manner she had decided to adopt, but at the crucial moment could not sustain the fiction:

> On Monday 4th October 1802, my Brother William was married to Mary Hutchinson. I slept a good deal of the night & rose fresh & well in the morning – at a little after 8 o clock I saw them go down the avenue to the Church. William had parted from me up stairs. I gave him the wedding ring – with how deep a blessing! I took it from my forefinger where I had worn it the whole of the night before – he slipped it again onto my finger and blessed me fervently. When they were absent my dear little Sara prepared the breakfast. I kept myself as quiet as I could, but when I saw the two men running up the walk, coming to tell us it was over, I could stand it no longer & threw myself on the bed where I lay in stillness, neither hearing or seeing any thing, till Sara came upstairs to me & said 'They are coming'. This forced me from the bed where I lay & I moved I knew not how straight forward, faster than my strength could carry me till I met my beloved William & fell upon his bosom.

For Dorothy William's day of happiness was the climax to her private tragedy (the phrase, 'coming to tell us it was over' is particularly eloquent, as it suggests the end of a period of suffering, such as death after a long illness), and her brief breakdown is pitiful but not surprising, given the intensity of her character and of her love for William. But just as feelings reached a climax, so did their opposite. The censorship that had frustrated correpondence between William and Annette for almost a decade, and the self-censorship that Wordsworth had developed as a way of regulating his own impulses and steering his thoughts in a direction that was socially acceptable, intervened dramatically to efface the trace of any improper act or feeling between brother and sister. The sentence, 'I gave him the wedding ring.... and blessed me fervently.' was heavily crossed out – and so successfully that even with the help of infra-red photography it is not possible to be sure what all the original words were: it may be that the phrase 'and blessed me fervently' should read, 'as I blessed the ring softly'. We do not know who crossed out this sentence, nor when, but the motivation for doing so is clear. That Dorothy should wear her brother's wedding ring on the night before his wedding, and that he should bless it – or her – as he slipped it on her finger again after she had removed it: all this raised too many uncomfortable questions about the nature of their relationship. Just as memories of Annette and Caroline had to be pigeonholed and hopefully forgotten, and William's marriage to his 'longtime sweetheart' elevated to the order of a natural event, a coming to fruition of seeds sown in innocent childhood, so his relationship with Dorothy needed to be brought into line. Whether or not it was Dorothy, or William, or some other member of the family, who was responsible for the censorship of Dorothy's account is unimportant: what matters is that the heavy black lines of ink stand as evidence of a need to keep intimate relationships private, and to present to others an image that corresponded to public expectations.[77]

From this time on Dorothy's instincts were to be bridled and harnessed, and her vision of the future framed by blinkers. William, though, exulted at his newfound liberty. The pent-up energy of his body was finally released, and his wife became pregnant before the echo of the wedding bells had died away.[78]

Chapter X

Masterclass

The entry in Dorothy's journal for May 21, 1802, reads:

> A very warm gentle morning – a little rain. Wm wrote two
> sonnets on Buonaparte after I had read Milton's sonnets to
> him.

This innocuous sentence conceals what would turn out to
be one of the most significant turning-points in Wordsworth's
career. For after trying his hand on the subject of Napoleon,
Wordsworth decided that the sonnet suited him as a form; and, in
this year of important decisions and profound changes, he adopt-
ed the genre without a moment's hesitation, at the same time
shelving his allegiance to the ballad form. For the rest of his life
he wrote sonnets regularly, and in 1838 gathered them together
in a single volume. By the time he died in 1850 he had published
489 of them – far more than any other major English poet, and
considerably more even than Petrarch, who had been the first
to master the form. For his contemporaries, who had no way of
getting to know *The Prelude*,[79] Wordsworth was to a large extent
defined by his ballads and his sonnets – indeed it is hard to exag-
gerate the importance of these fourteen-liners to him and to the
way he thought of himself as a poet.

The decision in 1802 to focus on the sonnet – it represented about ninety percent of his poetic output that year – was, super-ficially at least, a curious one. As a poetic form it was almost as traditional as the ballad, and hardly seemed to correspond to the state of mind of a thirty-two year old poet whose thoughts were concerned with the future: with marriage, starting a family, and making himself known. Moreover, while the ballad form had al-ways been linked to popular culture, the sonnet was traditionally associated with aristocratic manners and courtly love. It was the form of forms, constraining the heart and soul in a corset of rhythms, rhymes and patterns which celebrated the artificiality of art: what could such a form offer a penniless poet living in a cottage in the depths of rural Westmorland, whose concern had always been to express himself honestly and simply, and to use a language that matched the reality experienced by the people he lived among?

With hindsight we might see his adoption of the sonnet form as the first sign of that move towards conservatism for which Wordsworth became famous in middle age, but at the time his motivation was essentially practical. His work was hampered by two habitual tendencies: the first was that he almost always wrote about a subject or event long after the moment or time of expe-riencing it, and the second was his mania for correcting what he had written. Together these practices not only slowed down the process of composition, to a point where completion and even-tual publication of a poem became as mirages shimmering in the desert air, but actually threatened to jeopardise the whole creative process – by crippling the impulse of spontaneity and making every thought, idea and feeling susceptible to endless revision.

Resolution and Independence, which Wordsworth was working on when he began experimenting with the sonnet form, shows the kind of difficulties he had. The poem was based on a meeting with an old leech gatherer, during a walk that he and Dorothy had made on October 3, 1800.[80] *The Leech Gatherer* duly became the working title for the poem, when, one and a half years later, on May 4, 1802, Dorothy recorded in her journal that,

> I wrote the Leech Gatherer for him which he had begun the night before & of which he wrote several stanzas in bed this Monday morning.

The entry for May 7 was promising:

> William had slept uncommonly well so, feeling himself strong, he fell to work at the Leech gatherer – he wrote hard at it till dinner time, then he gave over tired to death – he had finished the poem.

However two days later it was clear that the end was not yet in sight: the entry for May 9 says that,

> William worked at the Leech-gatherer almost incessantly from morning till tea-time.

On June 14 Dorothy noted that William

> wrote to Mary & Sara [Hutchinson] about the Leech-Gatherer

and that on July 4

> Wm finished the Leech gatherer today.

Even this was not the end of the matter, for after showing the poem to friends such as Coleridge, and hearing their comments, Wordsworth made revisions to it, changed the title significantly – and eventually published it in 1807, seven years after the original meeting with the old man on the moor.

For someone who had as much difficulty in finishing his

poems as Wordsworth did, the sonnet had two significant advantages: it was short, and it was technically very demanding. The need to conform to strict metric rules and to obey well-defined rhyming patterns meant that there was less chance of wasting time in endlessly trying out alternatives to what had already been committed to paper. Once a sonnet had satisfied the requirements of its form there was very little likelihood of the poet changing it at all: for each phrase and each thought interlocked with another in a unique combination, and to change one or two phrases involved undoing almost the entire puzzle and starting again from scratch.

Being short and compact the sonnet was, one might say, easily transportable – and this may well have been the decisive factor in Wordsworth's decision to commit himself wholeheartedly to writing sonnets. It was the perfect form for a poet who found it easiest to compose while walking. It was relatively simple to hold fourteen lines in one's head, and there was pleasure in teasing out the rhymes while striding up and down the garden path or trampling through the heather. With practice it should become possible to 'do' a sonnet during the course of a single long walk, and once 'done' there would probably be no need to retouch it. And of course the sonnet could prove quite marketable, as it was always the same length, and therefore could be proposed to a publisher as a recognised unit of writing (two sonnets fitted neatly onto one page of a book or magazine). And for the same reason it could prove itself a steady source of income, as each sonnet could be priced at a certain amount, with no room for disagreement over length, style or genre. From being the preferred form of the lovesick courtiers of Elizabethan London the sonnet could perfectly well metamorphose itself into an eminently marketable product for the reading classes of early nineteenth-century England.

And so it was that Wordsworth began the first of his mature sonnets (he had written two already when he was in his teens) on May 21, 1802, when he had come to an impasse in his work on *The Leech Gatherer*. While that poem seemed to move even slower than either the leeches themselves or the old man who collected them, he managed to complete two sonnets in the course of a single day: one of these he later discarded, the other he offered to *The Morning Post* newspaper, which published it in September of that year.

A new phase of the poet's career had begun. During the summer and autumn of 1802 Wordsworth concentrated almost exclusively on writing sonnets, mostly on themes relating to national identity and politics. The subjects were varied, ranging from the revolt in Haiti against French colonial rule and slavery, to the death of the Venetian Republic, but the thread that ran through them all was the need to fight political oppression, and to resist the brainwashing of the individual mind that tyranny depends on to be effective. And once that theme becomes apparent, an interesting coherence in Wordsworth's thought-process also becomes clear, which weaves and ties his sonnets into the body of his other work. The definitive title of the poem Wordsworth was struggling with in the early summer of 1802, *Resolution and Independence*, sounds very much like *Revolution and Independence* – which could have served as a group-heading for the sonnets written between 1802 and 1806. In other words, poems like 'Resolution and Independence', which focus on individual destinies, are the indispensable counterparts to the sonnets which try to encapsulate general political and social truths, articulating them in more abstract form.

That said, the difference between the 's' and the 'v' – between 'resolution' and 'revolution' – is crucial. When tested by contemporary events Wordsworth's republican convictions, and his belief that revolution led to social progress, buckled. First the Terror in France, and then the way Napoleon's career evolved, led him to feel that there was a profound dichotomy between individual lives and the development of a society: more specifically, social progress was not something to be counted on, and therefore individuals needed to base their lives on personal values, and expect nothing from governments. *Resolution and Independence*, stark and reductive as a text by Samuel Beckett, takes this thought to its pitiless conclusion even as the 1802 sonnets sound a battle-charge in the name of liberty and the general good. The debate remained wide open in the poet's mind; time would tell which side he would come down on.

★ ★ ★

In 1802 Wordsworth wrote sonnets. But almost as significant as the choice of the sonnet form is the fact that many of these poems have dates included in the titles – or indeed the date is the only title that we have. For the first time in his career Wordsworth sought to fix a poetic statement in a precise moment of time. In some cases he gave only the year, in others the month also; and occasionally, especially with the sonnets written during the trip to France, he specified the day as well.

Given that a number of these poems are concerned with the ongoing political conflict between England and France, it may be that he wanted to make it clear at what particular moment he had expressed a particular thought or opinion about the relations between the two countries. But as some of the dated poems are personal in tone, and have no reference to political or historical events, that explanation is not in itself sufficient. It seems rather

that Wordsworth was trying to free himself from his cloying re-
lationship to the past – a bond that had structured and coloured
his vision of life since his late teens – and was doing his utmost
to place himself fair and square in the present tense, and to look
at and write about the world without the help (and hindrance)
of a powerful memory. In this the trip to Calais was a catalyst, for
the agreement he came to with Annette freed him from the sense
of moral obligation to her that had weighed on him for a whole
decade, and simultaneously allowed him to project himself into
the future – by clearing the way for his marriage to Mary and the
possibility of starting a (legitimate) family.

He wanted to live in the here and now. Having discovered
that the sonnet form enabled him to compose quickly, he began
to write in a direct and immediate manner. Thoughts came
cleanly out of specific situations, were articulated, formulated
and resolved according to the demands of the sonnet form – and
that was that. One poem was finished, and another was hatched.
For a season his poetry had a photographic quality: concise,
compact and situated firmly in the present – like the sketches
that Turner was busily making of the French and Swiss landscapes
at exactly the same time (the painter was also taking advantage
of the Peace of Amiens to make a journey to Europe). And for
a season his poetry was on almost the same wavelength as the
prose of his sister who accompanied him on this important trip
to Calais. His poems follow one another almost as regularly as
her journal entries, and the tone and subject matter are often
similar…

It is tempting to read in all this a moment of literary com-
plicity to match the personal intimacy that brother and sister
enjoyed: as if William moved closer to Dorothy during this cru-
cial and intensely lived experience in France, out of sympathy

for and gratitude towards his sister. But that would have been out of character. Wordsworth traced his literary trajectory on his own and according to his own goals and hidden agenda, and – as Coleridge learned to his cost – took no one else into account in the process. Indeed, while he addressed Dorothy as 'Dear fellow traveller!' and 'dear Companion' in the sonnet *Composed in the Valley, near Dover – On The Day of Landing*, nonetheless the feelings he expressed in the poem contradict the – supposedly shared – sentiments that Dorothy recorded in her journal on the same occasion. She remembered that

> We both bathed and sate upon the Dover Cliffs & looked
> upon France with many a melancholy & tender thought.

William, whose mind was set on marriage and whose poems at this time were scrupulously fashioned to demonstrate to his fiancée where his heart and loyalties lay, would have none of Dorothy's nostalgic tenderness. If he felt any such emotions, he certainly would not commit them to print. In his sonnet he exulted that, as he walked in the countryside near Dover, everything he saw or heard was English, and decided that,

> 'tis joy enough and pride
> For one hour's perfect bliss, to tread the grass
> Of England once again.

Not only was his attitude towards the French experience at variance with Dorothy's, but he also used the evening walks that they took together on the beach at Calais to establish a certain distance between himself and his sister, and to nudge her towards a new role in his life – one that would fit the new circumstances of his forthcoming marriage. For anyone accustomed to decoding Wordsworth's poetry – as Dorothy was well able to do after a decade of reading between the lines in order to understand the drift of her brother's mind – there was an allusion to her in

> It is a beauteous evening, calm and free,
> The holy time is quiet as a Nun[81]

Wordsworth had never used imagery from monastic life before this poem, and the comparison of the landscape to a nun's state of mind was striking. For Dorothy, tense and anxious in the run-up to her brother's marriage, and knowing that at this point she would never find a husband for herself, the image sounded as a reminder of her destiny, and as a tacit urging to be true to her calling as a faithful and undemanding companion, scribe, cook, housekeeper and dutiful maiden aunt. In recent years William had evoked his sister's passionate (and uncontrollable) character, admiring (in *Tintern Abbey*, written in 1798)

> the shooting lights
> Of thy wild eyes

and attributing to her, in the series of poems on the naming of places, a 'wild place' where a waterfall coursed freely among rocks and trees. But in August 1802 he had to reassure himself that this free spirit had in a certain sense been tamed – otherwise how would it be possible for her to live happily with Mary and himself? By evoking the image of a nun he no doubt hoped to inspire a certain serenity in his sister; and in another sonnet composed in the following months he reiterated the message, reminding her, even as she gave up her bedroom to the newly wedded couple and moved into a smaller room, that

> Nuns fret not at their Convent's narrow room

The evening walks that inspired these sonnets inevitably

recalled the long poem *An Evening Walk* published in 1793. But much had changed since that poem, which William had dedicated to Dorothy and in which he playfully evoked the image of a farmyard cock and his 'sister-wives'. For years Dorothy had assumed the role of wife to her brother; but that make-believe world had proved to be unsustainable, and the time had come for her now to bring her passions and her personal aspirations under control, and to acquire an inner spiritual freedom through the renunciation of passing desires and distractions.

It is interesting that at one of the most intense moments of her difficult life Dorothy retreated from the near-present tense in her journal, and instead waited until she had enough of a distance from the events she was relating to be able to write about them faithfully, that's to say with a sense of measure and proportion that would give the right degree of importance to the different elements in the story. During these crucial months she adopted her brother's way of writing about experience. He meanwhile for exactly the same period of time composed his poems as if he was writing a journal. He stepped into her shoes and she into his. What better example of their complicity could there be?

At the same time the way they were expressing themselves had never been so different. While Dorothy gave way in secret to the outpourings of her heart and soul, William was packaging his meditations into neat fourteen-liners, all metrically precise and ready for publication. His themes were duty, patriotism and politics; she wept over the loss of an exclusive relationship that had been priceless to her.

★ ★ ★

In conversation with Isabella Fenwick in 1845, Wordsworth

elaborated on his preferences where the sonnet was concerned. Recalling the day in 1802 when Dorothy read two of Milton's sonnets to him, he commented:

> I had long been well acquainted with them, but I was particularly struck on that occasion by the dignified simplicity and majestic harmony that runs through most of them – in character so totally different from the Italian, and still more so from Shakespeare's fine Sonnets.

Wordsworth's unmitigated admiration for Milton clouds his judgement here. Of the nineteen sonnets that Milton produced – a fraction of the number composed by either Shakespeare, Petrarch or Wordsworth – some are clearly derivative, owing a lot either to Shakespeare or to the Italian tradition (indeed five of them are even written in Italian). Maybe the sonnets that Dorothy read to William were two of the three that are most often anthologised – *'Avenge O Lord thy slaughtered saints, whose bones'*, *'When I consider how my light is spent'*, or *'Methought I saw my late espousèd saint'*, all of which are truly original in spirit and speak with a voice that is uniquely Milton's. Nonetheless, when one thinks of some of the best known of Shakespeare's sonnets, such as, *'They that have pow'r to hurt and will do none'*, or, *'Let me not to the marriage of true minds'* it is hard not to feel they have precisely the qualities of 'dignified simplicity and majestic harmony' that Wordsworth singles out for praise in Milton alone.

So was Wordsworth merely expressing his personal taste, and masking it in literary criticism? Maybe a little technical analysis will help us to understand what he was getting at. There were two traditions for the sonnet form, one that had been mastered by Petrarch and which formed the Italian tradition, and the other which has been defined as the Shakespearian sonnet. In both cases the poem is always fourteen lines long, but the rhyme schemes are quite different, and this in turn creates different emphases in the movement of the thought and the structure of the argument. The Petrarchan sonnet is composed of eight lines followed by six: the rhyme scheme in the first eight lines seldom varies, and usually goes, *'abba abba'*. After eight lines there is usually a turn in the thought, and the rhyme scheme changes completely: for the last six lines many variations are allowed (for example, *'cde ced'*, *'cdc dee'*, *'cde cde'*) – in other words the poet has as much freedom in the second part of the sonnets as he has constraints in the first part.[82] So the argument proposed in the first part of the sonnet can be developed in a number of ways during the second part. By contrast the Shakespearian sonnet was structured with three quatrains followed by two lines of conclusion, and the rhyme scheme was always the same, namely, *'abab cdcd efef gg'*. The lack of variations in the rhyme scheme made the form extremely demanding, and inevitably constricted the development of thought and feeling. The concluding two lines were conjured up on their own, either to summarise the argument that had preceded them, or to refute it. The Shakespearian sonnet was art married to artifice. In some ways it resembled the way a lawyer pleads in court: twelve lines of formal and controlled exposition of the case, followed by two lines of conclusion that wrap up the argument and (hopefully) convince the jury.

Milton's sonnets were composed according to the Petrarchan model, and that was the tradition that Wordsworth decided to follow. Not merely out of loyalty to Milton, but because the Petrarchan scheme meant that the poem remained open-ended, the argument could go this way or that as it progressed, new rhymes could be imagined and therefore new words drafted in. For Wordsworth, who related the poetry he composed to the movement of his body through space as he walked, or danced, or rowed a boat, or skated, or rode a horse, it was vitally important to maintain a sense of freedom within the form he was using. He found the tension between the constraints and the freedom of the Petrarchan sonnet exhilarating. While he respected the basic principle of the Petrarchan model, he also improvised a lot – indeed, one could say that the rule was to improvise and not to repeat (in itself a discipline!). The overall effect is of poems conceived of as variations on a theme – the theme being the Petrarchan model; and Wordsworth displays in this exercise a virtuosity worthy of Bach. On a purely artistic level, one can imagine the pleasure he had in meeting the challenge he had given himself. After years of writing poems that were largely organised around a narrative, he was now exploring the musical qualities of the English language and training his ear in a new way.

Wordsworth took to writing sonnets in a big way – a bit like Coleridge took to opium. Producing fourteen-liners at regular intervals was a harmless habit, with none of the side effects of drug addiction (though anyone who has waded through Wordsworth's 132 *Ecclesiastical Sonnets* might wish he'd tried opium instead). Certainly there was no shortage of criticism for the amount of time he devoted to writing sonnets, and Wordsworth himself was always ready to admit that his choice was difficult to defend: in April 1822, for example, he tacitly admitted in a letter to Walter Savage Landor that the time spent writing sonnets had been at the expense of other more important projects:

> I have filled up many a moment in writing Sonnets, which, if I had never fallen into the practice, might easily have been better employed. *The Excursion* is proud of your approbation. _The Recluse_ has had a long sleep, save in my thoughts.
>
> (April 20, 1822)

The women in the Wordsworth household, while maintaining a show of respect for everything the Poet did, came with time to despair of the abundance of sonnets which, like some strange weed, threatened to take over the beautiful garden of the Poet's Mind. In a letter to to her cousin in 1819 Sara Hutchinson, Mary's sister, wrote,

> William intends to publish a batch of small poems immediately ... then <u>he says</u> he will never trouble himself with anything more but *The Recluse*. (December 19, 1819)

Two years later Dorothy made a similar observation in a letter to Catherine Clarkson:

> William is quite well, and very busy, though he has not looked at *The Recluse* or the poem on his own life; & this disturbs us. After fifty years of age there is no time to spare, & unfinished works should not, if it be possible, be left behind....William is at present composing a series ofSonnets on a subject which I am sure you would never divine – the Church of England... In some of the sonnets he has, I think, been most successful.
>
> (March 27, 1821)

By 1829 however she was beginning to lose patience with his well-encrusted habits, and her language resembled that of Sara in her letter of 1819:

> He does intend to fall to the '*Recluse*' being seriously impressed with the faith that very soon it must be too late (His next Birth day will be his 6oth) – but, in the mean time he has been busy with other less important matters – polishing the small poems he wrote last year – and actually he has written another <u>Sonnet</u>! This we were not glad of – fearing it might be but the beginning as heretofore, of a <u>Batch</u>: he

has, however, promised that he will write no more…

(letter to John Wordsworth, November 18, 1829)

By 1833 Wordsworth's daughter Dora, now twenty-nine years old, joined the chorus (and added her mother's voice for good measure):

Father has written several 100 lines this spring but only 'tiresome small Poems' as Mother calls them who is vexed she cannot get him set down to his long work. I don't believe the Recluse will ever be finished…

(letter to Edward Quillinan, May 17, 1833)

In the face of all this nagging and reproachful cajoling from the women he shared his life with, Wordsworth did the only thing that any self-respecting man could do, and wrote more sonnets. And just to make the point clear that he had no intention of changing his habits he wrote a sonnet in defence of sonnets – 'Scorn not the Sonnet', probably written during the 1820s, and published in 1827. By this time the big project that the ladies of the household wanted him to focus on was in reality dead, and he had no scruples in concentrating on producing small pieces instead. Nonetheless the discourse about 'large and small'– according to which great poetry must by definition be long – was not one that Wordsworth found easy to ignore. It was a major part of the tradition in which he wanted to situate himself, and he was convinced that his vision could never stand comparison with that of a poet like Milton unless he were to write at length on a great theme.

The debate gave him sleepless nights for many years; and it is to Wordsworth's credit that he obeyed his instincts and wrote the poems that came to him more naturally, rather than follow a literary creed that he found artificial. And there was another aspect

to his predilection for 'small poems' (whether 'tiresome' or not),
and this had to do with his interest in all that was inconspicuous
and easily overlooked in nature. *Lyrical Ballads* had generally dealt
with people whose lives were modest and unassuming, but in the
'Lucy' poems this fact was more clearly articulated, particularly
in the couplet from *Song* (of 1799) in which Lucy was likened to
a wild flower:

> A Violet by a mossy stone
> Half-hidden from the eye!

In 1802, exactly at the time when he started writing sonnets,
Wordsworth returned to the thought implied by this couplet –
that even the smallest and least glamorous of nature's creations
are worthy of attention – and began writing poems about flow-
ers, birds and insects. Between March and July of that year he
composed four poems about birds (*To a Sky-Lark*; *The Sparrow's
Nest*; *The Green Linnet*; *To The Cuckoo*); two poems about butter-
flies; and four poems about flowers – two for the celandine, and
two for the daisy. It was rather as if the naturalist Gilbert White
had turned poet, and was offering tributes to all the fauna and
flora that he studied. And somewhat naturally the flowers, hardy
annuals as they were, resurfaced a year or two later. Another poem
on the celandine was written between 1803 and 1804, while the
humble daisy was called on twice in 1805 to evoke the spirit of
John Wordsworth, who had drowned that February. In the first
poem, *To the Daisy*, the flower was celebrated because John liked
daisies and Wordsworth imagined them gradually spreading to
decorate his brother's grave. The second poem, '*I only looked for
pain and grief*', reverted to the kind of analogy used for Lucy and
the violet, with Wordsworth affirming that the daisy could stand
for John –

this unknown Flower,
Affecting type of Him I mourn!   (lines 35-6)

on the grounds that John's character was as unassuming as the
daisy's:

He would have loved thy modest grace,
Meek flower!   (lines 81-2)

Typically with Wordsworth this rather fanciful association was
in fact underpinned by a sound biographical detail. In a letter of
August 7, 1805, William wrote that the poem *To The Daisy* 'was
written in remembrance of a beautiful letter of my Brother John'.
In that letter, written in 1801 when he had gone on shore from
his ship one afternoon for a walk, John had noted that,

the evening Primroses are beautiful – and the daisies after
sunset are like little *white* stars upon the dark green fields'.[83]

This feeling for all aspects of the natural world, whether great
or small, was common to William, Dorothy, and John, and no
doubt imbued the walks they took together with a special qual-
ity. Unsurprisingly though, the thought that God's presence is
revealed equally throughout His creation was lost on the general
public. When they were published in 1807 the poems on birds,
butterflies and flowers were looked down on as slight, and peri-
pheral to the true purpose of poetry: Byron spoke of 'the most
commonplace ideas' and 'puerile' language, while Frances Jeffrey,
writing in the Edinburgh Review, dismissed *The Small Celandine*
as 'a piece of namby-pamby...'. Later on the Victorians would
appreciate such poems, as the sort you could copy into an album,
placed next to a dried and pressed specimen of the same flower.
But that had nothing to do with Wordsworth's restless thinking,

which worried over the hierarchies within cultures which spec-
ified that certain subjects were intrinsically more worthy of at-
tention than others (rather in the way that poor people were
considered 'simple', and their lives less interesting and complex
than those of the middle and upper classes). Had he wanted to,
Wordsworth could have pointed to a Miltonic precedent in the
wonderful celebration of the birds, animals and plants of the
Garden of Eden in Book IV of *Paradise Lost*. And in his own
way Wordsworth achieved at moments a synthesis between the
humble lives of animals, and the noble and uplifting themes that
were considered the proper stuff of poetry. There is for example
the study of the shepherd and his dog in Book VIII of *The Prelude*
(lines 81-119) which stresses the interdependence of man and
dog, and sets them in a magical mountain landscape of swirling
mists – (the world beneath, where the shepherd is) – and autumn
sunshine (the world above, where the dog is leading the flock
to). Or there is the famous passage in Book XII of *The Prelude*,
narrating the ascent of Snowdon, which moves with cinematic
ease from the 'small adventure' of the guide's dog discovering a
hedgehog to the 'immense' panorama visible from the summit.
Nonetheless the tension between these two scales – between on
the one hand all that is small / short / modest, and on the other
all that is great / long / heroic – was very difficult to resolve; and
Wordsworth found it very hard to reconcile the expectations of
his readers with the values that were naturally his.

★ ★ ★

Milton's sonnets inspired Wordsworth to start working in the gen-
re, and that in turn offered him the opportunity to acknowledge
his debt to Milton, and to measure himself against the master.

Two of the sonnets of 1802 (*'Great Men have been among us'* and *'It is not to be thought of that the Flood'*) refer admiringly to Milton, while another sonnet, *London, 1802*, is addressed to him,

> Milton! Thou should'st be living at this hour:
> England has need of thee:

and elaborates on the qualities in Milton that Wordsworth would like to emulate. Meanwhile in Book I of *The Prelude* he confessed (in line 180) that he would have liked to treat a theme that had tempted Milton; and in Book V offered another tribute to his great masters,

> Shakespeare, or Milton, labourers divine! (line 165)

Wordsworth made no secret of his desire to follow in Milton's footsteps, and Milton haunts the whole of Wordsworth's oeuvre like a benevolent ghost. The challenge for Wordsworth was to remain true to the spirit of Milton without imitating him; and on the whole he was successful – thanks in part to the force of his own character, and his dislike of compromise. Milton's poetry was a vital reference-point, a landmark from which Wordsworth could take his bearings – but Wordsworth had to make the journey on his own. Still, his knowledge of Milton was so complete, and so well absorbed into his mind, that he could integrate a phrase or an idea from Milton into his poetry without disturbing the flow of his own thoughts. And then there were the private jokes he shared with Milton, which no one was invited to decode or understand. So, for example, he offered in Books IX and X of *The Prelude* a narrative to match Books IX and X of *Paradise Lost*.

Overleaf: Wordsworth, manuscript of the 'Ascent of Snowdon' passage from The Prelude. *Transcribed by Dorothy, and heavily revised by William*

& throughout the whole distance of the west
not so the Æthereal vault — encroachment none
was there, save only that the inferior stars
had disappear'd before the full-orb'd Moon
that front them sovere

and as we stood
hisher

for the press
before that silent shore   a Chasm appeared
(at distance not the thousand part of a mile)

fuller & blue, a fracture in the very

+ In plenitude of solitary state?
And while we stood, the hoary mist
Touching, we saw, at distance from the
                                        our feet
                        measure   shore
Not twice the distance of an arrow's
                                        flight
A dark blue chasm a fracture &c

I found myself - a billowy sea of mist
the meek and silent rested at my feet

over my head, and on the shore

myself of a huge sea of mist

meek and silent rested at my feet.

A hundred hills their dusky backs upheaved

All over this still Ocean, and beyond
against the usual dominion of Heaven;
the far beyond ____ the Solid vapours stretch'd
in headlands, tongues, and promontory shapes
Into the Atlantic

To dwindle and give up its majesty

Usurp'd upon as far as sight could reach.
The Moon look'd down upon this & fleece

X In single glory, and we ____ the mist

breach in the vapour,

A deep and gloomy breathing place thro' which
Mounted the roar of waters, torrents, streams
Innumerable, roaring with one voice

The universal spectacle ____ was shaped
____ for admiration and delight

____ that breach
Through which the homeless voice of waters
That dark deep thoroughfare had Nature lodged
The Soul, the Imagination of the whole.

In Milton's poem, Books IX and X are concerned with original sin and its consequences. Wordsworth responded to this by dedicating Books IX and X of his poem to his time in France. Book IX relates, through the story of Julia and Vaudracour, his own eating of the Tree of Knowledge, and his fall from grace – inevitable, as Caroline was conceived outside of marriage. The match of narratives is not casual: it is as a result of the original sin of Adam and Eve that Wordsworth inherits – genetically, as it were – a character that is sinful, and which prompts him to flout the moral code he was brought up on, to give way to sexual impulses that he ought to control, and to father an illegitimate child; while Book X extends this play of ideas by narrating the fall from grace of the French nation, through the Terror and the betrayal of the ideals of the Revolution.

History helped to consolidate the parallels between the two poems: both were written in the aftermath of revolutions in which the authors had been involved in one way or another, and which determined their political and social thinking for the rest of their lives. Superficially, though, it is the differences in the responses of the poets to these great historical events that is more striking than the similarities. Milton was in his mid-thirties when the Civil War began, while Wordsworth was just nineteen when the Bastille fell. Milton played an active role in Cromwell's government (as his Latin Secretary),[84] assumed all the consequences of that choice, and never wavered from his commitment to the republican cause, even after the restoration of the monarchy. Wordsworth on the other hand was caught up in the turmoil of the French Revolution quite unintentionally, became hopelessly entangled in the situation by virtue of the daughter he fathered in France, and then backed away as far as he could, gradually modifying his political position until he reached a point almost opposite to the one he had started at. It is almost as if Wordsworth repeated as farce what Milton lived through as tragedy; indeed Wordsworth was acutely aware of the huge discrepancy between Milton's ability to navigate through the most turbulent period of English history, and his own tendency to flounder when finding himself in stormy seas. Wordsworth was not proud of his record in the French Revolution, and hid the most embarrassing part of it from sight. For the rest, he simply attributed his own change of heart to the way the French had acted after 1792, and left it at that. But deep down he knew that, once again, he had failed when measuring himself against Milton – and this sense of inadequacy may have contributed to his decision not to publish *The Prelude*.

At another level, however, these historical earthquakes – the English Civil War and the French Revolution – nourished the imagination of each of the two poets in remarkably similar ways: for in both cases they had believed in the potential of the revolution and had then seen it fail; and they had begun writing the poem which referred (directly or indirectly) to the events they had witnessed some time after the last nail had been hammered into the last revolutionary coffin. So for both men there was an important 'before' and 'after' in their adult lives which could in some way or other be mapped onto narratives concerned with choice, growth and responsibility. Milton made no reference to the Civil War in *Paradise Lost*, and he was too sophisticated to want to suggest that Cromwell's Commonwealth was somehow like the Garden of Eden. Nonetheless he lived the restoration of the monarchy as a fall from grace for the English people, and to that extent contemporary history was ever present in his poem: it helped to imbue the work with its tragic quality, and offered a specific example of how easy it is for men to make the wrong choices, and how terrible the consequences can be when they do so.

Some of Wordsworth's references to Milton are oblique, others are explicit. But perhaps what matters most is that this mentor-pupil relationship existed at all, given the amount of time – almost two centuries – that separated the two poets. And, significantly, Wordsworth's contemporary Turner enjoyed a similar relationship with Claude le Lorrain. Claude (1600-82) and Milton (1608-74) were almost exact contemporaries, as were Turner (1775-1851) and Wordsworth (1770-1850). So we have the most famous painter, and the most famous poet, of British Romanticism, both claiming as their masters men who were far removed from them in time. This is not the place to go into detail about Claude's influence on Turner; enough to say that, like Wordsworth with Milton, Turner did not leave it to the scholars to establish a connection. The influence was publicly acknowledged – though in Turner's case the admiration was further spiced by a competitive impulse which was alien to Wordsworth. So when Turner gave his painting *Dido building Carthage* (of 1815) to the National Gallery, London, he did so on condition that it be hung next to Claude's *Seaport with the Embarkment of the Queen of Sheba* (of 1648), which the National Gallery owned, and which had been Turner's reference when composing his mythical-historical vision of Carthage. Turner invited the comparison of his work and Claude's: while he considered Claude inimitable, he reckoned that his own paintings, using the language of his day, could be placed on the same level as Claude's. Wordsworth, though, lacked Turner's assertive self-confidence. He always felt himself to be 'less than' Milton, and his attitude towards his master would have been close in spirit to Newton's remark that, 'If I have seen further it is by standing on the shoulders of Giants' (the irony being that Newton himself became the archetypal 'giant' for generations of scientists, with his discoveries providing laws for the physics of the universe that remained unchallenged for almost two hundred and fifty years).

Two men (Turner and Wordsworth) and two attitudes: but in both cases there is not just respect for, and understanding of, the art of previous centuries; there is also the sense of a continuum in time and culture, which made it possible for a writer or a painter to create what today we would call a virtual relation-ship, to place himself at the feet of someone who had lived and died two centuries earlier and to learn from that master's work. This kind of dialogue was placed under increasing strain during the nineteenth century, as the Industrial Revolution, capitalism, colonialism and imperialism together brutally transformed the societies of the western world. But it was still possible for Manet (1832-83) to point to Velasquez (1599-1660) as his master, or for Cézanne (1839-1906) to admire Poussin (1594-1665) to the point where he said that his aim was to, '*refaire Poussin d'après la nature*'. Indeed, with the disintegration of the centuries-old structures for the production of art (studios run by masters with pupils and apprentices in attendance, and the whole workshop reliant on aristocratic patronage for financing), artists in the nineteenth century were obliged to reconstitute their artistic environments through a process of individual initiative, creating for themselves new lines of paternity and succession based on affinities.

As long as there was a certain underlying continuity to the development of culture, these references, spanning even two centuries, could be made without irony. But the modernist movements of the early twentieth century subverted that sense of continuity, and the destructive force of the First World War left European societies shell-shocked and fragmented. *The Waste Land*

and *Ulysses* are crammed with literary and cultural references, but there is no longer the sense that a dialogue with writers and artists of the past is easily accessible; and while Ezra Pound aspired to have Dante as his model, his *Cantos* are above all proof of the yawning gap that separates him from the great Italian poet. Artists today are a bit like immigrants: whatever lineage they can claim belongs to another country and must remain a private affair. In the brave new world they have come to live and work in, they have to construct a new identity – a precarious affair made up of a patchwork or kaleidoscope of short-lived cultural references. It is almost impossible for an artist today to claim to be part of a long-standing tradition (should he or she want to): the family-tree has only shallow roots, that must spread wide to grip the soil as best it can.

Chapter XI

From Genesis to Revelation

The poem that we know as *The Prelude* was effectively finished in 1805, but was never published during the poet's lifetime. The title was chosen by Mary, William's widow, when the masterpiece finally went to press a few months after William's death in 1850 (a curious choice of title for a posthumous work, as it is hard to see what it is likely to be the prelude to). Students of Wordsworth today are taught that *The Prelude* was Wordsworth's finest creation, and central to his oeuvre as a whole. But it is not at all clear if this was how the poet saw it – otherwise, why did he not publish it at some point between 1805 and 1850?

To the handful of people who knew of the poem's existence and had had the chance to read it Wordsworth gave various reasons for not publishing. To start with he hated the whole process: the publishing milieu itself, the endless calculations and compromises involved in getting a work to press, and then the inevitable humiliation caused by the vitriolic scorn and abuse that was heaped on all his work by fashionable critics such as Francis Jeffrey of *The Edinburgh Review*. So, in a letter of 1798 to his friend James Tobin, he had written:

> There is little need to advise me against publishing; it is a thing which I dread as much as death itself. This may serve as

an example of the figure – by rhetoricians called hyperbole, but privacy and quiet are my delight…

(March 6, 1798)

The experience of publishing *Lyrical Ballads* in the same year, followed by the second edition in 1800, did nothing to change his feelings about the whole business. Nonetheless with time he overcame his reluctance to engage with the outside world: a collection of 115 poems, in two volumes, was published in 1807; *The Excursion* went to press in 1814, and the next year saw the publication of another two-volume collection, that included *Lyrical Ballads*. From then on till the end of his life most years saw the publication of a new work, or group of poems, or anthology, until virtually everything he had written had been published. Only a few significant pieces, such as *Home at Grasmere*, remained hidden away – along with, of course, *The Prelude*.

Clearly therefore Wordsworth's distaste for publishing does not hold as a simple explanation for the fate of *The Prelude*, though it was no doubt a contributing factor. More specific arguments appeared as the poem neared completion. In 1804 he wrote to Thomas de Quincey:

> I am now writing a Poem on my own earlier life;…. This Poem will not be published these many years, and never during my lifetime, till I have finished a larger and more important work to which it is tributary. (March 6, 1804)

And in June 1805 he wrote to his friend and patron Sir George Beaumont:

> …I finished my Poem about a fortnight ago… but it was not a happy day for me I was dejected on many accounts; when I looked back upon the performance it seemed to have a dead

weight about it, the reality so far short of the expectation;...

(June 3, 1805)

There are two quite separate reflections here. The feeling expressed in the letter to Beaumont is a version of post-natal depression which most artists have to live with: soon after a work is finished comes the sense of disappointment; then with time the merits of the work gradually reassert themselves; until eventually – maybe years later – one is able to judge a work fairly. A work as complex and ambitious as *The Prelude*, in which Wordsworth had invested so much, and which had cost him so much time and effort, would be likely to accentuate the feeling of anti-climax – the more so in that Wordsworth's physical isolation meant that he had very few people with whom he could share his 'work in progress', and who might have shown appreciation and given him encouragement.

The letter to de Quincey meanwhile asserted that *The Prelude* only made sense if considered as part of a larger work – implying that it was not autonomous, and could not be enjoyed as a poem in its own right. This must sound strange for modern readers who are invariably invited to read *The Prelude* in just that way. Nonetheless there is no doubt that Wordsworth did see *The Prelude* as existing in a greater context: and the 'larger and more important work' to which he referred in this letter was *The Recluse*. But what exactly was *The Recluse*? It's hard to say really: like some unquiet spirit it cast a long shadow over decades of the poet's life, without ever gaining substance or emerging into the light of day; and was finally laid to rest only in the mid-1830s, by which time Wordsworth's creative drive was exhausted.

As Wordsworth kept no diary or journal, and gave little away in the letters he wrote of what was going through his mind, it is often difficult to see any further than the texts of poems he did complete. However it seems clear that *The Recluse* did exist as a serious project, and that it was dreamed up in 1798, some months before Wordsworth wrote the first text of the poem that would develop into *The Prelude*. The best resumé of it that we have comes from a letter written by Coleridge to Wordsworth in 1815, following the publication of *The Excursion* (whose full title was *The Excursion, being a Portion of The Recluse, A Poem*):

> I supposed you first to have meditated the faculties of Man in the abstract [...] to have laid a solid and immoveable foundation for the Edifice by removing the sandy Sophisms of Locke, and the Mechanic Dogmatists. [...] Next, I understood that you would take the Human Race in the concrete, have exploded the absurd notion of Pope's Essay on Man, Darwin, and all the countless Believers – even (strange to say) among Xtians of Man's having progressed from an Ouran Outang state – so contrary to all History, to all Religion, nay, to all Possibility – to have affirmed a Fall in some sense, as a fact, the possibility of which cannot be understood from the nature of the Will, but the reality of which is attested by Experience and Conscience – Fallen men contemplated in the different ages of the World, and in the different states – Savage – Barbarous – Civilized – the lonely Cot, or Borderer's Wigwam – the Village – the Manufacturing Town – Seaport – City – Universities – and not disguising the sore evils, under which the whole Creation groans, to point out however a manifest Scheme of Redemption from this Slavery, of Reconciliation from this Enmity with Nature...[85]

The main thrust of Coleridge's resumé was to reproach Wordsworth for failing to keep to this grand scheme when composing *The Excursion*. But the real value of the letter lies in what it says about the 'larger and more important' project that both *The Prelude* and *The Excursion* were supposed to be parts of. The first thing that strikes one in reading the resumé is how impossibly ambitious the project was, and how different it was from Wordsworth's normal way of thinking and feeling about the world. It is a plan that bears the hallmark of Coleridge's mind – intellectually nervous and restless, and tending to move from the abstract to the concrete, from general theory to particular examples and experiences designed to illustrate and bear out the initial proposition. The manically feverish character of Coleridge's mind becomes apparent in the second half of the letter. Having listed some of the themes that he had expected Wordsorth to treat, he turns to questions of style, saying that he had hoped Wordsworth's epic poem would,

> conclude by a grand didactic swell on the necessary identity of a true Philosophy with true Religion, agreeing in the results and differing only in the analytic and synthetic process, as discursive from intuitive, the former chiefly useful as perfecting the latter – in short, the necessity of a general revolution in the modes of developing & disciplining the human mind by the substitution of Life, and Intelligence (considered in it's [*sic*] different powers from the Plant up to that state in which the difference of Degree becomes a new kind (man, self-consciousness) but yet not by essential opposition) for the philosophy of mechanism which in every thing that is most worthy of the human Intellect strikes *Death*, and cheats itself by mistaking clear Images for distinct conceptions, and which idly demands Conceptions where Intuitions alone are possible or adequate to the majesty of Truth.

And so on. One can imagine Wordsworth's despair at trying to decipher such convoluted thinking and impenetrable arguments; and Coleridge's letter may well have proved conclusively to Wordsworth that he would never complete *The Recluse*. But *The Prelude* was already written; and Coleridge's notes are invaluable in throwing light on the dialogue that existed between the two poets in 1798, when Wordsworth was sketching out the scheme for his autobiographical poem.

That Milton was a crucial reference-point for *The Recluse* is clear from Coleridge's notes, which emphasise the theme of fall and possible redemption within Western society. *Paradise Lost* was the paradigm, and *The Recluse* was to be its modern sequel. And once one is aware that Wordsworth had a Miltonic scheme in mind when working on *The Prelude*, one can see that he did his best to follow Coleridge's guide-lines when launching the great project. At the level of narrative *The Prelude* starts where *Paradise Lost* leaves off: the joyous declaration of Book I,

> Now I am free, enfranchised and at large,
> May fix my habitation where I will.
> What dwelling shall receive me?...
> The earth is all before me! (lines 9–15)

offering an optimistic reply to the last lines of *Paradise Lost*,

> The world was all before them, where to choose
> Their place of rest, and providence their guide:
> They hand in hand with wandering steps and slow,
> Through Eden took their solitary way.
> (Book XII, lines 646-649)[86]

But the carefree innocence of the opening passage is swiftly qualified by the childhood recollections that follow, which focus on moments of transgression, theft, and violence against the natural order – together with the feelings of guilt and anxiety that such episodes provoke. Clearly the Vale of Grasmere is no prelapsarian Garden of Eden: Wordsworth is not trying to transpose Milton's thinking onto eighteenth-century Westmorland, with childhood as an equivalent to the state of grace that Adam and Eve knew before the Fall. The Wordsworthian child is inclined to act in a way that is sinful; and to that extent the story of *The Prelude* does indeed start where *Paradise Lost* ends, not only at the level of narrative but also in its thinking concerning the human condition.

Likewise the 'manifest Scheme of Redemption…of Reconciliation from this Enmity with Nature' (noted by Coleridge in the letter above) can indeed be traced during the course of *The Prelude* – but with many ups and downs, dead ends and false dawns. Progress is never predictable, nor easy to locate: so while for example in Book VII we find an abundance of 'dissolute men / And shameless women' in London (as we would expect), it was also in London that Wordsworth encountered the blind beggar who so impressed him:

> And, on the shape of this unmoving man,
> His fixèd face and sightless eyes, I looked
> As if admonished from another world.
>
> (lines 620-622)

The encounter has a similar impact to that with the leech-gatherer on the moor, in *Resolution and Independence*: and the lesson to be drawn from such meetings is necessarily a hard one to decipher. Such redemption as is possible for man living in an age of industrial revolution and untamed capitalism and colonialism will not come easily, nor perhaps be easy to recognise where and when it does make itself visible.

With glimpses such as these we can begin to see how *The Prelude* might have fitted into a larger work that would, perhaps, have moved outwards from a personal narrative to explore wider social themes and issues (even if the title *The Recluse* makes such a movement seem unlikely). But in the hands of Wordsworth could such a project have had any hope of succeeding? Would he have known how to develop arguments that were not based on personal experience? If we compare the first lines of *The Excursion* (presented as the *Prospectus* for *The Recluse*):

> On Man, on Nature, and on Human Life,
> Musing in solitude, I oft perceive
> Fair trains of imagery before me rise,

with the opening lines of *The Prelude*:

> O there is blessing in this gentle breeze
> That blows from the green fields and from the clouds
> And from the sky: it beats against my cheek,
> And seems half-conscious of the joy it gives.

the difference is all too clear: the one is pompous rhetoric, the other poetry. *The Prospectus* has a distinctly eighteenth-century tone – a bit like Pope's poetry but without Pope's sharpness; and while it hopes to gain something of Milton's 'grand manner' by echoing his style – the opening line, 'On Man, on Nature, and on Human Life' having something of the effect of, 'Of Man's first disobedience…' (at the beginning of *Paradise Lost*) – it does not work. However great his admiration for Milton, Wordsworth could never hope to write like him. Milton's opening had a magisterial tone, that sounded like the beginning of a sermon or lecture:

Of man's first disobedience, and the fruit
Of that forbidden tree, whose mortal taste
Brought death into the world, and all our woe,
With loss of Eden, till one greater man
Restore us, and regain the blissful seat,
Sing heavenly muse

(*Paradise Lost*, Book I, lines 1-6)

Wordsworth may have wished that he had Milton's authority, but it was precisely his ability to doubt that mattered. His lack of dogmatic certainties, and his general sense of insecurity and insufficiency, allowed him to develop a language in which the external world continually impinged on the inner world; in which the human body and the natural landscape shared roles and imagery; and in which the narrator's voice could blend into the narrative. Nor did he have Coleridge's gift for abstract reasoning, or share Coleridge's interest in philosophy. His thinking was empirical and, left to his own devices, he would never have dreamed of writing anything as intellectually ambitious as the poem that Coleridge's letter suggests. That he did set out on this daunting journey is a testament to the seductive nature of Coleridge's company and conversation – indeed, the letter gives a good idea of how intensely stimulating and productive the dialogue must have been in the first five years of their friendship. Wordsworth found doors opening in his mind that he could never have opened on his own, and whole expanses of potential poetry being mapped out that, with Coleridge's unstinting enthusiasm and Dorothy's quiet encouragement to urge him on, he felt inspired to try and develop into a *magnum opus*.

The Prelude came into existence therefore for very particular reasons. Conceived of as part of The Recluse, it was Coleridge's brain-child, and a project that was quite alien to Wordsworth's character. Wordsworth was persuaded by Coleridge's discourse, just as he was tempted to follow in Milton's footsteps, even though this kind of writing did not come naturally to him. To that extent we have Coleridge to thank for the existence of *The Prelude*, as it is unlikely that Wordsworth would have embarked on the project of his own accord. At the same time we must not forget that the first passages for the poem were written in the solitude of Goslar, when Coleridge had left William and Dorothy to their own devices and was following a different German itinerary. Even as it evolved into a long and complex poem, *The Prelude* remained true to the spirit of that first composition, which was intensely personal in feeling. The difficulty therefore lay in reconciling a strong personal impulse with a structure that was suggested by others – it was a curious marriage, and one can understand why Wordsworth should have had doubts about the final product. Still, *The Prelude* is famous for being an autobiographical poem, so it makes sense to concentrate on the personal dimension of the writing. In fact it is autobiographical in more ways than one, as the poem evolved through three different manuscripts between 1798 and 1805, and was then revised at intervals for the next forty-five years (the 1850 version was the only one known to the general public until 1926, when the 1805 version was published). In a way the story of *The Prelude* and its various manuscripts and complicated life runs parallel to the story of the young Wordsworth that it recounts; so it is useful to have an idea of how the poem began its existence and then took shape.

★ ★ ★

It all started with a question. The embryo of *The Prelude*, a 150-line manuscript known as *'Was it for this?'* and conceived in the arctic austerity of Goslar in the winter of 1798-9, was as hesitant and fragile as the beginning of life itself:

> Was it for this
> That one, the fairest of all rivers, loved
> To blend his murmurs with my nurse's song,
> And from his alder shades and rocky falls,
> And from his fords and shallows, sent a voice
> To intertwine my dreams? (lines 1-6)

'Was it for what?' one might ask – and the answer is never given. For this is not a rhetorical device, but rather one of those questions one asks oneself continually without ever supplying an answer. Wordsworth in this passage gives us exactly the sense of a train of thought being ever so gently translated into poetry, the flowing musicality of the river being picked up and replicated in subtle wordplay:

> For this didst thou,
> O Derwent, travelling over the green plains
> Near my sweet birth-place, didst thou, beauteous stream,
> Give ceaseless music to the night and day,
> (lines 6-9)

Wordsworth was revelling here in the musical qualities of the language, and for once let himself go in a sort of careless abandon to pleasure, much as he would 'give his body to the wind' when ice-skating. The initial 'Was it for this?' is repeated and modulated a number of times – and answered by the echoes of 'Ah, not in vain' – until the verse feels like a Mozart aria:

> Was it for this (and now I speak of things
> That have been, and that are, no gentle dreams
> Complacent, fashioned fondly to adorn

The time of un rememberable being),
Was it for this that I, a four years' child,
Beneath thy scars and in thy silent pools
Made one long bathing of a summer's day,
Basked in the sun, or plunged into thy streams
(lines 16–23)

For this in springtime, when on southern banks
The shining sun had from his knot of leaves
Decoyed the primrose flower, and when the vales
And woods were warm, was I a rover then
In the high places, on the lonely peaks,
Among the mountains and the winds?
(lines 30–35)

Ah, not in vain ye beings of the hills,
And ye that walk the woods and open heaths
By moon or starlight, thus, from my first day
Of childhood, did ye love to interweave
The passions that build up our human soul
(lines 47–51)

Ah, not in vain ye spirits of the springs,
And ye that have your voices in the clouds
(lines 59–60)

For this, when on the withered mountain-slope
The frost and breath of frosty wind had nipped
The last autumnal crocus, did I love
To range through half the night among the cliffs
And the smooth hollows where the woodcocks ran
Along the moonlight turf?   (lines 76–81)

The writing here has the suppleness and relaxed lyricism

of *Tintern Abbey*, which had been composed just a few months earlier. In both poems the movement of thought and feeling is accompanied by a gracefully flowing river, which acts both as companion and as a benevolent natural presence; and the conclusion of *Tintern Abbey*, with its affirmation of nature's role as

> The anchor of my purest thoughts, the nurse,
> The guide, the guardian of my heart, and soul
>
> Of all my moral being.   (lines 110-12)

is remarkably similar to that of *'Was it for this?'*, in which the 'primordial feelings' inspired by nature are gratefully acknowledged:

> How serene,
> How calm these seem amid the swell
> Of human passions – even yet I feel
> Their tranquillizing power.   (lines 147-50)

In the winter of 1798 Wordsworth used *Tintern Abbey* as a springboard for launching this new experiment in autobiographical writing. It was an astute move, for *Tintern Abbey* was not only the most complex and intensely personal poem he had written up to that date; it had also been, paradoxically, one of the easiest to write – as we saw in the first chapter of this book, it had been composed in just a few days, and never revised or corrected. Wordsworth realised that there must be an untapped potential in himself for this kind of writing, if the composition of *Tintern Abbey* had been as uncomplicated as the poem itself was complex. And it is to Wordsworth's credit that he remained faithful to this first impulse throughout the next six and a half years in which *The Prelude* gradually took shape – always staying as close as possible to memories and sensations that came to him naturally, and allowing more general thoughts and theories to emerge from the narrative.

'Was it for this?' was clearly promising, and Wordsworth kept up the momentum, developing the text into a 978-line poem ('the two-part *Prelude* of 1799') which was copied out by the time he and Dorothy moved to Grasmere in December 1799. The poem is in two parts, corresponding more or less to the first two Books of the final poem, and explores further the realm of childhood memories. Interestingly, it is close in length to *Home at Grasmere*, which Wordsworth began to work on immediately after. It looks as if *Home at Grasmere* was intended to match and balance the two-part *Prelude,* by setting his emotional, spiritual and moral state of mind as an adult returning to the Lakes, against the condition and experiences he had known in the same place as a boy. Maybe in 1800 Wordsworth envisaged leaving the auto-biographical project there: with two poems, each of around a thousand lines, one on childhood and the other on adult life, that formed a pair. *Home at Grasmere* was predicated on the principle of the pair as a unit which united harmoniously two individual beings: could past and present, childhood and adulthood, not form a pair, thereby establishing that continuity across time that Wordsworth desired so strongly, and which the power of memory made possible?

Whether or not that might have been Wordsworth's intention, things worked out differently, in part because he was unable to sustain the myth that he subscribed to in *Home at Grasmere.* The poem was consigned to the archives, and he all but stopped writing. Instead he took the time to think through the dilemma in which he found himself. He must have realised that there were two quite separate aspects to the problem – one personal and the other literary. They intertwined and became as one, but they had to be dealt with separately. In courting Mary Hutchinson he moved towards a resolution of his personal frustration; and in the process turned his back on the proposition of *Home at Grasmere* (or at least heavily qualified it). Marriage involved the forming of another pair, certainly, but in Wordsworth's case it was at the price of the brother-sister pair which *Home at Grasmere* had sought to vindicate. So the basic notion of the pair lost some of its interest or validity. The premises on which the whole autobiographical project was based were called into question; and in the winter of 1800-1 it went into prolonged hibernation. At the same time Dorothy's journal either stopped or disappeared. But both her writing and his returned in force once William was able to plan his marriage to Mary, and organise a definitive 'settlement' with Annette. The new dynamic carried both of them through 1802 (Dorothy wrote twice as much during that year as in 1800), but faltered and then stalled just a few months after William and Mary's wedding. 1803 was another year of anti-climax. William had once again proved himself to be all too fertile physically – Mary gave birth to their first child after just eight months of married life – but from an artistic point of view he seemed almost sterile. He produced a few mediocre sonnets, and that was all.

In the winter of 1802-3 writing went on the back burner, along with the saucepans of porridge that constituted the staple diet of the Wordsworth household. And then that particular fire went out. The Poet stopped writing poems. At about the same time (January 1803) Dorothy's journal petered out without even the day or the date being completed. The last entry reads,

Monda

– (it should have read *Monday 17th*). The journal had been conceived as her part of an exclusive dialogue binding her to her brother; his marriage and the conception of his first child, which by January 17 Mary would have been confident of carrying, terminated the usefulness of her journal, her baby.

In Wordsworth's case one could see the unproductiveness of 1803 as a classic case of writer's block, or as showing the difficulty he had in realigning his personal life so as to accomodate both Dorothy and Mary satisfactorily. Whatever the reason, 1803 replicated the inertia of 1801. And then one day in the winter of 1803-4, while the waters of Lake Windermere slept under their cover of creaking ice, something happened. Just as the frost had performed its secret ministry during the bitterly cold winter at Goslar five years earlier, so he found stimulus once again in the dead waste and middle of the winter – and it was to the passages he had composed at Goslar that he turned, and that he decided to build on. Only this time he didn't stop. In the course of the next fifteen months he composed the 8,500-word masterpiece that we know as *The Prelude*, working regularly, blotting out the endless noises and problems of domestic life, with at least four adults and one baby – then two – cooped up in a tiny and unhygienic cottage, and concentrating as he had never done before.

★ ★ ★

What did he have to go on? The 'two-part *Prelude* of 1799' had not advanced the narrative much beyond boyhood, and had emphasised the strong and mysterious bond between child and nature. *Home at Grasmere* had come unstuck in glossing over the flaws and contradictions inherent to adult relationships. What he needed was to find a way of reconciling childhood and adult life, without reducing adult society to some utopian scheme that had no connection with reality, yet without losing sight of the vision and beliefs that had inspired him to jot down his childhood memories in the first place. It was a daunting task. Eventually he realised that if it were to work it would not be through adopting some grand scheme that overrode doubts and scruples, but, on the contrary, by admitting the difficulties, divisions, dissent and disappointments that are part and parcel of growing up. Accept the contradictions, then try and find a way of resolving them.

Abandoning the idea of 'pairs' he began instead to explore the different forces, experiences, and impulses that combined to create and form a person's character. Once the preamble and introduction of Book I had been dealt with, he engaged swiftly with the main themes of the poem:

> Fair seed-time had my soul, and I grew up
> Fostered alike by beauty and by fear
>
> (Book I, 305-6)

'Beauty and fear' was one of those pairings of impulses – like 'Sense and Sensibility', or 'Pride and Prejudice' – that formed themselves in that period, on the cusp of the eighteenth and nineteenth centuries, and which created a precarious sense of balance out of a marriage of complementary opposites . But the twinning of beauty and fear had none of the elegant poise of Jane Austen's inventions: it was more urgent, more dangerous – evoking almost Aristotle's formula for tragic drama, which the philosopher said should inspire pity and fear in order to achieve catharsis.

The verb 'fostered' is also significant as, knowing the story of Wordsworth's childhood, with his mother dying when he was eight and his father when he was thirteen, it suggests that beauty and fear were like foster parents to him. In that context the verb is wonderfully suggestive – in a way that 'nurtured' would not be;

but the verb is also significant in that it links, however discreetly, the beginnings of the process of growth with a time of traumatic bereavement. It is a signal that Wordsworth is prepared to absorb into his narrative elements and processes that go against the grain of his thinking, and that he is ready to delve into life's contradictions in a way that until then he had avoided.

The counterpoint in these two lines also alerts us to the way the poem would be structured – that is, through a dialectic of complementary opposites. For the poem as a whole the two protagonists would be 'nature' and 'the world of men', and their interaction would constitute the process thanks to which consciousness is formed and personality develops. And the narrative would be structured in a similar way – that is to say, Wordsworth spliced the storyline so as to alternate the forces at work, giving more or less precedence to each influence in turn. This becomes clear if we consider the contents of the poem in a schematic way:

Books I and II remain true to the spirit of the 'two-part *Prelude* of 1799', and lean heavily towards the child's intimate relationship with nature; and with the poem being set in one of the wildest parts of Britain, the influence of the natural world is powerful and omnipresent. The full title of Book I – 'Book I, Childhood and School-time' – points to the importance of education, as does the title of Book II – 'Book II, Schooltime (continued)'; but there is precious little about schooling in either of the Books, and the titles exist primarily to redress a balance in the narrative, which otherwise would seem to exclude 'civilising' influences from the period of childhood.

Book III makes an abrupt transition from the wilds of Westmorland to one of the capitals of the academic world, Cambridge University.

Book IV sees the undergraduate return to his rural birthplace armed with the baggage of schooling and learning; while Book V moves back to the world of books.

Book VI encapsulates the poem's debate in its title – 'Cambridge and the Alps' – while Book VII switches the reader's attention from the pristine summits of the Alps to the seething, noisy and dirty city of London.

Book VIII, set in rural Wales and subtitled 'Retrospect – Love of Nature leading to Love of Mankind', attempts the first of the poem's syntheses between the natural world and the process of civilisation.

Books IX and X (in the 1805 arrangement) abandon temporarily the promises offered by Book VIII and embark instead on an account of the most significant historical event of the age – the French Revolution.

Books XI and XII (of the 1805 version) see a sadder and a wiser man return from France to his birthplace to meditate on the human condition; while Book XIII, with its spectacular dénouement on the summit of Snowdon, reaffirms the possibilities of completeness of being that had been sketched out in Book VIII.

Even such a crude resumé as this shows that *The Prelude* was a carefully planned and intricately constructed work, closer in form to a musical composition than to an autobiography. Just to extend the musical metaphor for a moment, one could compare 'nature' and 'man' to major themes that are developed in the movements (or Books) of the work, while 'body', 'soul', 'heart' and 'mind' are the principal instruments in the orchestra. As the narrative proceeds the instruments are brought into play as and when necessary: the music they create, and the meaning they generate, vary from movement to movement as the work progresses.

Each of the major 'instruments' was solicited within the first sixty lines of the poem:

a heart / Joyous (Book I, lines 15-16);

mountings of the mind (line 20);

the sweet breath of heaven
Was blowing on my body (lines 41-42);

Pour out that day my soul (line 57)

The question then was, how would the instruments relate to each other? What music would they make when mixed and mingled? How best could the theme be developed and resolved?

★ ★ ★

In the beginning there was a small boy running wild in a sort of Garden of Eden:

Oh, many a time have I, a five year's child,
A naked boy, in one delightful rill,
A little mill-race severed from his stream,
Made one long bathing of a summer's day
(*The Prelude*, Book I, lines 291-4)

or...

...as if I had been born
On Indian plains, and from my mother's hut
Had run abroad in wantonness, to sport
A naked savage, in the thunder shower.
(Book I, lines 301-4)

During the period of childhood it is the body that is dominant as a conductor or filter of meaning – perhaps not surprisingly, since so much of the narrative is concerned with physical activity – and, crucially, because the other human faculties have yet to be developed. Once out of childhood, however, the body is more or less taboo as a subject: it is never referred to openly, though obviously it is very much present as a protagonist in the Book devoted to the long walk across France and Switzerland, or in crucial episodes like the ascent of Snowdon. But the body even then is a motor for the narrative rather than a subject in itself. At no point, once adulthood has been reached, does Wordsworth dwell on the body as a subject in its own right – nor does he anywhere else in his poetry.

This extreme reticence to express the body's needs, functions and appetites has led to Wordsworth's poetry being branded as 'bodiless' or 'disembodied'– a criticism that is hard to square with his love of strenuous physical exercise![87] Certainly there is in Wordsworth a sort of revulsion to the explicit 'language of the body' that we find in eighteenth-century writers such as Swift or Sterne, and even more vividly in the prints of Rowlandson and Gillray. But in this Wordsworth was typical of his generation, which during the first decades of the nineteenth century introduced and then imposed another, far more prudish way of relating to the human body, with a new vocabulary and a radically different set of values concerning morality and behaviour, as society moved inexorably towards what we now consider a Victorian mindset.

Actually Wordsworth's sense of the body in *The Prelude* is coherent and intelligent. The early passages (such as those quoted above) with their echoes of the Book of Genesis, make a tacit equation between childhood innocence and the state of grace that Adam and Eve knew before the Fall. And that equation is still maintained today, even in a society whose cultural values have been completely secularised. There is still the idea that children are born innocent ; and in the first years of their lives there is no shame in them running around naked – as one can see on any beach in Europe. The scheme of things that Wordsworth sketches out in *The Prelude*, whereby education and growing up involve an increasingly complicated relationship with one's own body, makes as much sense today as it did in 1800. What is remarkable is Wordsworth's ability to create a synthesis between the condition of man in an industrialised society, and the timeless message of the Bible. The retreat from nakedness and the loss of childhood innocence, that are both inevitable as we grow up, give a modern relevance and meaning to Genesis 1–3.

And, however obliquely, the body continues to assert itself in the later Books of *The Prelude*. As one might expect, London is the setting for the most sinful behaviour; however the sad condition of fallen women (i.e. prostitutes) in the metropolis is gallantly balanced by reference (in Book VII, lines 320–39) to a Westmorland girl who was unwittingly married to a bigamist (who was subsequently hanged for his crime). And then of course there is the Vaudracour-Julia episode in Book IX – or rather the absence of it in the 1850 version of the poem. The story of his own affair with Annette needed to be told, however obliquely; but then at a certain point he decided to cut it out of the personal narrative which is *The Prelude*, and publish it as something quite separate from his own life, as the stories in *Lyrical Ballads* had been. Once again, Wordsworth's realism was remarkable (though in this case unintentionally so): his way of both admitting the body's 'life story', and censoring it, corresponds perfectly with the way most of us deal with past (mis)adventures. He tells us there is a skeleton in the cupboard, but keeps the cupboard door locked – and then wears the key around his neck as if it were a necklace.

★ ★ ★

In the pairing game that intrigued him in this period of his life, expressions such as 'keeping body and soul together' suggested a good match of complementary opposites. As we saw in chapter II, Wordsworth used genders to dramatise the sexual element present in all that lives, and as part of that strategy he cast the soul in a female role, a sort of wife to his body:

> and my soul
> Did once again make trial of the strength
> Restored to her afresh; nor did she want
> Æolian visitations   (Book I, lines 101-4)

> ...but that the soul,
> Remembering how she felt, but what she felt
> Remembering not, retains an obscure sense
> Of possible sublimity, to which
> With growing faculties she doth aspire.
>   (II, 334-8)

Interestingly, Wordsworth's female soul seems to approach maturity in parallel with his masculine body, so that by the time of Book IV, when he was an undergraduate, his soul is described like a nubile young woman:

> Gently did my soul
> Put off her veil, and, self-transmuted, stood
> Naked, as in the presence of her God.
>   (lines 140-2)

As the demands of the body are seen to be animal, assertive and often aggressive, while the needs of the soul are impalpable and intuitive, there was nothing particularly original in Wordsworth's decision to make the soul feminine – indeed, it went along with Shakespeare's thinking when he wrote,

Since my dear soul was mistress of her choice
(Hamlet, III, II, line 61)

But what was quite original was Wordsworth's ability to pro-
ject this human concept into the natural world, endowing it with
a radically new dimension: speaking of images that came to him
while walking at night he wrote,

> ...they rose
> As from some distant region of my soul
> And came along like dreams;   (IV, 393-6)

The human soul here becomes part of the great natural land-
scape, it has its own geography and can be mapped like a coun-
try with its various regions. And, as a logical conclusion to this
thought-process, we understand that Nature also has a soul –
though in this case there is no tension of genders, as Nature is
obviously feminine (I, 362; 369; 371), and so is her soul:

> From Nature and her overflowing soul,
> I had received so much, that all my thoughts
> Were steeped in feeling;   (II, 416-8)

And then of course there was the presence of Dorothy, who
for years had been her brother's soul-mate: the complicity she
enjoyed with him, both at home and on their long walks to-
gether, made it easy for him to see the soul as the body's natural
feminine companion. At the same time his love for her obliged
him to sublimate his feelings, separating spiritual affinities from
sensual impulses: the dialectic between body and soul was for
Wordsworth not so much an intellectual debate as a tension that
he had to deal with in his everyday life.

Nature being feminine, and the soul being feminine, and

Dorothy being a woman, it was easier for Dorothy to absorb from Nature the qualities that Wordsworth identified with the soul – tenderness, sweetness, softness – than it was for him. That is in part the thinking in his tribute to Dorothy in Book XIII of *The Prelude* (lines 211-46), in which he thanks her for softening his 'over-sternness':

> Child of my parents, sister of my soul,
>
>   ... Thou didst soften down
> This over-sternness; but for thee, sweet friend,
> My soul, too reckless of mild grace, had been
> Far longer what by nature it was framed –
> Longer retained its countenance severe –
> A rock with torrents roaring....
>
>   thy breath,
> Dear sister, was a kind of gentler spring
> That went before my steps.

Intellectually the argument works; but the tension remains. 'Sister of my soul' proposes the same kind of synthesis – 'sister and soul-mate' – as 'sister-wives' had done in *An Evening Walk* almost twenty years earlier. William's relationship with Dorothy continued to elude definition, would not fit into any category, and could only be satisfactorily described as a hybrid of easily recognisable relationships.[88]

★ ★ ★

'Winning the hearts and minds' is another of those expressions, like 'keeping body and soul together', that have passed into the language, and which could have helped Wordsworth organise his thinking about human personality. Of the two, the heart interested him less: he saw it as the organ of straightforward, uncomplicated feelings, vital to the full development of an individual but less intriguing than the labyrinthine intricacies of memory, identity and intellect that were woven together in the creation of human consciousness. Nonetheless, as the expression 'far into his heart', in the famous 'There was a boy…' passage shows, he conceived of the heart as occupying a territory on the map of 'human geography', equal to that claimed by the soul or the mind:

> a gentle shock of mild surprise
> Has carried far into his heart the voice
> Of mountain torrents; or the visible scene
> Would enter unawares into his mind
> With all its solemn imagery,
>
> (Book V, lines 137–141)

Just as the body is omnipresent in childhood while the soul is unformed, so the mind in our early years is inarticulate while the heart speaks loud and clear. Wordsworth sees the mind in childhoood as a sort of blotting-paper on which nature and experience leave blurred, almost undecipherable writing, and in the opening Books of *The Prelude* it is more like a part of the natural landscape than the organ of human conscience. So, for example, after the boating episode of Book I, Wordsworth says that,

> huge and mighty forms, that do not live
> Like living men, moved slowly through my mind
> By day, and were the trouble of my dreams.
>
> (lines 425–7)

A similar idea is suggested in Book IV, as the poet reflected on his progress – or lack of it – as he moved out of his teens:

> Strange rendezvous my mind was at that time,
> A parti-coloured show of grave and gay,
>
> (lines 346-7)

His mind is seen here as a meeting-place – a crossroads or roundabout – rather than an entity in its own right. However it is during this same period – that of university studies – that the mind begins to define itself and to assert itself as a vital element in the intellectual and social life of an individual. At one point in Book III Wordsworth focuses on it in an almost obsessive way, referring to it five times in less than thirty-five lines:

> And more than all, a strangeness in my mind (79);

> by force of my own mind (88);

> As if with a rebound my mind returned
> Into its former self (96-7);

> my mind
> Seemed busier in itself than heretofore (103-4);

> turning the mind in upon itself (112)

Youth, Wordsworth suggests, is a time of fermentation in which the process of education helps the yeast of natural vitality to develop usefully: the adult, in acquiring a mind of his own, becomes master of his destiny and therefore answerable for his actions. Interestingly for someone whose *magnum opus* was supposed to be called *The Recluse*, Wordsworth suggests that social interaction is vital for the health of the mind in adulthood:

so Vaudracour's decision to withdraw from all social contact is treated with scathing contempt:

> but in those solitary shades
> His days he wasted – an imbecile mind.
> (Book IX, lines 933-4)

And it is significant that while the 1850 version of *The Prelude* reduces the whole Julia – Vaudracour episode from 379 lines to just 32, nonetheless the lines containing this severe judgement on Vaudracour are preserved intact (with only 'in those solitary shades' modified to 'hidden in those gloomy shades'). Wordsworth clearly saw responsible and mature adult human beings as social animals, and this view did not change with time.

In counterpoint to the individual mind stands the guiding and forming force of the universe, an ambiguous partnership of nature and religion:

> his mind,
> Even as an agent of the one great Mind,
> Creates, creator and receiver both   (II, 271-3)

This benevolent force works on the individual in a way that speaks of art, intuition and craftsmanship together:

> The mind of man is framed even like the breath
> And harmony of music; there is a dark
> Invisible workmanship that reconciles
> Discordant elements, and makes them move
> In one society.   (I, 351-5)

At the same time as this formative process helps to integrate the adult into society, it endows him with the means to transcend it. The vision which the poet had on the summit of Snowdon, with which the poem concludes, was of

> The perfect image of a mighty mind,
> Of one that feeds upon infinity,
> That is exalted by an underpresence,
> The sense of God, or whatsoe'er is dim
> Or vast in its own being, above all
> One function of such mind had Nature there
> Exhibited by putting forth
>
> (Book XIII, lines 69-75)

The teaming up of Nature and God to produce a single 'great Mind' capable of organising all life and offering order and meaning to human existence, is similar to the modern proposition of 'intelligent design' as a means of reconciling Darwinian principles of evolution with traditional religion. But unlike the proponents of 'intelligent design' Wordsworth was not fighting a rearguard action for a lost cause. Rather he was taking sides in a debate – concerning religion and the existence of God – that deeply divided European intellectuals at that time.

★ ★ ★

The Prelude reaches its climax with a vision worthy of the Book of Revelations in the Bible:

> I looked about, and lo,
> The Moon stood naked in the heavens, at height
> Immense above my head, and on the shore
> I found myself of a huge sea of mist,
> Which meek and silent rested at my feet.

A hundred hills their dusky backs upheaved
All over this still ocean; and beyond,
Far, far beyond, the vapours shot themselves
In headlands, tongues and promontory shapes,
Into the sea   (Book XIII, lines 40-49)

At that point nature's orchestra is brought into play, as the poet shifts his attention to

A deep and gloomy breathing-place through which
Mounted the roar of waters, torrents, streams
Innumerable, roaring with one voice![89]
(lines 57-9)

The symphony offered by the elements could be enjoyed and admired simply for its own sake, but Wordsworth goes a step further in locating precisely in 'that breach' 'The soul, the imagination of the whole' (line 65). Just as the human mind finds its complement in the 'mighty mind' that animates and orders the natural world, so that natural world is inspired and moved by a 'soul' and 'imagination', as if it were a human being. The synthesis between human and natural, between human and divine, and between natural and divine, is gracefully achieved; and one can hear the poet breathe a huge sigh of relief as he finally resolves the intellectual debate that had been central to the entire poem (he even does his best to integrate the language of an urban environment into the natural orchestra by describing the dark deep chasm as a 'thoroughfare').

But Wordsworth's mind was always that of a poet, not a philosopher; his sense of poetic truth was based not on the power of the ideas he engaged with, but on the force of personal experience. For him poetry was always born out of experience, then filtered and organised by memory; and meaning was generated primarily by the relationships established between different experiences lived at different moments in time. Language – in the sense of metaphor or allusion – was the thread which drew together apparently unrelated episodes, and gave meaning to the whole. In this way in his mind a web was continually being formed, extended, modified: and that web became, through writing, the expression of his identity. As a result he would trust no idea, however attractive, that went against personal experience.

The resolution of *The Prelude* on the summit of Mt Snowdon offers a perfect example of Wordsworth's labyrinthine mind at work, and shows how the ramifications of his thinking were potentially endless. For while that moment of revelation is triumphantly upbeat, it also evokes, like an unexpected echo, a passage from the holiday in the Alps in 1790 that was anything but euphoric. The episode in question (recounted in Book VI, lines 549-580) is set in 'a narrow chasm' that offers a clear precedent to the 'blue chasm' just below the summit of Snowdon, and has the same protagonists, interacting in a way similar to the elements described in Book XIII:

> Winds thwarting winds, bewildered and folorn,
> The torrents shooting from the clear blue sky,
> The rocks that muttered close upon our ears,
> Black drizzling crags that spoke by the wayside
> As if a voice were in them.   (lines 560-4)

Here, as in the Snowdon passage, Wordsworth sees the 'workings of one mind' – the expression of a natural logic that man can feel but not fully understand. But the episode in the Alps offers no promise of redemption: Wordsworth and his friend spent that night in an inn in the same valley, but found themselves unable to sleep,

> deafened and stunned
> By noise of waters, making innocent sleep
> Lie melancholy among weary bones.
>
> (lines 578-80)

There is nothing unusual in a bad night's sleep when travel-
ling, but the phrase 'innocent sleep' alerts us to the resonance of
other meanings. Clearly a quote from *Macbeth* – ('innocent sleep,
/ Sleep that knits up the ravelled sleeve of care' (II, II, 33-34) – it
comes of course from the passage in which Macbeth expresses his
sense of guilt and loss of peace of mind, after killing Duncan. The
state of innocence or grace is invoked once it has been lost. And
this reference will be picked up and developed in Book X when
the aftermath of the September Massacres in Paris provokes an-
other bad night's sleep:

> Until I seemed to hear a voice that cried
> To the whole city 'Sleep no more!'   (lines 77-8)

That sense of collective guilt – its seeds sown by the feelings of
personal guilt attached to some of the earliest experiences recount-
ed in Book I – will only be allayed when, later in Book X (lines
515-66), he learns that Robespierre is dead: he is told of this by a
passing traveller whom he meets while walking along the beach
of Levens Sands, one day in August 1794. For someone who had
witnessed at first hand the beginning of the Terror in France, the
news was profoundly meaningful, and it prompted Wordsworth to
meditate on the forces that shape political and historical events.
The passage though concludes with quite a different reflection, as,

> interrupted by uneasy bursts
> Of exultation, I pursued my way
> Along that very shore which I had skimmed
> In former times, when…

> ...a joyous crew
> Of schoolboys hastening to their distant home
> Along the margin of the moonlight sea,
> We beat with thundering hoofs the level sand.
>
> (lines 557...566)

Book X ends here, with a clear echo of the passage from Book II referred to on page 208, which recounted how, as boys, Wordsworth and his friends rode along that same beach:

> Lighted by gleams of moonlight from the sea,
> We beat with thundering hoofs the level sand.
>
> (Book II, lines 143-4)

And that sense of echo is important, because it creates a silent bond between two things that have nothing in common: namely, the boyish exultation felt in riding at full speed along a beach, and the man's intense joy at hearing of the overthrow of a tyrant. And what underscores the echo in meaning is the sound of the horses' hoofs themselves, as they reverberate like drumbeats on the damp sand. And – just to complete the puzzle – the hooves in Book II are 'thundering': when we read that in Book II we think only of the sound they make; but when we come across the repetition of these lines in Book X, it sounds as if they had been anticipating the storm (of the Revolution) that lies ahead. That storm though finally passes; and the facts recounted at the end of Book X resolve the (unsuspected) threat conjured up in the innocent episode of Book II.

This complicated way of relating time to consciousness – something that literature and cinema today revel in, but which was totally unheard of in Wordsworth's day – is here, as so often in his poetry, predicated on the sense of a specific place.[90] Just as Tintern Abbey, revisited in 1798 five years after his first visit, allowed Wordsworth to meditate on what had happened to him in the meantime, so in this case the beach of Levens Sands made it possible for Wordsworth to connect totally disparate events, and to establish a relationship between them across time – thanks to the working of his own consciousness, his own memories. But that consciousness cannot function in a way that is arbitrary and autarchical: had he not found himself on Levens Sands when he heard of the death of Robespierre, those particular lines of poetry would not have been written.

Echoes in time are crucial to the meaning of *The Prelude*, as they break up the one-way linear movement of the narrative, turning the ear back again and again to tune into another meaning, another context. Thanks to such strategies there is no straightforward progress from genesis to revelation, for memory establishes conections that thwart any easy resolution of the narrative. Writing in 1804, memories of a bad night's sleep in the Alps in 1790 remind him of a bad night's sleep in Paris in 1792, which reminds him of a walk on the beach in 1794 which in turn reminds him of riding a horse on the same beach about ten years earlier… Individual events reveal themselves to be crossroads of meaning, offering both positive and negative directions. The progress realised in life will therefore always be relative, and the poet will never be sure that the journey has been completed. Just as Milton, at the end of *Paradise Lost*, left Adam and Eve to wend their way through the world with few of the issues of the poem truly resolved, so the web of meanings created by memory in *The Prelude* deprive the reader of a proper journey's end at the end of the long poem.

★ ★ ★

The Prelude proposes itself, in the words of its subtitle, as an 'autobiographical poem' on the 'growth of a poet's mind'. Stated in those terms, the enterprise was likely to encounter various difficulties: first, because the genre of autobiography was in its infancy, so that there were almost no useful precedents to rely on;[91] and secondly, because of the intrinsic difficulty of reconciling autobiography with poetry. (Actually, for someone as secretive as Wordsworth, this was a godsend: the demands of poetry permitted him to interpret and refashion autobiographical material to his heart's content, until the version presented to the public had not so much autobiographical value, but read beautifully as poetry).

One can understand why Wordsworth should have faltered and lost faith with his great poem even as it neared conclusion. The fact that he was breaking new ground, together with his constant need to measure himself against masters of the past such as Milton, left him with the impression that he was not up to the task he set himself, and that in the end he didn't have anything of great value to contribute. Such doubts were underscored by the context in which the poem was conceived. For *The Prelude* was born out of a sense of cultural crisis, as much as out of a search for personal identity. Just as painters had lost a large part of their traditional vocabulary during the eighteenth century, so that it became harder and harder to produce religious or historical paintings which carried conviction and could be set alongside the masterpieces of the Renaissance, so writers found it increasingly difficult to work on an epic scale with any degree of satisfaction. One could ironise on such writing, as Pope did with mock-heroic works such as *The Rape of the Lock*, but irony did not appeal to Wordsworth. He had no great sense of humour, but neither did he like to mock others. He could only write on the basis of values which he did not doubt – and those values were being constantly eroded in the world he grew up in.

Different forces working quite separately from each other were combining to create a sense of fragmentation and discontinuity, and Wordsworth had found himself well placed to see them at work. In the so-called 'Age of Revolution' he had been caught up in the French Revolution, and had experienced it in a way that was so unexpectedly personal that he would be branded with memories of it for life. And while he had grown up in one of the wildest and most beautiful areas of England, the manufacturing cities of Manchester and Liverpool, epicentres of the Industrial Revolution, were less than seventy miles away.... He had been educated with sound religious principles, but at Cambridge had been obliged to reckon with intellectual arguments concerning man and the universe which left little place for God. He had been brought up with a strong sense of belonging to a particular place and a particular culture, and then had tried to come to terms with the anonymity and chaotic energy of London, the world's busiest metropolis. And so it went on: each personal progress or development that could be notched up had to be weighed against a reciprocal loss or sense of alienation. And that neutralising economy held good for the poem as well. For more than any other nineteenth-century text, *The Prelude* showed that it was still possible to write a long poem that could be considered both great and modern − but that it could only be done by renouncing the terms on which the masterpieces of the past had been created, and by inventing a radically new language instead. In its sense of failure lay its success.

★ ★ ★

Wordsworth set to work seriously on *The Prelude* at the beginning of 1804, and completed it by June 1805. So in the space of a year and a half he composed a poem almost as long as *Paradise Lost* (which Milton had taken nine years to write). By the time he was thirty-five (when Milton had nothing longer than *Comus* to his credit) he had achieved as much as Milton managed to do by the age of fifty-nine. He had proved himself a match for his model and master, and could lay the father-figure to rest once and for all. But of course he did not. At the last minute he held back. He decided not to publish his long poem, whose 'reality fell so far short of the expectation', and placed the bulky manuscript in a drawer of his writing-desk, and left it there. The little wooden drawer became the poem's coffin.

He buried his most important creation just a few months after burying the drowned body of his brother John. Was there a connection between these two moments? Did John's death somehow undermine his sense of a promising future to the extent that he no longer felt the energy or motivation needed to publish this radically original work, and then protect and defend it against the jibes and taunts of ignorant critics? Maybe. Maybe the depression he felt at that time would brand him for life. But the analogy between these two 'funerals' – that of his brother followed by that of *The Prelude* – only holds up to a point. For while John died young – aged only thirty-two – he had nonetheless lived in the adult world, he had had a career and had had the chance to be the man he aspired to be. The great poem was buried without having been granted a life. It was consigned to dust in the same way as Lucy was – or as two of Wordsworth's own children would be, in 1812 (Catherine, aged three, and Thomas, aged six).

In my experience, little or nothing is made by teachers of the fact that Wordsworth decided not to publish *The Prelude*. And yet it was a decision that influenced, maybe even determined, the course of his career over the next forty-five years. It also deprived younger poets of a work which was radically original, and which they might have responded to with poems of their own. Nineteenth-century English poetry might have taken a different course. And it blocked Wordsworth's sense of personal development at a critical moment in his life. Instead of moving on to a sequel or to something different (Milton did both when four years after publishing *Paradise Lost* he published *Paradise Regained*, in a volume that also contained *Samson Agonistes*), he began the process of endless revisions of the text. Like an old flea-bitten dog he scratched away for the next forty-five years at the sore that his poem became, improving next to nothing and changing nothing of substance.

In the final analysis what counts in art are results: the works done, signed, and made public. And once a work is definitive, and has an existence of its own, it alters the landscape for the artist in a way that no unfinished work, however beautiful, can do. It is the same as the difference between an unborn child and one that is born. The latter exists, has a life of its own – and the family will never be the same again. As a professional poet (and father) Wordsworth knew this all too well – so why did he not go ahead and publish? One can understand why he might have had misgivings when he finished the poem in 1805: there were no precedents for this kind of work, and it was open to all kinds of misinterpretation. Wordsworth was all too aware of this, as he showed in the letter to Sir George Beaumont written while finishing the poem:

> It will be not much less than 9,000 lines, not hundred but thousand, lines, long: an alarming length! And a thing unprecedented in Literary history that a man should talk so much about himself. (May 1, 1805)

But if he lacked the confidence to publish then, he could

have changed his mind at a later date, once his reputation was established and the critics looked more kindly on his work. By the mid-1820s the poem would surely not have been so controversial: it would have found its rightful place among the mass of other published work, and would have been read as a middle-aged man's assessment of his childhood and youth. But there is no evidence that Wordsworth ever considered this option. One reason that is sometimes given is that his political opinions had changed so much that *The Prelude*, with its fervent republicanism and its enthusiasm for the ideals of the French Revolution, would have been a source of embarrassment for the middle-aged Conservative that he had become. But that argument does not really hold, as just a few lines added to the poem would have been enough to situate the work in context, and to clarify any ambiguities about the poet's later thinking on politics. In any case, during the decades spent reviewing and correcting *The Prelude*, Wordsworth never made any attempt to modify or qualify the feelings and ideas he expressed as a young man. The 1850 version of the poem is in this respect almost identical to the 1805 version. Besides, Wordsworth's republicanism was never articulated coherently or developed into a serious and meaningful political discourse. At its most ardent it was a rallying-cry against injustice and oppression, but it never went beyond expressing the feelings that thousands of people must have shared at that time.

There is no logical explanation why Wordsworth refused to publish *The Prelude* during his lifetime, so maybe we should look for an explanation that eludes reasoning. It could be that his unconscious desire was that no one (apart from a few selected friends) should share the story that he told himself in his long poem; and the 'Lucy' poems might hold the key to this think-ing. Lucy's meagre consolation in dying young is that she can be returned to nature intact, without having had to endure the process of alienation from the natural world that is the inevitable counterpart of education and work and social life in general. Of course the whole thrust of *The Prelude* is towards reconciling the contradiction between two processes – of loss and of growing up. But while the text succeeds magnificently in this respect, it can only do so by creating another tension – between the intimate world of private memory, and the public terrain of a published work. In writing *The Prelude* Wordsworth had worn his heart upon his sleeve as far as he was able to do so; but in laying bare his most intimate thoughts and feelings, and in articulating his secret childhood memories, he had in a certain sense given away his birthright, the core of his identity. For in the final analysis his childhood and his memories were his and his alone – and not to be shared with anyone (except perhaps Dorothy, if and when he chose to). *The Prelude* was in this sense predicated upon an impossibility, and when it came to the crunch Wordsworth preferred to leave the work intact, in harmony with the memories it evoked and reflected on, rather than send it out into the world to earn a dreary living and a reputation of some sort.

Which would leave Wordsworth like Penelope in Homer's *Odyssey*, weaving and then undoing his work and then weaving again, all with the aim of never finishing.

Chapter XII

The Whirligig of Time

— and thus the whirligig of time brings in his revenges.
(Shakespeare, *Twelfth Night*, V, I, 373)

After *Lyrical Ballads* Wordsworth abandoned the idea of working exclusively in one genre or style. He began to experiment with different techniques, relying on his extensive knowledge of the poetry of the past as a guarantee of formal roadworthiness for his own compositions. Now that he was sure of his own poetic voice he could allow his mind to relax its grip, to dilate, to explore different themes and subjects for their intrinsic interest rather than harness them to a pre-defined structure. The result was that when his next collection of poems was published (in two volumes) in 1807, the reader was confronted by a bewildering variety of works: there were odes and sonnets, elegies, ballads and narrative poems; brief meditations like *'My heart leaps up...'* were wedged in between long and solemn masterpieces such as *Resolution and Independence* and *Intimations of Immortality*; political tirades were placed alongside personal meditations on wild flowers....the small celandine and the daffodils thus found themselves forming part of a herbaceous border in which the profusion of forms seemed to be the gardener's only guiding principle.

During the following years Wordsworth thought long and

hard about how he could present his work in a way that made sense; and when in 1815 he felt ready to publish his first anthology of *Collected Poems*, he decided on a radically new arrangement. He placed the poems under thematic headings such as 'Poems referring to the Period of Childhood', 'Poems Founded on the Affections', or 'Poems of the Imagination', disregarding completely the date of composition. No major poet before or since has ever organised his work in such an idiosyncratic way, and critics found his method confusing and unnecessary. Why not simply put the poems in chronological order, and allow the themes to reveal themselves naturally? As his friend Charles Lamb put it when, in 1827, Wordsworth was preparing his five-volume edition of *The Poetical Works of William Wordsworth*, 'there is only one good order – And that is the order in which they were written – That is a history of the poet's mind'.[92] Undaunted by the adverse response, Wordsworth remained faithful to the arrangement set out in 1815 for the rest of his life: as the poems accumulated with the years he either incorporated them into the existing categories, or created new categories or sections (especially when he wrote a series of poems on a specific theme). But the larger organisation didn't change; and for a long time after his death readers approached Wordsworth's oeuvre through this structure. The Victorian reading public were quite happy with it, and no doubt enjoyed distinguishing between imagination, fancy, the affections, sentiment and reflection, as the poet invited them to do. This legacy remained intact for about a century, until modern scholarship came to grips with it. From the 1980s onwards editors reinstated the primacy of chronology and discarded many of the corrections and revisions Wordsworth made to his poems, presenting as authentic and definitive texts which the poet later decided to modify. As a result all of Wordsworth's intentions have been undone, and his work is presented today in a way that would have annoyed him intensely.

The discrepancy between those intentions and the response of modern editors is sufficiently important to deserve examination in some detail. First we need to know how the poet would have liked his oeuvre to be presented. My oldest copy of the *Collected Poems*, which is from the end of the nineteenth century, is arranged as follows:

Poems Written in Youth

Poems Referring to the Period of Childhood

Poems Founded on the Affections

Poems on the Naming of Places

Poems of the Fancy

The Waggoner

Poems of the Imagination

Miscellaneous Sonnets

Memorials of a Tour in Scotland, 1803

Memorials of a Tour in Scotland, 1814

Poems Dedicated to National Independence and Liberty

Memorials of a Tour on the Continent, 1820

Memorials of a Tour in Italy, 1837

The River Duddon. A Series of Sonnets

The White Doe of Rylstone

Ecclesiastical Sonnets

Yarrow Revisited, and Other Poems

Evening Voluntaries

*Poems, Composed or Suggested during a Tour in the Summer
    of 1833*

Poems of Sentiment and Reflection

Sonnets Dedicated to Liberty and Order

Sonnets upon the Punishment of Death

Miscellaneous Poems
Inscriptions
Selections from Chaucer Modernised
Poems Referring to the Period of Old Age
Epitaphs and Elegaic Pieces
The Prelude, or Growth of a Poet's Mind
The Excursion

A quick glance at this summary reveals both the difficulties implicit in the system, and its underlying purpose. The problems are obvious: for example there is no reason why sonnets written in 1802 and 1803 on the theme of European politics should come after a series of poems composed in 1814 about a tour in Scotland. At the same time it is significant that those sonnets, ('Poems Dedicated to National Independence and Liberty'), are clearly separated from the 'Sonnets Dedicated to Liberty and Order' composed in the 1830s: for Wordsworth so much had happened during the intervening decades that for him it would have made no sense to group all the poems he had written on the theme of liberty together. His arrangement was designed to bear witness to the changes that take place in the mind of man during the course of a single life.

Within a single group of poems there are similar tensions. If we take for example the twenty 'Poems Referring to the Period of Childhood', those that are dated move forwards and backwards in time in the order that they are given in the late Victorian edition, the dates being: 1804, 1801, 1801, 1802, 1811, 1806, 1807, 1801, 1799, 1798, 1800, 1798, 1801, 1800, 1802, 1799, 1817. Wordsworth saw no problem in this: his concern within each group of poems was to arrange them in an order that was aesthetically satisfying – just as if he was a painter organising a retrospective exhibition of his work, and who would instinctively place canvases next to each other that went together well, rather than because one had been painted after the other. As if to demonstrate the absurdity of a purely chronological order, Wordsworth put at the beginning of this group the small poem *'My heart leaps up'*, which contains the famous line, 'The Child is Father of the Man'. That line gains its force precisely by inverting the natural order of events, and alerts the reader to a perception of time that is profoundly original and challenging.

Secondly, Wordsworth made it clear when he introduced this system that it was neither casual nor whimsical. The *Collected Poems* of 1815 were accompanied by a long Preface (of about thirteen pages) in which the poet explained the thinking that lay behind the arrangement he proposed. After distinguishing between the different poetic genres or 'classes' he continued:

> the following Poems have been divided into classes; which, that the work may more obviously correspond with the course of human life, for the sake of exhibiting it in the three requisites of a legitimate whole, a beginning, a middle, and an end, have also been arranged, as far as it was possible, according to an order of time, commencing with Childhood, and terminating with Old Age, Death, and Immortality. [93]

The significance of this passage seems to have escaped all those who, from 1815 to the present day, have rejected Wordsworth's arrangement out of hand. It shows that, far from ignoring the role of time in the development of an oeuvre, he wanted to integrate it fully into the creative process. What he chose to disregard was the idea of historical time as a continuum in which individual events and lives take place. Instead, the span of a human life became the standard by which time was measured. By extension time was considered as cyclical rather than linear, for the thinking implied that the birth of a new generation would follow the death with which the anthology closed. There was nothing un-reasonable in this proposition; what was radical was Wordsworth's decision to impose his thinking on the form of each collection of poems. (In a similar way James Joyce's *Finnegans Wake* resisted the linear drag of narrative: the end of his novel curved round to meet up with the point at which it had begun – the cycles of 'history repeating itself with a difference' mocking the notion of there being any ending to a story.)[94]

★ ★ ★

While modern editors have agreed in reverting to a chronological ordering of Wordsworth's work, they have not always agreed about which texts to adopt. Stephen Gill has edited two collections for Oxford University Press: the first – in the Oxford World's Classics series – in 1984, and the second – from the 21st-Century Oxford Authors series – in 2010. As these collections are both authoritative and easily available the line adopted by Professor Gill carries a certain weight, as it inevitably influences the way Wordsworth is approached by a large part of the reading public today. Professor Gill realised that the two issues – of text and arrangement – were intimately connected; and he decided to adopt exactly the same approach to both of them. In 1984 he commented on the last edition published during the poet's lifetime, that,

> For the reader interested in the development of Wordsworth's art, however, this last edition is most unsatisfactory. Many poems have been considerably revised from their first published state....There is a further objection to the last authorized edition, namely that its organization prevents a chronological reading. (Note on the text)

He therefore decided that in every case he would publish a poem in its first completed state (or as near to that as was possible), disregarding all revisions made by the poet – even while he quoted in the same Note on the text a remark made by Wordsworth in 1830, 'You know what importance I attach to following strictly the last copy text of an author'.

I can think of no other example in the history of literature where a major author has been subjected to the kind of treatment that Wordsworth has received at the hands of modern editors: his declared wishes overruled, his entire oeuvre reorganised, and each work that constitutes a part of that oeuvre reexamined, so as to determine whether the form that finally satisfied the artist can justly be presented to a public living two hundred years after the event. Such disrespect is so flagrant that one cannot help scratching one's head and asking oneself, why? Just what is going on here? Is all this really necessary?[95]

Let us consider first the element that seems to have irritated and perplexed all editors since the Second World War, namely Wordsworth's rejection of a chronological arrangement of his poems. As this was quite unheard of at the time it inevitably raised eyebrows; and since it coincided with the point in Wordsworth's life when his creative powers began to fail him, it has been suggested that the strategy was perhaps a skilful way of disguising that 'falling off', and of guaranteeing that sales of his poetry would be maintained at a respectable level. By mixing in earlier (and more successful) poems with new (and weaker) pieces – good apples in the same basket as less tasty ones – he could mask the fading of 'the visionary gleam' and continue to offer a decent product to his readers.

There is something in this argument, but not enough to be convincing. Over and beyond the cynicism it implies, which is far more typical of twentieth-century than of nineteenth-century artists, it suggests a degree of self-knowledge that seems unlikely. Would Wordsworth in 1815, aged just forty-five, have been convinced that his best writing days were behind him? And if so why did he continue to produce new work regularly for another thirty or so years? It is important to remember that phrases such as,

> Whither is fled the visionary gleam?

or,

> The things which I have seen I now can see no more

were almost certainly written in 1802, when he was at the very height of his creative powers: they do not refer to flaws in the creative process, but to patterns within a human life, which begin in early childhood and repeat themselves constantly until old age, and according to which we are caught up in a complex mechanism of loss and gain, whereby each experience involves something of each.

If, therefore, Wordsworth did not adopt his new system for commercial reasons, why did he do it? And why in the face of sustained criticism did he remain faithful to it? It can only have been because the arrangement he chose corresponded to his understanding of how time functions, and because he felt that a chronological arrangement of his poems would go against the vision that he sought to give form to in his work.

A simple linear representation of time ('first you do this, then you do that; you grow older, start a family, construct a career, etc.') would never have been good enough for Wordsworth. From the outset his brain operated a constant shuttle service between a well-defined past and a nebulous future, in which the present was merely a stop or a station where the train paused before continuing. The very first of the poems in his *Collected Edition*, written when he was sixteen, alerts us to this:

EXTRACT
*From the Conclusion of a Poem, Composed in
Anticipation of Leaving School.*

Dear native regions, I foretell,
From what I feel at this farewell,
That, whereso'er my steps may tend,
And whenso'er my course shall end,
If in that hour a single tie
Survive of local sympathy,
My soul will cast the backward view,
The longing look alone on you.

Thus, while the Sun sinks down to rest
Far in the regions of the west,
Though to the vale no parting beam
Be given, not one memorial gleam,
A lingering light he fondly throws
On the dear hills where first he rose.

The tension is there from the first couplet, with its rhyme of 'foretell' and 'farewell': at a moment of significant change he looks forwards and backwards at the same time; then projects himself far into the future so as to see the present in which he is writing as the past. The second half of the sonnet elegantly situates this movement in a natural context – saying that this is how it must be, that the laws of nature hold sway over the human heart just as they do over the evermoving planets.

Like a squirrel who in autumn makes a cache of nuts to provide food for the long winter, Wordsworth stored up intense sensations and significant moments for the future, placing them aside in his memory banks until the time would be right to feed on them in a creative way. This habit was well established by the time he was out of his teens: so, in a letter to Dorothy from Switzerland in 1790 (at the end of the famous walking tour) he wrote,

> At this moment when many of these landscapes are floating before my mind, I feel a high enjoyment in reflecting that perhaps scarcely a day of my life will pass, in which I shall not derive some happiness from these images.
>
> (September 6, 1790)

Phrased in this way the thought is in no way exceptional: any camera-clicking tourist on holiday might express the same feeling. But in *Tintern Abbey*, written eight years later, he articulated his thinking more precisely:

> The picture of the mind revives again:
> While here I stand, not only with the sense
> Of present pleasure, but with pleasing thoughts
> That in this moment there is life and food
> For future years.   (lines 62-66)

For Wordsworth an artist always lives twice, first in the immediate experience and secondly when that experience is revisited at a much later date. And since at any one moment in life he can be simultaneously working on past experiences and absorbing new ones, the activity of retrospection impinges on and qualifies the freshness of the present, making it difficult to give an absolute value to any transitory experience, however intense. Paraphrasing Sophocles, one might say, 'Count nothing real until it is past'.[96]

This unremitting cerebral activity must have been as tiring as it was potentially satisfying, and it is hardly surprising that composing poetry tended to make him physically unwell. '...only then, when memory / Is hushed, am I at rest', he wrote in another early poem: it is clear he had come to terms with the hold that the past had over him before he was adult. It meant that he was unlikely ever to write like Keats, who could cram a huge assortment of sensations and thoughts into a present tense that might be sustained for an indefinite period of time, and imbue the poet's vision with such amazing richness and intensity. But in remaining faithful to himself he was able to explore the relationship between past, present and future in a radically original way, and could chart new waters in literature, mapping out structures and patterns that consciousness creates inside all of us.

At the same time Wordsworth remained a very down-to-earth person, whose sense of his own body and whose love of physical exercise and movement provided a healthy counterbalance to the intellectual restlessness, keeping him firmly rooted in the reality of the present, and allowing him moments of intense satisfaction that resisted the constant process of revision and revisiting to which he was addicted. The faster the physical movement, and the less controllable it was, the more vividly it registered in the poetry. All-night dancing in Book IV of *The Prelude* (lines 316-345); horse-riding on the beach in Book II (lines 122-144); or ice-skating in Book I (lines 452-489) – all these experiences are told with a freshness and immediacy that transcends the act of memory involved in recounting them. The poetry is fluid and spontaneous, and gives us the sense of just what he was feeling at the time. In the ice-skating sequence, written during the winter of 1798 spent in Goslar (where the extreme cold no doubt made it easy for him to remember faithfully the sensations of ice-skating on Lake Windermere), the writing momentarily acquired an almost erotic quality:

And oftentimes,
When we had given our bodies to the wind
And all the shadowy banks on either side
Came sweeping through the darkness,

(lines 478-81)

The skating sequence was transcribed into the first draft version of *The Prelude* ('The two-part *Prelude* of 1799') almost a year after it was written, probably at the beginning of December 1799. The image clearly pleased Wordsworth, and was fresh in his mind when he wrote to Coleridge a few days after he and Dorothy began to set up house in Grasmere in December 1799:

> Rydale is covered with ice, clear as polished steel, I have procured a pair of skates and tomorrow mean to give my body to the wind – (letter of December 24)

Placed in the future tense – 'I... tomorrow mean to give my body to the wind' – the phrase loses some of its freshness, as anything premeditated must; while the same words, used in the past tense in the passage written a year earlier, are convincing as a record of something simply lived. For Wordsworth time was an intricate puzzle: past, present and future jostled continually in his head (the future, being as yet unknown, being by far the weakest of the three), and he often found it hard to situate his true response to anything, however trivial or however important, on this sliding-scale of time.

★ ★ ★

In the wet and water-sculpted landscape in which he lived, streams, torrents and rivers were his constant companions. He wrote of the rivers as if they were his friends, and as he walked beside one or other of them – the Derwent or the Duddon – he felt not only their soothing influence on him but also the clear analogy between running water and the movement of human thought. The very first text of the poem that would grow into *The Prelude* meditated on the interaction between the coursing of the river and the nurturing and development of the human mind – and the passage remained virtually unchanged when, six years later, it was transcribed into the 1805 version:

> Was it for this
> That one, the fairest of all rivers, loved
> To blend his murmurs with my nurse's song,
> And from his alder shades and rocky falls,
> And from his fords and shallows, sent a voice
> That flowed along my dreams? For this, didst thou,
> O Derwent, travelling over the green plains
> Near my 'sweet birthplace', didst thou, beauteous stream,
> Make ceaseless music through the night and day
> Which with its steady cadence tempering
> Our human waywardness, composed my thoughts
> To more than infant softness
>
> (Book I, lines 271-282)

A similar thought-process was evoked by Beethoven a few years later, in the second movement (entitled *Scene by a stream*) of his Sixth Symphony, where the music replicates the fluid gracefulness and rhythms of running water. For a moment the intentions of the German composer and the English poet coincided, as they sought to harmonise their art with the language of the elements. And Wordsworth's desire to speak with and on behalf of nature was sustained throughout *The Prelude*, culminating in the visionary passage in Book XIII when, from the summit of Snowdon, he listened to

> the roar of waters, torrents, streams
> Innumerable, roaring with one voice!   (lines 57-9)

that speak of

> The sense of God, or whatsoe'er is dim
> Or vast in its own being.   (lines 66-73)

Nothing in the conclusion of the poem comes to contradict the hope that this passage inspires, namely that the human mind can honestly find metaphors for itself in the natural world. Indeed when in 1799 Wordsworth wrote the initial passage 'Was it for this / That one, the fairest of all rivers...' he had good reason to believe in an active dialogue between running water and the movement of thought, for the previous year he had composed a long poem in a single concentrated fluid rush; he had held the poem in his head for several days without even setting pen to paper, and, once he had written it out, he had not changed a word of it either then or at a later date. The poem in question is of course *Lines written a few miles above Tintern Abbey,* and in it Wordsworth sang loud and clear of his love of rivers, both in the present –

> How oft, in spirit, have I turned to thee
> O sylvan Wye! Thou wanderer through the woods,
> How often has my spirit turned to thee!
>
>   (lines 57-59)

– and in his boyish past –

>   when like a roe
> I bounded o'er the mountains, by the sides

Of the deep rivers, and the lonely streams,
Wherever nature led   (lines 68-71)

One is tempted to see the ease with which the poem was com-
posed as matching the smooth flow of the river; and no doubt the
combination of walking, the river, and Dorothy's companionship
did help him to relax and focus creatively. But it would be wrong
to imagine that the beautiful and effortlessly produced love-song
to the natural world that makes up the poem was born out of that
moment alone – that the lines of poetry flowed in his mind as the
waters did in front of him. The subtitle, *On Revisiting the Banks of
the Wye during a Tour, July 13, 1798*, and the opening lines,

> Five years have passed; five summers, with the length
> Of five long winters! And again I hear
> These waters, rolling from their mountain-springs
> With a sweet inland murmur.   (lines 1-4)

remind us that the poem is controlled by memory: everything in
it depends on a constant comparison between past and present.
Unlike, say, Keats' *Ode to Autumn*, which springs from a sensual
response to the season in which the poem was being written,
Tintern Abbey moves restlessly backwards and forwards between
two points of time, establishing continuity or evaluating change as
the case may be. Thought is organised by memory, which shapes
the kaleidoscopic blur of immediate experience into patterns and
structures that can make sense of, and give an order to, what is
lived. In Wordsworth's poetry there was no place for a stream of
consciousness, no way of allowing the 'river of life' to spill over
into verse. Even when he was writing the most fluid and fluent
of his poems he was resisting immediacy and moving against the
straightforward course of events.

When he was writing about someone else, as in the *Lyrical Ballads*, Wordsworth was perfectly capable of producing a simple linear narrative. But when he himself was the subject of a poem he needed to engage both past and present tenses. The hold of memory on Wordsworth was absolute: it conditioned not only what he wrote in his poems but also the method of composition. Experience could not be written about directly; it had first to be lived, then laid to rest, and finally remembered. Remembering was a sort of test, which sieved and sifted through the mass of experience to separate the significant from the banal. This attitude was unprecedented for the age in which Wordsworth lived, even though it has since become so widely adopted among writers that it is now almost taken for granted. But Wordsworth went a step further still: the poem once written needed also to be laid to rest, and then at a later date reviewed and revised. In other words the poem with time became like another layer of experience superimposed onto the subject matter it narrated or articulated. It too could be seen in a different light at a later date – and might then be modified, rethought. Wordsworth's obsession with revising his work, that drove his team of unpaid secretaries (Dorothy, Mary, Sara and Dora) to distraction and that has irritated and baffled so many modern editors, was directly related to his method of composition: revision for him was an integral part of the creative process, and not simply a question of making corrections and improvements to a poem where necessary. It also means that the decision of a modern editor to systematically reject the revised version of a poem in favour of the first completed version – Stephen Gill in his introduction to the 1984 Oxford edition writes of poems 'encrusted with the revisions of perhaps forty years', as if corrections were barnacles that attached themselves to the smooth hull of a ship – goes diametrically against not only the wishes of the author, but also the spirit of the writing. Of course, corrections and revisions do not always improve a work – *The Prelude* being a case in point – but that is another question. The only fair solution to that problem – and it is the solution adopted by the Penguin edition of *The Prelude* – is to present both the first and last versions of a particular poem side by side, and to allow the reader to judge which is better.

★ ★ ★

Together with being the first truly autobiographical work written, *The Prelude* was the first work to explore the obscure world of memory. Superficially these two – autobiography and memory – go hand in hand, as writing about one's past is more or less a question of remembering. But in practice it is never as simple as that. For memory is selective just as affinities are elective. Forgetting is an essential part of memory – a deliberate act that streamlines experience, jettisoning the bits and pieces that for one reason or another upset us or hold us back, and discarding not only that which really is trivial and forgettable but also that which we prefer to consider unimportant because we are unwilling or unable to deal with its consequences. To this extent *The Prelude* is less about remembering the past than about the way the brain uses memory in order to move forward in life: selecting, re-arranging and erasing experiences so as to create a meaning which produces pleasure rather than pain and discomfort.

The selective processing of the past is a principle that we all apply; but in Wordsworth's case there were particular reasons for complying with this kind of censorship, and that had to do with his domestic situation. His intimate world was structured by relationships to different women, each of whom had an emotional claim on him. There was Annette (his mistress) far away in France, and Dorothy (his sister) by his side. Later there was Mary (his wife) + Dorothy + Annette. And later still there was Dora (his daughter) + Mary + Dorothy + Annette. Now many people have complicated love-lives, and emotional histories that require delicate management, and up to this point Wordsworth's situation was not exceptional. What made his case more complicated was his distaste for the act of writing. He simply did not enjoy putting pen to paper.[97] He had solved part of the problem by composing while walking, riding or lying in bed – but his poems still needed to be written down, and then more often than not corrected (a number of times), after which a fair copy would be made. Since he disliked writing he 'employed' the women of the household as scribes whenever possible. They were thus party to everything he composed, almost from the first spasm of inspiration to the last crossing of 't's and dotting of 'i's . With inevitable consequences: there were precious few secrets in Wordsworth's life that would not be passed under the microscope of female curiosity and suspicion, once they were committed to paper. And he knew it.

That said, he was incredibly lucky in being helped by women who were both discreet and unquestioningly loyal to him. Neither Dorothy nor Mary would have dreamed of querying anything that they copied out for William – nor would Dora, even though her letters, and the story of her life, show that she stuck to her own opinions even when they went against those of her father. The problem was in the mind of the poet. He did not want to upset unduly the women who shared his life, and who were closely involved in everything he wrote. So, while Dorothy had accepted Annette and Caroline's existence without much difficulty, and Mary had accomodated Dorothy's continual presence in her marriage with William, it would have been unreasonable to expect Mary to consider Annette as anything more than a part of William's history. Were he to dwell on that part of his life in his poetry at any length, and to attribute much significance to the relationship, it would not escape the notice of his loving wife and faithful scribe. For Wordsworth only his silent thoughts were private: the minute he articulated them in poetry they became public – and he knew all too well that he could be held to account for any feeling or idea that he uttered.

★ ★ ★

The remark by Charles Lamb concerning the arrangement of Wordsworth's poems, that was quoted above ('there is only one good order – And that is the order in which they were written – That is a history of the poet's mind') is echoed by the editor of the 2010 edition of Wordsworth's poetry in the Oxford Authors series:

> Convinced that a presentation which recognizes the claims of chronology can best reveal the growth of the poet's mind (the subject, after all, of his greatest poem, *The Prelude*), and record the historical unfolding of his career,... (Note on the selection and its ordering, p. xxxvii)

The use of the word 'history' or 'historical' betrays a tacit desire to establish a parallel between the life of an artist and the development of the society in which he or she lives. Both move forward, in obedience to the one-way movement of time; and the growth of the individual is matched by the progress of society. To the extent that one believes in social progress (as a man like Charles Lamb, living at a time when Britain was realising its dreams of empire and establishing itself as the world's major economic and industrial power, would have been inclined to do), the principle of chronology as a way of ordering an artist's work is fair enough. The artist learns his craft, practises, improves – he makes progress... themes are introduced, developed, brought to a conclusion... each new work, once finished, adds to those that preceded it, and enriches the oeuvre... in short, the whole of an artist's life can be studied on the assumption that he makes progress for as long as health and the ageing process allow. And the oeuvre of the artist is itself a contribution to the culture of the society in which he lives, and this contribution helps society to progress.

The problem is though that Wordsworth saw little evidence of progress in the world around him. His early enthusiasm for the French Revolution soon foundered, and its sequel – the Napoleonic period – left him dismayed and embittered. Closer to home he watched the Industrial Revolution transform lives and landscapes, and saw no good in it. He mistrusted capitalism, he hated the railways, he spoke out against the drift of people towards the cities: he simply did not believe that the lives of people were really improved by such things.

Wordsworth did his best to resist the drag of linear time, replicated in the onward march of history, in three ways: through the message of the poems themselves; by the powerful use of memory and retrospection; and by the non-chronological organisation of his oeuvre. The other great slave to memory and master of autobiographical fiction, James Joyce, counteracted the linear principle in narrative by other strategies, the most obvious of which was the cyclical pattern on which *Finnegans Wake* was structured. Joyce's concern was with the repetitive cycles of history, which undermined any idea of progress. For Wordsworth also, living close to nature in the wilds of Westmorland, the cyclical model was extremely important, but the thinking behind his use of that model was quite different. The most powerful rhythm in the natural world is of course cyclical, in clear opposition to a linear, chronological concept of time. While Wordsworth was well aware that he could not compose his poems in the same way as nature created her works, the voice that spoke to him from the untamed landscape in which he chose to live was strong enough to influence significantly the beliefs and wishes and intentions of his poems. And the elemental voice of nature found an echo in the all too visible cycle of life and death in rural communities: the sower of life being matched by the reaper of death, indifferent to individual destinies as his scythe brought down the infant, the healthy mother and the toothless grandparent indiscriminately.

Chapter XIII

The Child and the Man

My heart leaps up when I behold
A rainbow in the sky:
So was it when my life began;
So is it now I am a man;
So be it when I shall grow old,
Or let me die!
The Child is father of the Man;
And I could wish my days to be
Bound each to each by natural piety.

'The Child is Father of the Man', a single line in an untitled nine-line poem written in 1802 and published five years later, came to have a particular significance for Wordsworth: in 1815 he used it, together with the two following lines, as an epigraph to his *Ode: Intimations of Immortality*. Like a good mathematical formula the line acquired a universal validity with the simplest language, rearranging the order of words so that the sense was no longer trite – 'the man is father of the child' – but profoundly original, in that it pointed to the importance of childhood in the development of the individual.

This single line of poetry was a sort of signpost indicating a whole new territory that Wordsworth had staked out and claimed for himself. The territory was childhood, and the difference between how it is lived, and how it is later perceived by adults. The process of exploring this theme had begun nine years earlier with narrative pieces such as *Anecdote for Fathers* and *We are Seven*; it had then had been given greater depth by the 'Lucy' poems, and had provided *The Prelude* with some of its finest passages – as well as being crucial to the way the whole poem was structured. His *Ode: Intimations of Immortality*, written at more less the same time as *The Prelude*, took his thinking on the subject even further, and reached unexpected conclusions. So that before his last two children had even been born, Wordsworth had given shape to a vision of childhood that was complete, coherent, and profoundly original – and which called into question the way it had been considered in literature for more than two thousand years. In the past childhood had been seen as little more than a messy but necessary preamble to the serious business of adult life – an attitude neatly summed up by St Paul in his Epistle to the Corinthians:

When I was a child, I spake as a child, I understood as a child, I thought as a child: but when I became a man, I put away childish things. (I Corinthians 13, verse 11)

Wordsworth's intuition, based above all on memories of his own boyhood, was that the world in which children lived was not only quite distinct from the adult world, but was also just as valid and meaningful. The problem though was that what had profound meaning for children tended not to be articulated, and often remained outside of language: how then could it be approached and understood in writing? Courageously, Wordsworth began by making a stumbling-block of that difficulty, through the evident lack of communication that is the subject of *Anecdote for Fathers* and *We are Seven*. A few months after writing those poems he 'crossed the divide' and, delving into his own past, set out – in the first brief draft of the poem that would develop into *The Prelude* – to try and describe events from a child's point of view.

In this manuscript (the one known to us as *'Was it for this?'*, and written in Germany in the winter of 1798-9), he started by turning his back on received ideas about the relationship between childhood and adulthood, premised inevitably on notions of childhood innocence (and ignorance), set against adult experience (and knowledge) – ideas which underscored even such an innovative and visionary work as William Blake's *Songs of Innocence and Experience,* which had been published in 1794. Instead Wordsworth focused on acts of deliberate transgression in his childhood – such as hanging from a rock face while trying to rob a bird's nest; or running at night over the moors to steal birds' eggs; or stealing a bird that someone else had trapped. At the level of narrative he left these episodes hanging in mid-air, much as he had been while climbing the rock face: with no obvious context to circumscribe and define them, the memories were thus free to develop organically in the poet's mind – rather in the way bacteria is allowed to grow in dishes in laboratories. And those selected memories stood the test of time remarkably well: despite Wordsworth's mania for revision none of them were removed, or significantly altered, when he came to write the full-length version of the poem years later – nor during the countless changes made between 1805 and 1850. The core of the poem that was his childhood remained intact.

In the course of *The Prelude* these childhood experiences would form part of the slow process of growth towards adulthood. But at the same time as he meditated on this process he imagined another, quite different, movement: a circle that in closing in on itself refused the principle of development in time. This movement is most clearly seen in two of the untitled 'Lucy' poems written during the winter in Goslar: *'Three Years She Grew in Sun and Shower'* and *'A Slumber did my Spirit Seal'*. Here the intimate contact with nature which Wordsworth saw as being an intrinsic part of childhood remains intact, because the child dies before the painful process of educating the individual into adult human society can begin. In the first poem death is represented as a simple repossession by nature of the young girl,

> This Child I to myself will take,
> She shall be mine, and I will make
> A Lady of my own

while in the other poem the child's dead body is enfolded in an elemental embrace which, in focusing on the orbit of our planet around the sun,

> Rolled round in earth's diurnal course,
> With rocks and stones and trees

emphasises the circular dimension of time in the natural world. As we saw in the previous chapter, the tension between 'chronological' and 'circular' time, together with doubts as to the nature of progress, growth and development, would prove to be fundamental to Wordsworth's oeuvre as a whole; and it surely stems in part from this unresolved tension between childhood and adult life.

The same problem surfaces in the anecdote of the boy who imitated the owls so well that they responded when he called to them. Brooding on this memory while in Goslar, he wrote the passage 'There was a Boy...' which ended up in Book V of *The Prelude* (lines 389-413). The dialogue with nature is beautifully articulated by a boomerang of sound above Lake Windermere; and when the answering calls of the owls reach the boy, the communication is complete, for the boy has become an integral part of the landscape: his consciousness expands, transcending the limits of his body, so that the silence 'carried far into his heart', and the different elements of the landscape 'Would enter unaware into his mind' and reassemble themselves there. It reads like an intensely private and intimate experience, and originally was written in the first person; however at a certain point Wordsworth decided that the episode would gain in force if, like Lucy, the boy died young, and so he recast the passage in the third person. It's as if he could see no way of relating this kind of childhood experience to an adult perception of nature; the meaning could only be guaranteed if the experience remained self-contained and elusive. A child is like an animal, and has a knowledge of the natural world that is just as valid as that which a grown-up can feel and articulate, only it cannot be easily translated into the common currency of adult communication.

★ ★ ★

Apart from *The Prelude*, the *Ode: Intimations of Immortality* is the poem in which Wordsworth reflects most intensely on the relationship between childhood and adulthood. It is also the poem in which he articulates most fully his thinking on the cycles of birth and death, and meditates on the nature of time and on time in nature. Clearly a very ambitious poem, and generally considered one of his most important compositions, it had a particular significance for Wordsworth. In his arrangements he had the entire title printed in capital letters, and invariably placed it at the end of the *Epitaphs and Elegaic Pieces* (the last category of poems in the collection before the major statements of *The Excursion* and – after his death – *The Prelude*), just as *Tintern Abbey* was placed at the end of the different editions of *Lyrical Ballads*. In both cases these poems were seen, like the Fifth Act in a play, to provide a climax to and a resolution of the thoughts and feelings and arguments that had been elaborated in the preceding poems. Coming almost at the very end of his arrangement, the *Ode* looks and sounds like Wordsworth's poetic testament.

In fact it is two poems sewn together. The first four stanzas were written in March 1802, the remaining seven were completed in March 1804. Two years separate the questions that come at the end of the fourth stanza,

> Whither is fled the visionary gleam?
> Where is it now, the glory and the dream?
>   (lines 56-7)

from the unforgettable reply that opens the fifth stanza:

> Our birth is but a sleep and a forgetting:
> The Soul that rises with us, our life's Star,
> Hath elsewhere had its setting,
> And cometh from afar: (lines 58-61)

In *The Prelude* he was developing at this time the idea that consciousness, through the growth of the mind, gave an individual the means to transcend the limits of individual existence and to become a part of the infinite, and thus to rejoin the divine order that is nature. With the *Ode: Intimations of Immortality* his focus shifted abruptly from the mind to the soul. Unlike the mind, which was an elaborate construction – the result of character + education + experience – and therefore necessarily unique to each individual, Wordsworth saw the soul as a free and uncontrollable element that lodged within a human being but did not belong to anyone. This much was in accordance with traditional

Christian thinking, which considered the soul as a gift from God to each and every new-born child; but in the 'Ode' Wordsworth quite unexpectedly departed from the straight and narrow path of orthodox Christian theology. In a handful of lines he made it clear that his thinking on the life of the soul was close to that of the Ancient Greeks (as articulated in the concept of metempsychosis), was in tune with much oriental philosophy (of which he probably knew next to nothing), and had absolutely nothing in common with Anglican or Roman Catholic doctrine on the subject.

The elegance of the verse in these lines masks the density and complexity of the thought. The first line is particularly difficult: it compares the state of the new-born babe, usually seen as a process of gradual awakening to the world we live in, to the night's sleep that each of us know and enjoy at the end of a hard day – in other words, the birth of a baby is as much the end of something as the beginning of a new life. This is consonant with 'a forgetting', but that phrase begs the question, who is forgetting and what is being forgotten? Presumably 'forgetting' should be read with the word it rhymes with, namely 'setting': that's to say, what is forgotten is the previous life that was incarnated in the soul that sleeps in the new-born baby, alive but not yet awake. But of course what has been forgotten can also be remembered – indeed, we can't remember something unless we've first forgotten it. So just as memory preserves the continuity between past, present and future in our lives as individuals, so the birth of a child guarantees (according to Wordsworth's thinking here) a sort of immortality for the parents who conceived it, as the growing child will, consciously or unconsciously, 'remember' them in itself as it grows up. In waking gradually to consciousness it will emerge from that state of oblivion which goes by the name of birth; and the soul that wakes in it will, like the torch passed from runner to runner in a marathon relay, be carried forwards and onwards.

Wordsworth's image though is not of a torch that is passed from hand to hand, but of a star that appears and disappears during the constant movement of the planets. The linear thrust of time as represented by the movement from one generation to the next is thus tied in to a cyclical pattern that denies any sense of progress, emphasising the point that Wordsworth was simultaneously affirming in *The Prelude*.

★ ★ ★

The question-marks which ended the fourth stanza of the 'Ode' (quoted on page 329), and which found no sequel or reply for two years, are reminiscent of the first manuscript of the poem that would later evolve into *The Prelude*, which began with 'Was it for this?' and was then shelved, with the question unanswered, for a year. These questions were not rhetorical devices, introduced to break up the straightforward progress of an argument, or to cause it to pause and hesitate – as they would be for Keats in his Odes:

> Where are the songs of Spring? Ay, where are they?
> Think not of them, thou hast thy music too
> > (*Ode to Autumn*, lines 23-4)

> What men or gods are these? What maidens loth?
> What mad pursuit? What struggle to escape?
> What pipes and timbrels? What wild ecstasy?
> > (*Ode on a Grecian Urn*, lines 8-10)

Wordsworth had no skill in using rhetorical devices – just as he had no time for irony, or no wish to indulge in word-play for its own sake. To that extent his technical range as a poet was severely limited; but in the long run those limits proved to be his strengths, as they endowed all that he did write with a certain emphatic ring of conviction. In Wordsworth's poetry a question expressed a real doubt, one that could even cause a poem to stop short in its tracks and remain uncompleted – unless life in due course helped him to find an answer to the question. The self-questioning that made itself felt in the period before he married was a personalised form of the discontent and pessimism that ran through so much of the poetry he had written during the 1790s. Then his use of the ballad form meant that feelings such as doubt or despair, however intense and relevant to his own condition, were placed in a social context... but once he began to focus attention specifically on himself he became painfully aware of the mistakes he had made, of a lack of progress in his work and of a lack of direction in his life; and no amount of pompous patriotic sonnets would ease the sense of pain and dissatisfaction he felt when he made himself the subject of his verses.

The second part of *Ode: Intimations of Immortality* (stanzas 5 to 11, which make up almost three quarters of the poem), was written when Wordsworth had been married for a year and a half, was father of one child and was waiting for Mary to give birth for the second time. The tone in this part is different – more affirmative and balanced: the fact of being a father, of having created a new generation, offers a new meaning to the poet's life and also means that his centre of gravity shifts significantly. For now he must not so much find a balance inside himself as between himself and his children. His sense of time is modified also: he can begin to see his life as forming part of a bigger pattern, and not just having a design – a beginning, a middle and an end – that is sufficient to itself. Wordsworth articulates this tension between two visions by developing two distinct voices within the poem, in a sort of antiphony reminiscent of a Baroque cantata. On one side a world-weary adult piles on the pessimism, invoking 'grief', 'mourning', 'mortality' and 'death'; while another voice that feels itself 'strong', 'warm', 'fresh' and 'gay', sings of 'joy', 'jollity' and 'bliss' – the broken metrical pattern and irregular rhythms accentuating the impression of specific voices rather than of poetic diction. At moments the play of opposites has the tough bluntness of Elizabethan drama, as in:

> A wedding or a festival,
> A mourning or a funeral;   (lines 94–5)

or,

> To whom the grave
> Is but a lonely bed without the sense or sight
> Of day or the warm light.   (lines 120–22)

These alternating black-and-white, bleak-and-bright, visions of life and death rotate restlessly around the theme of childhood, which is itself reiterated in a way that is uncharacteristically obsessive for Wordsworth – 'child', 'birth', 'young', 'Child of Joy', 'Boy', 'Children', 'Babe', 'birth', 'infancy', 'Boy', 'Fosterchild', 'Child', 'Darling', 'Child', 'Childhood', 'new-born', 'Boy', 'Children', 'young' – and which bears witness to the extent and intensity of his anxiety.

★ ★ ★

Wordsworth's epigraph for the *Ode* in the 1815 edition ('The Child is Father of the Man...') replaced the one used in the

1807 edition, which was 'Paulò majora canamus'. However the editor of the present Oxford collection of Wordsworth's poetry has reinstated the original epigraph – on the grounds that it came first (just as he has invariably adopted the first text available of every poem in the collection). The notes to this edition offer a translation of the Latin, but make no comment on the choice of quotation, though it is actually quite revealing. '*Paulò maiora canamus*' ('Let us take a nobler tone') is the first line of Virgil's *Fourth Eclogue*, a powerfully optimistic poem that foresees a Golden Age in which a boy, part of a 'new breed of men sent down from heaven' ('*iam nova progenies caelo demittitur alto*'), will bring peace and prosperity to all people. While the poem could be set alongside Isaiah's vision of the coming of the Messiah ('a small boy shall lead them') the Eclogue's references and context are clearly classical and non-Christian, and to that extent fit well with the thinking on the rebirth of the soul that we find in the *Ode*, just as the vision offered by Virgil is in harmony with the affirmative mood of the *Ode*. Wordsworth's choice of epigraph was in no way casual.

And yet he changed it. The three lines he replaced it with were the second half of the short but very beautiful poem 'My heart leaps up when I behold', composed at the same time as the first four stanzas of the *Ode*, that's to say in March 1802. Or more precisely, the editor of the Oxford edition informs us, on March 26, 1802. Presumably that dating is based on the entry from Dorothy Wordsworth's journal for that day, which ends,

While I was getting into bed he wrote the Rainbow.

(referring to the opening lines of the poem, 'My heart leaps up when I behold /A rainbow in the sky'). Interestingly, the entry for that day begins,

A beautiful morning. William wrote to Annette then worked at the Cuckow.

As we have seen, Wordsworth's correspondence with Annette in 1802 had one overriding intention: to agree the conditions for an arrangement by which he would be freed from any moral obligation to her (and therefore free to marry Mary), while doing what he could to help Annette and Caroline financially (which wasn't much). March 26, 1802, was, therefore, a day which began with a letter whose purpose was to enable Wordsworth to sever his link with both his former lover and his daughter, and which ended with a poem which stressed the fundamental importance of continuity between generations. The contradiction is striking, the poem apparently working as an unconscious antidote to the thought behind the letter, rather as the second half of the *Ode* is affirmative while the first half is brooding and melancholic.

★ ★ ★

Wordsworth's most important meditations on childhood were composed by 1805, though the theme continued to interest him, and, as we have seen, was one of the headings – (*Poems referring to the Period of Childhood*) – for the collected edition of 1815. Not long after this date novelists began to experiment with the idea of setting a child's vision against that of adults – the early chapters of Jane Austen's *Mansfield Park* offering one of the first examples of its kind. But no other writer before the mid-nineteenth century came anywhere close to Wordsworth's intense and sustained involvement with the subject. Then came *Jane Eyre*, published in 1847; and above all there were the novels of Dickens, who from *Oliver Twist* through *Nicholas Nickleby*, *David*

Copperfield and *Little Dorrit* to *Great Expectations*, did more than any other nineteenth-century writer to give voice and form to the inner world of children's thoughts and feelings. It is tempting to see Wordsworth as an influence on writers like Dickens in this respect, but that would be misleading. To start with, the fact that Wordsworth did not publish *The Prelude* during his lifetime meant that the most important of his texts dealing with childhood, and the one that provided the vital link between the 'Lucy' poems and the *Ode: Intimations of Immortality*, giving coherence and depth to the vision that had inspired a large number of disparate poems, was unavailable until 1850 — by which time novels such as *Oliver Twist, Nicholas Nickleby* and *David Copperfield* had already been written.[98] In any case Dickens' concern was less with the realm of childhood as a subject in its own right, than with the — often painful or violent — confrontation between the world of children and that of adults. These confrontations showed up the vulnerability of children, and demonstrated the strategies children need in order to defend themselves against cruelty or oppression — or, quite simply, to deal with the tough realities of life. Like his contemporary Charles Darwin, Dickens was interested in the principle of struggle and survival. Wordsworth's thinking about the relationship between childhood and adulthood was different, and had more to do with loss and gain. The 'growth of the mind' was only possible through education, and through experience of the adult world; but that process necessarily involved an alienation from natural instinct — the priceless foster-parent to the child's soul. That is the price that adults pay in order to exist and function in society.

Wordsworth's thinking on childhood may not have been on the same wavelength as that of the Victorians, but it came into its own again in the twentieth century. His reliance on memory rather than imaginary narrative as the means to explore both childhood experiences, and the relationship between childhood and adult life, was shared by Proust and Joyce. In both their cases fiction could be said to develop out of memory (whereas with a writer like Dickens, the fictional impulse was dominant, and he simply delved into the archives of memory as and when it suited him). However, neither Joyce nor Proust expressed any interest in Wordsworth's work, so there is no question of establishing a sort of literary family-tree. Nonetheless we can say that Wordsworth proved to be a precursor for a large number of twentieth-century writers (and filmmakers), who relied heavily on autobiography to structure their writing; and who, within that aesthetic, saw childhood as an autonomous territory, to be explored and understood as a realm in its own right and with its own specific identity.

Chapter XIV

A Prayer for My Daughter

> Days I have held,
> days I have lost,
>
> days that outgrow, like daughters,
> my harbouring arms.

(Derek Walcott, 'Midsummer, Tobago')

One of the sonnets written in 1802 returned to the theme of a beautiful girl or young woman who is dead, which had been a central motif of the 'Lucy' poems a few years earlier. This time, though, Wordsworth overlaid the poem with a new layer of meaning: the opening line – 'Methought I saw the footsteps of a throne' clearly evokes the first line of Milton's famous sonnet, *'Methought I saw my late espousèd saint'*.[99] Wordsworth had been inspired to try his hand at writing sonnets a month or two earlier, after Dorothy had read some of Milton's sonnets to him one evening; and this sonnet is in part a tribute by Wordsworth to Milton. The poem obliquely referred to is one of Milton's most moving, and is itself a tribute to the most loved of his three wives, Katherine. She had died four months after giving birth to a daughter (also called Katherine) in October 1657; the little girl died six weeks later. Milton's poem recounts a dream or vision in which the dead woman appears to her blind husband (his sight began to deteriorate in the late 1640s, and he was completely blind by 1652): the force of the sonnet, beautifully encapsulated in the last two lines, comes from the stark contrast between inner vision and physical blindness, between the illusory hope that dreams offer and the bleak reality that returns with each new dark day:

> But O as to embrace me she inclined
> I waked, she fled, and day brought back my night.
>
> (lines 13-14)

In his sonnet Wordsworth retained both the narrative of a dream or vision, and the sharp confrontation of opposites, that together had given Milton's poem its particular quality. The subject remained more or less the same – a beautiful young woman who has died – but Wordsworth's viewpoint was significantly different. While Milton specified that the woman in question was his wife, who had died after giving birth ('Mine as whom washed from spot of childbed taint') Wordsworth was deliberately vague as to the age or situation of the woman in his vision. Indeed, she could perfectly well be a girl rather than a woman; and the ending of the sonnet replicated both the theme and the mood of the 'Lucy' poems written in the previous years:

> and I beheld the face of one
> Sleeping alone within a mossy cave,
> With her face up to heaven; that seemed to have
> Pleasing remembrance of a thought foregone;
> A lovely beauty in a summer grave! (lines 10-14)

The 'summer grave' epithet in the powerful last line has some of the macabre grimness of the grave evoked in Marvell's *To His Coy Mistress* –

> Nor in thy marble Vault, shall sound
> My ecchoing Song: then Worms shall try
> That long preserv'd Virginity　　　(lines 26-28) –

but in Wordsworth's verse sexual connotations are sublimated or effaced, depending on how one chooses to interpret the image of the young girl in her 'mossy cave', and the poem relies rather on contrasting opposites – youth, beauty and summertime set against death and the underworld – which have a timeless value.

Apart from the last line, *'Methought I saw the footsteps of a throne'* was not a very good sonnet – but it gained a haunting quality in retrospect when, ten years after it was composed, Wordsworth's daughter Catherine died at the age of three years and nine months. The ironies would have been all too obvious to Wordsworth: his daughter had the same name as Milton's second wife (and their daughter) who had been the subject of the poem that had inspired Wordsworth to compose his sonnet; and she died in the middle of summer – little Catherine was buried on June 8, 1812. Life imitating art? Events such as this, in which poetic vision and everyday reality marched sadly hand in hand, would gradually lead Wordsworth towards a certain kind of fatalism, according to which cycles of loss and gain, bereavement and renewal, death and life were everywhere present and irresistible; and in middle age this kind of fatalism would blend easily with political conservatism – with the sense that there was no point in trying to change the world, and that it was best to leave things as they were.

In the two years following Catherine's death in 1812, Wordsworth wrote two poems in her memory, which worked together in a kind of emotional counterpoint. The first, *Characteristics of a Child three Years old*, is a portrait of his daughter which, strangely for a posthumous tribute, is written entirely in the present tense:

> Loving she is, and tractable, though wild;
> And Innocence hath privilege in her
> To dignify arch looks and laughing eyes.
>
> (lines 1-3)

And so it goes on for another eighteen lines. Wordsworth's refusal to use the past tense, his evident desire to imagine his daughter still alive, speak clearly of his distress.[100] However another poem written at the same time unravels the fiction that the first poem constructs:

> Surprised by joy – impatient as the Wind
> I wished to share the transport – Oh! with whom
> But Thee, long buried in the silent Tomb
>
> (lines 1-3)

Here the message of irremediable loss is explicit; interestingly, to articulate his grief Wordsworth returned to the same sonnet of Milton's ('Methought I saw my late espousèd saint') that had served him ten years earlier. Avoiding the inimitable play on blindness and sight, darkness and light, that Milton handled so skilfully, he contented himself with a relatively simple play on the idea of blindness and sight. First he suggested that he himself was blind (which had the perverse benefit of making him feel closer to Milton) in refusing to admit his daughter's death:

> Through what power
> Even for the least division of an hour,
> Have I been so beguiled as to be blind
> To my most grievous loss!   (lines 6-9)

Then he concluded the sonnet by restoring his own vision but taking away the person he wanted to be able to see:

Knowing my heart's best treasure was no more;
That neither present time, nor years unborn
Could to my sight that heavenly face restore

(lines 12–14)

The logic is simple but pitiless: no inner vision, however in-
tense or beautiful, can be a substitute for whatever can be seen,
felt or known in the real world. For most of the time the inner
and outer worlds run parallel to each other, and at best they in-
teract in a dialectic which allows each to enrich the other. But
there are limits to what either memory can restore or imagina-
tion invent. For the poet who had relied on memory ever since
adolescence to structure his perception of the world, and who in
The Prelude had made of imagination one of the key elements of
the creative spirit, this was a sad and sobering assessment to make.

Book III of *Paradise Lost* had opened with an unforgettably
beautiful meditation on light and sight. The pivotal moment in
it came with Milton's suggestion that his own physical blindness
enabled him to see better in the inner world of ideas and beliefs:

Thus with the year
Seasons return, but not to me returns
Day, or the sweet approach of even or morn,
Or sight of vernal bloom, or summer's rose

(lines 40–43)

So much the rather thou celestial light
Shine inward, and the mind through all her powers
Irradiate, there plant eyes, all mist from thence
Purge and disperse, that I may see and tell
Of things invisible to mortal sight.   (lines 51–55)

For Wordsworth such a proposition was wishful thinking. It

might have been valid for Milton, living at a time in which religious convictions underpinned individual existences, but in the age of doubt and uncertainty in which Wordsworth lived an inner vision, however spiritual and uplifting, was unlikely to be convincing unless it could be seen and felt to be intimately related to empirical experience.

★ ★ ★

More than twenty years before Schubert composed his great D minor String Quartet, known as *Death and the Maiden*, Wordsworth had come to see death as the unwelcome chaperone of young girls. The sonnet of 1802 quoted above, with the dead girl 'Sleeping alone within a mossy grave', picks up where the 'Lucy' poems left off. And in that same summer he transposed a similar thought onto another young girl – this time his natural daughter Caroline. The only poem in which he ever refers to her directly – *'It is a beauteous Evening, calm and free'*, a sonnet composed while he and Dorothy, Annette and Caroline, were all at Calais together – consigns her to a kind of limbo, despite the fact that the healthy nine-year old girl, flesh of his flesh, was strolling beside him along the seashore:

> Dear Child! Dear Girl! that walkest with me here,
> If thou appear untouched by solemn thought,
> Thy nature is not therefore less divine:
> Thou liest in Abraham's bosom all the year;
> And worshipp'st at the Temple's inner shrine, God
> being with thee when we know it not.
>
> (lines 9-14)

The reference to Abraham's bosom is uncompromising, for it

is there that the dead rest (see Luke 16, verse 22). And of course Caroline had always been dead to him, as he hadn't once seen her during the first nine years of her life. Nonetheless she was clearly very much alive, and the last two lines of the sonnet go some way to reconciling the objective truth of the situation with the image he held in his mind. The idea that God is with her 'when we (adults) know it not' reverts to the thinking of Book I of *The Prelude,* which he was also working on at that time, and which suggests that children exist in an intimate relationship with nature (and by extension with God) that adults have difficulty in recognising.

It is both a moving and a clumsy tribute to his long-lost daughter: the emotion is intense but remains unclear and unresolved. And to that clumsiness must be added the fact that he refused to acknowledge in public that Caroline was his daughter. Although he did not disown her, and continued to help financially even after her marriage to Jean-Baptiste Baudouin in 1816 (which he did not attend), he could never admit the relationship openly. Caroline had no such difficulty. At her wedding she signed her name on the marriage certificate, 'A. C. Wordsworth' (the only time in France that William's surname was spelt correctly in an official document); and when at last she met up again with her father (in 1820, while he was passing through Paris on a tour in Europe) she embarrassed him by calling him 'Father' in company.[101] This may simply have been plain-speaking of the sort one finds in the few letters of her mother's that have survived; but one has the impression that she, like so many children who have grown up without knowing one or other of their parents, wanted the relationship to be made known, to be explicit. Not that she expected anything from Wordsworth other than recognition – but recognition mattered, as it constituted an important element in her own identity.

The man who wrote so eloquently about continuity between generations, about natural piety and about how 'the Child is Father of the Man' would not grant her that silent request. The 'French connection' would – must – remain a secret, with all traces obscured, all tracks covered over. Obviously there were reasons why Wordsworth, once married to Mary, would want to keep the affair with Annette under wraps. But what is striking is that he had the same attitude to that relationship throughout the 1790s. At a time of considerable sexual permissiveness he seems to have felt only shame at having fallen in love with a French woman and having fathered an illegitimate child; and he would not allow himself to see the affair as in any way enriching.

★ ★ ★

Even when married Wordsworth greeted paternity with a certain ambivalence. Having wasted no time in fathering his first legitimate child – Mary gave birth to John just eight months after her marriage to William – he seemed unwilling to alter his well-ingrained habits, or sacrifice his precious freedom, in order to accomodate the new arrival. On August 15, when the baby was less than two months old, he set off with Dorothy and Coleridge for a six-week tour of Scotland, leaving Mary with only her younger sister Joanna to help her and keep her company. It was a strange thing to do, as he knew all too well how easy it was for young babies to fall seriously ill and even die during their first few months, and one would have imagined him unwilling to leave his wife's side at that time.

As if to compensate for his insouciance, he celebrated the birth of his daughter Dora the following year with an overdose of fairly incomprehensible angst. A 76-line poem, pompously entitled *Address To My Infant Daughter Dora, On Being Reminded That She Was A Month Old That Day, September 16,* started off with all the joy and gaiety of a funeral address:

> —Hast thou then survived—
> Mild offspring of infirm humanity,
> Meek Infant! Among all forlornest things
> The most forlorn – one life of that bright star,
> The second glory of the Heavens? – Thou hast;
> Already hast survived that great decay,
> That transformation through the wide earth felt,
> And by all nations.   (lines 1-8)

In due course, though, the world-weary mood passed, and the Poet went back to the happy business of procreating offspring at two-yearly intervals: Thomas was born in 1806, Catherine in 1808, and Willy in 1810. At that point the family was complete – and then Wordsworth had to find a way of making sense of the situation as a whole, of understanding how each individual (including himself) might fit into the bigger picture. It was no easy task, given the complicated set of relationships that he had to juggle with by this time. There was an unmarried ex-lover in France; an illegitimate daughter in France; an unmarried sister with whom he lived; his wife; a sister-in-law-in-residence; and five legitimate children. Ten people whose needs and desires had to be considered – and of these only three were males. That's to say that in the context of his personal life Wordsworth's time and mental space were above all taken up with trying to understand female preoccupations, and negotiating with the female charac-ter. All the signs are that he was unprepared for the task and un-suited to the role in which he found himself.[102] It was simply too much for him: the best he could do was to burrow into his own private world (where no one else could come), while preserving a calm and polite exterior which guaranteed a sense of order, and enabled each person to find his or her place in the real or imaginary household. Outside of his poetry he kept his thoughts very much to himself, keeping no diary and seldom expressing his feelings in the letters he wrote. So, apart from the comments made by others concerning the way Wordsworth conducted his relationships, together with basic biographical facts, all we have to go on are the poems. The picture they offer is of a man who had great difficulty in entering imaginatively into a woman's inner world; and of a father who, while he loved to evoke and explore the hidden mysteries of his own childhood, showed no such interest when it came to considering his children's lives.

The first hint of this lack of empathy came as early as 1802, before he had even married. The sonnet composed while in Calais in August of that year, and quoted above, opened with the lines:

> It is a beauteous evening, calm and free;
> The holy time is quiet as a Nun
> Breathless with adoration;

The relevance of these lines to William's relationship with Dorothy has already been discussed in chapter ten (page 245); but the image of the nun would prove to have wider implications. The image itself was surprising – in no way related to the kind of metaphors a reader had come to expect in Wordsworth. But then this was a poem composed in Catholic France, where the monastic life flourished undisturbed, whereas in England it had been abruptly terminated by the Dissolution of the Monasteries in the sixteenth century (Tintern Abbey was one of the victims of that policy, having been disestablished in 1536). The journey he and Dorothy made to Calais together provided Wordsworth (for whom experience was intrinsically linked to a specific time and place) with this new vocabulary. Once anchored in his brain, he could deploy it again whenever it was relevant. And so, in another sonnet written later in 1802, he followed up the theme of the earlier poem with a more explicit and emphatic message:

> Nuns fret not at their convent's narrow room;
> And hermits are contented with their cells;
> And students with their pensive citadels:
> Maids at the wheel, the weaver at his loom,
> Sit blithe and happy;

The poem goes on to trace a parallel between the limits within which such people live and work, and the limits a sonnet imposes on the poet. In so doing it brings Dorothy's nun-like condition onto the same plane as her brother's, making it clear that she should not feel her life-choices to have been wrong, nor herself inadequate. All well and good, were it not for the fact that the future he was fashioning for himself was a lot more attractive than the one that Dorothy could contemplate – and that her active participation in his new life as husband and father-to-be was essential to his happiness and creativity.

Everything worked out as William would have wished: Dorothy remained chaste and virginal, and if she ever fretted at the conditions in which she lived, she kept her discontent to herself. Time passed, their lives moved on. Interestingly though, the image of the nun returned punctually when William and Dorothy made their next trip to the Continent – eighteen years later. After staying at Bruges during the summer of 1820, Wordsworth ended his sonnet *'Bruges I saw attired with golden light'* (composed once they were back in England) by evoking the charm of the old town where,

the Forms
Of nun-like females, with soft motion, glide!

Needless to say, Dorothy was at his side during the walk referred to; but the image of nuns here is less significant as a comment on his sister's lifestyle, than as indicating how his brain worked. For Wordsworth, for whom all experiences were clearly fixed both in time and space, returning to a place where he had been before inevitably moved him to return also to the poetry written at or about that place years (or even decades) earlier. Certain images or passages, and certain poems, belonged not just to specific moments in his life, but also to specific places. The 'Lucy' poems would always be inseparable from the winter at Goslar, for example, for the simple reason that once he was back in Continental Europe his mind returned instinctively to reflecting on his relationship with Annette and on his daughter Caroline. Similarly, when he went back to France in 1802 to meet Annette and Caroline, he revived the thinking of the 'Lucy' poems (in the sonnets *'Methought I saw the footsteps of a throne'* and *'It is a beauteous Evening, calm and free'*) and introduced the imagery of nuns (again with a geographical logic – that convents are associated with Catholic countries – underpinning the choice of imagery).

In 1802 it was Dorothy, and not Caroline, who was cast in the role of nun; and the same was true when he wrote the sonnet *'Bruges I saw attired with golden light'* (Caroline by that time was married and mother of a little girl). But when he returned to Bruges in 1828, in the course of his 'Continental Tour', it was in the company of his daughter Dora (Dorothy remained at home). Inevitably their brief stay in Bruges stimulated him to compose a sort of 'Bruges Revisited' – in this case not a sonnet but a poem of forty lines on the subject of – English nuns! *Incident at Bruges* describes how, during a walk he and Dora made through the old town, they heard voices from inside a convent singing in English. The poem ends with Wordsworth noting that his daughter's response echoed his own:

> Such feeling pressed upon my soul,
>   A feeling sanctified
> By one soft trickling tear that stole
>   From the Maiden at my side;
> Less tribute could she pay than this,
>   Borne gaily o'er the sea,
> Fresh from the beauty and the bliss
>   Of English liberty?

According to Wordsworth, father and daughter are both moved by the idea that these English nuns live as in a prison, and he contrasts their situation with that of women in England who cannot be shut up in convents, and for whom freedom is part of their birthright. The assumption is therefore that Dora herself is free as air, and mistress of her own destiny – and that the last thing her father would want would be to consign her to a convent and deprive her of fulfilling herself as a woman. In July 1828 Dora was almost twenty-four, and certainly of an age to marry.... So how will the story end: do we hear wedding bells in the distance, challenging the plaintive plainsong that drifts through the iron grating of the convent windows?

★ ★ ★

Following the deaths of both Thomas (aged six) and Catherine (aged three) in 1812, Wordsworth's family was cruelly re-dimensioned. Of the three children who survived, Dora (the only girl) was his favourite. Unlike the two boys she was intellectually bright, and, far from being the 'most forlorn' girl that her father had judged her to be in the poem written for her first birthday, was by nature cheerful and helpful. Although she was no great beauty, having inherited the Wordsworth nose in all its Roman splendour, she had a positive energy that was attractive. With so many good qualities to her credit a happy childhood seemed assured – but that promise had been severly compromised by her father's decision to send her away to a boarding-school at Appleby (about thirty miles from Grasmere) when she was just six years old. Although she was able to stay with relatives there, she was deprived of regular contact with her parents and siblings from then until the age of eighteen.

Why did Wordsworth chase his favourite child away from home when she was so young? By all accounts it was a very odd thing to do, and given that (as usual) he made no attempt to explain or justify his action, one can only make some sense of it by piecing together disparate elements of the puzzle. To start with, it would seem that the initiative lay with Dorothy, who had never felt the affection for Dora that she had for John (Dora's elder brother). As the girl grew Dorothy had no trouble in finding fault with Dora's character, and didn't hesitate to point out that such or such a trait needed to be corrected. But if William decided simply to go along with his sister's opinion (which was rather unlikely, as he was strong-willed and stubborn, generally preferred to take important decisions on his own, and in any case would have had to take his wife's feelings into account before his sister's), it can only have been because in one way or another Dorothy's promptings suited him. (Her part in all this is hard to understand, for Dora found herself replicating the drama that Dorothy had been forced to enact, when she was separated from her brothers for eleven years after their father's death. One would have imagined that Dorothy would have wanted to spare her niece a similar experience – yet it seems that it was she who prompted her brother to send his daughter away).

If one wants to be generous to Wordsworth one can attribute his decision to send Dora away to a desire to provide her with a better education than could be had locally. *The Prelude* had shown just how important he felt education to be in the growth of personality, and all his children were at school by the age of three (indeed Thomas was only two years and ten months when he began). As Dora looked like being the brightest of his children, maybe he wanted to offer her the best chance possible of developing her natural talents. However such a theory stubs its toe on a couple of inconvenient facts. The first is the obvious point that at that time a girl's education always took second place to a boy's – and Dora had three brothers (two after 1812): it was unheard of to give priority to a girl's education over a boy's, if for no better reason than that the career prospects for an educated girl were so limited, and usually only mattered if the girl was unmarried and without financial support (in which case she might become a governess or lady's companion). And then Wordsworth, as if to underline this social principle, made no attempt to promote Dora's personal interest once she had finished her education. On the contrary. He made it clear to her that she was indispensable to him in a number of ways, and did everything he could to keep her by his side, domesticated and useful, once she reached adulthood.

A poem of 1817, written shortly before Dora's thirteenth birthday, and entitled, *The Longest Day – Addressed to my Daughter*, makes Wordsworth's stern and joyless attitude towards Dora clear at the moment when the girl is about to enter adolescence.

Setting the poem at the midsummer solstice, Wordsworth considers the sunwarmed landscape with all the cheerfulness of Eeyore the donkey in *Winnie the Pooh*, and concludes that from now on it's downhill all the way:

> Summer ebbs; – each day that follows
> Is a reflux from on high,
> Tending to the darksome hollows
> Where the frosts of winter lie.　　　(lines 29-32)

He then urges his daughter to ignore the joys of summer and the fruitfulness of autumn and, even before she reaches the peak of her youth and beauty, to fix her eyes on the inevitability of the winter that will conclude the year (and her life):

> Be thou wiser, youthful Maiden!
> And when thy decline shall come,
> Let not flowers, or boughs fruit-laden,
> Hide the knowledge of thy doom.
> Now, even now, ere wrapped in slumber,
> Fix thine eyes upon the sea
> That absorbs time, space, and number;
> Look thou to Eternity!　　　(lines 41-8)

As a guide to this end the girl should remember what her duty is:

> Duty, like a strict preceptor,
> Sometimes frowns, or seems to frown;
> Choose her thistle for thy sceptre,
> While youth's roses are thy crown.　　　(lines 65-8)

The nature of that duty soon became all too clear: it was to stay next to her father, keep him company, copy out his poems, and generally make herself useful in the household....The parameters for a nun-like existence were clearly set out before Dora had even reached her teens, and for the next twenty years Wordsworth never wavered from that line.

It was a strange version of fatherly love (though perhaps less unusual in real life than in art). The curious thing is that the poet who for decades had eulogised personal and national liberty, should want to write and publish a poem that went so drearily against the grain of the thinking for which he had become renowned. Those who (like myself) find the first two Books of *The Prelude* particularly powerful and moving may find it hard to accept that Wordsworth preferred to know that his young children were sitting at their desks and learning basic arithmetic rather than running free as the wind through the heather, in a kind of sustained ecstasy which offered them a form of education through nature. That surely was what *The Prelude*, and to a lesser extent much of Wordsworth's finest poetry, was all about. Yet as far as one can tell Wordsworth made no attempt to offer his children a childhood that in this respect was similar to his own, despite bringing them up in the same gloriously untamed landscape that he had revelled in when he was a small boy. There were outings and picnics of course, but none of the freedom that he had enjoyed and which had made his childhood so precious and unforgettable. Why?

A number of reasons are possible, which in one combination or another may explain Wordsworth's attitude. First and foremost, he may have been jealous of his own experience. Having consecrated his own childhood in poetry he perhaps wanted at all costs to avoid an imitation or repetition of the same journey by his children. It was up to them to find the path which made their childhood memorable: that was not something that could be bestowed on them by someone else. And as if to emphasise the private nature of the experience recounted in *The Prelude*, Wordsworth simply refused to publish the poem. It may also have been that Wordsworth's antennae were picking up a shift in values that could be felt across British society. He had grown up in a very particular historical moment, in which the French Revolution had called into question the stability of governments throughout Europe; and, following on from the American Declaration of Independence of 1776, with its assertion that it was a 'self-evident truth' that all men were born free, had led to the idea of both personal freedom and political self-determination being 'inalienable rights'. By the time Dora Wordsworth was growing up, this attitude was yielding ground to principles of duty and individual responsibility – values that would be later defined as typically Victorian. In doing his best to repress in his daughter's breast the aspirations that he had enjoyed as a young man, Wordsworth may in part have been anticipating the parental role of the Victorian father. And lastly, his childhood had been in a sense the happy product of neglect: if he had been free to roam the hills and valleys of the Lake District it was at least in part because his mother was not there to watch over him, and because his father was too busy to take care of his five children on his own. The young Wordsworth had made good use of that freedom; but when he had his own children he may have felt that there were better ways of bringing them up than the one he had known.

Having said all that in an attempt to understand Wordsworth's thinking, the fact remains that the poem, addressed to a girl as she entered puberty and adolescence, is chillingly repressive and morbid. And no doubt Dora was invited at some point to read it, just as she would read, or have read, the funeral dirge composed for her first birthday. All this while she was being brought up and educated miles away from her family, and deprived of simple parental affection in her daily life. It's not hard to imagine the effect such verses could have had on her... As it turned out, however, Dora proved to be remarkably resilient. She refused to be either meek or forlorn, and while she was dutiful towards her father, she was never submissive in the way she expressed herself. She probably did not tell him when she disagreed with something that concerned his poetry, but she did not hesitate to comment on his work in letters she wrote to friends – just as Dorothy had done in the past. And she was alone among the women in the Wordsworth household in having a sense of humour, and in being ready to laugh at the Poet from time to time. (For example, she described Wordsworth and Coleridge, travelling with her by coach, as 'perched on the roof exactly like a pair of monkies'; she referred to some of his lesser poems as 'stuffing' to help make up a volume; and she openly laughed at his odd appearance when out walking with him (see pages 389-90)).

★ ★ ★

For Wordsworth the separation from Dora – when he sent her away to boarding-school – awoke painful memories. Not only that of his separation, at the age of thirteen, from his beloved sister, but also of his abandoning of Caroline, his first daughter, even before she was born. These events, along with the stories of childhood deaths and fragmented families that he regularly heard of, had branded him with the conviction that loss was an integral and quite inevitable part of normal human existence. Premature death had been the theme of the 'Lucy' poems – and it could only be resolved, it seemed to him, by fatalistic resignation in the face of loss, and by an insistence on the values of domesticity and static family life. Only that kind of stability offered an adequate response to the capricious and unpredictable calendar of events that unfolded year by year in every human life.

In Wordsworth's imagination girls remained wild, elusive and vulnerable up until the age at which they married; after which the butterflies were supposed to metamorphose into home-loving, maternal and useful angels. And if, as in the case of Dorothy or his sister-in-law Sara, they passed the age of marrying and were clearly destined to remain spinsters for the rest of their lives, then they should be integrated into the household in such a way as to guarantee that they never needed or wanted to leave it. 'Sister-wives' was the term he had coined for this status when he was just eighteen (line 130 of *An Evening Walk*), and in middle age he put it into practice. His possessive love for Dora was such that he did his best to make her a permanent member of his 'harem' (as Coleridge had called it) without giving her the chance to be courted. Being a man, and having lost both parents by the time he was thirteen, Wordsworth had never had to consult, or ask permission of, anyone when it came to the subject of marriage. But he had no intention of offering his daughter the kind of freedom that he had enjoyed. When Dora was twenty-one Tom Robinson, a lieutenant in the Royal Navy who was also her second cousin, formally asked Wordsworth's permission to marry his daughter. He was immediately and unequivocally rejected. The next year William Ayling, a clergyman with an independent income, was likewise turned down (almost certainly it was Wordsworth who refused his consent, rather than Dora being uninterested in the proposal). It seemed that no suitor would suit Wordsworth's taste; and Dora seemed destined to follow in her aunt's footsteps, and become the steady companion to her father as he grew older. To fulfil this role various qualities and conditions would have been important: virginity (less because of the purity it represented, than because it meant she had no sexual history or identity, and no man other than himself should have a claim on her), and intelligence being the most important. Dora shared with Dorothy a true intellectual independence, and was not afraid to speak her mind – and this was very stimulating to Wordsworth. With Dora he had the pleasure of young female company, the intimacy of a close family tie, and the possibility of lively dialogue on subjects that interested him (which his placid wife Mary certainly didn't offer him), all in one. He was not going to surrender Dora to another man if he could avoid it....For her part Dora's health from this time on deteriorated gradually: she became anorexic, and also suffered from severe colds, particularly during the winter, which sometimes immobilised her for weeks or even months at a time.

As it turned out the real threat to Wordsworth's peace of mind came from where he least expected it, and when he thought all danger was past. Dora was in her early thirties, and well past the marrying age, when Edward Quillinan declared his love to her. Quillinan was thirteen years older than her and a widower; he was also a very good friend of the family, a regular house-guest who followed Wordsworth's work closely, and whose opinions were much appreciated by the Poet. One can imagine the shock Wordsworth felt when his very good friend turned out to be a worm in the bud, a traitor who wanted to carry off his daughter and have his way with her. Still, Dora had known Quillinan since she was seventeen, so if she responded to his courting fifteen years later she must have known what she felt for him and what she was doing (in fact it was a bit like Wordsworth's courtship of Mary – they also had known each other for years before becoming lovers). For over a year the betrothal remained a secret, no doubt because both Dora and Quillinan knew what Wordsworth's reaction would be when he found out. And they were not to be disappointed: when Quillinan finally wrote to Wordsworth, in the winter of 1837-8, to ask his permission to marry Dora, Wordsworth responded with all the fury of a winter storm. Quillinan was banished and Dora heavily censured.[103] Dora being Dora, however, she did not give up or submit to her father's will. She stuck to her commitment to Quillinan and waited, while good friends of the family like Isabella Fenwick tried to persuade Wordsworth to change his mind. More than three years passed before he gave up the struggle, and gave his consent. Dora eventually married Quillinan when she was three months short of her thirty-seventh birthday. Wordsworth, replicating Dorothy's behaviour at his own wedding thirty-nine years earlier, announced at the last moment that he didn't have the strength to attend the ceremony, and left it to his youngest son, Willy, to give the bride away.[104]

Dora and Quillinan enjoyed a few years of married life together, despite Dora's poor health – until that degenerated dramatically: she contracted tuberculosis and died, childless, in 1847, at the age of forty-three.

★ ★ ★

Wordsworth's relationship with his daughters had something of the quality of the drama of *King Lear* or *Little Dorrit*. It was a major preoccupation for him throughout his adult life: he was only twenty-two when Caroline was born, so one can fairly say that there was never a time in his poetic career when that relationship was not present in his mind. And it is significant that while he wrote poems that were addressed directly or indirectly to each of his three daughters, not a single poem was ever addressed to any of his three sons. (For the record, the sonnet of 1802, 'It is a beauteous Evening, calm and free', can be said to be addressed to Caroline; Characteristics of a Child three Years old and 'Surprised by joy – impatient as the Wind', both of 1813-14, were for Catherine; while the Address to my Infant Daughter Dora... of 1805, and The Longest Day of 1817 were composed for Dora). It is depressing to note that of these five poems the only one that celebrates pleasure and vitality is Characteristics of a Child three Years old, written when the little girl was already dead; the other poems systematically negate the perspectives and promises that a girl might look forward to when young: independence, love, marriage, and maternity. By comparison the lines by Derek Walcott quoted at the beginning of this chapter, written when his daughters were between the age of ten and fourteen, anticipate with wonderful concision the moment when they will move beyond his protective love. Or consider how the poem by Yeats, A prayer for my daughter, written just after his daughter was born, already envisages the time when she will cease to be a girl and will become a woman:

> May she be granted beauty and yet not
> Beauty to make a stranger's eye distraught,
> Or hers before a looking-glass, for such,
> Being made beautiful overmuch,
> Consider beauty a sufficient end,
> Lose natural kindness and maybe
> The heart-revealing intimacy
> That chooses right, and never find a friend.
>
> (lines 17-24)

And the last stanza of the poem looks forward, with a mixture of hope and concern, to his daughter's marriage:

And may her bridegroom bring her to a house
Where all's accustomed, ceremonious; (lines 73-4)

For Wordsworth there was no space in his head for such lyrical daydreaming, as he was obsessed by the need to have women constantly around him, women he could trust and whom he could rely on not to disappear in order to lead lives of their own from which he was excluded. He exerted a form of tyranny, but one that was Dickensian rather than Shakespearian in this respect, as it stemmed from a weakness of character of which he was scarcely aware, rather than from the desire to impose his will on other people (so, for example, he wrote to Dora from Florence in 1837, when he was touring Italy with his good friend Henry Crabb Robinson,

Of this be assured, that I never shall go from home for any time again, without a female companion.)[105]

Wordsworth's problem was that he was unable or unwilling to match his needs with consideration for the needs of others. There was no reciprocity. Instead there were a variety of strategies engineered more or less unconsciously, which together enabled him to reconcile the tensions inside himself and allowed him to function, to work, to write. The emotional demands made on him by those he loved most being more than he could cope with creatively, Wordsworth tried to keep the peace within himself by creating categories within which each relationship, or each literary project, could be contained and managed. It was a sort of 'divide and rule' approach to life – but it was complicated by the need to divide himself as well in the same process. The most obvious example of these divisions occurred in his major works. On one side there was *The Prelude*, which was finished but never

published in his lifetime, and which remained a secret to all but
a handful of people. On the other side was *The Recluse*, which
he never stopped talking about to friends as being his '*magnum
opus*' but which never actually existed. *The Prelude* was private,
The Recluse was public. And following this one all-defining fault-
line that ran down the middle of his life, there were people who
belonged to the world of *The Prelude*, and others who belonged
to the world of *The Recluse*. His illegitimate daughter Caroline
clearly belonged to the private world of *The Prelude*: she was
one of Wordsworth's secrets, and besides, she was in a way hid-
den inside the narrative of *The Prelude*, in the story of Julia and
Vaudracour – though Wordsworth made sure that no one would
track her down and identify her while he was alive. Dora, his
other daughter, belonged to the public world of *The Recluse* –
and she was continually urging her father to work on it, and kept
her friends informed of his progress or lack of progress. Long
after he had abandoned the project she still believed in it.

Another fault-line separated Dorothy from Mary. Dorothy
was the woman with whom he felt completely at ease in private,
who shared with him moments of extreme complicity and inti-
macy, while Mary was his partner, his wife. And of course Dora
belonged to the same sphere as her mother Mary (that of England
and of Wordsworth's official family), while his illegitimate daugh-
ter Caroline belonged with Annette and France and the unoffi-
cial family…Nonetheless the compartmentalisation of his mind
was subverted by the power of his memory, which instinctively
related people to specific events and places that made an impres-
sion on him. Hence, for example, the references to Dorothy and
to Dora in poems concerning nuns – when nuns should belong
exclusively to the French Catholic world inhabited by Annette
and Caroline – neither of whom had anything nunlike about

them. In the end it proved very difficult to organise Life properly, and to make it neat and obedient!

And in the end memory would prove a more powerful organiser of consciousness than any self-imposed scheme. A nice example of this was provided by Wordsworth's friend Henry Crabb Robinson, who accompanied the poet on his last Continental tour, in 1837 (he had also been present when Wordsworth met up with his daughter Caroline in Paris, in October 1820 – the time when she embarrassed him by calling him 'father' in public – and we owe it to him that we know anything of this encounter, as both Dorothy and William passed over it in silence). Robinson related in his diary that after visiting Annette and Caroline in Paris, they travelled south to Nimes, where they visited the Roman arena, which left Wordsworth completely indifferent.

> He was, on the other hand, delighted by two beautiful little girls playing with flowers near the Arena; and I overheard him say to himself, 'Oh, you darlings! I wish I could put you in my pocket, and carry you to Rydal Mount.' (Robinson's diary, April 6, 1837)[106]

Wordsworth's whispered wish was innocent, but also revealing – in that it showed to what extent time and memory structured his perception of the world. The little girls in the arena confused in his mind with the daughter that he had just visited in Paris and who remained for him still a little girl – the girl who had been a preoccupation for him throughout the 1790s, and whom he would have liked to carry home with him. No matter that the little girl was now a woman, a wife and a mother; for him she remained the nine-year old that he had walked with along the beach at Calais in 1802. He only had to return to France in 1837 in order to trigger off memories of France in 1792 and 1802: and the experiences superimposed like two colour slides, but with the immediate experience of the present serving to reinforce rather than qualify the past experience.

Caroline, the daughter 'who never was', nonetheless had the last word. She outlived both of Wordsworth's legitimate daughters, as well as her father. Dora and (of course) Catherine died childless, but not Caroline. Her father did his best to ignore and neglect her, but in the end she probably had a happier and richer life than Dora, who was 'banished' from home at the age of six; became anorexic; was prevented for years from marrying; and was expected above all to satisfy the needs of a difficult and demanding father. Caroline, in keeping with the spirit of *The Prelude* which she helped embody, preserved in her life a degree of freedom which none of Wordsworth's legitimate children ever enjoyed.

Chapter XV

The Long Yesterday

Age did not weary them, nor the years condemn: in the space of
just three years the most gifted among the second generation of
English Romantic poets – Keats, Shelley and Byron – all died in
the prime of their lives, leaving their loved ones to mourn the
loss – and with their artistic reputations as wholesome and un-
blemished as their young skin. Keats was the first to go, dying of
tuberculosis in Rome in 1821, when he was just twenty-five. The
next year Shelley, who was also living in Italy, drowned when his
boat sank near Livorno during a storm. He was twenty-nine. And
in 1824 Byron's colourful life came to an abrupt end at the age
of thirty-six, when he caught a fever in Greece – where he had
been engaged in trying to help the Greeks achieve independence
from the Turks.

These premature deaths dealt a body blow to English
Romantic poetry, and more or less guaranteed that it wouldn't
develop any further. At that point, with Coleridge too unwell
or erratic to be relied on for any consistency of production,
Wordsworth came to be seen as the uncontested figure-head of
the Romantic movement – even as his poetry moved further

and further away from the tone and spirit of all that we consider as Romantic. After being ridiculed by critics when he was in his thirties, he came to be respected and appreciated in middle age for a vision which he had given shape to twenty years earlier but no longer truly embodied. Moreover the early deaths of Keats, Shelley and Byron had imbued the Romantic aesthetic with a special quality, which was (or seemed to be) the antithesis of everything that Wordsworth represented. The younger poets had lived with a passion that had both inspired and destroyed them: their lives were in harmony with their poetry; and, like the self-destructive rock stars from the 1960s onwards whose careers have been snuffed out by drug overdoses, they suggested that the price to pay for true creativity was tragically high.[107] William Wordsworth esq., Distributor of Stamps for Westmorland and living in a fine property at Rydal Mount in the Lake District, was badly placed to speak on behalf of those who, like Marianne Dashwood in Jane Austen's *Sense and Sensibility*, embraced Romanticism wholeheartedly and wanted – needed – to suffer for their convictions.

First Keats, then Shelley, and finally Byron: Wordsworth would have witnessed these losses with mixed emotions. While he liked the gentle and melancholy Keats, and found his poetry full of promise, he would have had little sympathy for the mixture of atheism, political radicalism and random womanising that made up Shelley's personal portfolio. As for Byron, Wordsworth considered him a hangover from the libertine culture that had in a way tainted his own youth, and which he had done so much to correct in himself and take a distance from. It was bad enough to watch this depraved aristocrat waltz from one affair to another, nonchalantly leaving illegitimate children in his wake, and then crowing about it all in his poetry; but then for him to die while presuming to aid an oppressed European nation in its fight for liberty! It was as if a whole host of ghosts and skeletons from Wordsworth's French adventure had come back to haunt him and to mock the path that he had chosen to take. And the fact that Byron probably had an incestuous relationship with his half-sister Augusta, and was probably the father of her daughter Elizabeth, would have cut Wordsworth to the quick, given his own intense feelings for Dorothy and the self-control he used to manage his relationship with her.

Wordsworth was right to consider this English Don Juan a bit anachronistic — indeed, Byron was forced to leave England to escape not only his creditors but also the censure of a society which no longer upheld eighteenth-century morals; nonetheless, the real problem with Byron was that he came too close to the bone for Wordsworth. Byron's life waved Books IX and X of *The Prelude* under Wordsworth's nose, and called into question the choices he had made. In Book IX Wordsworth emphasised his solidarity with the French Republican cause, saying that,

> my heart was all
> Given to the people, and my love was theirs.
> (lines 125-6)

And in the following Book he declared that only a lack of money forced him to return to England in the winter of 1792, and that otherwise

> I doubtless should have made a common cause
> With some who perished   (lines 194-5)

But, unlike Byron, he did not make common cause with those who were fighting for their freedom; instead, after returning to England at the end of 1792, he turned his back on Europe and adopted an increasingly nationalistic and insular attitude in his writing. After the frontiers reopened following the end of the Napoleonic wars he made a few trips to the Continent (in 1820, 1828, and 1837), but always as a tourist (and often an unenthusiastic one at that). He consigned his French experiences to the archives and set out to define his own identity in terms of Englishness, and, more specifically, as a northerner from the Lake District. So while Shelley and Byron, after leaving England to get away from the threats of censure and the claims of creditors, and Keats, who had gone south in a desperate attempt to fight tuberculosis, all ended their lives in the Mediterranean, Wordsworth completed a sequence of thirty-four sonnets on the River Duddon, and carried on working on the sequence of 132 *Ecclesiastical Sonnets* that would make up his mind-numbingly boring history of the Church of England.

Shelley, Keats and Byron all died prematurely; similarly, the first obituaries for Wordsworth were premature, beng composed when he still had several decades of life ahead of him. In 1826 his friend Henry Crabb Robinson offered an unflattering assessment of Wordsworth's creative output in middle age:

> This great poet survived to the fifth decennary of the nineteenth Century, but he appears to have died in the year 1814 as far as life consisted in an active sympathy with the temporary welfare of his fellow creatures – He had written heroically & divinely against the tyranny of Napoleon, but was quite indifferent to all the succeeding tyrranies which disgraced the succeeding times –

Robinson then referred to wars and uprisings in Spain, Greece and Germany, all of them ignored by Wordsworth, before concluding,

The poet's eye was not a prophetic one – There is proof that he was alive about 1823-4 when new churches were built in London but otherwise he took no care about any of the events of the day[108]

Coming from someone whom Wordsworth considered a good friend, Robinson's mock obituary must have been hurtful – but for the same reason it shows how widespread was the sense of disappointment felt by those who followed Wordsworth's work closely. However the most incisive epitaph had already been written about ten years earlier – by Shelley, who was not a friend, but whose opinion mattered because he was a practising poet. As if to mock Wordsworth's regular production of often mediocre sonnets, Shelley composed a sonnet of his own (in about 1816) to mourn the disappearance of a great talent:

> Poet of Nature, thou hast wept to know
> That things depart which never may return:
> Childhood and youth, friendship and love's first glow,
> Have fled like sweet dreams, leaving thee to mourn.
> These common woes I feel. One loss is mine
> Which thou too feel'st, yet I alone deplore.
> Thou wert a lone star, whose light did shine
> On some frail bark in winter's midnight roar:
> Thou hast like to a rock-built refuge stood
> Above the blind and battling multitude:
> In honoured poverty thy voice did weave
> Songs consecrate to truth and liberty, –
> Deserting these, thou leavest me to grieve,
> Thus having been, that thou should'st cease to be.

Shelley's lament dovetails neatly with Robinson's; interestingly, given that Shelley had not had the chance to read *The*

Prelude, he nonetheless picks out three themes that dominate that poem – childhood, youth, and the sense of loss – and which we today see as central to Wordsworth's vision. The sonnet is both perceptive and fair in the criticisms it makes; but neither this sonnet nor Robinson's 'obituary' made any difference to the way Wordsworth's writing evolved.

Almost everything Wordsworth wrote in the last forty years of his life is tedious and heavy, lacking the freshness of his early work but without the richness and density that one associates with maturity in art. Anthologies of his poetry pay lip service to the second half of his life by including a handful of pieces from that time, and leave it at that. The comment, if one is made at all, is invariably that Wordsworth's inspiration ran out at an early date – and maybe a remark or a verse of Wordsworth's is quoted to show that he was aware of his failing powers. The *Ode: Intimations of Immortality* is seen as pivotal in this respect, both because it represents a high point in his career (soon after that, it would be downhill all the way); and because the retrospective tone of the poem suggests that Wordsworth knew that his best years were behind him (even though, as we have seen in chapter XII of this book, that kind of interpretation does not match Wordsworth's intentions).

Wordsworth tempered his melancholy with a form of stoicism that would permeate everything he wrote – letters as well as poems – as he got older, and which resolved satisfactorily the intense anxiety which the *Ode* expressed. Nonetheless such lines as,

> The things which I have seen I now can see no more.
>
> (*Ode: Intimations of Immortality*, line 9)

do beg the question whether Romantic poetry – like rock music – was inevitably short-lived? Was the impulse that inspired such art something that could not be developed beyond a certain point, so that youth and maturity were obliged to fuse in a single onward rush? Maybe it would be fair to see Romanticism as a land like the one evoked by Yeats in his poem *Sailing to Byzantium*,

> That is no country for old men. The young
> In one another's arms, birds in the trees
> – Those dying generations – at their song,
> The salmon-falls, the mackerel-crowded seas,
> Fish, flesh, or fowl, commend all summer long
> Whatever is begotten, born, and dies.
> Caught in that sensual music all neglect
> Monuments of unageing intellect.   (lines 1–8)

Imagine for a moment that Wordsworth had died like Byron at the age of thirty-six. What then would have been his legacy, with *The Prelude* just completed, so many fine poems already written and published, and the great project of *The Recluse* clearly present in his mind? It is hard not to think that his premature death would have been seen as one of the greatest losses ever to English literature, and the Romantic muse would have been considered as potentially inexhaustible. Instead of which we have to deal with a radically different picture, in which the poet's lifetime's inspiration was packed into eight to ten years (roughly 1798 to 1807), followed by almost half a century of constipated mediocrity. Was this the inevitable pay-off for listening to the Romantic muse, and would it have been the same sad story for Keats, Shelley and Byron, had they lived longer?

★ ★ ★

By the mid-1830s only Wordsworth and Turner were left of the

artists and poets we now group together under the wide um-
brella of English Romanticism. In many ways Turner's career had
followed a similar course to Wordsworth's, with the two paths
converging at different points in significant ways. They were con-
temporaries (Turner was born in 1775, five years after Wordsworth,
and died a year after him, in 1851), and as artists they shared sim-
ilar concerns – at times even treating the same subject. Turner
painted Tintern Abbey three years before Wordsworth wrote
about it; and in 1797 he made a tour of the Lake District, pro-
ducing a number of watercolours of the mountains and lakes that
Wordsworth had not yet claimed as 'his', before following these
sketches up with a carefully worked oil painting of Buttermere
Lake with a rainbow, once he was back in his studio. A large and
powerful gouache and watercolour study of Snowdon and the
surrounding hills, painted in 1799-1800, is very close in spirit to
the landscape evoked by Wordsworth in Book XIII of *The Prelude*,
after reaching the summit of Snowdon: while Wordsworth uses
the light of the moon to create an unreal world that transcends
the human dimension, Turner achieves a similar effect by includ-
ing an army of ant-like soldiers in the foreground – insignificant
scratches and scribbles of human beings that are dwarfed by the
magnificent snow-capped mountain and the surrounding hills.

Although the two men never met, it looked as if they were
heading in the same direction – parallel lines whose destiny would
be to meet at infinity. But in 1802 their paths diverged in a way
that was significant. The Treaty of Amiens made it possible for the
English to visit France again, after a gap of almost ten years, and
both Wordsworth and Turner took advantage of the opportunity.
But while Wordsworth remained at Calais, as near to England as
was possible, and used his time in France to close his personal ac-
count there, Turner began to explore the continent that had been

closed to him by the Napoleonic Wars. His route through France and Switzerland was similar to that taken by Wordsworth on his epic walking tour of 1790, and in the course of his journey Turner made over four hundred drawings and watercolours – material which could then be developed in oils once back in London. He also studied the paintings in the Louvre (whose collection had recently been greatly enriched thanks to Napoleon's Italian campaigns). As a painter he was well aware that English art belonged heart and soul to a European tradition which transcended any kind of nationalistic sentiment. For him the Napoleonic Wars were above all a major source of frustration, as they prevented him from travelling freely in Europe; but they made absolutely no difference to the way he looked at the world or the way he felt about his own identity. So while Wordsworth spent 1803 sounding off against Napoleonic France and reasserting the special qualities of Englishness, Turner worked up sketches done during his Continental trip, and wondered when he would next be able to take the passenger boat to Calais.

He was back in France in 1817, once the grass had begun to grow again on the fields of Waterloo, and Napoleon was safely – and definitively – cooped up on St Helena. By this time he was probably the best known painter in England, with nothing left to prove, and nothing obvious to gain by embarking on new adventures. But his curiosity was as limitless as the horizons he liked to paint, and Europe called to him. Between 1817 and 1845 he visited the Continent almost every year, gradually developing a dialectic between home and abroad that enriched his art enormously. The contact with Italian light, for example, made his palette more luminous and less earthy, giving him the confidence to experiment with primary colours, and to explore the no-man's land where colour and light meet. The long series of watercolour studies in which he worked out these ideas from about 1820 onwards, and which we know as the 'Colour Beginnings', are at the heart of his artistic legacy. Whether left as simple studies – amazingly fresh and profoundly intuitive – or developed into larger oil paintings, the work on colour and light that Turner did in the second half of his career has had an enormous influence on painting ever since. For the Impressionists, and for Monet in particular (who stayed and worked in London several times for long periods), Turner was an important reference-point. While the pictorial language the Impressionists developed led them in a different direction to him (they were more interested in the vibration achieved by dividing a single colour into two complementary opposites than by the brilliance and luminosity obtained by fusing a colour with its light source), the courage and insatiable curiosity of the Englishman, coupled with his all too evident technical skill and professionalism, made of this shy and awkward man a model for generations of painters.....And when, 120 years after his death, the terms of his will were finally respected and the whole Turner legacy was put on display in a museum designed for that purpose, the public was able to take stock of the range of his achievement – and to note, among other things, how that spectrum was continually enlarged as the years passed, as if a sort of mental and visual diaphragm in the painter's head was being constantly opened wider and wider.[109]

The Swiss Alps fascinated Turner, and inspired some of the finest watercolours of his later years; and as they also had a particular significance for Wordsworth, they offer a good way of comparing the work done by the two men in middle age. Turner's landscapes of the Alps tended to be structured (rather as Cézanne's paintings would be) on geometrical lines. He used the basic pyramid shape of a mountain to create compositions with strong diagonals – often with two or more mountains converging, so that the eye is drawn down to the dark valley, and sent rushing skywards again on the other side. The energy created by these compositions is similar to that of Turner's storm scenes, in which a central vortex in the painting sends the spectator's eye round and round in an unresolved turbulence. Unlike Friedrich, who always maintained a distance from the mountains that he painted, and who often placed the mountain at the centre of the canvas, thereby giving a sense of symmetry and stability to the composition, Turner placed himself, with his sketchbook and box of watercolours, in the middle of the landscape that was his subject. You can feel the scene 'happening' all round him; and this sense of immediacy, together with the dynamic movements generated by the compositions, released or unleashed a powerful energy in Turner, that made itself felt in the brushwork and in the increasingly radical and daring treatment of colour and light.

There are a couple of passages in Book VI of *The Prelude* which are very close in feeling to these alpine studies of Turner's. One in particular, in which Wordsworth describes a narrow mountain pass he and his friend walked down, summons up the unbridled power of natural forces exactly as Turner did in his later watercolours:

> Downwards we hurried fast,
> And entered the road which we had missed
> Into a narrow chasm. The brook and road
> Were fellow-travellers in this gloomy pass,
> And with them did we journey several hours
> At a slow step. The immeasurable height
> Of woods decaying, never to be decayed,
> The stationary blast of waterfalls,
> And everywhere along the hollow rent

Winds thwarting winds, bewildered and forlorn,
The torrents shooting from the clear blue sky,
The rocks that muttered close upon our ears,
Black drizzling crags that spoke by the wayside
As if a voice were in them, the sick sight
And giddy prospect of the raving stream,
The unfettered clouds and regions of the heavens,
Tumult and peace, the darkness and the light –
Were all like workings of one mind, the features
Of the same face, blossoms upon one tree,
Characters of the great apocalypse,
The types and symbols of eternity,
Of first, and last, and midst, and without end.

(lines 551–72)

The passage ends with Wordsworth's recollection that the sound of the rushing water just outside the inn they were staying in made it almost impossible for him to sleep that night:

A dreary mansion, large beyond all need,
With high and spacious rooms, deafened and stunned
By noise of waters, making innocent sleep
Lie melancholy among weary bones. (lines 577–80)

The conclusion is perfect, and needs no further elaboration. Nonetheless, Wordsworth manages to add another layer of meaning to the experience by picking up the reference to Macbeth in 'innocent sleep' and developing it in Book X of the poem (lines 62–77), to establish a clear relationship between the unease provoked by the 'violence' of nature and the fear inspired by anarchy or uncontrollable social unrest. Politics and nature in (discordant) symphony – in moments such as these Wordsworth's poetry acquires a Shakespearian quality.

When he returned to Switzerland in 1820, Wordsworth's attitude had changed radically. That tour seemed to have been planned with the past as much in mind as the present. At every step he was weighing memory against sensation: a familiar technique for him, but by now memory had so much the upper hand on sensation, that it left him little room to feel things freshly, or for the first time. Both Mary and Dorothy went with him, and this already complicated his response to the landscapes and situations they found themselves in – not because of any preordained tension inside the trio, but because Dorothy had been William's exclusive companion on so many walking tours and expeditions – and in particular during their memorable winter in Goslar in 1798-9 – that he could not embark on a tour such as this one without memories of other journeys he had made with his sister resonating continually in his ears. In William's mind Mary was associated indelibly with England, just as his daughter Caroline was part of Europe.[110] But Dorothy's position was more complicated: had it not been for the Goslar experience, together with the fact that she kindly accompanied him to Calais in 1802, she would have been part of his English world, like Mary – but as it was, the 1820 tour revived memories not only of his 1790 walking tour with Robert Jones, but also of the Goslar winter and the Calais summer. Needless to say, Dorothy was eager and willing to participate in that massive act of memory – as long as it included her.

Neither of them were disappointed, as Dorothy's account of one moment at Trientz – in the Swiss Alps – demonstrated:

> While standing on the brow of the precipice, above this shady deep recess, the very image of pastoral life, stillness and seclusion, William came up to me; &, if my feelings had been

moved before, how much more interesting did the spot be-
come when he told me it was the same dell, that 'aboriginal
vale', that 'green recess' so often mentioned by him – the first
of the kind he had passed through in Switzerland, and 'now,'
said he, 'I find that my remembrance for thirty years has been
scarcely less vivid than the reality now before my eyes!'…
We left the hut of Trientz musing on the strange connexions
of events in human life; – how improbable, thirty years ago,
that William should ever return thither! – and we to be his
companions! – And to pass a night within the hollow of that
'aboriginal Vale' was a thing that the most romantic of our
fancies could not have helped us even to dream of! (Dorothy
Wordsworth, *Journal*, September 14 and 17, 1820)[111]

The anecdote reads as yet another example of what had by
now become an ingrained habit of Wordsworth's – that of weigh-
ing the present against the past. But if we follow Wordsworth
upstream in time we see that the mechanism was actually more
complicated. For even when he first discovered the Alps his reac-
tion involved weighing two sentiments against each other, as he
made clear in Book VI of *The Prelude*:

> That day we first
> Beheld the summit of Mont Blanc, and grieved
> To have a soulless image on the eye
> Which had usurped upon a living thought
> That never more could be.   (lines 452–6)

The tension here is not between the present experience of a
particular place or situation, and the memory of a similar experi-
ence in the past. Rather it sets personal experience against precon-
ceived ideas and expectations: the young Wordsworth had a clear
idea of the impact that Mont Blanc should make on him (derived

from travellers' accounts, poems, prints and paintings, etc.), and was disappointed to discover that the image he had formed in his mind did not correspond to what he really felt when confronted in person by the mountain. The tension is then heightened by inverting the values that one would have expected: that's to say, the mountain he observes is 'soulless' while the idea he had of it was 'living'; and the idea held in the mind can only be removed by being 'usurped'. In other words, Wordsworth tends to see all perception as conflictual and contradictory, and human consciousness as a battleground between the inner and outer worlds, each of which is constantly modifying the other during the long journey through life. But, despite his instinctive preference for empirical experience and his mistrust of abstract concepts, he comes down here on the side of concepts and ideas, and refuses to smooth over the conflict between the two forms of perception.

The resolution of that conflict is one of the unstated aims of *The Prelude*; so it is hardly a coincidence that the disappointment of Mont Blanc finds a clear reply in Wordsworth's exultant vision from the top of Mount Snowdon in Book XIII. Here the magnificence of the vision from the summit is set against the downbeat tone of the narrative during the ascent, in which the only sound to punctuate the silence comes from the guide's dog barking at a hedgehog – in other words, Wordsworth's appreciation of the sublime vision offered by the mountain landscape is grounded firmly in precise and clearly seen details of a specific moment, a particular experience.

In moments such as this Wordsworth's writing has the directness and spontaneity of Turner's watercolours. But whereas Turner's larger works seem, throughout his long career, to coagulate from hundreds of sketches that are constantly suggesting new approaches and perspectives, Wordsworth had difficulty after the age of forty in letting go and experimenting with new or un-familiar ideas. He found it increasingly hard to look at or consider any subject without referring back to something which provided a benchmark against which to measure his thoughts and feelings. That tendency had always been there, even when he was in his teens, but it became inexorably stronger as he grew older, and he did little to resist it. Like an ageing computer Wordsworth's crea-tive drive lost gradually in power and speed, as his brain became clogged up with layer upon layer of 'indispensable' memory and reference, through which every new perception needed to be fil-tered. The very impulses that had made his poetry unique ended up by leaving him stranded like a whale on the sand, as they pre-vented his vision from renewing itself. Turner on the other hand was free of these restraints. If in middle age he looked backward at his earlier work, it was to learn from it, not to return to it. But in any case he doesn't seem to have been particularly interested in his own finished work. It's true that once he was financially comfortable he made less and less effort to sell his paintings; but although he accumulated quantities of canvases and hundreds – then thousands – of sketches and watercolours in his London home, he didn't pay much attention to them or look after them properly – with the result that some of them started to suffer seriously from damp and neglect.

Like Picasso, Turner recognised only one creative direction: forwards. Work, live in the present, produce. Whether or not one likes the later style of Turner, it is clear that it represents a devel-opment, that the paintings done in his sixties and seventies draw on and carry forward the thought-processes of previous decades. That Wordsworth didn't develop in the same way is, however, only in part a question of character. As a poet, his relationship to the outside world was essentially cerebral: the 'inner world' he constructed was always at least as important as the 'outer world' he lived and moved in. For a painter like Turner the balance was different. A large part of his days was spent in observing and recording all that was going on around him. His sense of reality was conditioned by what he saw as much as by what he felt or thought. The inner vision could never stray too far from the empirical facts of any situation; and by the same token the endless observation and studying of nature kept the painter mentally agile and supple, far less inclined to slip into a rut than an elderly poet accustomed always to listen to the sound of his own voice.

★ ★ ★

The man who as a boy had listened to the owl echoing his own imitation of the bird's call, now began to hear and see life echoing across the years. It was an attitude that could work for or against him: either enriching immediate sensation by linking it back to previous experience, or dulling it by bogging it down in the archives of memory. His habit of constantly referring the present back to the past meant that his poetry ran the risk of presenting endless variations of itself. At times this might even appear in the titles: *Yarrow Unvisited*, written in 1803, would be followed by *Yarrow Visited* in 1814, and *Yarrow Revisited* in 1831.... On the other hand he could treat the lines of poetry he had written decades earlier as no more than a pack of cards: shuffle them, deal a new hand, and so produce a new thought or feeling out of the old stock.

One of the best examples of this practice starts with the earliest poem he chose to publish, entitled *Extract, from the Conclusion to a Poem, composed in anticipation of leaving School* (I shall call it *Extract* for short). It has already been quoted in full and discussed in chapter XII, but for the sake of convenience it is worth quoting the relevant lines again. These are lines 9–14, that make up the second half of the sonnet:

> Thus, while the Sun sinks down to rest
> Far in the regions of the west,
> Though to the vale no parting beam
> Be given, not one memorial gleam,
> A lingering light he fondly throws
> On the dear hills where first he rose.

The poem had known a curious history. It was included in the first collected edition of his works, in 1815, with the title making it clear to the reader that it had been composed in 1786. But in fact the version of the poem Wordsworth had written as a schoolboy read slightly differently:

> As Phoebus, when he sinks to rest
> Far on the mountains in the west,
> While all the vale is dark between
> Ungilded by his golden sheen,
> A lingering lustre softly throws
> On the dear hills where first he rose.[112]

The differences in style are obvious – above all 'Phoebus' with his 'golden sheen' belongs to the eighteenth century. What is interesting is that, rather than present his early work to the world as he had thought it and felt it then, he preferred in middle age to make revisions where he felt like it, and then say that what he wrote in his forties had been composed in his teens. In a sense he was cheating – but of course he did not see it like that. And for her part Dorothy, who knew her brother's methods all too well, would not have raised an eyebrow at his manipulation of an early text. The entry in her journal for January 28, 1802, shows that this kind of thing was all part of a working day:

> Thursday 28th. A downright rain, a wet night. Wm
> slept better – better this morning – he had [writ-
> ten an] epitaph & altered one that he wrote when
> he was a Boy. It cleared up after dinner.

It could well be that the epitaph he altered that day was the poem quoted above. What is certain is that the lines he had com-posed as an adolescent remained alive for him long after he had written them: they, and the moment they gave voice to, con-tained a particular significance whose full potential had not been exploited by those early verses. He returned to that moment, and those verses, in the second part of the 'two-part *Prelude*' of 1799:

> It was a joy
> Worthy the heart of one who is full grown
> To rest beneath those horizontal boughs
> And mark the radiance of the setting sun,
> Himself unseen, reposing on the top
> Of the high eastern hills. And there I said,
> That beauteous sight before me, there I said
> (Then first beginning in my thoughts to mark
> That sense of dim similitude that links
> Our moral feelings with external forms)
> That in whatever region I should close
> My mortal life I would remember you,
> Even as that setting sun, while all the vale
> Could nowhere catch one faint memorial gleam,
> Yet with the last remains of his last light
> Still lingered, and a farewell lustre threw
> On the dear mountain tops where first he rose.

'Twas then my fourteenth summer, and these words
Were uttered in a casual access
Of sentiment, a momentary trance
That far outran the habit of my mind.

(lines 156-178)

It is perhaps worth noting that Wordsworth, who was born on
April 7, situates this moment in his 'fourteenth summer' – pre-
sumably therefore when he was thirteen, and three years before
the poem *Extract* was composed. If it was so, then the habit of
writing about an event long after it took place was well and truly
formed right from the beginning of his career. For the rest, the
passage from the manuscript of 1799 remains faithful both to the
spirit and to the language of *Extract*. However it develops the
experience in a totally different direction from the earlier poem.
Picking up on the Shakespearian reference – the evocation of the
sun 'reposing on the top / Of the high eastern hills' (lines 160-1)
being a clear echo of Horatio's,

But look, the morn in russet mantle clad
Walks o'er the dew of yon high eastern hill

(*Hamlet*, I, I, 167-8) –

Wordsworth leads into a panegyric of the sun as the source of
life, in which dawn is just as suggestive as sunset:

Already I began
To love the sun – a boy I loved the sun
Not as I since have loved him (as a pledge
And surety of my earthly life, a light
Which while I view I feel I am alive),
But for this cause, that I had seen him lay
His beauty on the morning hills, ... (lines 217-223)

The original poem, written before leaving school, had been about looking back on something that was ending. Thirteen years later Wordsworth grafted the same initial experience onto a radically different thought-process – one that exulted in the creative life force, and looked forward to the future.

That was in 1799. By the time *The Prelude* was finished six years later, he had rearranged the thought-process once again. The panegyric on the sun remained in place in Book II (lines 181-93), while the preceding passage, which in a certain sense had inspired the panegyric, disappeared. But not completely: something of it was preserved in the account in Book VIII of the shepherd and his dog, with the dog leading the flock of sheep up into the sunshine at the top of the mountain:

> the flock
> Fled upwards from the terror of his bark
> Through rocks and seams of turf with liquid gold
> Irradiate – that deep farewell-light by which
> The setting sun proclaims the love he bears
> To mountain regions.   (lines 114-9)

And that, one might think, would be the end of it. But not quite. For that whole episode was subsequently removed from the poem: in the 1850 version of *The Prelude* not a trace remains of the *Extract* Wordsworth had written as a schoolboy, and that had done him such good service. Instead, the original poem was granted autonomous status, and joined the collected edition of his poems in 1815 (in the same way as the 'Vaudracour and Julia' episode was removed from Book IX of *The Prelude* and published as a separate poem in the edition of 1820). So in a sense the poem returned gratefully to its starting-point (even if the *Extract* that appeared in 1815 was not, as we have seen, exactly the one he had written in 1786), having nurtured and nourished other poetic thoughts and helped other narratives along their way.

★ ★ ★

In 1829 Dorothy fell ill, and took to her bed. Her condition did not improve, and following the deaths of Coleridge in 1834, and Sara Hutchinson (William's unmarried sister-in law, who like Dorothy had been a long-time resident at Rydal Mount) in June 1835, something snapped in Dorothy's mind. She spiralled downwards into a state of mental confusion from which she would never recover. Both physically and mentally she was completely transformed, becoming almost the exact opposite of the person she had been. The woman who had measured her days by the miles she walked alongside her brother, was confined to a room at the top of the house, and only occasionally taken out in a wheelchair into the garden. After decades of following a meagre diet, in line with William's taste, she took to eating in a big way, so that her wiry body swelled like a balloon; and from being a quiet and discreet presence in other people's lives she became an embarrassment, as she shrieked and hooted and demanded attention for herself when in company....

Obviously it is difficult, at this distance in time, to diagnose what her illness was, or whether it was linked to and in part caused by the difficulties and deprivations of her adult life with William − though the fact that in illness she reacted so visibly against the way she had always behaved in the past might suggest that her breakdown was at least in part connected to the lifestyle she had accepted in order to be close to her brother.[113] Be that as it may, William's mental and emotional world must have been deprived of much of its meaning by his sister's illness and breakdown – and he knew it. She had been his constant companion, both indoors and out, for forty years; he had enjoyed a dialogue with her, where both his own poetry and literature in general were concerned, that was unique; he trusted her as completely as he trusted his wife... she was his soul-mate, the female version of himself, born just a year after he had been. And all of this he lost at the age of sixty-five, to discover instead a person with whom he had absolutely nothing in common, and who went from being a helper to a burden almost overnight. In the passage from *The Prelude* quoted above he had described how his idea of Mont Blanc had been usurped by reality; but here, in the sickroom at Rydal Mount, he could honestly claim that Dorothy had been usurped by another person – by someone who made a mockery of the principle of continuity through memory that he held sacred, and that had informed all the poetry he had written.

There were occasional moments of lucidity for Dorothy over the next fifteen years, but no improvement of her condition – and in the end she outlived her brother by five years. For William those fifteen years represented a trial by ordeal which he could never hope to win. Still, he never complained, or expressed bitterness or anger. Just as he had accepted his brother John's death in 1805, and those of his two children in 1812, so he met Dorothy's 'death-in-life' with the same brand of fatalism. These events brought out the Roman in Wordsworth's character, and showed how far he was in many respects from being a Romantic. The man who during the 1830s wrote fourteen *Sonnets upon the Punishment of Death*, which advocated acceptance of the death penalty, was never likely to indulge in the histrionics that accompanied the display of true Romantic feeling. But he was consistent with the man who, in a poem such as *Expostulation and Reply*, had, at the age of twenty-eight, preferred passivity coupled with attention to activity bolstered by rhetoric. Over the decades the language Wordsworth used in his poetry went through a sea-change, but the man himself changed much less – and given that he had always made a virtue of continuity and consistency, that much was only to be expected.

★ ★ ★

Unlike Allan Bank, the chimneys in Rydal Mount didn't smoke; but it was there that the Romantic flame flickered and went out. Not that Wordsworth would have necessarily thought of himself as a Romantic poet, even in his most inspired moments – or have imagined that future generations would coin that term to define much of the great art, literature and music produced in the first half of the nineteenth century. On the rare occasions that Wordsworth used the adjective 'romantic' he did so with a certain diffidence: for example, when recounting a funeral he had been to in a letter to Sir George Beaumont, he said that,

> The Churchyard is romantically situated: Duddon Sands on one side, and a rocky Hill scattered over with antient trees on the other. (January 6, 1821)

Dorothy remained more alert to the connotations of the adjective, as the excerpt from her journal of 1820 (quoted above) shows: for her a night spent with her beloved brother in a valley in the Swiss Alps went beyond her most romantic dreams. Of course there is a blurring of meanings and associations in the confusion between 'romantic' and 'Romantic'; nonetheless, one gets the impression that it was easier for the Victorians to define what was or wasn't 'Romantic' than it was for the artists and writers of the Romantic period.[114]

Certainly, there was precious little about Wordsworth that was obviously romantic – and that little (such as his affair with Annette) he did his best to hide and ignore. Even in youth his appearance and manner were ungainly and awkward, worlds away from the smooth and seductive elegance of Byron; and as the years passed, and he became increasingly entrenched in his ways, the portrait became more and more unprepossessing. One of the best sketches was offered by a friend of his daughter Dora, Ellen Ricketts, who accompanied Dora and her father (then aged sixty-eight) on a walking tour of the Duddon Valley in 1838:

I do not think I shall ever forget our dear old Poet's *Quixotic* appearance on this eventful little tour, or rather I should say he resembled more the representations of one of the Weird Sisters in Macbeth than anything else I can think of. He had been lately recovered from a very severe attack of Sciatica, he had suffered so much, and 'felt for himself (as he said) so much', this being almost the only serious illness he had ever had, that he was determined to take every precaution against cold. He had a little cloth cap on his head with a piece of fur falling from the back of it, and serving occasionally as a Collar. He had one of those Sheppard Scotch Plaids, used in the Highlands, and the gift of one of his many fair admirers, this plaid being sewn up one side and end, he threw over his head; it formed a conical peak at the top of it and then hung down shapeless and lank straight down his back, and being too long for him the remainder generally trailed on the ground like a train. It is true he suddenly recollected (when he stumbled over it every now and then) to hold it up on one arm, but this never lasted *long* for in his eagerness in talking and walking, away went the poor train again, sweeping the ground. He had on a pair of dark glass spectacles, as he was suffering from inflammation in his Eyes, and as a further protection to them whenever there was the least wind, up went an old weather-beaten faded green Umbrella with some of the points coming out, but from the flexible state to which it was alto-gether reduced by constant usage, it accomodated itself most agreeably to its owner's wishes and suited itself to every point of the compass. This completed our Hero's *turn out*, and a fund of amusement did it occasion us, for we were saucy enough to laugh at him repeatedly, which seemed much to divert him.[115]

This is – must be – the real Wordsworth. Unlike the insipid engravings and busts which, helped by his Roman nose, sought to metamorphose him into an Augustan poet, Ellen Rickett's por-trait presents us with the man himself: the same who, when mak-ing his marathon march across France and Switzerland in 1790, looked like a tramp and knew it:

> Our appearance is singular, and we have often observed that in passing thro' a village, we have excited a general smile. Our coats which we had made light on purpose for our journey are of the same piece; and our manner of bearing our bun-dles, which is upon our heads, with each an oak stick in our hands, contributes not a little to that general curiosity which we seem to excite.
>
> (letter to his sister Dorothy, September 6, 1790)

The man's consistency is impressive: it unites Wordsworth the undergraduate with Wordsworth the old age pensioner in a single image of cheerful shabbiness, and it unites the poet with the long series of travellers, beggars and vagrants that he had met on the open road and whose lives he had tried to understand. His scornful disregard for appearances and superficial impressions also gives us an insight into his understanding of Romanticism. For him Romanticism was closely linked to Puritanism: it depended on a contradiction between the visible and the real, and involved transcending the banal and ordinary appearance of things to reach the true beauty of nature. Of course he belongs to the Romantic period, and his vision of nature as an awe-inspiring and mysterious force that transcends the human dimension is in perfect harmony with the landscapes of Turner or Friedrich. But the wild and 'romantic' natural world in which he lived and worked was above all a context – without which his work would not have existed, no doubt, but which did not in itself make or explain his art – a bit like London would be for Dickens. Wordsworth's abiding concern was with time, memory and consciousness, and in itself that was not specific to Romanticism. On the contrary, they are themes which would preoccupy twentieth-century writers and thinkers far more than they interested those of the eighteenth or nineteenth centuries.

★ ★ ★

It was perhaps inevitable that a man who spent his life looking backwards in his poetry should develop a similar reflex in his political opinions and social thinking. For Wordsworth the future was an alien element – like the open sea, unreliable and undefinable. He preferred to measure change or progress (or the lack of it) by comparing the past with the present, rather than by projecting present conditions into an abstract future. And while he did not subscribe to the puritan myth of a 'golden age' – being well aware that life had always been hard for the poor, whether in the country or the city – he could see that England in the early nineteenth century was going through a particularly turbulent phase of its history, and he felt the stresses and strains that were being placed on the social structures that he understood and was at ease with.

One of the most dramatic changes to English society at this period was caused by the Industrial Revolution, and for someone living in the Lake District its impact was all too clear. The great manufacturing cities of Manchester and Liverpool were only seventy miles away from the pristine wilderness that Wordsworth loved to walk in. And the cities were not just the 'noisy neighbours' of the rural communities. Because of them more and more people were leaving the country – and it was this erosion of the rural way of life that Wordsworth opposed more than anything else. While he had been fascinated by the colour, energy, and drama of London as a young man, he had no true feeling for urban or metropolitan life, and he could not translate into art whatever he saw or witnessed in the cities he passed through or spent time in during the second half of his life. To that extent his range or scope was more limited than Turner's (though the latter had the advantage of being a Londoner by birth). There is no equivalent in Wordsworth to Turner's extraordinary painting of *Keelmen heaving in Coals by Night* of 1835. Nor did Wordsworth show any interest in the forms of transport that the Industrial Revolution introduced, while for Turner they were the subjects of some of his best known later works. *The Fighting Témeraire* of 1839, showing the old battleship being taken by a tug to be broken up, is explicit about the passage from sail to steam as a form of locomotion. Courageously, Turner also sought to integrate the 'artificial monsters' that were steam-boats into landscapes that were powered by purely natural forces: *Staffa, Fingal's Cave*, of 1831-2, showing a steam-boat in a storm, being the precursor to the even more dramatic *Snow Storm – Steam-Boat off a Harbour's Mouth* of 1841-2, in which the boat and its plume of black smoke are totally integrated into the swirling vortex of the storm. And then of course there was the famous *Rain, Steam and Speed* of 1844, in which a strong diagonal composition emphasised the acceleration of the train as it crosses the bridge, the painter responding to the surge of mechanised energy.

Wordsworth, who, if he could, would have gone everywhere on foot or on horseback, had little sympathy for modern forms of transport; and when he learned in 1844 of the plan to bring a railway line as far as Lake Windermere, he reacted furiously and did everything he could to oppose the project, lobbying, attending meetings, and – of course – writing sonnets on the theme.... The aptly named *Sonnet on the Projected Kendal and Windermere Railway*, published in the Morning Post in October 1844, shows us Wordsworth at his most rhetorical:

> Is then no nook of English ground secure
> From rash assault?

he asked at the beginning of the poem; and concluded with the same vehemence,

> Speak, passing winds: ye torrents, with your strong
> And constant voice, protest against the wrong.

In the end the trajectory of the railway line was modified, and Windermere was left in peace, though it is not clear how much influence Wordsworth had in getting the plans changed. Certainly, the debate did nothing to improve his public image: already considered out of touch with contemporary society, he was now criticised for wanting to preserve his own peace at all costs at the expense of the greater good. An important motive behind the construction of this line had been to make it easy for the working population from the manufacturing cities to have direct access to the Lakes, and so to be able to enjoy a day out in some of the most beautiful landscape in Britain. In opposing this scheme Wordsworth was seen to be selfish and élitist. A statement by the Board of Trade to Parliament, referring to Wordsworth's campaign, made this criticism quite clear:

> We must [...] state that an argument which goes to deprive the artisan of the offered means of occasionally changing his narrow abode, his crowded streets, his wearisome task and unwholesome toil, for the fresh air, and the healthful holiday which sends him back to work refreshed and invigorated – simply (so) that individuals who object [...] may retain to themselves the exclusive enjoyment of scenes which should be open alike to all [...] appears to us to be an argument wholly untenable.[116]

It would surely have surprised the participants in this debate to know that the same conflicts and tensions were being expressed a hundred and seventy years later, and the same arguments used to justify one course of action or another. Today almost all of the Lake District is a National Park, but that does not mean it can simply remain as it has always been, and exist according to the laws of nature alone. It is a national treasure and a resource, and as such needs to be managed. So who manages it, and in whose interest? The pressures exerted are greater than ever, as the few remaining wild spaces in Britain soak up the needs of an ever increasing number of people who want to get away from it all – but without wanting to let go of the habits and comforts that they are used to in daily life. Yacht marinas on Lake Windermere; three-star hotels; mountainous theme parks – these are the kind of facilities that are developed in the Lake District nowadays – and with inevitable results. The area loses its original identity, and becomes instead something that (hopefully) gives pleasure to a large number of people. In a relatively small and definitely overcrowded island like Britain, the Lake District today is as precious as an oasis; but it is also expected to function as a major holiday destination – which is not the same thing. However the change in the role and character of the region over the last two centuries has been gradual enough for it to seem natural, or at least inevitable.

Wordsworth's argument was that such a change was neither welcome nor inevitable. For him, the Lake District was a wild animal that had to remain untamed in order to have dignity and meaning. The fatigue and discomfort involved in exploring it was part of the point. The landscape, and all it contained, was not a utility placed there to enrich people's lives, but an intrinsic part of God's creation that existed for its own ends, and with its own mysterious logic and meaning; and one that could only be appreciated by someone who was prepared to take the time, and make the effort, to get to know it on its own terms.

It is easy to see the later Wordsworth as just a boring reactionary, but his conservatism was neither bland nor straightforward. If he was alive today it would be hard to place him in the political spectrum, especially since the traditional political categories, represented by the mainstream parties, no longer satisfy a large proportion of the electorate. As someone who mistrusted capitalism, and advocated respect for the environment and sustainable economies above all else, he would be far more likely to vote for a Green party than for the Conservatives. Be that as it may, it is important not to pigeonhole Wordsworth as a man whose thinking remained stuck in the eighteenth century, and to appreciate instead that many of the issues that interested him still provoke debate today, and show no signs of being resolved.

★ ★ ★

The 'Windermere Railway Episode' provided a good example of how Wordsworth's mind worked, and how his feelings were engaged. Put simply, his opinions on the subject became clear because his personal interest was at stake. Up to a point that is true for most people – but most people also try to think outside themselves from time to time, to take into consideration wider parameters than they are familiar with when trying to work out what is for 'the general good'. Otherwise how could any political thinking be possible?

It was one of Wordsworth's strengths and weaknesses that he had great difficulty in engaging with a subject that did not in one way or another resonate with his own predicament. I suggested above that his tendency to refer backwards in his political think-ing was intimately connected to the habit of using memory to structure his poetry. In a similar way the opinions he expressed about politics or society seem to have been provoked by specific events or circumstances that touched him personally. When he was a young man, his resentment of the aristocracy was fuelled by the grudge he and his siblings held against Lord Lonsdale; reciprocally, his attitude towards the landowning classes changed in middle age as a result of the kindness shown to him by Sir George Beaumont and by Lonsdale's heir, Sir William Lowther.... While he ascribed his nationalistic stance after 1802 to the shame-ful way the French had acted under Napoleon, his desire to set a distance between himself and his own (mis)adventures in France was crucial in determining his opinions.... His warm feeling for the small landowners who lost out at the time of enclosures, or his concern with the drift of the rural population towards the cities, was underscored by his passionate desire to reconstitute the sense of family, stable and emotionally secure, that he had lost in childhood.... His mistrust of capitalistic economics stemmed

from having had to survive on a very modest budget for dec-
ades, and knowing that risk was a dangerous luxury which he
could not afford. But then his brother's death, which left his and
Dorothy's investment, along with John's, at the bottom of the
English Channel, was decisive in turning Wordsworth against
the principles of free-market economics which, through a heady
mixture of capitalism, colonialism, and imperialism, were setting
Britannia on a course which was designed to guarantee that she
would rule the waves for the rest of the nineteenth century....

And so on. For Wordsworth history and his story were always
overlapping, and it was always going to be difficult to disentangle
one from the other.

Chapter XVI

The Poetry That Endures

Prospero: *No tongue, all eyes! Be silent.*
(Shakespeare, *The Tempest*. IV, I, 59)

In 1838 George Ticknor, Professor of Belles Lettres at Harvard University, paid a visit to the Wordsworths. On May 8 he recorded in his journal that

> Mrs. Wordsworth asked me to talk to him about finishing the *Excursion*, or the *Recluse*; saying, that she could not bear to have him occupied constantly in writing sonnets and other trifles, while this great work lay by him untouched, but that she had ceased to urge him on the subject, because she had done it so much in vain....On my asking him why he does not finish (*The Recluse*), he turned to me very decidedly, and said, 'Why did not Gray finish the long poem he began on a similar subject? Because he found he had undertaken something beyond his powers to accomplish. And that is my case.'[117]

Wordsworth's reply echoes the assessment that he had made of *The Prelude* in two letters to Sir George Beaumont, written in May and June 1805 as he was completing the poem:

I began the work because I was unprepared to treat any more arduous subject & diffident of my own powers (May 1, 1805)

when I looked back upon the performance it seemed to have a dead weight about it, the reality so far short of the expectation; it was the first long labour that I had finished, and the doubt whether I should ever live to write *The Recluse* and the sense of this Poem being so far below what I seem'd capable of, depressed me much (June 3, 1805)

Wordsworth's expectations of himself were based not on the quality of the writing he produced, but on the length of a poem, and on the grandeur, scope, and nobleness of its theme. It is a way of thinking that may be hard for a writer today to take seriously, but there is no doubt that Wordsworth thought of his career in those terms. The poets he admired – such as Chaucer, Dante, and Milton – had all created masterpieces whose length was as impressive as the breadth of the poets' vision. The principle was straightforward: a small thought could be expressed in a few lines, while a large and complex idea needed a lot of space in order to find its form. However, pithy gems such as *'My heart leaps up when I behold'*, and many wonderfully dense and suggestive passages in *The Prelude*, show clearly that this kind of arithmetical equation makes little or no sense when assessing the quality of Wordsworth's poetry. Nonetheless he remained faithful to the principle that achievement could be measured by size; and it was only with great reluctance, after decades of trying to maintain the fiction that he would complete his epic poem, that he finally abandoned it. As far as he was concerned, the *'Prelude-Excursion-Recluse'* project may have ranked as the biggest failure of his life.

The likelihood of failure was clear to Wordsworth from the

outset. After listing at the beginning of *The Prelude* a variety of
noble themes that he could have tackled, he admitted that,

> either still I find
> Some imperfection in the chosen theme,
> Or see of absolute accomplishment
> Much wanting – so much wanting in myself
> That I recoil and droop   (Book I, lines 263-6)

Nonetheless he went ahead, and gave the project all he had
to give. Looking back, we may say that *The Recluse* was doomed
from the beginning; nonetheless, if Wordsworth had not had the
aspiration to realise his great and ambitious dream, then almost
certainly *The Prelude* would never have existed – at least not in
the form that we know. The jewel in the crown of Wordsworth's
oeuvre would be missing, and we should have a completely
different conception of his poetry. Luckily for us, he was close
enough in time to the great masters of the past to feel he could
take on a major project like *The Prelude*. And luckily for us he was
far enough from them in time to be able to produce a complete-
ly different kind of long poem from those he admired, one that
was profoundly personal and original. Though he didn't realise it,
the timing of Wordsworth's life – (that's to say, its bookend dates,
1770-1850) – was crucial in defining the poetry that he would
feel able to write.

★ ★ ★

Wordsworth's desire to be worthy of the great masters of the
past led him to envisage his poetic career in terms of a long
and patient construction. Great art, he believed, should have the
qualities of fine architecture – slow to build, but also long-lasting.

Writing to Sir George Beaumont in June 1805 about *The Prelude* (which he had just finished), he said,

> This work may be considered a sort of portico to The Recluse, part of the same building, which I hope to be able erelong to begin with, in earnest; and if I am permitted to bring it to a conclusion, and to write, further, a narrative Poem of the Epic kind, I shall consider the <u>task</u> of my life as over.
>
> (June 3, 1805)

The analogy was developed a little further nine years later, in the preface that he wrote when publishing *The Excursion*. Having made it clear that *The Excursion* was a portion of a larger project, *The Recluse*, he then referred to the relationship between the as yet unpublished *Prelude* and *The Recluse*:

> the two Works have the same kind of relation to each other [...] as the ante-chapel has to the body of a Gothic church. Continuing this allusion, [... the] minor Pieces, which have been long before the Public, when they shall be properly ar-ranged, will be found by the attentive Reader to have such connection with the main Work as may give them claim to be likened to the little cells, oratories and sepulchral recesses, ordinarily included in those edifices.[118]

The allusion continued to please him, even when it was clear that the *Recluse* project was not making headway. His sonnet of 1820, *Inside of King's College Chapel, Cambridge*, meditated on the qualities of a particularly beautiful building in a way that invested the Chapel with values that went beyond architecture. In admiring

this immense
And glorious Work of fine intelligence! (lines 4-5)

he could have been referring to any great work of art; and when
he considered the building in some detail, the language he used
was poetic rather than technical:

> the man who fashioned for the sense
> These lofty pillars, spread that branching roof
> Self-poised, and scooped into ten thousand cells,
> Where light and shade repose, where music dwells
> Lingering – and wandering on as loth to die;
> Like thoughts whose very sweetness yieldeth proof
> That they were born for immortality.   (lines 8–14)

As always, Wordsworth's imagery was grounded in straightfor-
ward observation. The elaborate fan-vaulting of King's College
Chapel, which runs the whole length of both nave and choir
without any modification, comes as close as is possible in a
building to suggesting an avenue of trees; and this metaphor is
brought into play in the sonnet with the 'branching roof / self-
poised'. The image was not in itself dazzlingly original: indeed,
Shakespeare must have had something similar in mind when re-
ferring to 'choirs' in his sonnet (no. 73):

> That time of year thou mayst in me behold
> When yellow leaves, or none, or few, do hang
> Upon those boughs which shake against the cold,
> Bare ruined choirs where late the sweet birds sang.
>
> (lines 1–4)

But the significance of the metaphor for a poet like
Wordsworth was that he was clearly looking to integrate the ar-
tificial construction that is a building into the larger order of the
natural world – to create a synthesis between the principles of
construction and creation. To this end he abruptly changed tack

in the middle of the line, and turned his attention from trees to beehives ('that branching roof / Self-poised, and scooped into ten thousand cells'). And the use he made of that image was original. The crucial idea came from the cells of a honeycomb, in which worker bees store honey. Honeycombs are of course amazing constructions, and Wordsworth seized on this link between artifice and nature by giving a twist to the words used in the preface to *The Excursion* of 1814 (as quoted above). There he had compared minor poems to 'cells', meaning small chapels or other enclosed spaces that are part of a large church or cathedral. This architectural connotation was reinforced thanks to the common use of the same word to describe the room in which a monk or nun lived; and that meaning had been deployed by Wordsworth in his sonnet of 1802, *'Nuns fret not at their Convent's narrow room'*:

> Nuns fret not at their convent's narrow room;
> And hermits are contented with their cells;
>
> (lines 1-2)

However the 'ten thousand cells' that are 'scooped' out of the chapel ceiling – (referring to the complex pattern of spaces between the ribs of stone that make up the fan-vaulting) – point to a different context, namely the organisation of a beehive. In this context cells are not symbols of monastic solitude and austerity, but rather act as 'traps' which hold and contain beauty and life: Wordsworth imagines the music sung by the choir floating up to the ceiling and 'lingering' in the 'cells' that articulate the ceiling. And it is surely the idea of honey that imparts 'sweetness' to the thoughts that such a building can inspire, and which, like the building itself, can hope to stand the test of time, to endure. Or rather, the building itself, being made of stone, endures, while the thought that inspired it is 'born for immortality'. Like the soul in *Intimations of Immortality* which passes from body to body, so poetry (or music, or any creative thought) is housed for a while in some form or other, but belongs nowhere.

For Wordsworth the true poetic voice had always been no-madic, nameless and placeless as the wind. And early on he had sensed a relationship between the will o' the wisp that was poetry, and the wanderers that he encountered on the open road – a similarity that was not casual, since it was precisely the vagabond lifestyle of the travellers that ensured that they remained close to nature. This vision was first given form in the portrait of the Pedlar from *The Ruined Cottage* (of 1797-8):

> To him was given an ear which deeply felt
> The voice of Nature in the obscure wind,
> The sounding mountain and the running-stream.
> To every natural form, rock, fruit, and flower,
> Even the loose stones that cover the highway,
> He gave a moral life; he saw them feel
> Or linked them to some feeling. In all shapes
> He found a secret and mysterious soul,
> A fragrance and a spirit of strange meaning.
> Though poor in outward shew, he was most rich;
> He had a world about him – 'twas his own,
> He made it – for it only lived to him
> And to the God who looked into his mind.
>
> (lines 80–89)

In fact the description of the Pedlar was less a portrait than a self-portrait, as Wordsworth himself admitted decades later. Speaking to Isabella Fenwick in 1843 he remarked that,

had I been born in a class which would have deprived me of what is called a liberal education, it is not unlikely that, being strong in body, I should have taken to a way of life such as that in which my Pedlar passed the greater part of his days. At all events I am here called upon freely to acknowledge that the character I have represented in this person is chiefly an idea of what I fancied my own character might have become in his circumstances.[119]

Wordsworth's identification with the Pedlar in 1798 set the young poet on a course that was barely compatible with the grand scheme (for *The Recluse*) postulated in the same year by Coleridge. The affinities Wordsworth felt with poor, hardworking and uneducated men whom he felt had much to teach him, together with his decision in 1799 to settle in a remote and wild part of Britain – as far as possible from the sophisticated metropolitan world of salons, coffee-houses and publishing-houses, with their passion for fashion and gossip, and their dogmas about what constituted good taste and fine art – all this created tensions which no small measure of compromise was likely to resolve. And the description of the Pedlar emphasised the importance not merely of living close to nature, but also of being extremely attentive to the voices of the natural world, however obscure or slight they may be. Attentiveness, and the permeability of human consciousness, are seen as the keys to creativity. The implication is that the true poetic voice does not really need a social context. It has no respect for class or hierarchy, no need for justification or explanation. It simply is – in the way that everything in nature 'simply is'.

How could such ideas be reconciled with the baroque intellectual fantasies that Coleridge dreamed up, and with which he sought to seduce the mind of his talented young friend? Throughout 1798 the debate inside Wordsworth's head went on and on – yet each time he committed himself to paper he came down on the same side, merely advancing the argument a little further. *Expostulation and Reply*, probably composed in May 1798, suggested that poetic awareness came via the body's five senses:

> The eye – it cannot choose but see;
> We cannot bid the ear be still;
> Our bodies feel, where'er they be,
> Against or with our will.
>
> 'Nor less I deem that there are Powers
> Which of themselves our minds impress;
> That we can feed this mind of ours
> In a wise passiveness.   (lines 17-24)

The 'wise passiveness' advocated here was well expressed in Wordsworth's personal life by the stoicism with which he responded to the 'slings and arrows' that life sent his way, in particular the early deaths of two of his children; his brother John's death at sea; and Dorothy's long illness. But in his poetry the principle of passiveness was qualified by the fact that our bodily organs are constantly active, processing or interpreting whatever they receive or absorb. This idea had already been expressed in the description of the Pedlar quoted above:

> he saw them feel
> Or linked them to some feeling

and was explored further a couple of months later in *Tintern Abbey*:

> Therefore am I still
> A lover .... of all the mighty world
> Of eye and ear, both what they half-create
> And what perceive (lines 103-8)

The idea that we 'half-create' the world that we like to think of as 'real' was also present in the description of the Pedlar:

He had a world about him – 'twas his own,
He made it – for it only lived to him
And to the God who looked into his mind.

There were no precedents for thinking and writing about consciousness in this way: it opened up a completely new territory for literature – but it was one which was difficult to reconcile with the 'noble themes' and epic narratives that Wordsworth admired. Squaring that circle was one of the aims of *The Prelude*, and it is easy at this point to understand why he kept losing faith in the poem, and why he decided not to publish it. *The Prelude* existed on a fault-line in Wordsworth's psyche. It continually aspired to be one kind of poem – an important element in the great work of intellectual architecture that he planned to realise; and yet it stubbornly decided again and again to be something else – namely, an exploration of the inner world of the human mind, based on the premise that consciousness is, like a thumbprint, unique to each individual.

The debate acquired particular intensity in the famous dream-sequence in Book V of *The Prelude* (lines 56-139). The passage begins with Wordsworth sitting by the sea on a warm summer's day, reading Cervantes' *Don Quixote* (in the 1805 version it is a friend – maybe Coleridge – who recounts the dream, but Wordsworth later recast the narrative in the first person, and I prefer this reading). After a bit he closes the book, and, while gazing out to sea, reflects

On poetry and geometric truth
(The knowledge that endures), upon these two
And their high privilege of lasting life
Exempt from all internal injury   (lines 64-7)

until, lulled by the sound of the sea and the warm air, he falls asleep, and his intellectual daydream flowers into a true dream. In the dream, which takes place in the middle of the desert, a Bedouin comes riding towards him on a camel, holding a stone in one hand and a bright shell in the other. The Bedouin tells Wordsworth that the stone is in fact Euclid's *Elements* (Wordsworth's reference-book for learning geometry when he was at school), while the shell is also a book – one which is even more precious than Euclid's masterpiece. This book which, given that it accompanies Euclid, must (given the daydream that precedes the dream) represent poetry, is a conch. The Bedouin tells Wordsworth to hold it to his ear. When he does so he hears

> an unknown tongue,
> Which yet I understood, articulate sounds
> > (lines 94-95) –

that's to say, the raw material of which poetry is made. The promise implicit in this thought is that the language of nature can be translated into the language of poetry – as long as one is prepared to be patient and listen. Hence the wisdom of the passiveness Wordsworth had advocated years earlier.

The choice of a conch as symbol for poetry works perfectly within the context of the passage, since the setting for the dream-sequence has been made quite clear: the episode takes place beside the sea, and in those conditions anyone who holds a conch-like shell to their ear will have the impression of 'listening to the sea' as the sound of the wind and water resonate in the shell. As usual with Wordsworth, there is a plausible empirical basis for even his most imaginative fantasies. What is more striking is the twinning of geometry and poetry – a more unlikely marriage of disciplines would be hard to imagine. Wordsworth's thinking goes against all the received ideas of what Romanticism

stood for: Romantic art, music and literature should give prec-
edence to feeling over rational thought, it should be intuitive,
expressive, passionate, and not consort with the most rigorous of
sciences....So what was Wordsworth up to? Is this another exam-
ple of a retreat by him to an eighteenth-century way of think-
ing, to the world of the Encyclopédistes and the masters of the
Enlightenment, with their belief that creativity and intellectual
knowledge and social progress all went hand in hand?[120]

No, not quite. The synthesis that Wordsworth aimed for was a
bit different. As we saw in chapter XI of this book, the whole of
The Prelude was structured on a dialectic between the two agents –
nature and education – that together enable the healthy growth
of human personality. The dream sequence of Book V functions
in the same way: geometry and poetry are shown there as equals,
yes, but also as complementary opposites rather than partners; the
stone and the shell are symbols that balance each other – but they
are not held in the same hand. Poetry for Wordsworth was essen-
tially a form of creation that belongs to the natural world, while
geometry was the product of an intellectual education.

Poetry and geometry may be strange bedfellows, but between
them they represented for Wordsworth all that was noblest in
human culture. As the dream-sequence progresses we learn that
the end of the world is at hand, and that, in order to preserve the
'essence of civilisation' the Bedouin

> Was going then to bury those two books –
> The one that held acquaintance with the stars
> And wedded man to man by purest bond
> Of nature, undisturbed by space or time;
> The other that was a god, yea many gods,
> And voices more than all the winds, and was
> A joy, a consolation, and a hope.　　(lines 103-9)

Wordsworth here perhaps comes closer than anywhere else to
defining what poetry is for him. It is above all an art of interpre-
tation, which depends as much on listening as on speaking, since
the meaning it proposes depends on understanding the obscure
meaning(s) offered by nature. The role of the poet is not so far
removed from that of the Delphic oracle – and it is interesting that
Wordsworth in the passage just quoted places poetry in the con-
text of a culture in which there are 'many gods', many sources of
meaning and inspiration. There is a strong tension here between
on the one hand a vision of art that looked back to the classi-
cal world, and on the other the monotheistic Christian tradition
that Wordsworth subscribed to, according to which there is only
one source of meaning, which is God. And it is significant that
at crucial moments in his writing Wordsworth refuses to submit
to orthodox Christian dogma, when it comes into conflict with
other ways of thinking – this is one important example, while
his thinking about the life of the soul in the 'Ode: Intimations of
Immortality' is another.

Cunningly – master craftsman of his art that he was by this
time – Wordsworth achieved his own synthesis of the classical and
Christian visions later in *The Prelude*. After reaching the summit
of Mt Snowdon in Book XIII, the chaotic force of the elements
is evoked in a way that reminds us of how the poetic impulse was
described in Book V:

> A deep and gloomy breathing place through which
> Mounted the roar of waters, torrents, streams
> Innumerable roaring with one voice!
>
> (Book XIII, lines 57-59)

Wordsworth's trump card was to use the Pentecost to reconcile
the classical and Christian worlds, for on that day the assembled

apostles spoke with many different tongues, many voices; but in so doing they made it possible for the single truth of God's Word to be disseminated widely.[121]

★ ★ ★

The theme Wordsworth chose to explore in *The Prelude* – the growth of the human mind – opened up for him the perspective of a new poetic language: one in which the workings of the mind, and the voice that articulates them, are hard to distinguish. The thought process and the verse blend and become as one. The result was that when his poetry was at its most intimate the language was deceptively casual. It's as if we were listening to Wordsworth having a conversation with himself, and could follow the movement of his thoughts this way and that, changing tack as one idea modified another. For example, in the passage in *The Prelude* – (Book IV, lines 247-268) – in which he meditates on the act of remembering while being rowed across Lake Windermere, the writing seems to drift as aimlessly as the boat itself. Nonetheless the thought process reveals itself to be as complex and subtle as anywhere in his poetry.

If we try to visualise the scene represented in this passage, we come close to the long sequence of water-lily paintings that Monet elaborated between 1903 and 1927. Those paintings relied on a tension (between the surface of the water as mirror, and water as transparent) that allowed Monet to juggle with the elements of air and water and earth – with the floating lilies and the weeds swaying underwater and the trees and clouds reflected on the surface of the pond – to create endless variations on a theme in a way which challenged traditional notions about composition and perception. Wordsworth indulges in a similar confusion of images: the passenger in the boat 'sees many beauteous sights' and 'fancies more', yet

> cannot part
> The shadow from the substance – rocks and sky,
> Mountains and clouds, from that which is indeed
> The region, and the things which there abide
> In their true dwelling – now is crossed by gleam
> Of his own image, by a sunbeam now,
> And motions that are sent he knows not whence
>
> (lines 254-60)

At this point however Wordsworth introduces a new direction or dimension to the thinking. The still water of the lake is equated with past time, that is to say the lake contains water just as the present contains memories of the past, the present being the surface of the lake, and its contents being the past. Memories rise to the surface, reflections about the past that rebound from the surface... only Wordsworth could write in this way, translating difficult intellectual concepts into words and images that are accessible to any reader, and imbuing the passage with a lightness and ease worthy of Mozart.

The passage begins and ends with the word 'still': 'still water' in line 249 echoed by 'where we still are lingering' in line 268. Same word, but quite different meanings – the adjective describing something that is static, the adverb referring to an action that continues in time. Wordsworth enjoyed playing these contrasting meanings against each other. The obvious counterpoint was between a human conception of time (linear and progressive) as expressed by the adverb 'still', and the ordered realm of nature, with its complex structure of cycles, evoked by the adjective 'still'. The passage from Book IV of *The Prelude* just referred to provides a perfect example of that word-play. But Book I of *The Prelude* complicates matters considerably, for there nature is shown to be a living force, a protagonist in the drama rather than a backdrop to it. The boating episode (Book I, lines 372-427) at first evokes a placid natural landscape, in which even the ripples made by the oars lie 'still' and 'glittering idly in the moon'. But the idyllic vision is subverted by the image of the 'huge cliff' which,

> still,
> With measured motion, like a living thing
> Strode after me.   (lines 410-12)

Objectively a cliff is static and inert (except to a geologist), and by placing the word 'still' at the end of the line Wordsworth offers first that meaning – before refuting it in the following line, so that 'still' can no longer be read as an adjective but only as an adverb.

This tension – between human activity and the forces that propel the natural world – is developed in the very next scene – the famous skating episode. Wordsworth picks up the theme explored in the boating episode and deploys an almost identical arrangement: 'still / The rapid line of motion' of lines 481-82 seeming to echo deliberately 'still / With measured motion' (lines 410-11). But the emphasis is different. The boy stops short on his skates, but the scene around him continues to spin past:

> yet still the solitary cliffs
> Wheeled by me, even as if the earth had rolled
> With visible motion her diurnal round!
>   (lines 484-86)

Here the cliffs 'wheel' rather than 'stride', in other words their movement is not voluntary but involuntary, and they can be said to be 'still' in both senses of the word – that is to say, both static and in continuous motion. For here we are no longer in the realm of childish imagination, in which cliffs and hills move through the boy's troubled mind; rather we are coming to terms with the laws of physics — and in particular the principle of inertia — as defined by Newton.[122] The world turns on its axis round the sun, and we turn with it. Following this reasoning, the real precedent for the thought behind the skating episode is to be found not in the boating episode that preceded it, but in the 'Lucy' poem *'A slumber did my spirit seal'* composed a few year earlier:

> No motion has she now, no force;
>   She neither hears nor sees,
> Rolled round in earth's diurnal course
>   With rocks and stones and trees.

This is where we approach the essence of Wordsworth's understanding of stillness. It has to do with order — in the sense that nature is based on a principle of order which it is hard for us to perceive, but which we must listen to and yield to if we intend to live in harmony with the rest of creation.

In *Tintern Abbey* also he places 'still' at the end of a line, to produce an effect similar to that of the lines from the boating episode in Book I of *The Prelude* (quoted above):

> Therefore am I still
> A lover of the meadows and the woods,
> And mountains; and of all that we behold
> From this green earth;   (lines 103–6)

'Still' functions here as an adverb, but by placing it at the end of the line, with the inevitable break or pause that that implies, it almost becomes an adjective: we almost read 'Therefore am I still' as a complete phrase. Through his love for 'the green earth'

and all that it contains, the poet is led towards the primeval still-
ness and quietness of all those beings that live in harmony with
nature – that same 'settled quiet' that the old Cumberland beggar
possessed, and which the young envied him. The ambiguity of
meanings is perfectly registered by the most delicate of touches,
by a simple matter of phrasing.

★ ★ ★

There were periods in Wordsworth's life that were crowded and
noisy with human activity – the months spent in London, for
example, or the time in Dove Cottage when babies were teething
and children were growing fast. But mostly he lived in an envi-
ronment which by our standards was very quiet, even oppres-
sively so: in houses where the hours might be punctuated only
by the creaking of a floorboard or the rattling of a window pane;
and in the vast outdoor spaces where only wind and running wa-
ter – streams, torrents, waterfalls – could be relied on to provide
background music and company. Silence was his natural habitat
to a degree which we can only with difficulty imagine. But he
also knew that the silence was textured by an infinity of almost
inaudible voices: he could identify a tree in the dark from the
sound the wind made in its leaves; he could recognise the calls of
all the local birds, or distinguish the cry of a pine-marten from
that of a stoat or a weasel. His ear was finely tuned and attentive
to the least sound; and in the same way he was able to hear clearly
the stories of the people he met on the open road – even though
much of what they had lived through remained unsaid, or was
muted by massive understatement.

Whether in relation to the natural or the human world, a
major dynamic of Wordsworth's poetry involved giving a voice

to silence: making sense of the ballet of the elements as they un-
furled across the mountains and lakes, or listening to the coded
messages of his unconscious. Perhaps his most lasting achievement
has proved his ability to make of this no-man's land between the
inarticulate and the articulate the natural terrain for poetry: there
he has been a model for generations of poets, whether or not
they agreed with his politics or were interested in the Romantic
aesthetic.

In what may be the only revision to the text of *The Prelude*
that is a definite improvement, the 1850 version adds two lines
to the description of Newton's statue in Trinity College Chapel:

> The antechapel where the statue stood
> Of Newton with his prism and silent face.
>
> (Book III, lines 58-59; 1805 version)

becoming,

> The antechapel where the statue stood
> Of Newton with his prism and silent face,
> The marble index of a mind for ever
> Voyaging through strange seas of Thought, alone.
>
> (Book III, lines 60-63)

Apart from the beauty of the added lines – which could just
as well serve as a tribute to Wordsworth the poet as they do to
Newton the physicist and mathematician – the significance of
the addition lies in the idea that silence is expansive. Far from
representing a closure on language and thought, silence opens
doors, and creates new perspectives onto worlds that are 'strange'
but also exciting and enriching.

Wordsworth the poet of silence, who loved above all to listen?
At any rate, 'silent' and 'listen' are true anagrams, better even than

'poetry' and 'poverty'. And just as there is a profound silence at the core of his personality – a silence and a private space that he was ready to defend at all costs, against anyone who came too close – so the best of his poetry seems to emerge out of silence and doubt, like elements of a landscape in the mist, which acquire form and substance and then disappear again. Poetry that was impalpable, undefinable – yet memorable, and instantly recognisable as Wordsworth's. Poetry that has endured because it did not try to endure, but was content simply to live in the wind's embrace.

A Note on Editions and Texts

Wordsworth had difficulty in letting go of his poems once published. He continued to brood over them, and quite often made changes to the texts, which were then incorporated into later editions. Sometimes these revisions are minute, but in other cases they modify the tone or meaning of a poem significantly. Editors have therefore often had to choose between two distinct versions of a poem – either the first published text or the final version from near the end of Wordsworth's life (what one might call the authorised version).

Until the 1980s editors printed the 'authorised version' of the poems, thereby respecting the poet's declared wishes and following (one might say) the legalistic principle that the last version of a person's will is the one that has validity in law. But in recent decades most editors have chosen to use the first published version of each poem, on the grounds that what counts is the original poetic expression, and that subsequent revisions only compromise the integrity of that statement. Occasionally a footnote containing a variant made by Wordsworth is included, but more often than not the reader is simply presented with a single text which is proposed as definitive, when it may well not be.

Editors are obliged to be consistent, so an anthology of Wordsworth's poetic output spanning sixty-four years will necessarily be organised according to the same criteria from start to finish. I do not have the same constraints as editors, and have given myself the freedom of choosing which version of a poem to quote from. For poems written from 1798 onwards I have referred to the final ('authorised') version of a text (with the exception of *Nutting* and *The Prelude*). For poems written between 1787 and 1797 on the other hand, I have chosen the first published version of a text. Wordsworth revised his early work in middle age, as he sought to establish a distance from what he had thought and felt as a young man, without losing sight of past experience. The process involved the toning down or suppression of erotic or sexually suggestive imagery – a form of 'revisiting' which I find unhelpful if one is trying to understand an artist; and so I have invariably chosen the first version of Wordsworth's early poems, such as they existed before self-censorship hid or obliterated the impulses of his youth. (*Home at Grasmere*, mostly written in 1800, remained unrevised as it was never published during Wordsworth's lifetime; it is discussed in chapter VI, *Adam and Eve*).

Given Wordsworth's tortuous working methods, it is very difficult for any single edition of his collected poetry to present the oeuvre in a way that is wholly satisfactory. The Penguin edition of *The Prelude* is exemplary, offering both the 1805 and 1850 texts on facing pages. Ideally one would want the same arrangement in every anthology of Wordsworth (with the first and last version of each poem on facing pages), but such an edition does not exist. The nearest one gets to it is the Project Gutenberg archive online: all of Wordsworth's published poems are available there, with the 'authorised' version printed, and virtually all variants given.

Some of the editions available today are noted in the bibliography that follows.

The way that Wordsworth has been edited is discussed in chapter XII, *The Whirligig of Time*.

Bibliography

SOME OF THE EDITIONS AVAILABLE

Editions using first published text of the poems:

William Wordsworth, The Major Works; ed. Stephen Gill, Oxford University Press (Oxford World's Classics series), 1984 (paperback edition, 2008)

William Wordsworth, Selected Poems; ed. Stephen Gill, Penguin (Penguin Classics series), 2005

William Wordsworth; ed. Stephen Gill, Oxford University Press (21st-Century Authors series), 2010

Poems of William Wordsworth (3 volumes), Cornell University Press, 2009

Editions using last published text of the poems:

William Wordsworth, Collected Poems, Wordsworth Poetry Library, 1994. (This edition also preserves the thematic and non-chronological arrangement of the oeuvre, established by Wordsworth in 1815)

William Wordsworth, Selected Poems; ed. John Hayden, Penguin (Penguin Classics series), 1994. (This edition is out of print, but can be obtained online)

The Prelude:

William Wordsworth, The Prelude: The Four Texts; ed. Jonathan Wordsworth, Penguin, 1995

DOROTHY'S JOURNALS

Dorothy Wordsworth, The Grasmere and Alfoxden Journals; ed. Pamela Woof, Oxford University Press, 2002

LETTERS

Wordsworth, A Life in Letters; ed. Juliet Barker, Viking, 2002. (Unless otherwise indicated in the notes that follow, all letters quoted can be found in this selection)

BIOGRAPHIES

Wordsworth, A Life; Juliet Barker, Penguin, 2001. (Referred to in the notes that follow as *Wordsworth, A Life*, this is the abridged version of a similar biography published by Viking in 2000, which I have also referred to once in the notes)
The Hidden Wordsworth; Kenneth Johnston, Norton, 2001
The Ballad of Dorothy Wordsworth; Frances Wilson, Faber and Faber, 2008

FURTHER READING

Thomas De Quincey, *Recollections of the Lakes and Lake Poets*
The Fenwick notes of William Wordsworth, ed. Jared Curtis
Emile Legouis, *William Wordsworth and Annette Vallon*
The Love Letters of William and Mary Wordsworth

MATERIAL AVAILABLE ONLINE

Much of Wordsworth's work is available online. The *Project Gutenberg* is particularly useful and complete as a source. Among many other elements of interest, Isabella Fenwick's notes can be found there: they are given after each of the relevant poems, in *Wordsworth's Poetical Works*, vol. 1.

The text of both Emile Legouis' book, and that of Thomas De Quincey, can be found online. The letters of Annette Vallon to William and Dorothy can be found, in the original French, in a facsimile version, by googling 'William Wordsworth and Annette Vallon letters mocavo', then by going to Appendix II at the end of the book.

I have not found the text of William and Mary's love letters online.

Notes

1. The complicated history of *The Prelude* is discussed in chapter XI.
2. This part of Wordsworth's life is discussed in chapter III.
3. William and Dorothy's relationship is discussed in chapters VI & IX.
4. References are to the 1805 version of *The Prelude*, except when otherwise stated.
5. They took cheap lodgings when they could, and otherwise slept rough. Everything was done as cheaply as possible: William told Dorothy that in seven weeks of travelling he and Robert Jones had spent just £12 between them.
6. For men like Wordsworth – middle-class and well-educated, but without private means or property – there were generally three choices for a career: the law, the army, or the Church. Of these, the Church was the only option he felt he could even begin to consider seriously. Within the family pressure was put on him to follow this path, and uncles who were in a position to help him materially made it clear that they would do so. But Wordsworth refused to engage, and then thought up tutoring as an alternative form of employment (but made no efforts to find work in this way)… In the end, the 'classic' choices were pretty much respected by William's three brothers: Richard became a lawyer; Christopher was ordained and was also made a Fellow of Trinity College, Cambridge (ending up as Vice-Chancellor of the University); while John, though he did not follow a military career, entered the Navy.

7.   In 1843 Isabella Fenwick, a long-standing friend of the Wordsworths, invited the poet to dictate to her any comments or reflections that came into his mind about the poems he had written. The result of this lengthy collaboration was an informal but invaluable collection of notes, the only document of its kind where Wordsworth's work is concerned (see bibliography for details).

8.   The 'Lucy' theme is discussed in chapter V of this book.

9.   Newton's so-called 'law of inertia' corresponds to his first law of motion, which stated that objects remain either at rest or in movement (at a constant speed), unless acted upon by an external force. The significance of this law for Wordsworth was that it eliminated the distinction between movement and stasis: things which seem to us to be static are in fact in movement, while things which move may be doing so because they have no choice, rather than because they want to. Given the interest Wordsworth showed as a teenager in Newton's *Opticks* (see page 136), it is reasonable to assume that he also read some of Newton's writings on gravity and motion. At any rate, his admiration for the great scientist was clearly formed by the time he went to Cambridge (see pages 136-7), and did not lessen as he got older: the reference to Newton in Book III of *The Prelude* (1805 version) became an explicit tribute in the 1850 version (see page 416 – the two lines were added in 1838-9). Wordsworth's move towards established religion in middle age did not in any way involve a denial of the value of scientific thought and research.

10. Wordsworth acknowledged on a number of occasions the influence his sister had had in shaping his poetic vision and voice. One of the most eloquent tributes came in *The Sparrow's Nest*, a short poem written in 1802, quoted on page 227 of this book. See also page 287.

11. Recorded in the *Memoirs* of Charles Grenville, entry for February 27, 1831; quoted in *Wordsworth: A Life in Letters*, p. 207.

12. See note 13.

13.   Quoted by Frances Wilson in *The Ballad of Dorothy Wordsworth* (p. 45). Earlier in the book Wilson offers a variant on this scene which may come from the same source:

> '"Mr Wordsworth went bumming and booing about," one local recalled of Wordsworth's muttering as he paced up and down the path, "and she, Miss Dorothy, kept close behint him, and she picked up the bits as he let 'em fall, and tak 'em down, and put 'em on paper for him."' (z3)

These observations clearly date from the Dove Cottage period, as the path there was very close to the road and visible to any passer-by... Almost thirty years later Dora, William's daughter, wrote to a friend,

> 'I must tell you what a neighbour of ours said when he heard Daddy was about to return after a long absence "Why than we shall hae him *booing* agen int' that wood; he boos like a bull enough to *freighten* a body" – Poetical is it not?' (letter of 1 December 1828)

One has the impression that with the years Wordsworth's method of composition passed into local folklore, and became something of a standing joke.

Wordsworth himself (who was not known for having a sense of humour), was also able to see the joke. In Book IV of *The Prelude* (lines 109-20) he recounts how he liked to walk on the roads with a dog he was fond of, while composing poetry aloud 'like a river murmuring / And talking to itself'; and how the dog would bark to warn if someone was coming, so that Wordsworth would be spared from 'piteous rumours such as wait / On men suspected to be crazed in brain.'

14.   Milton's eyesight deteriorated during the late 1640s, and he became totally blind in early 1652, when he was forty-three. Most of his great poetry, including *Paradise Lost* and *Samson Agonistes*,

was composed after he had gone blind. *Paradise Lost* (which took Milton about eight years to 'write') was composed early in the morning – between the autumnal and spring equinoxes – as he lay in bed. He would store about forty lines in his head, and then wait for someone to whom he could dictate them. As one of his friends put it, 'hee waking early (as is the use of temperate men) had commonly a good Stock of Verses ready against his Amanuensis came; which if it happened to bee later than ordinary, hee would complain, Saying, *hee wanted to bee milkd*.' (Cyriack Skinner, quoted in: Barbara Lewalski, *The Life of John Milton*, Blackwell, 2003, p. 448).

15. Long journeys, and seemingly endless highways, had of course been an intrinsic part of life for North Americans ever since the migration westward of the early European settlers; but it was only in the 1950s that Americans began to think of such travelling as something that could be done for pleasure rather than necessity. For the characters of John Steinbeck's pre-war novel *Grapes of Wrath* (1939) travelling was an ordeal; while for Jack Kerouac, in *On the Road* (1957), it was synonymous with personal freedom. However it was the cinema – and the rock music that made up the films' soundtracks – that truly consecrated 'road culture', with a long sequence of road movies from *Easy Rider* (1969) to *Thelma and Louise* (1991) and beyond.

16. Wordsworth paid tribute to Anne Tyson in Book IV of *The Prelude*, lines 16-32:

> 'Glad greetings had I, and some tears perhaps,
> From my old dame, so motherly and good,
> While she perused me with a parent's pride.
> The thoughts of gratitude shall fall like dew
> Upon thy grave, good creature!...'

17. Anacreon lived from 582-485 BCE Several translations of his poem, *Instructions to a Painter*, are available online: in them the relevant passage is translated as follows:

(1) And o'er all her limbs at last
A loose purple mantle cast;
But so ordered that the eye
Some part naked may descry,
An essay by which the rest
That lies hidden may be guessed.

(2) And let her tender limbs be drest,
In a translucent, violet vest,
Which, while it slightly veils her skin,
The whole discloses from within.

(3) Now let a floating, lucid veil,
Shadow her limbs, but not conceal;
A charm may peep, a hue may beam,
And leave the rest to Fancy's dream.

In *The Hidden Wordsworth* (p. 74) Kenneth Johnston discusses Wordsworth's reading of the poem, and offers another translation of the relevant passage:

'the rest
Be in a chastened purple drest,
But let her flesh peep here and there
The lines of beauty to declare.'

While these four translations vary considerably, they are consistent in focusing exclusively on the woman's body. Wordsworth's invention was to introduce the metaphor of the landscape, and through that metaphor to suggest the woman's sex, which is nowhere evoked in the original poem.

18. The poem was never published, but the full text can be found online, by googling 'Wordsworth Beauty and Moonlight' then (for example) www. poetrynook.com. (See also note 52).

19. The print is reproduced in *City of Laughter*, by Vic Gattrell, Atlantic Books, London, 2007, page 369.

20. A part of the relevant passage – lines 205-10 of *An Evening Walk* – is quoted on pages 149-50.

21. The incident, as recalled by Wordsworth at the end of his life, is quoted in *Wordsworth, A Life in Letters*, p. 2.

22. Quoted in *Wordsworth, A Life*, p. 67.

23. The narrative of Book VII of *The Prelude* develops these metaphors by weaving observations of the people in the streets with visits to actual circuses, fairs, etc. So, for example, lines 227-79 move from contemplating the variety of racial types in the cosmopolitan crowd (227-43) to an animal menagerie (244-7), and from there to an art gallery (248-79). Next we visit Sadler's Wells, with its tight-rope-dancers and dwarfs and clowns (lines 288-309), before making a trip to the theatre (lines 439-87). The tour of London's sights and sounds culminates with a day at St Bartholomew's Fair (lines 648-94), which is evoked by a long list of the strange and colour-ful people and animals to be seen there. Wordsworth's London is remarkably vivid and fresh: it comes alive in a way one would not expect from a nature-poet, and cries out to be filmed (it would have been perfect material for Fellini).

24. From *London* (*Songs of Innocence and Experience*, 1794)

25. *Little Dorrit*, Book I, chapter 3. Work on constructing an adequate sewer system for London began in 1857, the year that *Little Dorrit* was completed. When Wordsworth says, 'How often in the over-flowing streets / Have I gone forwards with the crowd…' (*The Prelude*, Book VII, lines 594-5) the word 'overflowing' carries two meanings, even if the sense of the flow of people is primary – and backed up a little further on by, 'When the great tide of human life stands still,' (line 630). (I imagine T. S. Eliot had these lines in mind when in *The Wasteland* he wrote, 'A crowd flowed over London Bridge, so many, / I had not thought death had undone so many.' (*The Burial of the Dead*, lines 62-3)).

26. *The Early Lives of John Milton*, ed. Helen Darbishire, London, 1932, p. 63. Quoted in: Barbara Lewalski, *The Life of John Milton*, p. 156.

27. *The Life of John Milton*, p. 165.

28. Op. cit. pp. 171-2.

29. In January 1793 Richard Watson, Bishop of Llandaff, republished a sermon he had preached years earlier, and added an Appendix to it. Watson wrote the Appendix in reaction to the execution of King Louis XVI earlier in the month; and in it he denounced the violence and civil unrest in France, while praising the (largely unwritten) constitution thanks to which the British preserved the status quo in their country. Wordsworth's *Letter* set out to refute the arguments put forward by Watson: in particular he attacked the principles of monarchy, aristocracy and primogeniture that Watson defended, advocating instead the virtues of a republic based on universal suffrage. The *Letter* showed Wordsworth at his most rebellious (the exact opposite of the man who, almost forty years later, would oppose the Reform Bill of 1832); and had it been published he would have risked being arrested and imprisoned. As it was, the tract remained in a desk drawer.

    The tracts in which Milton attacked the status of the monarchy and advocated republican values – *Tenure of Kings and Magistrates* and *Eikonoklastes* – were published in 1649, following the execution of Charles 1 in January of that year. After the restoration of the monarchy in 1660, Milton feared for his life as a direct consequence of his writings and political actions. He spent several weeks in prison, and hid for more than three months in a friend's house, before finally being pardoned.

30. *Wordsworth, A Life*, pp. 83-4.

31. Op. cit. p. 84.

32. Voltaire, *Candide* (1759), chapters 5 and 23.

33. Following the death of William's father in 1783, William's uncle Richard assumed responsibility for the finances of the estate: when William needed money he had to ask his uncle for it. Richard died in 1794, and at that point the responsibility passed to William's elder brother (also called Richard) who by then was

a qualified lawyer. Given that William and Dorothy were continually penniless, and that a considerable part of the estate remained blocked (because of the money owed to the Wordsworths by Lord Lonsdale), administering the family finances was a thankless task, and relations between the siblings were not always easy. In the end Richard, the elder brother on whom everyone relied, and who was a model of success and respectability, got his own back on all those who had unreasonable expectations of him. At the age of forty-five this confirmed bachelor decided to marry his servant, Jane Westmorland, who was just twenty-two years old. After fathering a son he died the next year, leaving huge debts, and the family finances in disarray – having made bad investments of William and Dorothy's money on their behalf.

34. Jane Austen, *Sense and Sensibility* (1811), chapter 49. Comparing accurately the value of money then and now is a tricky business. In *The Hidden Wordsworth*, Kenneth Johnston offers 'A Note on Money' (pp. xxiii–iv), which gives an idea of incomes and expenses in the early 1790s – though he adds that during the second half of that decade 'the cost of living approximately doubled as a result of economic dislocations caused by the war with France'.

35. We know nothing about how Wordsworth spent his time in Paris. Probably he followed debates in cafés and salons (his French was fluent by this time), went to the theatre, and walked in the streets. There were also groups of English people sympathetic to the republican cause – he could have spent time with them.

36. The censorship cannot in fact have been complete. In May 1800, for example, Wordsworth mentions writing to Annette, and there is also evidence of correspondence between William and Annette in 1812. The three surviving letters from Annette to William and Dorothy can be found online (see bibliography).

37. While in Blois Wordsworth made friends with Michel Beaupuy, an officer in the Revolutionary army. There was a Lieutenant Vaudracourt in Beaupuy's regiment – Wordsworth borrowed his

name for the hero of his story. In *The Prelude* Wordsworth also said that it was Beaupuy who told him the story of Vaudracour and Julia – but this was merely to make the narrative smoother. In fact, as he told Isabella Fenwick in 1843, the 'Vaudracour and Julia' romance was based on a true story that he had been told by a woman at Blois (he had also learnt, many years after the events, that Dupligne – the real-life Vaudracour – had ended up as a monk in a Trappist monastery). To this must be added another source for the Vaudracour – Julia story, namely the opening episode of Helen Maria Williams' *Letters from France*, of 1790. Helen Williams' story of lovers thwarted by parental opposition (over which they finally triumph) has a number of points in common with the Vaudracour–Julia story; and Wordsworth would surely have read it, for he had been an admirer of Williams' poetry since he was in his teens – indeed, his first published poem, written in 1787, was a glowing tribute to Helen Williams (entitled, *Sonnet on Seeing Miss Helen Maria Williams Weep at a Tale of Distress*)... and when he left for France in November 1791 he carried with him a letter of introduction to Miss Williams (though we have no record of whether they actually met).

However, if I mention these details in a note devoted to the name 'Vaudracour', it is above all because Wordsworth did not sign his teenage tribute to Miss Williams (*Sonnet on Seeing...*) with his own name, but as 'Axiologus'. This is a Greek version of his surname, 'axios' in Greek meaning 'worthy' and 'logos' meaning 'word'. As an adolescent Wordsworth was already alert to the word-play that his surname allowed; and when, in around 1804, he came to write the coded version of his affair with Annette for Book IX of *The Prelude*, he summoned back to his memory both Helen Maria Williams' story as a reference, and the name of Lieutenant Vaudracourt; with, linking the two, the fact that he had used a pun on his surname when writing a tribute to Miss Williams in 1787. It is a neat example of the labyrinthine nature of

Wordsworth's mind, in which memory proved itself the supreme organiser of material and constructor of narrative.

38. Christopher Wordsworth, *Memoirs of William Wordsworth* (London, 1851), vol. I, p. 74.

39. It is hard however to know in what way Wordsworth might have respected this commitment. The one letter from Annette to William that has survived makes it clear that in March 1793 she was hoping and expecting that he would marry her; but he may have felt that it was enough for him, having openly acknowledged paternity of Caroline, to help Annette financially. It is possible that he never considered marriage with Annette as a viable option, even during the relatively calm summer of 1792, and felt that the fact of not repudiating the relationship was the best he could do.

40. See the theme of chapter XIII.

41. £250,000 is the figure that Juliet Barker proposes in *Wordsworth, A Life* (p. 13).

42. It is often suggested that Wordsworth used the time spent with young Basil to try out Jean-Jacques Rousseau's ideas on education (especially as set out in *Emile, ou De l'Education*), according to which the natural and physical world have an essential role to play in forming a child's character. Unfortunately there is no proof (as far as I know) that Wordsworth ever acknowledged Rousseau's influence on his own thinking, or even mentioned the French philosopher at all. *Emile* was published in 1762, and it is likely that Wordsworth read it (as a young man he read more widely in European literature than his poetry would superficially suggest – in a letter of June 1791 Dorothy says that, 'He reads Italian, Spanish, French, Greek & Latin' – and it would be surprising if he took no interest in Rousseau). However there is no evidence to support the theory that Wordsworth set out to put Rousseau's ideas into practice during the time spent in Dorset, or that he grafted Rousseau's thinking onto memories of his own boyhood experiences, as recounted in *The Prelude*. While in retrospect we may trace

a continuity of ideas from Rousseau to Wordsworth, any linking of the two men must remain a matter of conjecture. See also note 91).

43. Quoted in *Wordsworth, A Life* (p. 225).

44. The *Elegaic Stanzas* were written in 1805, shortly after William's brother John died at sea. Wordsworth used the image of the castle in a storm to explore his feelings of grief and bereavement; and lines such as, 'A power is gone, which nothing can restore; / A deep distress hath humanised my Soul' imbue the writing with an emotional force which belies the poem's elaborately formal title.

45. The title of Earl of Lonsdale died with the childless Sir James Lowther in 1802. It was recreated for his heir, Sir William Lowther, in 1807 – at which point he became 'Lonsdale' rather than 'Lowther'. Between 1802 and 1807 he could be referred to (it seems) either as Sir William Lowther or Lord Lowther; after 1807 either as Lord Lonsdale or the Earl of Lonsdale. Similarly his predecessor seems to have been known either as Sir James Lowther, or Lord Lonsdale, or the Earl of Lonsdale.

46. While there was no official salary, it was estimated that Wordsworth would earn between £400 and £500 a year from this job.

47. Another part of the same letter is quoted on pages 28-9.

48. There are two main areas for the law of intellectual property, where writers and artists are concerned: one concerns their production while they are alive, the other concerns their estate once they are dead (who inherits what, who has the right to what, etc.). While the prime issue in the second category is usually money, there is also the question of the artist's reputation. In cases where evidence comes to light after the death of an artist, that would affect his or her reputation – extra-marital affairs being the most common example – families tend to close ranks in order to preserve an image of the artist that suits them. To this end they demand that incriminating evidence – letters, poems, photographs, songs or whatever – be kept secret; and judges have to decide whether or not to prohibit publication. Not all such cases come

to court, however, as the family almost always has a headstart over the general public, simply by virtue of having immediate access to relevant papers, letters and documents, and can often effectively determine the outcome of a debate before it even begins. Destroy incriminating evidence, and there is nothing of substance for people to enquire into. Wordsworth's relationships with Annette (and, to a lesser extent, Dorothy) were a good case in point, with his heirs taking pre-emptive measures necessary to guarantee the integrity of the poet's reputation (see notes 73 and 77).

49. Published in Wordsworth's *Collected Editions* as one of the *Poems of Sentiment and Reflection*, with the title, *Written in Germany, on one of the coldest days of the century.* The poem is composed of seven verses of five lines each; the passage quoted is of lines 15-25.

50. Quoted in *Wordsworth, A Life* (pp. 89-90).

51. Wordsworth's use of the name 'Emma' for Dorothy is discussed on pages 156-7.

52. Dorothy may have been aware of this poem, as Wordsworth certainly showed it to Coleridge – who then reworked it in 1798 into a longer poem called *Lewti, or the Circassian Love-Chant.* Coleridge's poem was due to be included in the 1798 edition of *Lyrical Ballads*, but at the last minute was replaced by another poem – though it was published in *The Morning Post* on April 13, 1798. In Coleridge's *Lewti*, the relevant lines are rephrased as,

> 'I then might view her bosom white
> Heaving lovely to my sight,
> As these two swans together heave
> On the gently swelling wave'

– (the full text of the poem can easily be found online). Had the poem been included in *Lyrical Ballads*, it would have introduced a quietly erotic note which would have modified considerably the tone of the collection – but that was not something that Wordsworth wanted. Nonetheless, the fact that Wordsworth let

Coleridge use his own verses in this way is a clear indication of the complicity that existed between the two men in those years.

53. We find the same epithet in *Nutting*, written two years earlier than *Home at Grasmere*, in which Wordsworth admires the hazel trees 'with milk-white clusters, / A virgin scene!'. (The poem *Nutting* is referred to on pages 52-3). And it appears in Book I of *The Prelude* (line 511) in a passage that evokes outdoor pleasures enjoyed in adolescence.

54. *The Recluse* was designed to be a long philosophical poem about the spiritual and social condition of modern man. It is referred to at different points in this book (see index). The best resumé we have of the would-be poem's themes and arguments comes from a letter of Coleridge's to Wordsworth written in 1814, and quoted on pp. 266-7.

55. As we saw in chapter I of this book, movement was central to Wordsworth's understanding of life; and in his poetry he evoked many different kinds of motion. With 'moveless', which Dorothy here refers to, he was feeling his way towards expressing a certain kind of motion, namely movement in space without any apparent exertion. This fascinated him all his life, and he returned to it at different moments and in quite different contexts. For example, in '*A slumber did my spirit seal*', Lucy is 'rolled round in earth's diurnal course' thanks to the rotation of the world around the sun. While it is clear in the poem that Lucy is dead, this is not specified: in reality we are all 'rolled round...' whether we are alive or dead. (See also note 9).

56. The extent to which William read his sister's journal remains a mystery. My intuition is that the notebooks were private, and that William would not read them – but that Dorothy would read to him from them. For example one can imagine situations in which brother and sister reminisced about a particular experience – at which point Dorothy might look for the relevant reference in her journal, and read it to William.

Pamela Woof discusses this topic in her notes to the *Grasmere Journals* (p. 161, note for 'Pleasure').

57.　Frances Wilson considers this debate in chapter 7 of *The Ballad of Dorothy Wordsworth* (in particular pages 145-7). Beginning with F. W. Bateson's suggestion (in 1954) that while they were in Goslar, William and Dorothy realised they were falling in love, she then quotes other biographers and scholars who considered the relationship to have been 'profoundly sexual' or 'excessively close'; and characterised by 'strong erotic attraction' or by 'an agonising frustration'. Wilson's own opinion is that, 'The relationship between the Wordsworths was organised around a notion of perfect and exclusive brother-sister love which was imaginatively assimilated by them both to the point where it became the source of their creative energy, but its physical expression would have been of no interest to them.' She attributes this lack of sensual desire to Wordsworth's inability to think of other people as existing in flesh and blood; and she cites another writer, Camille Paglia, who 'calls this type of disembodied desire "Romantic incest", which she sees as "a metaphor for supersaturation of identity"'. (For Wilson's judgement on Wordsworth's sexuality see also note 87).

I agree with Wilson's opinion that William and Dorothy did not look for a physical expression to the love they felt for each other, but I disagree with the reasons she puts forward. I think it is more helpful to think of them as living in a state of profound symbiosis, rather as we see sometimes with identical twins. In such cases sexual frustration or satisfaction is simply beside the point; what matters is both the intensity of the current that passes between the siblings, and the ease with which thoughts and emotions are shared.

58.　The universal character of this taboo fascinated anthropologists throughout the twentieth century. Claude Lévi-Strauss's *Les structures élémentaires de la parenté* (1949) is one of the best known texts on the subject. In it he came to the conclusion that the

prohibition of incest is vital to social life because it – (the taboo) –
promotes the exchange of women in a way that both extends the
network of relationships and encourages the development of what
one might call the 'social economy': '*La prohibition de l'inceste est
moins une règle qui interdit d'épouser mère, soeur ou fille, qu'une règle qui
oblige à donner mère, soeur ou fille à autrui. C'est la règle du don par ex-
cellence.*' ('The prohibition of incest is less a rule that forbids a man
to marry his mother, sister, or daughter, than a rule which obliges
him to give his mother, sister or daughter to another man. It is
the perfect example of the rule of giving.'). Later on in the book
he developed the idea of an economy of the emotions: '*Comme
le dit justement un observateur, "il en est du couple incestueux comme
de la famille avare: ils s'isolent automatiquement de ce jeu consistant à
donner et à recevoir, à quoi se ramène toute la vie de la tribu."*' ('As one
observer has noted, "an incestuous couple is like a miserly family:
they automatically distance themselves from the play of giving
and receiving on which the whole life of the tribe is based."')...
In the 'library episode' of *Ulysses* James Joyce expressed a not dis-
similar thought, with this reflection on the writings of Thomas
Aquinas: ' – Saint Thomas, Stephen, smiling, said, whose gorbellied
works I enjoy reading in the original, writing of incest from a
standpoint different from that of the Viennese school Mr Magee
spoke of, likens it in his wise and curious way to an avarice of the
emotions. He means that the love given to one near in blood is
covetously withheld from some stranger who, it may be, hungers
for it.'... For Lévi-Strauss the dominant impulse in the prohibi-
tion of incest throughout history has been the desire to develop
beneficial social relations; any sense of moral outrage at incestuous
relationships has been secondary, if not irrelevant. It is the point
of view of an anthropologist rather than of, say, a sociologist or
a psychologist. But whatever the reasoning that one adopts, it is
clear that the taboo on incest is as strong today as ever – even
though the structure of societies in the western world today bears

little resemblance (superficially at least) to those of the primitive cultures that Lévi-Strauss studied. Incest is considered a crime in over half the countries of the world; and with the sustained campaign against paedophilia and child sex abuse that we have seen in the last decade or so, any kind of sexual impropriety is likely to be censured heavily. Attitudes in general are probably far less tolerant today than they were in Wordsworth's time.

59. According to de Quincey, Dorothy refused any potential suitors because she did not want anyone to come between her and William. In his *Recollections of the Lake Poets* he states this quite clearly: '...few women live unmarried from necessity. Miss Wordsworth had several offers; amongst them, to my knowledge, one from Hazlitt; all of them she rejected decisively.' De Quincey's assertion is generally ignored by scholars and biographers as being unreliable and unsusbstantiated; but what reason would he have had to invent a marriage proposal which was never made? On the contrary, given William's possessive attitude to the women who were close to him, the idea that Hazlitt proposed to Dorothy could help to explain the way Hazlitt's friendship with William deteriorated after 1803 (see note 60). If we allow that de Quincey's assessment of Dorothy's actions and motivations could well be true, then the language of her *Grasmere Journal* where William is concerned, and her selfless devotion to her brother, make perfect sense...and the intrinsic imbalance in their relationship also becomes even clearer, Dorothy having committed herself to chastity in order to live with her brother, while he set about looking for a wife and then starting a family.

60. Wordsworth met Robert Southey in 1795, at the same time as he met Coleridge, and they remained friends until Southey's death in 1843. At that point Wordsworth succeeded Southey as Poet Laureate, a position that Southey had held since 1813. Today Southey's poetry and essays have passed into obscurity, and he is best known simply for the fact of having been part of 'the Lake

School'. Charles Lamb, whom Wordsworth met in 1797, was another lifelong friend. He was primarily an essayist, as was William Hazlitt, whom Wordsworth met in 1798 – though Hazlitt was also a painter. The friendship with Hazlitt cooled after 1803. Likewise Wordsworth's friendship with Thomas de Quincey started well and then went sour. In 1807 de Quincey made what amounted to a pilgrimage to the Lake District to meet Wordsworth. He was happy to join the circle, and in 1808 he took over the tenancy of Dove Cottage when the Wordsworths moved to a larger house. But with time they lost contact, and Wordsworth was mortified by the portrait that de Quincey drew of himself and Dorothy in his *Recollections of the Lake Poets*, which first appeared in 1839.

61. Some details of the 'Christabel crisis' are given on pages 218-19.

62. Wordsworth's thinking here was underwritten by the concept of limbo, that had been introduced at the time of the Reformation to counter the Catholic concept of purgatory. According to the Protestants, an individual sleeps after death, until being reawakened on the Day of Judgement – hence the inscriptions on gravestones one occasionally comes across, 'Not dead, just sleeping'. (However it could be said that the English later returned to an idea of purgatory that was close to that of Roman Catholics, by inventing the boarding-school system).

63. Allan Bank, the house (also in Grasmere) they moved to, was spacious but turned out to be cold and draughty – and the chimneys smoked badly. In 1813 they moved again to Rydal Mount (also close to Grasmere). The move to Rydal Mount coincided with the falling-off in Wordsworth's creative energy and output: eventually the house came to be known informally as 'Idle Mount'.

64. Caspar David Friedrich's trademark composition was of a figure in the foreground, seen from behind, contemplating a vast and majestic landscape.

65. See chapter XV, and note 113, for a discussion of Romanticism.

66. The etching is reproduced in *Wordsworth, A Life*, facing p. 299.

67. Letter of September 12, 1802; quoted in *Wordsworth, A Life*, p. 185.

68. In *The Ballad of Dorothy Wordsworth* (pp. 150-4), Frances Wilson traces a parallel between Dorothy's relationship with William, and Catherine's relationship with Heathcliff. It is unclear from what she writes whether Wilson believes that Dorothy served Emily Bronte as a model for Catherine, or whether she (Wilson) simply sees the two women – Dorothy and Catherine – as having much in common. As Wilson admits, the material concerning Dorothy that was available to Bronte in 1847 (when *Wuthering Heights* was published) was scarce and fragmentary: at that date *The Prelude* had not been published; and extracts from Dorothy's *Grasmere Journals* would only be published in 1851, included in the *Memoirs* of Wordsworth written by his nephew Christopher. The only material from the Wordsworth family that Bronte could have relied on in order to have a sense of the William-Dorothy relationship were a few poems (*Tintern Abbey* in particular). However, as Wilson points out, Bronte could also have drawn on the portrait of Dorothy offered by De Quincey in his *Recollections of the Lake Poets*, which suggested a woman of great passion and intensity (as in the following passage, for example:

> 'Miss Wordsworth was too ardent and fiery a creature to maintain the reserve essential to dignity... Beyond any person I have known in the world, Miss Wordsworth was the creature of impulse.')

De Quincey's *Recollections* appeared in serial form in 1839, and it is very likely that the Brontes would have read them. As Wilson also notes, the Bronte siblings were well aware of the Wordsworthian model: in 1837, Emily's brother Branwell sent some of his poems to Wordsworth, 'entreating' the poet to give an opinion of their worth, 'because from the day of my birth to this the nineteenth year of my life I have lived among wild and secluded hills where I could neither know what I was nor what I could do'. Branwell's letter points to the common ground that the Brontes shared with Wordsworth – the fact of living and working in a remote part of northern England, and the problems that such isolation created for a writer. In *Wuthering Heights* geographical isolation and the force of nature can be felt as unseen protagonists in the human drama that unfolds: they contribute to the idea, crucial to the dynamics of the novel, that human relationships may be truer, more honest, when they follow natural instinct and disrespect civilised notions of law and propriety. Might we not see something similar bubbling up in William and Dorothy's relationship, with the only significant difference being the degree of self-control, and respect for social norms and conventions, shown by the Wordsworths?

69.   A total of thirty-one love-letters were discovered in 1978: fifteen were from William to Mary, and sixteen from Mary to William. They all date from either 1810 or 1812.

70.   Wordsworth offered a rare glimpse into this aspect of his character in a letter written to Sir George Beaumont after the death of his brother John: 'At first I had a strong impulse to write a poem that should record my Brother's virtues & be worthy of his memory. I began to give vent to my feelings, with this view, but I was overpowered by my subject & could not proceed: I composed much, but it is all lost except a few lines, as it came from me in such a torrent that I was unable to remember it; I could not hold the pen myself, and the subject was such, that I could not employ Mrs Wordsworth or my Sister as my amanuensis. This work must therefore rest awhile till I am something calmer' (May 1, 1805).

71.   £20,000 in goods and money is the figure that Juliet Barker gives for John's investment at the beginning of the fatal China voyage (*Wordsworth, A Life*, p. 233). Kenneth Johnston assesses the investment at 'nearly £20,000', and adds that John 'expected a profit of £10,000 on the first leg alone, even more from the cargo of rice and forbidden opium from Bengal to China, and still more

from the teas he would carry on his voyage home.' (*The Hidden Wordsworth*, p. 584). De Quincey however reckoned that £20,000 represented what John could hope for as a return on his investment if the voyage proved to be successful. Very approximately, we might reckon John's investment for that voyage to have been worth about one million pounds today – (so much for the modest and unassuming 'silent poet', who preferred the uncomplicated world of nature to the tedious demands of human society!)... As for William and Dorothy's part in the financial venture, it seems that their brother Richard invested several hundred pounds of their money on their behalf, but took out insurance for them. Therefore they probably did not lose money; however John's mercantile adventures had represented the only hope they had of making an interesting profit from the sums they had inherited: following his death they had to radically lower whatever expectations they may have had of improving their financial situation.

72. Three different poems have *To the Daisy* as their title, and are best identified by reference to their opening words. So, *To the Daisy ('Sweet Flower!')*, William's tribute to John, was written in late May – July 1805; while *To the Daisy ('In Youth')*, and *To the Daisy ('With little here')* were written in April-June 1802 (as was another poem entitled *To the Same Flower*).

73. Quoted in *The Hidden Wordsworth*, p. 517. Johnston says that this sentence is 'all that remains of a letter that Gordon Wordsworth destroyed.'

74. Certainly the Wordsworths understood the gesture in that way. When in 1817 Southey called in on Caroline and her daughter in Paris, on Wordsworth's behalf, he reported back that 'the little French Dorothy is very like her mother'.

Annette, it should be said, did not leave it to her daughter to pay a tribute to Dorothy's generous efforts. In her letter to William of March 1793 she sang Dorothy's qualities loud and clear: '...*elle fait l'honneur de son sexe. Je désire bien que ma Caroline lui resemble.*

Que j'ai pleuré, mon cher Williams! Quel coeur, quel ame! Comme elle partage bien les malheurs qui m'accablent...' ('...what a woman she is! I do hope that my Caroline grows up to ressemble her. Dear William(s), she moves me to tears with her kindness and her capacity to understand. I feel she shares my troubles intimately...'). Although the written evidence is slight – (given that no other letters to William survived) – Annette's way of expressing herself – direct and heartfelt – seems to have been curiously similar to Dorothy's. This would have complicated things considerably for Wordsworth during the 1790s. He could have listened to the sister he loved so intensely, and with whom he had so much in common, expressing herself in much the same way as the woman he had fallen in love with in France, and who was the mother of his child. And it seemed that there was a kind of bond established between the two of them... it was a difficult cocktail for Wordsworth to handle, given that all reasonable arguments urged him to place a distance between himself and Annette.

75. See pages 178-9.

76. Wordsworth's association of the colour white with Frenchmen is presumably based on the fact that white (in reality the off-white of unbleached wool) was the dominant colour in French military uniforms between 1750 and 1789 (the other colour usually being blue). These were also the two colours of the French flag under the Ancien Régime: blue being the colour of the Capet family (the ruling dynasty), and white representing the monarchy; (after the Revolution red – symbolising revolution – was added, to make the *tricolore* that we know today).

77. It seems to me unlikely that it was Dorothy who crossed out these lines, as the journal was never intended to be read by others (except perhaps William), and she had no reason to retract what she had felt and done. And William was unlikely to interfere in a heavy-handed way by obliterating the expression of such a spontaneous and intimate sentiment between brother and sister. It is

much more probable that the culprit was either William's nephew Christopher, or his grandson Gordon. Christopher was William's official biographer, and executor of the literary estate (see note 48), and as such he would have had access to material that had never been edited or analysed carefully. It is certainly possible that he decided that passages such as this one were best forgotten, as he set out to provide the public with a definitive image of the great poet. However, the true vandal turned out to be Gordon, who in time became the guardian of the family archives. Brought up on good Victorian values, he destroyed anything that could possibly conflict with the idea of Wordsworth that by this time (around 1900) had become set in stone (see note 73). During their life-times both William and Dorothy exercised self-censorship in less conspicuous ways than crossing out or destroying texts: for exam-ple, in her journals and letters, Dorothy had nothing to say about their meetings with Annette and Caroline in 1802 or 1820, and William likewise removed the 'Annette episode' from *The Prelude*. And there was continual self-censorship in their own relation-ship: feelings that were not put into words, so that the relationship could continue to function.

After the poet's death censorship continued to flourish, mod-elling the image that the public was offered of the Wordsworths. Christopher Wordsworth's *Memoirs*, published in 1851, offered a bland version of the poet's life, from which all embarrassing details were removed. Likewise, the first publication of substantial extracts of Dorothy's *Journals*, in 1889, edited by William Knights, was extremely selective. As Pamela Woof notes in the Oxford edi-tion of 2002 of the *Grasmere Journals*, the extended edition of 1897 was not much better:

'Knight's Victorian editorial principle prevailed: the omis-sion of what he deemed "trivial details", i.e. most mentions of concern about the bodily conditions of Wordsworth, Dorothy, and Coleridge, from boils to bowel problems, from snoring to sleeplessness; such physical activities as shaving, eating and white-washing; there is no brotherly kiss of greeting in this edition, no riding snugly, buttoned up "both together in the Guard's coat"; fewer poor people litter the roads. The poet lived in an elevated world.' (Note on the texts, p. xxii).

78.   It seems likely that Wordsworth enjoyed no sexual relations be-tween the autumn of 1792, when he left Annette to return to England, and the autumn of 1802, when he married Mary. Certainly we know of no such relationship during those ten long years; and given the attitude towards prostitution that he expressed in Book VII of *The Prelude* (in particular lines 382-94, and 412-34), it could well be that the prime of his life was spent in a state of unhappy abstinence. If so, then it would mean that his physical and sexual condition when he did marry, at the age of thirty-two, was actually not so different from that which Milton had known when he married at the age of thirty-four.

79.   See chapter XI for the story of *The Prelude*.

80.   Medicinal leeches were used for bloodletting: demand grew dur-ing the first half of the nineteenth century, until leeches were almost extinct in Europe. Collecting the leeches from ponds and bogs was hard work and badly paid: leech-gatherers quite often used their own legs as bait, with the result that over time they lost quantities of blood (and got very cold). Wordsworth's poem uses considerable licence. Dorothy's account specified that the man they met no longer worked in this way: 'His trade was to gather leeches, but now leeches are scarce, and he had not the strength for it. He lived by begging, and was making his way to Carlisle, where he should buy a few godly books to sell.' In Wordsworth's poem however the meeting with the leech gatherer takes place beside a pool, where the old man is seen stirring the water in search of leeches; and the man is likened to a boulder, immobile and totally integrated into the landscape.

81.   These are the opening lines of an untitled sonnet – one of those

inspired by the trip to France in the summer of 1802. While a few of the sonnets have dates as titles, most were not published until 1807, so it is impossible to say precisely when a particular poem was composed. However it is likely that most of these sonnets were begun in August 1802.

82. Petrarch sometimes used '*abab abab*' as a rhyme scheme in the first eight lines; and occasionally '*abab baba*' or '*abab baab*'. His favourite arrangement for the last six lines was '*cde cde*', but he also used '*cdc cdc*'; '*cdd dcc*'; '*cdd cdd*'; '*cde ecd*'; '*cde dec*'; and occasionally '*cde edc*'.

83. Details of this reference are given in the note to the poem *To the Daisy*, on p. 766 of the *Oxford 21st-Century Authors* edition of Wordsworth's poetry (OUP, 2012).

84. Milton served as 'Secretary for Foreign Languages' from 1649 until the collapse of the Commonwealth and the Restoration (of the monarchy) in 1660, despite going blind during this period, and remaining in his post after Cromwell's death in 1658. Milton's duties consisted mainly of translating letters (from foreign governments) into English, and composing letters in Latin (which was used then as the language of diplomacy). While he had no official role in determining policy, he took part in the Council of State when necessary, and met regularly with Cromwell and the other leaders of the Commonwealth, so one can imagine that his views and opinions would have been listened to.

85. Letter of May 30, 1815, quoted in *Wordsworth, A Life*, p. 330. The 'Darwin' referred to is Erasmus Darwin (1731-1802), grandfather of the more famous Charles. Erasmus Darwin was a physician and natural philosopher. His key scientific work, *Zoonomia,* published in two parts between 1794 and 1796, reflected at length on theories of evolution and postulated life existing 'perhaps millions of ages before the commencement of the history of mankind'; it was later read and commented on by his grandson Charles. Wordsworth read it in March 1798, having borrowed a copy from his publisher Joseph Cottle. Coleridge's argument in this letter is

perverse. He uses Wordsworth's unqualified admiration for Milton to try and persuade Wordsworth to expound a seventeenth-century view of history and science in a poem to be composed in the early nineteenth century, completely ignoring (or rejecting) any relevant thinking of the intervening two centuries. Wordsworth was never going to adopt a scheme of that kind. Apart from his admiration for Newton's work, he was clearly aware of recent developments in scientific thinking; and he was never going to devote years of his life to trying to refute two hundred years of scientific thinking. By bundling everything together in a characteristically confused and confusing way, Coleridge completely lost sight of Wordsworth's way of looking at the world. Wordsworth made (rightly or wrongly) a fundamental distinction between art and science. In his view arguments that were valid for one were not necessarily valid for the other. Miltonic thinking about the fall and possible redemption of the human race made sense in literature, thanks to the working of human consciousness, but did not have a scientific validity. Scientific thinking functioned according to other laws and principles, which, while they complemented the thinking which human beings use to make sense of their own lives, nonetheless remained quite distinct. As conceived by Coleridge *The Recluse* project was therefore doomed at a purely theoretical level, even from the moment it was dreamed up. The wonder is that Coleridge did not realise this.

86.   The editor of the Penguin edition of *The Prelude* says that lines 1–54 of Book 1 'seem to have been composed on November 18–19, 1799 and inserted in *The Prelude c.* late January 1804. They are the record of a mood of exuberance and optimism as Wordsworth walked from Ullswater to Grasmere to arrange the renting of Dove Cottage, where he and Dorothy would live until 1808.' This would suggest that the departure-point for *The Prelude* was the same as for *Home at Grasmere* (which Wordsworth began to compose soon after settling in to Dove Cottage) – and with

the parallel between the Lake District and the Garden of Eden evoked more or less explicitly in both poems. At a certain point in time the two poems divide in the poet's mind, with *The Prelude* carrying forward the autobiographical narrative, while *Home at Grasmere* contained the more theoretical reflections that developed out of that personal experience. Both poems were intended to form part of *The Recluse*; and given the importance that that project had for Wordsworth, it seems fair to say that the act of setting up house with Dorothy, which inspires the openings of both *The Prelude* and *Home at Grasmere*, was seen by him as marking the beginning of all that gave significance to his adult life.

87.   Kenneth Johnston, for example, speaks of 'a pervasive sexlessness in much of his work' (*The Hidden Wordsworth*, p. 6). Frances Wilson, in *The Ballad of Dorothy Wordsworth*, referring to de Quincey's opinion of Dorothy that she was not womanly, writes that 'It is Wordsworth and not his sister who comes across as having never experienced or aroused a physical feeling. His poetry is startlingly without sexuality, his landscapes are peopled by children, old men, widows, and idiots; there is not a sexually active creature among them.' (pp 43-4). Such a drastically literal reading of the poetry leaves little room for discussion; but it is only an extreme version of the customary assessment of Wordsworth, according to which he achieved a kind of intellectual alchemy, sublimating the impulses of the body until they became as agents in the working of the human mind. Against that we could set, for example, Iain McGilchrist's study of Wordsworth in *Against Criticism* (Faber, London, 1982): 'In the physicality of Wordsworth's language lies the origin of all its special qualities, and all of its most striking effects.…We have seen that the heart, for Wordsworth, is not a vaporous assemblage of emotions, but the central organ of the physical system, a point that is emphasized by explicit references to blood, breathing, and often to the pulse itself. But even the mind, Wordsworth often reminds us, is part of the physical organism' (p. 187). Later on

McGilchrist qualifies one of his own observations 'because it suggests a split between physical and intellectual existence which had no reality for Wordsworth. True thought incorporated itself with "the blood and vital juices of the mind", in his striking expression. Movements of the mind and soul were literally experienced in the body.' (p. 190). It is perhaps not a coincidence that McGilchrist, who, when he wrote *Against Criticism*, was a Fellow of All Souls College, Oxford (where he taught English), then moved from literature to medicine. He works today as a psychiatrist. His book *The Master and His Emissary – The Divided Brain and the Making of the Western World* (Yale University Press, 2009), which includes a section on Wordsworth, offers fascinating insights into the way art and the human body are inextricably linked – in particular in the way the human brain operates in the production of what we know as culture. Given the way the literary academic world in general has decided to consider Wordsworth as 'unfeeling' and 'bodiless', it may be that we need to look outside the traditional parameters of literary scholarship in order to understand better Wordsworth's sense of the body, and its relationship to the mind.

88. It may be that William's relationship with Dorothy also offers a key to understanding his use of the concepts of 'Fancy' and 'Imagination', about which he wrote at length in the Preface of 1815. One way of approaching Wordsworth's understanding of these faculties is to consider them as complementary, 'fancy' being an essentially feminine quality, and 'imagination' masculine. This distinction can be simply linked to gender stereotypes ('fanciful' is an attribute used almost exclusively of women); but in Wordsworth's case it could well be linked to his own relationship with Dorothy. At one point in the Preface he writes, 'Imagination is the power of depicting, and fancy of evoking and combining. The imagination is formed by patient observation; the fancy by a voluntary activity in shifting the scenery of the mind. ... Fancy depends upon the rapidity and profusion with which she scatters

her thoughts and images, trusting that their number, and the felicity with which they are linked together, will make amends for the want of individual value...' Wordsworth could have been thinking here of the difference between his way of composing poetry, and Dorothy's way of writing her journals. The workings of fancy as described by Wordsworth remind us very much of the disjointed, patchwork style of Dorothy's journals: following this line of thought, William, the man, would incline instinctively towards imagination as a form of expression, and Dorothy, the woman, towards fancy. However it is important to remember that Wordsworth insists that both Fancy and Imagination are faculties to be found in the same person. To that extent we might say that Wordsworth anticipates the idea – developed well over a century later – that each human being contains a male and female side to their character. What is also striking, if we admit the possibility that Wordsworth was thinking along these lines, is that it suggests that in a way he saw Dorothy as part of himself, even as he respected her as a person in her own right.

89. With these lines Wordsworth's Biblical references do a very fast rewind from Revelation to Genesis – specifically, to the story of the Tower of Babel in Genesis XI. In that story, the attempt by men to approach God by building a tower high enough to reach heaven is thwarted by God, who sows confusion among them by creating many languages, so that the people cannot understand each other. Wordsworth here inverts the image of Babel by evoking a dark chasm – precisely the opposite of a manmade tower; and listens admiringly to the unison of voices produced by the innumerable torrents and streams – again, the exact opposite of the confusion of sounds and meanings generated by the people of Babel. For Wordworth it is one of those precious moments in which Nature offers a possibility of redemption by returning us close to a point of origin – in this case the vision evoked in the opening verse of Genesis XI (before the construction of the

tower): 'And the whole earth was of one language, and of one speech.' Wordsworth's ability in *The Prelude* to suffuse a secular narrative with religious sense, without ever making his Biblical references obvious or heavy, is remarkable.

90. The narrative of Laurence Sterne's *The Life and Opinions of Tristram Shandy, Gentleman*, published in nine volumes between 1759 and 1767, was radically original in the way that it moved backwards and forwards in time, dramatising the play of consciousness and memory in everyday lives. Wordsworth mentions reading the first three volumes of *Tristram Shandy* in a letter of August 1791, so although we do not know if he read the entire book, he was certainly familiar with Sterne's writing. There is however an essential difference between the two men: Sterne delights in the capricious agility and inventiveness of the human mind, and these are the qualities which determine the flow of the narrative; while for Wordsworth consciousness is formed without our being aware of it, and language is subordinate to the gravitational pull of memory.

91. Nothing in art comes completely out of the blue – there are always precedents of some kind or other. In the case of autobiography, there was confessional literature going back as far as Saint Augustine, but the aim of such writing was not so much to enjoy and understand the story of the writer's life as to draw lessons from specific episodes in that life. Similarly, philosophers like Montaigne or Pascal integrated personal memories into essays, but always with the ulterior purpose of using personal experience to make a moral or philosophical point. Samuel Pepys' diaries no more constitute an autobiography than do Dorothy Wordsworth's journals, even though they give us a good idea of how the writer lived and felt about life – the day to day writing up of one's experience is a completely different operation from writing about it in the past tense....Casanova's *Histoire de ma Vie* was indeed written a few years earlier than *The Prelude*, but was not published until 1821. A more significant precedent to *The Prelude* is

Jean-Jacques Rousseau's *Confessions*, published in 1769. *Confessions* could indeed claim to be the first true autobiography. Stylistically it reads like a lightweight eighteenth-century novel (as indeed does Casanova's *Histoire de ma Vie*), and bears no relation to the intensely interiorised language of *The Prelude*. Nor do we know if Wordsworth read the *Confessions*. As with Rousseau's writing on education (see note 42) establishing a connection between Rousseau and Wordsworth is problematic.

92. Quoted in *Wordsworth, A Life* (unabridged 2000 edition), pp. 591-2.

93. Quoted in the Oxford World's Classics (1984) edition of Wordsworth, p. 628. This edition offers the entire Preface of 1815, while the *Oxford 21st-Century Authors* (2012) edition of Wordsworth gives about two-thirds of the original text. A considerable part of the 'Preface' is devoted to a treatise on the concepts of 'Fancy' and 'Imagination' – two of the headings used in the 1815 edition of *Collected Poems* – and of the way in which they relate to each other. Wordsworth's reasoning is not easy to follow – theoretical thinking was never his strong point – but that is less important than the fact that he wrote these pages. The concept of 'Imagination' was central to his vision of poetry – after all it was the title for two Books of *The Prelude* – and in this Preface he tried to make clear what he understood by the term… Even harder to follow than Wordsworth's reasoning is that of the Oxford editor: why does he devote so many pages to Wordsworth's 1815 Preface (fourteen in the 1984 edition and eight in the 2012 edition), while at the same time categorically rejecting the principle of arranging poems by categories (rather than chronologically), which the Preface sets out to explain and justify?

94. *Finnegans Wake* begins with a few lines on the landscape of Dublin. At the end of the book the River Liffey, which had been evoked in the first word of the novel ('riverrun'), is given a voice, and talks to the reader as it flows through Dublin and out into the sea. The last sentence of the novel remains unfinished – 'A way a lone a last

a loved a long the' – with the final 'the' linking back to 'riverrun' at the beginning of the book. With this device Joyce invited the reader to start the book all over again – (he joked that the novel was intended for 'that ideal reader with an ideal insomnia') – in a movement which in a way replicated the cycle that water follows (freshwater – saltwater – rainbearing clouds – rain – freshwater…).

95. A similar problem was posed by the Greek poet C. P. Cavafy (1863-1933), who from 1918 organised the editions of his verse thematically rather than chronologically. The categories he devised – 'philosophical'; 'historical'; 'sensual'; as well as hybrids such as 'philosophical-sensual' – correspond well to the kind of categories that Wordsworth thought up ('poems founded on the affections'; 'poems dedicated to national independence and liberty'; 'poems of the imagination', etc.). As with Wordsworth, editors of Cavafy reverted to a chronological arrangement of the oeuvre once the author was dead and out of the way. However the Oxford University Press has now produced an edition in which, to quote from the introduction, 'the thematic or chronological sequence established by Cavafy has been scrupulously followed'. So much the better. It is worth noting that this new edition belongs to the same series – (Oxford World's Classics) – as the collection of Wordsworth's poetry that I have referred to, whose editor decided to ignore completely the poet's wishes over the arrangement of his oeuvre: ('The decision to break with the poet's wishes both as to text and to arrangement means that I have taken the text of the first appearance in a Wordsworth volume…') . One can only conclude that Oxford University Press has no guiding principle concerning the way poetry should be presented to the public, and leaves the matter up to individual editors. Cavafy has been luckier than Wordsworth.

96. For *The University of Chicago Press* (1960), David Grene translated the last two lines of *Oedipus the King* as, 'Count no mortal happy till / He has passed the final limit of his life secure from pain.'

97. Wordsworth was eloquent on the subject of letter-writing: in a letter of January 1804, to his friend Francis Wrangham, he lamented, 'You do not know what a task, it is to me, to write a Letter; I absolutely loathe the sight of a Pen when I am to use it.' While he did not make the same comments about working on his poems, the impression Dorothy invariably gives in her *Journals* is that he derived no pleasure from writing: it was a necessary means to an end, but it exhausted him physically and tended to give him headaches. Not once does she evoke a sense of satisfaction for the Poet at the end of a day's work.

98. Interestingly, Dickens did buy a copy of *The Prelude* soon after it was first published.

99. Both Wordsworth's and Milton's sonnets have as 'titles' the first lines, which are quoted here.

100. In giving this date to the composition of the poem I am following the Oxford editor, who notes that the poem was 'composed most probably Jan. 1813–May 1814'. He does not say on what basis he makes this dating, but I find it convincing for two reasons: first, because Wordsworth's sense of the interrelationship of past and present could well inspire him to write about the past as if it was present; and secondly, because he was more likely to write about the loss of a young person who had died than to celebrate youth for its own sake (except when it was his own, fondly remembered youth). The 'Lucy' poems were about loss, and I would place this poem in that lineage.

101. This was noted by Crabb Robinson (who was accompanying Wordsworth) in his diary, and is quoted on p. 372 of *Wordsworth, A Life*.

102. Evidence for this is fragmentary, as none of the women in the Wordsworth household liked to criticise the master of the house. But it is clear that William made no effort to participate in domestic life: so, in a letter written just after they moved to Allan Bank in 1808, Dorothy writes that she and her brother-in-law

Henry are working hard to get settled in to the new home – 'there is much to do for Henry & me, who are the only able-bodied people in the house except the servant and <u>William</u>, who you know is not expected to do anything.' And it would seem that the household revolved around William's wishes, the programme for each day being decided according to his needs and feelings. The entry in Dorothy's *Journal* for June 7, 1802, is typical in this respect: 'William was walking when we came in – he had slept miserably for 2 nights past so we all went to bed soon.' Such evidence as one can glean from letters or from Dorothy's Journals, together with the story of his relationship with his daughter Dora, gives the impression of a self-absorbed and inflexible man; and suggests that while the dialogue with Dorothy was vital to him, he made little effort in daily life to go towards her, to put her needs first or to indulge her wishes.

103. One of the consequences of this rupture was that Wordsworth did not invite Quillinan to be his official biographer, although he was ideally suited for that role, and would have done the job far better than William's nephew Christopher did. Had Quillinan presented Wordsworth's life story to the world in 1851, the poet's image and legacy might have been quite different.

104. With reference to Lévi-Strauss's observations on the exchange of women through marriage (see note 58), it is interesting to note that even today the bride is 'given away' (usually by her father) during the wedding ceremony.

105. Quoted in *Wordsworth, A Life*, p. 455.

106. Quoted in *Wordsworth, A Life in Letters*, p. 239.

107. It could fairly be said that this is not true of Keats – one does not will tuberculosis on oneself. Nonetheless the transience of life is a major dynamic in Keats' poetry: most clearly articulated in *Ode to a Nightingale*, but palpable throughout his oeuvre, which in a sense depends for its meaning on the idea that life and sensual pleasure are shortlived.

108. Quoted in *Wordsworth, A Life*, p. 396.

109. Turner made a bequest of about 300 paintings and 30,000 works on paper (watercolours, drawings and small sketches) to the nation, on condition that they be kept together and made available to the public. For a variety of reasons nothing was done to this end for over 120 years (the story of the Turner Bequest, with all its complications, can be found online). Eventually the Clore Gallery, designed to house the Turner legacy, was opened in 1987, as an annexe to what is now 'Tate Britain'. Without the generosity of the Clore family, who provided most of the financing, it is unlikely that the Gallery would have seen the light of day, as the British government showed no wish to spend money on respecting the will and testament of the nation's greatest painter. In any case, it would be more accurate to say the terms of the will were not properly respected, as some of Turner's most important works remain in the National Gallery. Turner's wish to have his work kept together and viewed as an ensemble resonates with Wordsworth's desire to arrange his oeuvre in a thematic and non-chronological manner: in both cases there is the desire to demonstrate the overall coherence and unity of a lifetime's work.

110. Given that Mary rarely left the north of England during her long life, the association of her with England was straightforward. But as we saw in chapter VIII, her Englishness was an important element for resolving tensions in William's mind, and was celebrated in the poem he wrote while courting her ('*I travelled among unknown men*'), in particular in the lines, 'And She I cherished turned her wheel / Beside an English fire.' (see pp. 205-6).

111. Quoted in *Wordsworth, A Life in Letters*, pp. 205-6.

112. Quoted in *The Hidden Wordsworth*, p. 78.

113. Frances Wilson considers Dorothy's illness in some detail in *The Ballad of Dorothy Wordsworth* (pp. 240-3; 245-9).

114. Today we have a fairly clear idea of what we understand by 'Romantic' and 'romantic'. We know that they are not the same

thing, but with both terms being used all the time, a grey area has developed in which one term can easily be confused with the other; and in order to understand Wordsworth's intentions and achievement, it is useful to clarify what is meant by the two words.

Romanticism was a nebulous phenomenon, that meant quite different things to different people – (so, for example, the Oxford English Dictionary proposes Wordsworth, Goya and Wagner as three examples of Romantic artists, but what does Wordsworth's *The Prelude* have in common with Goya's *Disasters of War* etchings, or Wagner's *Ring Cycle*)? It is also hard to define because it made itself felt in the work of artists who often did not know each other: the connections and affinities that we can point to may not have been apparent to the artists themselves. For example, while we can say today that English and German Romanticism had much in common, Wordsworth almost certainly knew nothing either of Holderlin's poetry, or Friedrich's painting – though he would have heard Beethoven's music… With regard to Wordsworth's achievement, there is also a problem of dates. The term 'Romanticism' began to be used in the 1820s, by which time all of Wordsworth's major poetry had been written. Only in retrospect could he be considered a Romantic. He had worked on his own, creating largely in isolation: only with hindsight would it be possible to see his oeuvre as forming part of a larger picture – that of 'Romantic literature'. And the idea that artists and writers like Wordsworth might have thought of themselves as belonging to or participating in a movement, is complicated by another factor: the lack of precedents. Unlike neoclassical artists of the seventeenth and eighteenth centuries, Romantic artists had no model from the past against which to measure their work, and to help define their aims. This lack of precedents, together with his sense of isolation, no doubt contributed to Wordsworth's uncertainty as to the value of some of his work, and probably helps to explain his reluctance to publish *The Prelude*.

Unlike 'Romantic', the adjective 'romantic' had a long history. It traced its pedigree back through French to the *'romans'* – ('romances' in English) – of the Middle Ages, which recounted chivalrous adventures in which the ideals of courtly love were often evoked (the modern French for 'a novel' is *'un roman'*: this is further proof that the novel as it developed in the eighteenth and nineteenth centuries was seen as a descendant of the medieval *'roman'* / 'romance'). Our use of 'romantic' today stems from that etymology, and has no direct link with 'Romantic'. In the one use of 'romantic' that I have located in Wordsworth's poetry, it is clear that this was how he understood the word: in Book VII of *The Prelude* he writes of the times spent at the theatre in London, 'Enchanting age and sweet – / Romantic almost' (lines 473-4: the word 'romantic' has a capital letter here only because it is at the beginning of the line); and he goes on to compare the theatre with 'some bright cavern of romance' (line 485), meaning by that the world of fantasy and chivalrous adventure. Whatever we may think today about 'romantic love' or of 'the Romantic spirit', we need to be very careful when using these words in relation to Wordsworth and his poetry.

115. Quoted in *A Life in Letters* (p. 247).

116. Quoted in *Wordsworth, A Life* (pp. 492-3).

117. Quoted in *Wordsworth, A Life in Letters* (p. 246).

118. Quoted in *Wordsworth, A Life*, (p. 321).

119. The autobiographical nature of Wordsworth's portrait of The Pedlar was made clear when, in December 1801, Wordsworth rephrased and expanded the same verses to speak of himself as a young man, in Book III of *The Prelude* (lines 121-67).

120. However extraordinary Wordsworth's dream may be, the themes it gives voice to were not new: the debate about the relationship between religion, science and nature, and the place of art in that matrix, had been a constant in intellectual life in Europe since the discoveries of Galileo. The subject is vast; but we can get

an idea of Wordsworth's thinking if we compare it with that of the great eighteenth-century poet, Alexander Pope (1688-1744). Pope's proposed epitaph for Isaac Newton, written in about 1730, was typically pithy and succinct: 'Nature and Nature's Laws lay hid in Night. / GOD said, *Let Newton be!* and All was *Light.*' Pope's couplet establishes a clear hierarchy, in which God is supreme. Below God are Nature and Science, both of which are governed by laws. Science has tools which enable us to understand the laws of nature; but the ordering of nature – and of the human scientific mind which is trained to perceive that order – stems from God. He is the great lawmaker. In *The Prelude* Wordsworth proposes a different arrangement: he sees the universe as being ordered by 'a mighty mind' inspired by 'the sense of God', rather than by God himself. This macrocosmic mind functions in one way in nature, and in another way in science. Human beings find themselves in the middle: they are part of nature, but also have the capacity to understand the laws of science. Artists incline towards that part of consciousness where God's presence (i.e. religion) is felt more strongly, because art is informed by a multitude of inchoate voices that would die if an artificial sense of order were imposed on them. These voices come from nature – hence the dichotomy between nature and science for Wordsworth.

121. The play of ideas here is complicated. To start with we have to consider the account of the Pentecost (as related in Acts 2). On that day the apostles were filled with the Holy Spirit, and began to speak in different languages (despite all being from Galilee, and naturally speaking the same language). These 'different tongues' were the languages spoken in different parts of Asia Minor and North Africa. The mission of the apostles being to spread Christ's teaching throughout these lands, it was obviously crucial to be able to speak in the language of the country they travelled to if they wanted to communicate. The episode of the Pentecost is a step on the way to neutralising the harm done by the construction of the

Tower of Babel in Genesis XI (see note 89). The Tower of Babel split meaning ('God's Word') into innumerable components (languages) that could not understand each other: confusion reigned. The Day of Pentecost reproduced the same movement (splitting a common language into a variety of tongues), but it did so to achieve the opposite effect: namely, to make it possible for the truth of God's Word to be communicated to people who had no common language. The Pentecost thus replies to Babel through one of those counterpoints that enable the New Testament to resolve problems and arguments explored in the Old Testament.

Subtle theological arguments were not however Wordsworth's main concern. He was looking to reconcile monotheistic and polytheistic cultures; and it may be that Newton helped him in this respect. In his *Opticks*, which Wordsworth read avidly when he was in his teens (as noted on pages 136 of this book), Newton analysed the way that light and colour interacted. He demonstrated that light passing through a prism was split into the various colours that composed it. Reciprocally, the combination of all the colours of the spectrum produced white, the 'colour' of light. Wordsworth might have found here a model for understanding the creative process in poetry. According to the analogy that Newton's discoveries offered, light could be said to correspond to truth, while colours are the voices (or languages) through which we express meaning. In poetry truth is split into a spectrum of meanings – many voices – just as light is split into a spectrum of colours; but at the same time these voices can form a chorus, and sing in unison, just as the spectrum of colours when brought together rejoin the source of light. It was the principle underlying the rainbow effect, and Wordsworth's walks in the Lake District offered him regular opportunites to marvel at the rainbows that briefly spanned the landscape. Their beauty was in itself enough to inspire the poet; but other layers of meaning were offered both by Newton's optical theories and by the reference to the rainbow in Genesis 9, verses 8-18: in that passage the rainbow symbolised the covenant that God made with man after the flood. For someone like Wordsworth the rainbow was thus imbued with a triple significance: poetic, scientific and religious.

The equation of God with light (which in Christian thinking was indisputable) tended to polarise the mind, committing all that was alien to God to varying degrees of darkness (a principle that became more and more rigid during the nineteenth century). Newton's discoveries concerning the relation of light to colour offered a vital alternative to the Manichean light-dark confrontation: instead of opposing one force (light) with another (dark), it split light into innumerable components, and also showed the process of splitting and unifying to work both ways. As such, these discoveries not only offered a way of reconciling (up to a point) scientific thought with religious belief, but also suggested a way in which a monotheistic vision (based on a single source of truth) could be reconciled with a polytheistic system, in which meaning is generated from a multitude of sources.

122. See note 9.

Biographical Notes

Entries in *italics* refer to events taking place in France.

1770   April 7: William Wordsworth born at Cockermouth, Cumberland, second son of John and Ann Wordsworth (Richard, the eldest boy, was born in 1768).

1771   December 25: Birth of Dorothy Wordsworth, only sister of the poet.

1772   December 4: Birth of William's younger brother John.

1774   June 9: Birth of William's youngest brother, Christopher.

1778   March: William's mother Ann dies aged 30.

June: Dorothy sent to live with relatives in Halifax.

1779   William and his brothers sent to Hawkshead Grammar School. He lodges with Ann and Hugh Tyson.

1783   December: William's father John dies aged 42.

1787   Early summer: William reunited with Dorothy for the first time in nine years.

John, aged fifteen, enrols in the navy. For the next ten years he is generally at sea, mainly on the route to India and China.

October: William begins his studies at St John's College, Cambridge.

1789   *July 14: Fall of the Bastille in Paris.*

1790   July 13–September 29: Continental walking tour, with Robert Jones; 2,000 miles on foot, averaging 30 miles a day. Route taken: Calais – Dijon – Chalon-sur-Saone – Lyons – St. Vallier – Grenoble – Geneva – Lausanne – Martigny – Simplon Pass – Domodossola – Lake Como – Gravedona – Hinterrhein – Great St Gothard Pass– Lucerne – Lake Wallen – Appenzell – Lake Constance – Schaffhausen – Lucerne – Interlaken – Berne – Basel – Cologne – Aix-la-Chapelle. (Chalon-sur-Saone – St Vallier; and Basel – Cologne, by boat, the rest on foot).

1791   January: Finishes studies at Cambridge, and moves to London.

        June–August: Walking tour in Wales with Robert Jones, including ascent of Mt Snowdon (see, *The Prelude*, Book XIII).

        November: Goes to live in France.

        December: Takes lodgings in Orléans, which is probably where he meets Annette Vallon.

1792   March: Annette pregnant.

        August: Assault on palace of Tuileries. French royal family imprisoned.

        September: 'September Massacres' (of prisoners in Paris).

        September 20: the Convention established.

        September 21: the monarchy abolished. France declared a Republic.

        October–December: Wordsworth in Paris.

        December: Returns to England. December 15, birth of his daughter Anne-Caroline (generally known as Caroline). Baptism of Caroline the same day.

1793   *January: Louis XVI guillotined.*

        February 1: France declares war on England. 1793–4: Reign of Terror.

        Tour of West Country and Wales with William Calvert (Isle of Wight – Salisbury – River Wye – Wales).

1794   William and Dorothy are reunited. They make the first of their walking holidays together (in the Lake District).

        July–August: Arrest and execution of Robespierre. End of the Reign of Terror.

1795   *The Directoire established in France.*

        Wordsworth's friend Raisley Calvert dies of tuberculosis,

leaving Wordsworth £900 (payable in the form of annuities), to allow him to concentrate on his writing.

William and Dorothy take up residence in Dorset, then in Somerset, where they look after Basil Montagu.

Wordsworth meets Coleridge and Robert Southey for the first time.

1796 *Beginning of Napoleonic military campaigns.*

1797 Beginning of regular dialogue and friendship with Coleridge.

1798 *Recluse* project first thought out by Wordsworth and Coleridge.

July: Walking in the Wye valley, with Dorothy (composition of *Tintern Abbey*).

September: Publication of *Lyrical Ballads* (for which Wordsworth is paid £30). Uncomplimentary review of the work by Southey. William and Dorothy, together with Coleridge, leave for Germany. After a fortnight Coleridge separates from the Wordsworths. William and Dorothy settle in Goslar for the winter. Between October 1798 and February 1799 Wordsworth composes five 'Lucy' poems, and the 'Was it for this?' manuscript, containing elements later developed in Book I of *The Prelude*.

1799 February: William and Dorothy walk over the Hartz mountains, then spend two months travelling in Saxony.

Composition of 'two-part *Prelude*' manuscript.

Successful coup led by Napoleon against the Directoire. Napoleon becomes First Consul.

October–November: walking in the Lake District with Coleridge. William's brother John joins them for a week.

December: William and Dorothy walk 44 miles over the hills of the Lake District to reach their new home at Grasmere.

1800 January–September: John lives with William and Dorothy at Dove Cottage.

July: Coleridge, with his wife Sarah and son Hartley, arrive to live in the Lake District.

Work on second edition of *Lyrical Ballads*. Composition of *Home at Grasmere*.

October: Wordsworth decides not to include Coleridge's poem *Christabel* in the second edition of *Lyrical Ballads*. Coleridge effectively excluded from the second edition.

1801 January: Second edition of *Lyrical Ballads* published (dated 1800), including Wordsworth's Preface.

John made captain of the *Earl of Abergavenny* (the largest ship in the merchant navy) at just 28 years. He needs money to invest privately in trade: William and Dorothy lend what they can. By the time he sails, John has invested almost £10,800 in the voyage to China.

Some work on Books I–III of *The Prelude*.

September: trip to Scotland.

Coleridge announces that he is returning to the south of England.

October (1801)-September 1802: Treaty of Amiens, with renewed contact between England and France.

November: probable date of William's engagement to Mary (Hutchinson).

1802 May: composes first of his 'mature' sonnets.

Lord Lonsdale dies. His heir, Sir William Lowther, acknowledges debt of £4,660 (plus interest) payable to the Wordsworth family.

July–August: trip to France (Calais) with Dorothy, to meet Annette and Caroline.

September: John, just returned from China, meets with William (just back from France) in London. John's investment in the China expedition had not been very successful financially, but he wants to reinvest in the next journey.

October: wedding of William and Mary. Dorothy has a breakdown and does not attend the service.

1803 William's brother Richard reaches settlement with Sir William

Lowther, the debt to be paid in three instalments. John asks
for the first instalment, of £3,000, to be entirely invested in
his next voyage. The request leads to a family quarrel, but
eventually John has his way.

June 18: birth of William's son John.

August: Sir George Beaumont offers Wordsworth a small estate
near Keswick.

August–September: trip to Scotland, with extensive walking in
the Highlands.

Wordsworth meets Walter Scott for the first time, while in
Scotland.

William Hazlitt a visitor to the Lakes. He is forced to leave
quickly after sexually molesting a local girl.

1804 April: Coleridge leaves for the Mediterranean (Madeira, then
Malta).

August: birth of William's daughter Dora. Lady Beaumont
stands as godmother.

John returns from China. During the following winter he
prepares his next voyage to China. William and Dorothy again
persuaded to invest. John's personal investment amounts to
about £20,000 in goods and money.

December: *Napoleon declared Emperor.*

1805 February 1: the *Earl of Abergavenny* sets sail for China.

February 5: the ship capsizes off Weymouth, and John drowns
(William and Dorothy apparently insured against loss for
their investment).

May: *The Prelude* completed.

August: Walter Scott visits Wordsworth in the Lake District.

1806 June: birth of William's son Thomas.

August: first meeting with Sir William Lowther, who had
helped Wordsworth buy a small property in the area.

Coleridge returns to England.

October: Wordsworth accepts Beaumont's invitation to make

use of a farmhouse on his estate in Leicestershire.

The Wordsworth family remain there until June 1807.

(The invitation is again taken up in 1810).

1807   *Poems, in Two Volumes* published.

First visit of De Quincey to Grasmere.

1808   Wordsworth begins to lobby for changes to the law on
copyright.

May: the Wordsworths move to Allan Bank.

September: Coleridge arrives, and is a regular visitor for the
next two years.

Birth of William's daughter Catherine.

1809   De Quincey takes over tenancy of Dove Cottage.

1810   Breakdown in relationship with Coleridge.

May: birth of William's son Willy.

1811   July: Dora sent to boarding-school (aged six).

Winter 1811–12: Shelley in the Lake District, but does not meet
Wordsworth.

1812   June: death of Catherine (aged three).

December: death of Thomas (aged six).

1813   Lord Lonsdale nominates Wordsworth for post of Distributor
of Stamps. He and Beaumont together provide the necessary
sureties. Wordsworth holds the post for the next 29 years.

1814   Summer: tour of Scotland.

Publication of *The Excursion, Portion of The Recluse*.

First edition of *Collected Poems*, with thematic and non-chrono-
logical arrangement.

1815   *Battle of Waterloo*.

1816   Marriage of Caroline to Jean-Baptiste Baudouin. Wordsworth
promises annuity of £30 p.a. to Caroline.

1817   Meeting with Keats in London.

Turner returns to Continental Europe for the first time follow-
ing the Napoleonic Wars. From then on he travels, and paints,
in Europe almost every year until 1845.

1818   Wordsworth supports the Lonsdale family in election campaigns – in particular, doing what he can to assist Lonsdale's candidate son, William, Viscount Lowther (and offers help similarly in 1826 and 1832).

1819   First major revision of *The Prelude*.

1820   July–October: Continental tour, with Mary, Dorothy, and friends. (France – Flanders – Belgium – Germany – Switzerland – northern Italy). Meeting in Paris with Caroline and her two daughters, during the tour.

     Turner begins experimenting with primary colours, and exploring relationship of colour to light – the 'Colour Beginnings'.

1821   Death of Keats.

1822   Death of Shelley.

     Dora's schooling concluded, she returns to live at Rydal Mount.

1823   May–June: tour of Flanders, Holland, and Belgium, with Mary.

1824   August: tour of Wales, with Mary and Dora.

     Death of Byron.

1825   Tom Robinson, a lieutenant in the Royal Navy, asks Wordsworth's permission to propose marriage to Dora. Wordsworth refuses.

1826   Revd. William Ayling proposes to Dora, but is turned down – probably by Wordsworth rather than by Dora.

     Dora's health begins to be a problem; within a few years she is also anorexic.

1827   Beaumont dies. He leaves Wordsworth £100, plus an annuity of £100 for life.

     Publication of five-volume *Poetical Works*, with older poems revised.

1828   Lord Lonsdale finds a living for Wordsworth's elder son, John, but is unable to find a job for his younger son, Willy.

     June–August: tour of Flanders and Belgium, with Dora and Coleridge.

1829   August–September: tour of Ireland, with friends. On one day
he noted:

> 'breakfasted at 5, set off from Kenmare at half past, rode 10
> Irish miles, took to our feet, ascended nearly 1,500 feet, de-
> scended as much, ascended another ridge as high, descended
> as much, and then went to the top of Carrantuohill, 3,000
> feet, the mountain being the highest in Ireland, 3,410 feet
> above the level of the sea. We then descended, walked nearly
> two hours, and rode on bad horses an hour and a half or
> more, and reached Kilarney at ten at night, having eaten
> nothing but a poor breakfast of spongy bread without eggs
> and one crust of the same quality, and drank milk during the
> whole day. I reached Killarney neither tired nor exhausted
> by this.'

1830   Rides pony from Lake District to Cambridge.

1831   September: trip to Scotland with Dora to visit Walter Scott.
Tour of the Highlands together.

1832   Second major revision of *The Prelude*.

1833   July: journey up West coast of Scotland, with Robinson, to visit
Inner Hebrides.

1834   Death of Coleridge.

1835   Dorothy has a mental breakdown, and becomes a permanent
invalid.

1836   Beginning of Dora's relationship with Edward Quillinan.
Winter 1836–7: publication of six-volume *Poetical Works*.

1837   March–August: Continental tour, with Robinson (Paris –
Avignon – Nimes – Rome – Assisi – Florence – Italian
Lakes – Venice – Munich). Meeting in Paris with Caroline
and her husband during the tour.
December: Quillinan asks permission to marry Dora.
Wordsworth refuses.

1838   Wordsworth's sonnets collected in a single volume.

1839   Third major revision of *The Prelude*.

1841 Marriage of Dora and Quillinan.

1842 Copyright Bill passed.

1843 Death of Southey. Wordsworth succeeds him as Poet Laureate.

1847 Dora dies of tuberculosis.

1850 Death of Wordsworth.

1851 Death of Turner.

1855 Death of Dorothy Wordsworth.

1859 Death of Wordsworth's wife Mary.

List of Illustrations

Front dustjacket, foreground: William Shuter,
*Portrait of William Wordsworth at the age
of 28*, 1798; Cornell University Library,
courtesy of Wikimedia
Front dustjacket, background: Wordsworth's
chest (detail); collection of the author
Back dustjacket: Wordsworth chest; collection
of the author

TEXT FIGURES

COLOUR PLATES

Index

ABOUT THE AUTHOR

Andrew Wordsworth, a collateral descendant of William Wordsworth, is a painter and sculptor. He studied at Winchester College and Jesus College, Cambridge, where he read English and studied Wordsworth in detail. Following in the steps of his ancestor, he then moved to France for several years, studying at the École des beaux-arts in Paris and teaching English at the École nationale de l'administration. From Paris, he moved to the Italian countryside, where he still lives.

Information about Andrew Wordsworth's artistic work can be found at www.andrewwordsworth.com

First published 2020 by
Pallas Athene (Publishers) Ltd,
Studio 11A, Archway Studios
25-27 Bickerton Road, London N19 5JT
For further information on our books please visit
www.pallasathene.co.uk

 pallasathenebooks   PallasAtheneBooks

 Pallas_books   PallasatheneO

ISBN 978 1 84368 194 6

Printed in England